Engendering
Rationalities

SUNY series in Gender Theory

Tina Chanter, editor

ENGENDERING
RATIONALITIES

EDITED BY

NANCY TUANA

AND

SANDRA MORGEN

STATE UNIVERSITY OF NEW YORK PRESS

Published by
STATE UNIVERSITY OF NEW YORK PRESS, ALBANY

© 2001 State University of New York

For information, address State University of New York Press,
90 State Street, Suite 700, Albany, NY 12207

Production by Marilyn P. Semerad
Marketing by Dana E. Yanulavich

Library of Congress Cataloging-in-Publication Data

Engendering rationalities / edited by Nancy Tuana and Sandra Morgen.
    p. cm—(SUNY series in gender theory)
    Includes bibliographical references and index.
    ISBN 0-7914-5085-6 (alk. paper)—ISBN 0-7914-5086-4 (pbk. : alk.
paper)
    1. Knowledge, Sociology of.   2. Feminist theory.   I. Tuana, Nancy.
II. Morgen, Sandra.   III. Series.

BD175 .E54 2001
121'.082—dc21   00-050955

10 9 8 7 6 5 4 3 2 1

Contents

Preface   vii

Chapter One   Introduction   1
Nancy Tuana

I. RETHINKING EPISTEMOLOGY: REALISM, TRUTH, OBJECTIVITY

Chapter Two   Epistemology Resuscitated: Objectivity as Trustworthiness   23
Naomi Scheman

Chapter Three   On Judging Epistemic Credibility: Is Social Identity Relevant?   53
Linda Martín Alcoff

Chapter Four   How to Be Really Responsible   81
Lisa Heldke

Chapter Five   Beyond Epistemology: From a Pragmatist Feminist Experiential Standpoint   99
Charlene Haddock Seigfried

II. UNVEILING RATIONALITY

Chapter Six   Resisting Rationality   125
Sarah Lucia Hoagland

Chapter Seven   Memory, Suggestibility, and Social Skepticism   151
Sue Campbell

Chapter Eight   Relativism and Feminist Science Scholarship   175
Lynn Hankinson Nelson

Chapter Nine   The Bias Paradox in Feminist Epistemology   195
Richmond Campbell

III. ON THE MATTER OF KNOWING

Chapter Ten   Material Locations: An Interactionist
                     Alternative to Realism/Social Constructivism   221
                     Nancy Tuana

Chapter Eleven   Participatory Knowledge and the World
                     in Virginia Woolf   245
                     Louise Westling

IV. WHOSE STORIES? WHICH BIASES?

Chapter Twelve   Rational Imaginings, Responsible Knowings:
                     How Far Can You See From Here?   261
                     Lorraine Code

Chapter Thirteen   The Epistemology of Moral Voice: Displacing
                     Hegemony in Moral/Legal Discourse   283
                     Susan Hekman

Chapter Fourteen   Objectivity and the Role of Bias   297
                     Susan E. Babbitt

Chapter Fifteen   The Struggle to Naturalize Literary Studies:
                     Chicana Literary Theory and Analysis   315
                     Judith Richards

Chapter Sixteen   Epistemological Deliberations: Constructing
                     and Contesting Knowledge in Women's
                     Cross-Cultural Hair Testimonies   335
                     Lanita Jacobs-Huey

Chapter Seventeen   Standpoint Epistemology in the Physical
                     Sciences: The Case of Michael Faraday   361
                     Barbara L. Whitten

Bibliography   Feminist Epistemologies   381

Contributors   393

Index   397

PREFACE

Conferences have long been an important vehicle through which feminist knowledge has been developed and shared. From the Seneca Falls gathering in 1848 to the International Women's Conference in Beijing in 1995, conferences have facilitated the face-to-face sharing of ideas, intensive discussion, nourishment of bonds, and networks that fostered further development of ideas. The enGendering Rationalities conference, planned and hosted by the Center for the Study of Women in Society (CSWS) at the University of Oregon in 1997, was no exception. One of the challenges in preparing this volume has been our hope to capture on the printed page some of the intellectual exhilaration the conference exuded.

A foundational insight of one of the major intellectual traditions in feminist epistemology is the claim that we know in communities, that contexts of inquiry and social relationships profoundly shape who we are and what we know. My own allegiance to this idea has been the ground root for a series of activities that the Center for the Study of Women in Society, which I direct at the University of Oregon, has developed to encourage collaboration and scholarly community. Over the past five years, CSWS has allocated significant human and financial resources to nourishing intellectual communities, interdisciplinary exchange, and collaborative scholarship through support of a series of Research Interest Groups (RIGS) and the research and scholarly programming they have spawned. One of the exciting results of this process was the national conference that brought hundreds of feminist scholars from philosophy, anthropology, physics, English, political science, psychology, German, art history, history, religion, linguistics, earth sciences, education, sociology, comparative literature, and women's studies together to explore how feminist research and practices challenge and transform dominant conceptions of rationality and knowledge. Although this volume is not as interdisciplinary as the conference, we are excited to have been able to include a number of papers from outside philosophy, the discipline traditionally concerned with epistemological investigation. Indeed, epistemological questions continue to interest and animate feminist scholarship in the humanities, social sciences, natural and physical sciences, and the professions.

One of the great joys of collaboration is the opportunity to work closely with and learn from our colleagues. This was certainly my experience working on both the conference and this book with Nancy. We collaborated on every aspect of the conference and on the selection and editing of papers for this volume. Our intent was to produce a book that would serve the dual goals of engaging the most important, current issues in feminist epistemology, and to do so in ways that are accessible to, and valuable for, philosophers *as well as* other feminist scholars and practitioners.

The questions explored by the authors of the following chapters are at the heart of feminist theorizing today. But their importance extends beyond the walls of the academy. Understanding how particular knowledge practices are authorized or delegitimized, examining how more or less diverse communities shape what and how we know, and revealing the relationships between power and knowledge are ultimately issues each of us who envisions a more just society must grapple with in the process of theorizing or working toward social transformation.

Nancy and I wish to thank the staff of the Center for the Study of Women in Society who helped with the enGendering Rationalities conference: Judith Musick, Lin Reilly, and Roxanne Livingston. Shirley Marc, CSWS' office manager, has provided ongoing, invaluable assistance with the preparation of this volume. We owe her a huge debt of thanks for her attention to detail and commitment to this book. We are grateful to Lori Howard, of the University of Oregon publications office, who designed stunning conference materials. And finally, we wish to thank everyone who participated in the conference for their individual contributions to the conference and for their role in fostering an exciting and productive community of knowledge.

Sandra Morgen

CHAPTER ONE

Introduction

Nancy Tuana

This anthology and the intersecting lines of influence between the scholars included in it have a long and significant history. In the summer of 1996 I directed an NEH Summer Seminar for College Teachers on the topic of Feminist Epistemologies. Not only was this conference the first ever NEH Summer Seminar in the area of philosophy to focus on issues of gender and feminism, it was the first NEH Summer Seminar to have the term "feminist" in its title.[1] Many of the contributors to *Engendering Rationalities* were involved in that seminar, either as participants, visiting scholars, or as authors whose work was studied during those six exciting weeks of collaboration.[2]

Those of us who were involved in the NEH Summer Seminar not only enriched our understanding of feminist epistemological positions, but we also discovered the importance of collaboration and community in developing new areas of research. It was this realization that gave birth to the idea of a conference devoted to the topic of the seminar. Through the support of the Center for the Study of Women in Society and in collaboration with Sandra Morgen, the Director of CSWS, the conference "enGendering Rationalities" was held at the University of Oregon in April 1997. Many of the original NEH Seminar participants and visiting scholars returned to continue the dialogues begun a year earlier and were joined by over one hundred scholars who came to the University of Oregon to present their work and share in the development of this exciting area of feminist scholarship. All of the authors in this anthology participated in "enGendering Rationalities," and the initial formulations of the ideas contained in their chapters were presented at that conference.

FEMINIST EPISTEMOLOGIES

Feminist work on epistemological issues is now well enough established to have given rise not only to numerous journal articles, but also to be the subject of dozens of books and anthologies.[3] Those of us in the United States who work in this area often acknowledge our debt to the 1983 anthology *Discovering Reality: Feminist Perspectives on Epistemology, Metaphysics, Methodology, and Philosophy of Science* edited by Sandra Harding and Merrill B. Hintikka. This anthology, and the chapters contained in it, established the need for developing feminist perspectives in areas like epistemology, metaphysics, and philosophy of science. In the decade and a half since the publication of that anthology, feminist epistemological work has not only had a chance to develop, but has begun to be included in general epistemology textbooks and classes.

The study or acceptance of feminist work in epistemology has not, of course, been universal. Many theorists whose epistemological inquiries would be enriched by feminist scholarship—examinations of the role of values in knowledge processes or concerning the role of cognitive authority in issues of testimony—often include no reference to our work. Others who do make reference to our work sometimes present an oddly distorted view of it. The most typical error, and one I do not fully understand, is to assume that because scholarship is "feminist" that all who claim to do feminist epistemological research must hold the same views. This is an odd error in that no one would ever assume that all theorists who embrace the label "analytic" (or Continental, or pragmatic) would hold identical epistemological positions. Yet the fact that our work is feminist leads many to assume that we must have a uniform platform and if we don't, then referring to our work as "feminist" makes little sense.[4]

To say that our work is "feminist" is to acknowledge that gender is a central lens through which we conduct inquiry, but it does not follow from this that our theorizing is homogeneous. Feminist epistemologists, in holding gender as a central analytic category, investigate the influence of conceptions and norms of gender and gender-specific interests and experiences on accepted accounts of knowing and on the actual production of knowledge. But our interests, methods, and arguments often take us in different directions, and though we frequently build upon each other's work, we do not always agree with one another.[5] Feminist philosophical scholarship is best seen as a methodology, that is, a way of doing philosophy that has similar aims and concerns, and emerges from a common history, but where there will be welcome and productive disagreements and differences between practitioners. On this account, feminist philosophy should be counted as a philosophical tradition along with American pragmatic philosophy, analytic philosophy, and continental philosophy.[6] Like theorists from those traditions, feminist philosophers work in all areas of philosophy from aesthetics to philosophy of science, and, as with theorists from those traditions, individual theorists often share common concerns and approaches, but do not all hold identical or even similar views on all topics. Feminist philosophy, however, is somewhat unique in this group of methodological approaches in that feminist philosophers work within and across the other traditions. This uniqueness is reflected in this volume. Although the majority of the theorists working in the area of feminist epistemology are most influenced by analytic philosophical approaches, our volume also includes voices like those of Charlene Haddock Seigfried and Lisa Heldke who work in the tradition of classical American pragmatism, and Susan Hekman and Louise Westling whose work is influenced by continental philosophical approaches. It is also important to note that not all feminist epistemological scholarship is done by those trained in or housed in departments of philosophy. Epistemological theorizing is increasingly being formulated by scholars from other disciplines as part of a critique and development of alternative epistemologies in the humanities and social sciences.

Feminist scholarship in epistemology is perhaps best summarized through the concept of family resemblances. It is possible to identify a set of themes that describe the central concerns of feminist epistemologists, though not all of these themes will be present in a particular feminist epistemological writing, nor will feminist epistemologists concur on the importance or import of each theme. As with a family resemblance, though there is no one position or approach that is the same across all feminist epistemological studies, there are, as Wittgenstein would say, "a complicated network of similarities, overlapping and crisscrossing" (Wittgenstein 1958, section 66). Indeed, in this vein, Naomi Scheman in "Feminist Epistemology" (1995) identified four themes common to feminist epistemologists, and Helen Longino in "In Search of Feminist Epistemology" (1994) identified six theoretical virtues found in the work of feminist epistemologists. Here I would like to build on the foundation they provided to offer a list of thirteen themes that often figure in feminist epistemological studies.

By way of removing another common misunderstanding of feminist work, it is important to note that the themes I'll delineate are not uniquely feminist. Versions of many of these themes can be found in the work of nonfeminist epistemologists. Indeed, it is important to remember that feminist philosophers who work in the area of epistemology are trained as philosophers within particular traditions and are influenced by the methods in which they were trained. Though we keep gender as a central lens of our analysis, we employ and adopt methods from the traditions in which we were raised in order to best accomplish our goals. In this sense, there is nothing uniquely feminist about the methods of feminist epistemology. It is rather in the practice and aim of keeping a clear focus on issues of gender in order to identify and remove practices and institutions that contribute to the oppression of women that renders our investigations feminist.

Critique of "S Knows That p" Models of Knowledge

Few, if any, feminist epistemologists are interested in arguing that traditional models of knowledge that posit a "generic" knowing subject "S" are problematic *because* they rule out innate differences between the sexes. Nevertheless, the notion of generic knowing subjects has been the subject of feminist critique for two reasons. First, there has been the suspicion, one that numerous theorists have argued is warranted, that the so-called generic knowing subject as it has actually been constructed within modern philosophy has manifested traits and characteristics associated with privileged males, namely, White, propertied, Christian, heterosexual, and able-bodied.

Some feminists have also argued that the attempt to make the knowing subject "truly" generic (i.e., not modeled on privileged male characteristics, but reflective of innate characteristics of human knowledge) will not provide an accurate model of knowledge in that human knowledge practices emerge out of and are influenced by social structures, including those of gender. In other words, this second line of argument holds that the goal of a generic knower is misguided in that subjectivity is always at least partially socially constituted. On this position, none of us, regardless of gender, race, class, or ability, are generic subjects. If, as some have argued, epistemic authority, judgements of warrantability, or belief formation are inextricably shaped by features such as gender, then models of knowledge that posit generic knowers will be inadequate. As Scheman argues, "to position the knowing subject somehow outside of these differences, somehow able to take them into account—as though they simply constitute differences in situations in which one finds oneself . . . —is to underappreciate the depth at which such structures operate in our lives" (1995, 178).

Lorraine Code, in the chapter entitled "Rational Imaginings, Responsible Knowings: How Far Can You See From Here," argues that the orthodox epistemic subject, who is distinct but not *distinctive*, arises from the uncontested assumption "that anyone can 'stand in' for anyone else, as knower or known," a tenet that exerts "a continuous pull on regulative epistemic even within theories committed to modifying or evading its reductive excesses." She argues that epistemologies based on or influenced by this conception of the epistemic subject are not adequate to responsible knowing projects.

A Nonindividualist Conception of Knowledge

"S knows that p" models of knowledge posit an individual knowing subject. Many feminist epistemologists have critiqued the individualism of this account. In *Who Knows? From Quine to a Feminist Empiricism*, Lynn Hankinson Nelson answers the title question of her text with the answer that "in the primary sense it is communities, rather than individuals, that know" (1990, xi). Others, like Helen Longino, have offered a modified position, a model I have labeled "individuals in communities" (Tuana 1996), to embrace the individual as the holder of knowledge, but reject an individualist account of knowing by arguing that knowledge is so held only by persons who are part of complex social communities where both the knower and what is known are marked by that relationship.

Just by way of reminder that this list is designed only to identify common themes, but not ones universally held by feminist epistemologists, it is important to mention that not all feminist epistemologists reject individualist conceptions of knowledge. Though one might characterize the work of Helen Longino as a modified individualism, Louise Antony (1997) has argued that nonmodified individualist accounts are adequate to feminist epistemological concerns.

In shifting from individualist accounts, many feminist epistemologists have also replaced attempts to construct general standards of valid knowledge acquisition with analyses of the contexts of inquiry. Charlene Haddock Seigfried, in "Beyond Epistemology: From a Pragmatist Feminist Experiential Standpoint," calls for an abandonment of "the epistemological turn" in contemporary Anglo-American philosophy. It is her goal to replace it with a pragmatic theory of knowledge that "show[s] the connection of knowledge with values, of understanding with transformation, which argue[s] that the quest for certainty too easily became a means of hegemonic control, and which equate[s] the quest for understanding with resolving problematic situations and overcoming oppressive conditions." For Seigfried this means not a reconstruction but an abandonment of epistemology. "Feminist theories have been ignored or derided in mainstream epistemological circles because these mainstream views are 'abstract, nonempirical, universalist, and elitist,' because they resist efforts to historicize knowledge claims, and because they claim epistemological authority on the grounds that their analyses are not influenced by concrete circumstances that distort everyday knowledge, such as historically specific references and political, gender, class, or racial relations. The point is not that someone doing philosophy in this epistemological vein could not recognize the error of their ways, but that doing so entails abandoning epistemology as it has been constructed and doing something else."

Naomi Scheman has argued that one central theme of nonindividualist accounts of knowledge that has been overlooked by mainstream epistemological accounts is a realization of the epistemic significance of the fact of human interdependence and the epistemic centrality of trust. On this model, knowledge practices are social and our epistemic dependency on others is pervasive; thus the social institutions and practices that permit or limit such interactions become epistemically significant and must be subject to epistemological investigation. In "Epistemology Resuscitated: Objectivity as Trustworthiness" Scheman argues for the importance of a full-blown notion of trust and the dependency that necessitates it as an essential component of epistemological theorizing, but one often minimized or missing from contemporary epistemological theorizing. She argues that the recognition of the fact of epistemic dependency foregrounds the need for theorizing about "diversely situated subjects and about the possibilities for and barriers to trust between them." In this way, an adequate epistemology requires attention to forms of social organization to determine how social, political, or economic injustices may impact who is deemed worthy of trust and whose experiences and interests are and are not treated as epistemically significant.

Linda Martín Alcoff in "On Judging Epistemic Credibility: Is Social Identity Relevant?" continues the exploration of trust raised by Scheman's emphasis of the centrality of epistemic dependence. Alcoff argues that traditional epistemological standards are often inadequate to the task of adjudication of testimonial knowledge where epistemological questions are "not about perceptual reliability or perceptual memory but about trust and the basis of interpersonal judgement, credibility and epistemic reliability." With this in mind, Alcoff explores the question of the epistemic roles social identities like race or sex can play in assessing epistemic credibility.

Engaged Knowers, Local Knowledge

The model of the generic knowing subject posits knowers that are distinct but not *distinctive*. Neither the body nor any "subjective" aspect of an individual's mental activity is seen as affecting the proper pursuit of knowledge. In rejecting the impartiality ideal, feminists argued for replacing the traditional model of the knower as a detached, disinterested individual with the dynamic model of engaged, committed individuals in communities. Many feminist theorists, following the lead of Lorraine Code, began to investigate the epistemic value of "taking subjectivity into account" (Code 1991).

Code and others analyzed the ways various aspects of subjectivity play a constitutive role in the construction of knowledge, including one's historical and cultural location, the worldview and values one inherits in being raised in a particular culture; one's various social locations, including class, race, gender, religion, and other identifications; and the cognitive role of emotions.

In investigating new models of knowers designed to replace the disinterested knower with the engaged knower, feminists also argued that traditional accounts of the generic knower were not sufficient for more complex instances in which knowledge requires constant learning, is open to interpretation at various levels, admits of degree, and is not primarily propositional. These investigations not only included nonpropositional knowledge by going beyond the limitations of "knowledge that x is the case" to "know-how," that is, skills and habits, it also revealed that knowledge itself bears traces of knowers. That is what we know is both shaped and constrained by the specific subjective locations of which we are part.

In "The Struggle to Naturalize Literary Studies: Chicana Literary Theory and Analysis," Judith Richards applies Code's epistemology of local knowledges to the production of Chicana feminist literary theory in which who knows and how, as well as standards of evidence and authority, are locally conceded. Richards argues that the Chicana literary theory of Gloria Anzaldúa, in ways similar to the epistemological tenets of Code, "works simultaneously back into histories (personal and cultural), forward to the time when the feminist *mestiza* consciousness will be a leader in the structuring of global survival, and inward to the creative self that is always reconstructing (retheorizing) itself."

Lanita Jacobs-Huey in "Epistemological Deliberations: Constructing and Contesting Knowledge in Women's Cross-Cultural Hair Testimonies" investigates how Black women's concrete experiences play a role in their ways of knowing. Using the case study of Black women's discourses about hair care, Jacobs-Huey argues that Black women's narratives are filtered through their experiences of marginalization. "These shared experiences socialize them into similar ways of knowing and experiencing their body, particularly their hair," and emerge out of their specific memberships in lay and professional epistemological communities.

The Role of Imagination, Empathy, Storytelling

While embracing the importance of taking subjectivity into account, many feminist epistemologists have advocated the role of affective dimensions of cognition in the knowledge process: the importance of the imagination, empathy, and affective connection as a source of understanding, and the role of narrative. Lorraine Code, for example, in "Rational Imaginings, Responsible Knowings: How Far Can You See From Here," argues that those who attempt to know, and work to liberate those whose lives are in danger, "need to practice a particularly imaginative, discursively responsible knowing that is wary of replicating the very silencings and other oppressions it aims to counteract.

But embracing the epistemic role of subjective components of knowledge practices is not limited to acknowledging their presence. Feminist epistemologists argue that it is crucial to ensure a reflexive analysis of the subjective components of epistemic practices. That is, we must go beyond simply demonstrating the role of imagination in knowledge practices, but look critically at whose imaginings are taken as credible, whose stories are allowed to be told.

Code provides a careful study of the limits, indeed the danger, of a recognition of the role of imagination crafted out of a position of privilege—class, race, sex, ability—that reinforce assumptions of universal sameness of the self constructed by the liberal tradition. She argues that "orthodox epistemic subjects are trained only to know instances not particulars; and to fit those instances into ready-made universals, generalities." This, Code concludes, precludes subjects able to imagine "well enough to respond adequately to the particularities of suffering, the specificities of a situation whose horror is exacerbated by its being so unlike anything hitherto known or imagined."

Sue Campbell's study of the False Memory Syndrome Foundation (FMSF) in "Memory, Suggestibility, and Social Skepticism," for example, illustrates the means by which the FMSF has worked to create a shared imagining about the malleability of memory, an imagining she sees as paralleling Descartes's argument from misdesign and his metaphysical skepticism. "This imagining is meant to promote both a shift in epistemic project and in relations of epistemic reliance, but, in fact, promotes a metaphysical skepticism that leaves knowledge unavailable." Studying the narratives of the FMSF, Campbell examines how we are encouraged to imagine that we are prone to undetectable errors—the inability to distinguish memory from visualization and our proclivity to suggestibility—and we are urged to imagine the therapist as a potential deceiver, creating visualizations we are then urged to embrace as memory.

In a similar vein, Susan E. Babbitt in "Objectivity and the Role of Bias" argues that "in order to hear some stories *as* important, we often need *not* to hear other stories, or at least not to take them as seriously." In other words, in recognizing the epistemic role of bias and interpretation, and of storytelling and imagination, feminists cannot advocate a simple pluralism or risk slipping back to a version of the impartiality ideal that allows all stories equal rhetorical space. Babbitt urges us to be sensitive to the ways certain beliefs and practices render other perspectives and stories meaningless. Given this, we must sometimes "in order to properly appreciate stories, take a moral and theoretical position about those stories first."

The Role of Embodiment

An additional aspect of the knowing subject that some feminists take to be epistemically significant is the fact and nature of our embodiment. The model of the generic knower has traditionally ignored or minimized the epistemic role of embodiment and has rejected the epistemic relevance of our bodily differences. Attention to the body calls attention to the specificities and partiality of human knowledge, as well as reminding us of the importance of acknowledging the role of materiality, including the relations between human materiality and the materiality of the more than human world, in the knowledge process. But once we admit the body into our theories of knowledge, feminists argue that we must also recognize its variations; we must, for example, examine the ways in which bodies are "sexed" or "raced" or differently "abled." Alcoff, as one example, argues that racial and sexual difference is manifest "in bodily comportment, in habit, feeling and perceptual orientation." The move to including "knowing how" as an important source of knowledge, also brings up the significance of "bodily" knowledge, that is, skills or habits that are a blend of bodily and cognitive practices.

In "Participatory Knowledge and the World in Virginia Woolf," Louise Westling outlines the "dynamic epistemology of enmeshment in the web of life" found in the fiction of Virginia Woolf. In my chapter "Material Locations: An Interactionalist Alternative to Realism/Social Constructivism," I argue that feminist epistemology will be enhanced by embracing an enriched version of the embodiment hypothesis in which we recognize that material interactions are central both to what we know and to what there is—that is, to both epistemology and ontology. I delineate three aspects of material interactions: "(1) The particularities of human material configurations are epistemically significant, but it is important to see these as neither fixed nor as developed in the same ways in all communities; (2) The types of material interactions we engage in with the human and more than human world are materially shaped by our interests and our particular materiality; and the material agency of the more than human world in turn shapes our particular materiality and our interests; and (3) Our best theories, including but not limited to science, indicate that the world is a flexible fabric of interconnections, where many but certainly not all the most important interconnections involve humans. This realization demands a new ontology that renders any type of 'out there/in here' 'nature/culture' dichotomy nonsense, and carries a recognition that we (all we's) are of and in the world, or, to speak more poetically, that worlding is always part of our relationality."

Complexity and Change as Values

A common theme of feminist epistemological accounts is the view of reality as both complex and as emergent. As noted by Helen Longino, "many feminist scientists have taken complex interaction as a fundamental principle of explanation" (1994, 478). Many feminist epistemologists embrace theories of biological interaction in which the models that best describe natural events are those that incorporate dynamic interaction not only between organisms but also between organisms and environments. This conception of the world as constituted through interactions can be found in the chapters by Lisa Heldke, Charlene Haddock Seigfried, Louise Westling, as well as my own.

Westling carefully illustrates how Virginia Woolf's writings, read through the lens of the philosophies of John Dewey and Maurice Merleau-Ponty, encourage a "recognition of the dynamic interplay between human life and the myriad other lives and energies surrounding us" that supports a new epistemology of "enmeshment, reciprocity, dynamism, and continuity as the qualities of our knowing and being."

Similarly, in "Material Locations," I propose an interactionalist account based on an acknowledgment of the complex interactions between individuals, the environment, and the social contexts of knowledge acquisition. On such a view, the goal of epistemology is not to create a list of a priori standards but to develop a nuanced account of the complex interplay of material, conceptual, and social practices. "We are not just bodies existing independently from the external world; we are subjects committed to the world. Material locations are shaped by many forces including physical, social, linguistic, political, economic, historical. And all of these forces, including the physical, are not fixed but emergent. The world that we are of and in is, in the words of Haraway, a 'multifaceted set of interactions' between human and material agency. Neither the materiality of the more than human world nor human materiality is an unchanging given. What exists is emergent, issuing from complex interactions between our embodiment and the world."

Empirical Adequacy

Much of our work in feminist epistemology arose out of research in feminist science studies questioning the empirical adequacy of scientific research that claimed to demonstrate a biological origin for alleged intellectual or physiological deficiencies of women in comparison to men or to establish a biological basis for gendered social roles. Early work in this area by Ruth Bleier, Anne Fausto-Sterling, and Ruth Hubbard[7] demonstrated that sexist and androcentric bias had resulted in bad science. Hubbard, for example, argued that feminist science criticism could "lead us to more accurate, hence truer, accounts of nature than we now have" (1990, 5).

Lynn Hankinson Nelson, in her chapter "Relativism and Feminist Science Scholarship," argues that the critiques of feminist science studies overlook the role of evidence in feminist science critiques. She investigates examples of feminist scientific work such as Ruth Bleier's, Ruth Hubbard's, and Evelyn Fox Keller's critiques of linear, hierarchical models of gene action to demonstrate that a key concern of the work of feminist scientists is the empirical adequacy of scientific models and theories. Nelson argues that this concern is not in tension with or even separate from the other values and themes of feminist science scholarship. She argues that feminist values, such as "preventing gender from being disappeared" (Longino 1994) are not only political values, they are also "*epistemic* values, the rationale of which lies in the value feminist scientists attribute to empirical adequacy, explanatory power, and generality of scope." Although empirical questions are not separate from social factors, Hankinson Nelson argues that we make a serious mistake, and one that provides the basis through which critics of science studies reject our work, when we see the political values of feminist science studies as separate from questions of empirical adequacy.

Critiques of Objectivity

Feminist philosophy, like other feminist scholarly and activist practices, is one of a number of liberatory theories. I use the phrase "liberatory theorist" to refer to those who are committed to using the skills they have, whether they be philosophical, literary, scientific, sociological, or whatever, to address contemporary injustices and attempt to overturn oppressive practices.[8] Given our awareness of oppression and our commitment to developing theories and methods that will serve to remove such injustices, feminist epistemologists are concerned to develop accounts of knowledge and epistemic practices that will contribute to this goal. In the process of identifying androcentric or sexist values, feminist theorists not only began to identify their pervasiveness, many feminist epistemologists questioned the impartiality ideal in science and other knowledge practices.

While insisting that sexist or other oppressive biases must be identified and corrected, a number of feminist epistemologists and science theorists argued that accounts of objectivity that advocated impartiality were not the most effective way of doing so. Sandra Harding argued that the impartiality ideal in science was often the cause of racist or androcentric science because it "provides no resistance to the production of systematically distorted results of research. . . . It certifies as value-neutral, normal, natural, and therefore not political at all the existing scientific policies and practices through which powerful groups can gain the information and explanations that they need to advance their priorities" (1992, 568–69). In other words, Harding argued that the impartiality ideal served only to mask dominant values by identifying and eliminating those social and political values and interests that differed between individuals who constitute a research community. In sum, in a culture where dominant knowledge practices are conducted primarily by members of privileged groups, the impartiality ideal serves to reinforce dominance and inequality.

To correct this problem Harding proposed the practice of "strengthened objectivity" to identify and correct for institutionalization and normalization of oppressive biases. On this account, objectivity includes research designed to identify background beliefs and values, and the roles that they play in knowledge practices. Harding argued that the best way to do this is not to insist on value neutrality, but to maximize the participation of those who work from different perspectives, both as a way to identify the values imbedded in dominant practices and to provide alternative practices and values from which knowledge can be developed and evaluated.

As noted by Scheman in "Epistemology Resuscitated," feminist epistemologists are examining the history and social contexts from which current conceptions of objectivity emerged. Rather than simply accepting objectivity at face value, feminist epistemologists have argued that epistemological concepts and standards are shaped in part by social context. When those social contexts are sexist or racist or classist, it is reasonable to ask if the epistemic standards reflect and/or reinforce such values. Though most feminist epistemologists do not see their goal to be the removal of social influences from knowledge projects in order to obtain pure knowledge, we do think it is possible to develop better epistemic standards—ones that emerge out of and reinforce a more just social order.

Building on this belief, Lisa Heldke in "How to Be Really Responsible" argues for an expanded notion of objectivity as acknowledging, fulfilling, and expanding responsibility. Recognizing the centrality of relationships between participants in inquiry, Heldke advocates a more fluid account of subject/object roles than found in traditional epistemology and develops an account of inquiry as becoming more objective as participants expand the number and nature of their responsibilities, taking responsibility both for their actions and for the values out of which inquiry emerges.

The Bias Paradox

Such linkages of objectivity and value engender a related concern, one Louise Antony has labeled the bias paradox (Antony 1993). Antony queries "If we don't think it's good to be *im*partial, then how can we object to men's being *partial?*" or, put another way, if we think bias is ineliminable and we attempt to develop better methods, such as strengthened objectivity, to put values to positive epistemic use, then "*how do we tell the good bias from the bad bias?*" (Antony 1993, 189).

In "The Bias Paradox in Feminist Epistemology," Richmond Campbell responds directly to Antony's query by arguing that a realist understanding of truth and objective justification can resolve the paradox and show how particular biases—for example, feminist biases—can be effective guides to truth in a context of systemic gender bias. Campbell argues that a realist interpretation of evidential support is compatible with feminist epistemology and embraces the epistemic ideal of reflexivity included within it. He also holds that his account does not presuppose the impartiality ideal and includes the thesis that there are multiple, equally accurate or true perspectives about reality rather than a single, all-encompassing truth. He offers a conception of objectivity as pursuing "inquiry in a way that is conducive to finding out the truth about the subject of inquiry," and argues that inquiry that is truth-conducive need not be value-free. Campbell demonstrates that the concept of truth-conducive objectivity can be used to explain the difference between good and bad biases without presupposing that we already understand the difference. Campbell, like Nelson, believes that good biases are good *because* they contribute to empirical adequacy. Both would agree that the values of feminist epistemology are truth-conducive and thus are not simply political but are also epistemic values.

As with all the characteristics of feminist epistemologies that I list here, not only will feminist theorists disagree with one another, but the question of the context in which such themes are raised must also be taken into consideration. Without such attention to context we risk engaging in a form of cultural universalism in which we assume that the epistemically significant contexts for Western knowledge practices are true transculturally. As Uma Narayan argues, it has pragmatic value to reinsert the question of values into knowledge projects in Western epistemology given the European history of positivism, but this same strategy will have quite negative consequences if employed in India with its history of infusion of religious values in knowledge projects (1998).

Attention to Diversity

Harding's account of strengthened objectivity focused attention on the importance of supporting a diversity of knowers and knowledge projects as a means
to help insure the adequacy of research projects. On this model, difference becomes a potential epistemic resource. By including those working from different perspectives and with different methods, we help to encourage an
identification of the role of values in the production of knowledge and provide a means to assess which values provide the most reliable knowledge—both
in terms of empirical adequacy and in terms of addressing the needs and concerns of a wider spectrum of society.

This attention to diversity originally emerged from feminist concerns
about the low numbers of women scientists, particularly in the areas of physics,
chemistry, mathematics, and computer science. However, as feminist science theorists and epistemologists began to argue that the inclusion of women and other
under-represented groups was not only an issue of equity, but would actually
strengthen objectivity and would enhance what is known, attention to diversity
was transformed from a concern about equity to an issue of more adequate
knowledge practices. In the words of Linda Martín Alcoff, "social identity is relevant to epistemic judgment not because identity determines judgment but because identity can in some instances yield access to perceptual facts that
themselves may be relevant to the formulation of various knowledge claims."

In "Standpoint Epistemology in the Physical Sciences: The Case of
Michael Faraday," Barbara L. Whitten provides a case study of the work of
Michael Faraday that supports Alcoff's claim that social identity can be relevant to epistemic judgment. Whitten argues that the view that science and
other knowledge projects are adversely affected by the homogeneity of their
epistemic communities can be shown to hold even in the physical sciences.
Through a close study of the life and work of Michael Faraday, and through
the lens of the variable of class, Whitten illustrates her claim that even those
sciences where the objects of inquiry are not gendered (physics in this case) can
be affected by the social and cultural background of the scientist. She uses this
study to support the claim that science and other knowledge projects would "be
better off, the knowledge we construct would be more reliable, more authentic,
more objective, if the scientific community included more diverse standpoints."

Attention to diversity and a displacement of the impartiality ideal creates the need for epistemological alternatives that are open to multiple methods and perspectives. Articulating such an epistemology for moral theory is
the goal of Susan Hekman in "The Epistemology of the Moral Voice: Displacing Hegemony in Moral/Legal Discourse." Hekman argues that the work
of Carol Gilligan contains an "alternative moral epistemology that places dif-

ferences at its center." She notes that any epistemology that is based on differences raises the question of how to choose among perspectives and how to
decide which perspectives are appropriate in a particular context. Arguing that
truth, whether in the moral or the empirical realm, is local and contextual,
Hekman delineates an alternative moral epistemology that posits many paths
to moral truth. "This reading produces an understanding of moral truth that
is situated, particular, and, most importantly, multiple." She argues that explicit recognition of this pluralism is central to the articulation of an epistemology adequate to feminist goals.

Also dealing with the topic of difference, Susan Babbit in "Objectivity
and the Role of Bias" presents a lens that complicates the pluralistic impulse
in feminist epistemology. Babbit cautions that "sometimes proper understanding requires, not consideration of difference, but rather concern about the perspective according to which we see some differences as more important than
others in specific ways." The theme of Babbit's concern is contemporary development theory and the conceptions of human development it presupposes.
Babbit argues that in assessing cultural norms and traditions, multiple perspectives and appreciation of difference are often insufficient. Through an examination of the contexts of the Cuban revolution, Babbit concludes that "in some
cases of understanding, there must first be resistance to available, more comfortable explanations and, second, commitment to narrowly focused, *biased*,
pursuit of a specific sense of importance and meaningfulness." Through the
lens of Babbitt's analysis we see the danger of succumbing to a version of the
impartiality ideal even as we embrace difference and pluralism.

The Question of Authority and the Role of Power

Feminist epistemologists moved from the simple query How do we know? to issues of cognitive authority—that is, Which individuals are authorized as knowers and by which means? Which methods are deemed epistemically valuable?
And these questions began to reveal the complex relationships between power
and knowledge: Who benefits from or is disadvantaged by what we know? Who
benefits from or is disadvantaged by what we don't know? Who benefits from or
is disadvantaged by having only certain methodologies accepted as legitimate?

Feminists in numerous disciplines began to investigate the processes
though which women and their experiences were excluded or rendered invisible. Whether in the social sciences where social stratification studies classify individuals according to jobs, thereby rendering women and atypical men who do
not have jobs invisible, or in the medical sciences where research on heart attacks was conducted primarily on male subjects, or in the sciences where our

stories of evolution focused attention on male activities, feminist theorists documented the ways those in privilege frame the concepts and concerns around which knowledge is developed. An adequate feminist epistemology, then, is one that includes an analysis of the structures of cognitive authority and maps the complex links between issues of power, privilege, and knowledge.

Lynn Hankinson Nelson's chapter, "Relativism and Feminist Science Scholarship," includes a case-study analysis of the social and conceptual mechanisms of cognitive authority through an investigation of the complaints of science studies critics that science studies "in general constitute a threat to objectivity and rationality." She carefully documents the techniques used to deny the cognitive authority of feminist scientists and feminist science scholars.

Sue Campbell's study of the politics of the recovered memory versus false memory debate in "Memory, Suggestibility, and Social Skepticism" provides a powerful case study of how certain experiences and particular knowers can be rendered unreliable. Campbell examines how the False Memory Syndrome Foundation (FMSF) has successfully targeted the competence and epistemic authority of those who experience memories of abuse and the therapists who counsel them. She documents that one aim of the FMSF is to develop policy that "excludes the woman with a troubled past from participating as an agent in an understanding of her past and in contributing to social knowledge of childhood sexual abuse."

Epistemic Responsibility

Feminist epistemologists are concerned not only with descriptive analyses of our current knowledge practices, they are also committed to developing accounts of how our knowledge practices can be improved. Given that many feminist epistemologists hold that knowledge and justification involves trust, dependency, values and interests, community, power and privilege, feminist normative accounts of knowledge often employ notions of epistemic responsibility, that is, the belief that we have a responsibility to consider how social structures impact the generation of knowledge in addition to the complex effects of knowledge projects on the lives of other men and women as well as on the more than human world. Notions of epistemic responsibility mark the belief of many feminist epistemologists that we as individuals and members of social orders must take responsibility for how cognitive authority is established, for the values that knowledge practices embrace, and for those values that are rejected or rendered invisible. In this sense, the goal of developing better methods for gaining knowledge and the goals of creating a just society and more equitable human-nature interactions go hand in hand.

Lorraine Code, who introduced the notion of epistemic responsibility in her book of the same title (Code 1987), argues that an epistemology based on what real, variously situated knowers actually do makes ethical deliberation integral to epistemic discussion (1995, vii). In her chapter, Code argues that epistemic responsibility requires "an epistemology capable of engaging with particularity [that will] unsettle the epistemic subject; to require him (and now her) to come out of the shadows . . . undermine the self-certainty of the subject's vanishing act—into the shadows, into an allegedly ubiquitous 'we.' Fully visible/audible specificities require him and now her (for the generic self dissolves) to engage in ways that put his/her subjectivity also on the line; to assume responsibility for what and how he/she claims to know."

Sarah Hoagland, in "Resisting Rationality," provides an exploration of the importance of epistemic responsibility. Hoagland questions the feminist goal of strengthening objectivity by including within mainstream dialogues those whose voices and experiences have been rendered invisible. Providing a powerful case study of how the stories of the disenfranchised can be used against them, even when this is the unintended effect of well-meaning feminist scholars, Hoagland worries about the ability of those in power, including feminist scholars, to recount the stories of those who have less power in ways that will enfranchise rather than endanger them. It may be, following Hoagland, that certain epistemic reforms can only be safely instituted *after* certain social and economic reforms.

Hoagland's alternative to the dangers of seeking common ground within a tradition that oppresses us is resistance to mainstream paradigms through conceptual separatism. She defines conceptual separatism as an activity of refusal and disloyalty designed to disrupt conceptual coercion and to render oppressive systems of rationality nonsense, but "it is also a creative project, embodying shifts in language-games, shifts in logic which make new ways of engaging possible." Hoagland rejects the idea that feminists have no alternative to working within the dominant tradition, thereby risking not only having their knowledge used against them and others who are oppressed, but also unwittingly reiterating and reinforcing the conceptual coercion that keeps oppression in place.

Sue Campbell provides another cautionary tale of how feminist scholars have been dangerous to women by allowing the FMSF to frame the conceptual terrain such that even feminist actions have been influenced by the foundation's strategies. Campbell argues for rejecting the powerful rhetorical strategies of the FMSF designed to shift our support from women who have been abused. She argues that political support to create "contexts in which women can explore and articulate their experience of harm and of taking their testimony as fundamental to our own understanding of childhood sexual harm" is not compatible with accepting or being influenced by the imaginings of the FMSF concerning the malleability of memory. In the words of Sarah Hoagland, what we require is conceptual separatism: "strategies of resisting rationality both in the sense of resisting (dominant) rationality and also of finding nondominant resisting rationalities."

A Liberatory Epistemology

An acceptance of the value of epistemic responsibility and the related awareness of the linkages between power and knowledge lead many feminist epistemologists to embrace epistemology as a liberatory activity. Rather than an ideal of knowledge for knowledge's sake or abstract reconstructions of ideal knowledge practices, feminists concerned with creating liberatory epistemology focus on the applicability of knowledge practices to current needs and to the type of society we want to live in. This has led many feminist epistemologists to advocate the creation of a pluralistic and democratic epistemology.

But concern regarding epistemic responsibility noted above also suggests that the goal of creating better knowledge practices requires more than philosophical theorizing or empirical studies. It requires working toward a more just social order. Once again we see that, for many feminist epistemologists, we cannot and should not separate ethical deliberation and practice from epistemology.

For those who worry that feminist epistemology, like other aspects of feminist philosophy, is motivated by political concerns and thus is propaganda and not pure philosophy, Linda Martín Alcoff reminds us that much work in the history of Western philosophy emerged out of particular political motivations, including the work of Kant, Locke, and Russell. As Alcoff explains, "like Kant, feminist philosophers are committed to using philosophical methods to clarify and disempower the current dogmatisms that inhibit political advance." The authors represented in this anthology are committed to using the methods of their disciplines to reveal and transform the current dogmatisms concerning rationality to further the important goal of working toward a more just society. We hope this exciting conversation will motivate others to use their knowledge and wisdom to advance similar projects.

Notes

1. There had been a number of NEH Summer Seminars and Institutes on the topic of gender in other disciplinary areas, including history and literature, but all of them used the terms "woman/women" or "gender" to demarcate the focus rather than "feminism."

2. Seminar participants included: Alison Bailey, Philosophy, Illinois State University; Karen Barad, Physics, Pomona College; Drue Barker, Economics, Hollins College; Sara Farris, English, University of Houston; Ruth Ginzberg, Philosophy, University of Kentucky; Lisa Heldke, Philosophy, Gustavus Adolphus College; Ran-Joo Herr, Institute of Philosophy and Culture, Seoul; Sarah Hoagland, Philosophy, Northeastern Illinois University; Amber Katherine, Philosophy, Saint Mary's College; Shelley Park, Philosophy, University of Central Florida; Judith Richards, Romance Languages, Rockhurst College; Phyllis Rooney, Philosophy, Oakland University; Shijun Tong, Philosophy, East China Normal University; and Janet Varner Gunn, English, University of Pittsburgh. Visiting scholars who presented their work to the seminar included: Linda Martín Alcoff, Syracuse University; Lorraine Code, York University; Sandra Harding, UCLA; Lynn Hankinson Nelson, University of Missouri, St. Louis; Libby Potter, Mills College; Alison Wylie, Washington University, St. Louis.

3. The bibliography included in this anthology, though not exhaustive, includes many of these texts.

4. See Haack 1998.

5. A good example of this disagreement can be seen by comparing the use of Quinean scholarship in the work of Lynn Hankinson Nelson and Louise Antony, and subsequent research on the bias paradox, one of the topics of the chapters in this volume.

6. To my knowledge, the philosophy department at the University of Oregon is the first department to explicitly embrace this view of feminist philosophy. For more information about this conception of philosophy see our website at http://darkwing. uoregon.edu/~uophil/.

7. Bleier 1984; Fausto-Sterling 1985; Hubbard 1990.

8. In this group I include those working in areas such as race theory, queer theory, liberation theology, materialism, and disability studies, as well as the various areas of study included within multicultural studies.

References

Antony, Louise. 1995. Sisters, please, I'd rather do it myself: A defense of individualism in feminist epistemology. *Philosophical Topics* 23, 2: 59–94.

———. 1993. Quine as feminist: The radical import of naturalized epistemology. In *A mind of one's own: Feminist essays on reason and objectivity*, ed. Louise M. Antony and Charlotte Witt. Boulder, Colo.: Westview.

Bleier, Ruth. 1984. *Science and gender: A critique of biology and its theories on women.* New York: Pergamon.

Code, Lorraine. 1995. *Rhetorical spaces: Essays on gendered locations.* New York: Routledge.

———. 1991. *What can she know? Feminist theory and the construction of knowledge.* Ithaca, N.Y.: Cornell University Press.

———. 1987. *Epistemic responsibility.* Hanover, N.H.: Published for Brown University Press by University Press of New England.

Fausto-Sterling, Anne. 1985. *Myths of gender: Biological theories about women and men.* New York: Basic.

Haack, Susan. 1998. Reflections of an old feminist. In *Manifesto of a passionate moderate.* Chicago and London: University of Chicago Press.

Harding, Sandra. 1992. After the neutrality ideal: Science, politics, and "strong objectivity." *Social Research* 59, 3: 567–87.

Hubbard, Ruth. 1990. *The politics of women's biology.* New Brunswick, N.J.: Rutgers University Press.

Longino, Helen. 1994. In search of feminist epistemology. *Monist* 77, 4: 472–85.

———. 1990. *Science as social knowledge.* Princeton, N.J.: Princeton University Press.

Narayan, Uma. 1998. Essence of culture and a sense of history: A feminist critique of cultural essentialism. *Hypatia* 13, 2: 86–106.

Nelson, Lynn Hankinson. 1990. *Who knows? From Quine to a feminist empiricism.* Philadelphia: Temple University Press.

Scheman, Naomi. 1995. Feminist epistemology. *Metaphilosophy* 26, 3: 177–98.

Tuana, Nancy. 1996. Revaluing science: Starting from the practices of women. In *Feminism, science, and the philosophy of science*, ed. Lynn Hankinson Nelson and Jack Nelson. Dordrecht; Boston; London: Kluwer.

Wittgenstein, Ludwig. 1958. *Philosophical investigations*, trans. G. E. M. Anscombe. Oxford: Blackwell.

PART I

RETHINKING EPISTEMOLOGY: REALISM, TRUTH, OBJECTIVITY

CHAPTER TWO

Epistemology Resuscitated: Objectivity as Trustworthiness

Naomi Scheman

Introduction:
With Friends Like These, Who Needs Enemies?

A growing chorus of scientists, historians, and philosophers, many of whom self-identify as on the left of the political spectrum, would have us add objectivity, along with truth and rationality, to the endangered species list, with feminist epistemologists and philosophers of science among those responsible for the cultural environmental degradation that poses the threat.[1] As with efforts to protect endangered animals and plants, however, it is not always obvious just which forces endanger and which protect, or even how to characterize what it is we should be trying to preserve. Much as environmental preservationist projects need to be grounded in an understanding of the value of biodiversity, so objectivity preservationist projects need to ask just what it is about objectivity that makes its preservation so important. I want to argue that feminist epistemologists and philosophers of science are not the enemies of objectivity they are made out to be by the critics (as I will follow Elizabeth Lloyd in calling those who charge feminist epistemology, along with science studies and postmodern critical theories, with endangering objectivity). What the critics misidentify as a threat is better understood as an attempt to save objectivity by understanding why it matters and why and how it is truly threatened.

Objectivity, along with reason, truth, and rationality, is a normative concept with which we evaluate our own and each other's assertions and beliefs. Central to what we do when we call an argument, conclusion, or decision "objective" is to recommend it to others, and, importantly, to suggest that they *ought* to accept it, that they would be doxastically irresponsible to reject it without giving reasons that made similar claims to universal acceptability. Objective claims, that is, are always disputable, but they are not, without dispute, rejectable—as one can, without disputing a film critic's judgment, reject their recommendation of a particular movie simply on the grounds that one doesn't share their taste. Although some feminists and others have argued, on a wide range of grounds, against the value of objectivity as a norm, the disputes I want to focus on are not between objectivity's self-declared enemies and its self-declared friends but between self-declared friends who charge each other with being enemies in friends' clothing.[2] I'm concerned, that is, not with feminist arguments *against* objectivity, but rather with those feminist arguments that explicitly take their aims to be the articulation and defense of alternative conceptions of objectivity, and with the critics who insist that these feminists cannot possibly mean what they say.

In order to break up the logjam of disputes over who the "real enemies" of objectivity are, I am suggesting that we start by asking what it is about objectivity that makes a sustainable claim to being a real friend so valuable, why it is that objectivity and its similarly endangered relatives *matter*. Although I agree with Lorraine Code that the ground rules for legitimate philosophical argument have problematically framed these issues in ways that foreclose discussion by setting up relativism as a dismissably irrational position (Code 1995a, 185–207), my approach is somewhat different from hers: Rather than defending relativism (or some other alternative to objectivity as an ideal), I want to start with the fact that we (diversely) do often want or need knowledge claims to be acceptable by broader constituencies, or criticizable by those constituencies. I take it to be an open question, not to be answered in advance or in general, how broad such a constituency can, or should, be—that is, how broad a consensus we ought to seek or can plausibly expect for particular sorts of knowledge claims: when, for example, we might want not to exempt ourselves from what we take to be a problematically broad assertion but rather *contest* it. I will focus on the case that can be made for the objectivity (the universal acceptability) of the paradigm cases—namely, the claims of the sciences. Stated more broadly, the issue is: When, and insofar as, it actually matters that knowledge claims be acceptable to—or criticizable by—a broader constituency, what do we actually have to *do*, and what counts as doing it right? I take this project to be complementary to Code's defense of relativism, in particular in the attention that I will argue we need to pay to the particularities and, especially, social locations of the subjects, objects, and (passive or active) audiences of knowledge claims.

In the disputes over who are the real friends and who the real enemies of objectivity one point of agreement is that other things that we care about depend on it and are imperiled by its actual or perceived enfeeblement or demise (whether as a consequence of the head-on attacks of its alleged enemies or as a side-effect of various social and cultural developments). What are these other things, and why might their well-being depend on the well-being of objectivity? According to Paul Gross and Norman Levitt, "What is threatened [by, *inter alia*, feminist science studies, which, they allege, attack or repudiate objectivity] is the capability of the larger culture, which embraces the mass media as well as the more serious processes of education, to interact fruitfully with the sciences, to draw insight from scientific advances, and, above all, to evaluate science intelligently."[3] The underlying assumptions here are that the sciences produce something of value ("advances"), and ("above all") that "science" ought not to be accepted uncritically but ought to be subject to intelligent evaluation by "the larger culture." While the details of this formulation will turn out to be contentious—What are the consequences of acknowledging the nonhomogeneity of "the larger culture"? What makes some processes of education "more serious"? How do we identify scientific "advances"? What makes an evaluation of science "intelligent"? What are the relevant objects of evaluation: scientific results, scientific practice, or both?—the general formulation and the assumptions behind it would, I think, be acceptable to the feminist epistemologists and philosophers of science who are cited as objectivity's alleged enemies.

How does objectivity figure in this story such that its real or perceived enfeeblement or a widespread loss of belief in its possibility or desirability would pose such a threat? Rather than defining what objectivity *is*, I want to propose an answer to a different question, one about what objectivity *does* (what it's good for). The proposal is this: A sustainable attribution of objectivity serves to underwrite a significant degree of—objectively refutable—authority, and it does so by rationally grounding trust. When we characterize something (an epistemic practice or product) as objective, we commend it or its results to others than those who engaged in or produced it, including to those whose perspectives and interests might differ.[4] It comes into importance as a virtue to the extent that we are epistemically dependent on others who are in a range of ways—spatially, temporally, culturally, attitudinally, cognitively—distant from us. Given the extraordinary and increasing degree of both interconnectedness and technological complexity of the contemporary world, the need for objectivity cannot be overstated: We are all downwind of the activities of the sciences and other culturally authoritative sites of knowledge production, dependent on them both for much that we need and desire and for much that we cannot avoid. If objective judgments are judgments we can rationally trust, we need them more than ever; and the "we"s that need them are, especially, the "we"s least in a position either to identify with or to independently check out the judgments produced by socially recognized authorities. Furthermore, and perhaps even more importantly, we (diversely located "we"s) need to be able to enter into dialogue with authoritative knowledge producers, to become and be recognized as credible even if nonexpert critics—to, in Gross and Levitt's terms, "evaluate science intelligently"—and to have our perspectives recognized as potentially contributing to fuller, more adequate accounts.

If something like this is what objectivity is good for, what can we say about the disputes over who its real friends and enemies are? The antifeminist friends of objectivity are, I want to argue, the sorts of friends alleged to render enemies superfluous. Like snake oil salesmen, they purvey a quack remedy for a real problem. And like most quack remedies, this one is worse than useless: worse, because in purporting to be the real thing, it effectively diverts us from pursuing an effective remedy for what actually ails us.[5] By contrast, feminist epistemologists and philosophers of science such as Donna Haraway, Sandra Harding, Evelyn Fox Keller, and Helen Longino[6] (to cite just those most widely targeted by the antifeminists), along with others engaged in related projects of what can be called "liberatory epistemology," are developing accounts of objectivity that take seriously our need for it: If objectivity is an instrumental good, then it has actually to function so as to produce the good it promises; what we label "objective" has actually to be worthy of our trust and the trust of a diverse range of others.

In the tradition of analytic philosophers' giving acronyms to the theses they argue for, I want to suggest "CPR" as an acronym (sort of) for the projects of liberatory epistemology. As befits a loose collection of projects, as opposed to a clearly specifiable thesis, the acronym doesn't stand for any one label, beyond that of marking the connection to the practice of cardio-pulmonary resuscitation—reviving by breathing life back into a moribund subject. Rather, oddly and for no particular reason that I can think of, those letters jointly cover a large number of the central concepts that characterize epistemology resuscitated: critical, contextual,[7] committed, "corresponsible,"[8] and commonable;[9] perspectival, pragmatic,[10] practical, political, participatory, pluralist,[11] and partial;[12] and radical, relational, and responsible[13]—all of which characterize revised notions of reason, rationality, and realism.[14]

I will not be surveying these feminist objectivity projects or addressing the sometimes contentious differences among them. Rather, my aim is to provide a framework within which to understand them and to argue that projects within such a framework give us the most *useful* ways of understanding and defending objectivity. Briefly, my argument will be that liberatory politics such as feminism are intrinsically related to objectivity in their commitment to struggling for social institutions that are worthy of trust on the part of all those whose lives are affected by them: A "bias" in favor of such struggles is a bias in favor of the conditions that would make objectivity a real possibility, rather than a merely theoretical gesture.[15] Ironically, as Stephen Kellert points out, "the imposition of Modern Western Scientific Knowledge and its applications on people without their involvement and consent" is a "barrier to the achievement of genuinely universal scientific knowledge," which requires "a kind of radical democracy" (Kellert 1999, 196). Whether, when, and why objectivity *is* a real possibility—and whether, when, why, and how various "we"s ought to struggle to make it so—are deep and divisive political questions, not avoidable by metaphysical or methodological fiat.

The Case for Scientific Objectivity

Objectivity's antifeminist defenders locate the threat to objectivity presumed to be posed by feminist epistemology, philosophy of science, and science studies primarily in the feminist analyses of the sciences as social practices, in the claims that as such science is typically problematically implicated in the inequities of the broader society, and in the conclusion that such implication undermines science's claims to objectivity. For the critics of feminist science studies, science is the paradigm example of objectivity; hence such arguments are taken to be an attack on objectivity itself. There is, in fact, good reason for thinking of objectivity as the defining virtue of modern science—that is, as the guiding aim of scientific method and practice—but it doesn't follow from that connection that we cannot meaningfully ask about how it is that scientific practices achieve that aim to the extent that they do and why and how they might fall short of it, or even about whether the particular conceptions of objectivity embedded in scientific method as usually understood (especially by philosophers of science) might not be fundamentally flawed. By attending to the function of objectivity in rationally grounding the trust we are called on to have in what scientists do, we can get a handle on understanding both why and how scientific practices are objective and why and how they are not.

We can start by noting that objectivity has a history—one intimately and honorably bound up with the democratization of knowledge, the wresting of epistemic authority away from those with entrenched religious, political, or economic power—and a track record—comprising all of the successes of modern science. Defenders of scientific objectivity need not argue that the methods of science always work or even that they are not subject to systematic distortions, owing, in part, to their contamination by the injustices that characterize universities, primary and secondary educational systems, scientific funding establishments, and the society at large. There is no reason why those defenders have to argue that anything about the doing of science can entirely rule out any of those influences, nor even that good science could possibly thrive in a seriously unjust society. That there are external conditions that set the stage for the effective working of scientific methods is surely something that can be conceded by those who nonetheless maintain that it is adherence to those methods, whenever and whyever they are adhered to, that constitutes objectivity and gives us good reason to believe what scientists come up with.

Furthermore, the critics can grant that the plural ("scientific *methods*") is crucial: There is no one such method, nor is there even a codifiable range of them. Science is a complex set of social practices governed by a complex set of norms that share little more than the aim precisely of ensuring that the results of scientific investigation will be trustworthy, meaning that those results will be credible not only to the scientists who came up with them but also to others who may not share their particular experiences, biases, perspectives, interests, and the like. The norms of science work—when and to the extent that they *do* work—by factoring out of scientific knowledge claims the biasing effects of, among other things, the sorts of injustices that characterize the world in which science is done. When the rest of us trust what scientists come up with, what we are trusting them to do is to conform to the norms of good scientific practice; and we trust their results to the extent that we believe that they have done so and because we trust that conforming to those norms reliably tends to lead to the truth.

Certainly (the critics can concede), political considerations come into play around questions of research priorities, notably decisions about funding; and there is reason to argue for the greater involvement of a diverse range of scientists and nonscientists in these decisions, and for specific attention to the perspectives of those whose voices have been silenced, ignored, or distorted. But when it comes to the research itself, and to the evaluation of research results, it will be claimed that such diversity is idle. Certainly, it is a loss to science that some potentially productive researchers are undiscovered or unsuccessful for reasons having to do with discrimination and other social inequities, but there is no reason to believe that the loss is of some *distinctive* contribution— beyond, for example, that of bringing a particular passion to questions that have special relevance to their own lives and to the lives of those they identify with. If they bring anything *else* from the specificities of their lives into the doing of science, they are importing the same sort of bias that has led to sexist, racist, or homophobic science. The passion they bring ought to fuel a desire to discover the truth, whatever it might be, not to come up with answers that will accord with the political interests of a particular group, no matter how justified those interests might be.

I could go on, along what I take to be familiar lines, articulating the reasons for regarding science as an epistemically privileged means of revealing the truth (or an approximation to it) about a real world that exists independently of our needs, interests, and desires, as well as for thinking that especially those on the left—in solidarity with the subordinated and marginalized—have good reasons to believe in science so conceived.[16] For one, being less powerful, we have a need for the sort of neutral referee science promises to be, and, for another, we are (presumably) confident that the objective truth will, if it has political implications at all, support our judgments (that, for example, those who are White men are not intrinsically superior to those who are not).

The central point is this: According to the critics, feminists are claiming that trust in scientific method is misplaced, amounting to trust in those who wield unjust forms of privilege and who use that privilege—buttressed by the cultural capital of scientific expertise—to shield themselves from possibly legitimate forms of criticism. Rather, the critics claim, trust in scientific method is trust in a set of mechanisms and practices that are designed precisely to *rule out* these sort of abuses. Expertise, on this model, is acquired and justified not through the possession of various forms of unjust privilege but through the necessary talent, time, and energy that go into becoming able to understand, hence to be both a contributor to and a credible critic of, a difficult and complex area of knowledge. Given the extraordinary difficulty and complexity of contemporary science, we have no choice but to delegate epistemic authority to those who understand what we never will and to trust that what they come up with is what we would come up with if we had the talent, time, and energy to acquire their expertise; and that their being different from us in a whole range of ways other than their being experts (their being, for example, at the present time overwhelmingly White, male, middle class, heterosexual, and relatively able-bodied) is morally and politically lamentable but epistemically irrelevant.

Dependency and Trust

Certainly these defenses of scientific objectivity are apt and the beginnings of serious arguments, the playing out of which has produced a voluminous literature. But rather than review those arguments, I want to focus on a central and (so far as I can tell) indisputable but oddly under-acknowledged fact about the vast majority of what we know or believe; namely, the extent to which we are irremediably dependent on others. I want to argue that taking this fact seriously gives us good reason to be suspicious of what I will call "internalist" defenses of scientific objectivity, such as those of the critics of feminist science studies.

The fact of our epistemic dependency, and the implication that knowledge rests on trust as much as it rests on such epistemological staples as perception, reason, and memory, has only recently come to play a significant role in analytic epistemology and philosophy of science.[17] Even now that role is deeply disputed: The fact of epistemic dependency might not be contestable, but its centrality to epistemology is hardly universally acknowledged. Taking trust to be a central epistemological issue tends to mark one as belonging to a particular, still academically marginal, subfield—that of social epistemology.[18] It is, as usual, interesting to note what is and what is not linguistically marked: the contrast (unmarked epistemology proper) is presumably nonsocial, individualist, taking as its subject the generic knower-as-such—what Lorraine Code (1991) has dubbed "S knows that p" epistemology. The issue of epistemic dependency, when it arises in "unmarked" epistemology, is addressed as the specific and separable problem of "testimony"—whether and, if so, when and how and why and to what extent S (the generic knower) should believe some particular claim because someone else says it is so.[19]

What is masked by S's generic nature are not so much S's individual properties but rather the particularities of S's relationships to others as a fully social being, including the relationships that constitute S's gender, race, class, sexual identity, and so on. With respect to generic knowers, if "trust" is used at all, it is only as (roughly) a synonym for "believe," as in "I trust the train will be here any minute." And certainly some of my own uses of it thus far can be understood that way. But it is one of the central claims of this chapter that thinking about objectivity requires thinking about diversely situated subjects and about the possibilities for and barriers to trust between them. What is needed for that task is a much more full-blown notion of trust, involving an indefinite range of moral, political, and interpersonal factors that we can never fully spell out. Even when we do enumerate what we take to be the grounds for accepting what another tells us, that explicitness depends on webs of social connection that lie below the level of what we can check out. Such dependence, I want to argue, is ineliminable, but it can be more or less rational, and the trust that rests on it more or less justified. It is this "full-blown" notion of trust, and the dependency that necessitates it, that have been largely ignored in modern epistemology and that I want to argue need to be at the center of discussions of objectivity.[20]

The marginality of epistemic dependence within epistemology reflects the emergence of the field in its distinctively modern form in the seventeenth century, in the attempts to liberate the individual knower from dependence on various, particularly religious, forms of authority. The strongly individualist slant of the field reflects the religious, political, and economic individualism of early modernity; and the fact that on the most fundamental theoretical level individuals were and are taken to be generic reflects modernity's democratic egalitarianism. Difference is always relational: generic subjects are subjects who (for purposes of analysis) are understood as standing in no particular relation either to specific others or to social norms and institutions. The crises of trust out of which modern science arose—the need to find foundations for knowledge that would survive challenges to authority—were resolved by finding firm ground on which such individual generic knowers could stand and by articulating a notion of rational personhood that guaranteed that each such knower would come up with the same answers as any other, if only each followed a proper method. In the first instance (for example, in the founding texts of the field, Descartes's *Meditations* and *Discourse on Method*), this guarantee is meant to underwrite extreme epistemic autonomy: Each of us should pursue knowledge on our own, confident that if we follow the rules we will end up with the same results.

In practice, however, what the guarantee has underwritten is our dependence, oddly grounded in the denial of the relationships that make us different from each other. We are meant to trust each other epistemically only to the extent that we are assured that each of us is acting in ways uninflected by any of our actual relationships. My confidence in the generic nature of our arithmetic abilities, for example, allows me to ask you to count the candies and to divide them equally among the children at the party: I needn't worry that for you the correct answer would be different from what it would be for me.

Such dependence has not been, in practice, comfortable to acknowledge. Even if I can be confident that arithmetic is not different for you from what it is for me, I cannot be confident that you will not make a mistake, either inadvertently or in order to give some favored child more than a fair share of candies. I need to trust *you*, not just arithmetic-for-you, and no amount of nonrelativist absolutism about the truths of arithmetic can deal with the worries I might have about whether or not you are trustworthy. In theory, that is, your doing arithmetic is the same as my doing it; in practice I have all sorts of reasons to worry about the consequences of trusting you to do it. These worries are, in part, what motivated Descartes's emphasis on epistemic autonomy: Even if he can satisfactorily conclude that others are, like him, conscious, rational beings, he cannot so confidently rule out the possibility that they are careless or mendacious.

Such extreme epistemic autonomy is of a piece with Descartes's rationalism. Though observation had a place in his scientific method, that place was subsidiary to the workings of reason, which in his view were not in any essential way social.[21] Considerations of trust, specifically of those one took to be peers, were, by contrast, central to the development of experimental science, as Steven Shapin argues in *The Social History of Truth* (1994). As important as it was that experimental results be replicable, it was clearly impractical for every knower actually to replicate every experiment the results of which contributed to something he took himself to know. That, by and large, knowers were men was, in fact, one of the consequences of the need to provide socially salient signs of one's credibility, signs that rested on indications of competence and character that were, most explicitly, focused on class, with consequences for gender—notably, the economic independence of gentlemen, which was taken to be a necessary condition for intellectual independence, and the related importance for gentlemen of an honorable reputation, marked, for example, by a willingness to duel to defend that honor against suggestions of lying (Shapin 1994, chapters 2 and 3; on dueling, 107–14; on women, 87–91). By contrast, the significant number of women Cartesians can be seen as a consequence of the absence of any such demand in the case of knowledge conceived as Descartes did: If you can and think you should check anyone else's reasoning yourself, there is no need to rely on socially recognizable marks of integrity.[22]

No one thought, of course, that some experimental result was true *because* it was reported by a gentleman, still less that being so reported was what truth *was*. But we can say that a significant part of the justification for believing such a report was that it was made by a gentleman: In other words, its being so reported was a good reason for taking it to be (likely to be) true, and those who believed the report did so in part because it was so reported. Epistemologically, issues of honorable character and the ways of giving recognizable demonstrations of such character, were in practice ineliminable—as are the present-day ways of ensuring the integrity of scientific results: peer review of research and researchers, replication of experimental results, and the like. To argue for a distinctively feminist epistemology, therefore, is not to argue for some dubious claim about sex differences in individual cognitive capacities: Rather, it is to argue, far more plausibly, for the relevance of gender to the ways in which different people regard—and ought to regard—others as more or less worthy of trust.[23] And whatever one wants to say about the nature of truth claims, claims to credibility—what makes our beliefs justified—rest in large part on such socially grounded reasons for trusting.[24]

We can, of course, meaningfully ask if such trust is well or ill-placed: Was it in fact the case that the social and economic position of gentlemen made them better observers and more trustworthy informants, or that the present-day oversight mechanisms of peer-reviewed journals are effective in inhibiting and screening for fraud? Recent efforts in the United States to deal with highly publicized cases of alleged scientific fraud are cases in point: It is an empirical question how effective various mechanisms are for guiding the justification of belief, and when we discover that some mechanism has been working badly, we can attempt to make it work better.[25] But our ability to check on particular means for giving evidence of trustworthiness does not mean that we can, even in theory, eliminate the need for trust altogether—as, for example, I could in the case of asking you to count the candies. In that case, whatever I might be relying on in taking you to be trustworthy (both arithmetically competent and honest) can be independently verified: All I have to do is count and divide the candies myself and see if I get the same result. I don't *have* to trust you, and I can, without trusting you or anyone else, determine whether, when I *did* trust you, I was justified. In this case, it appears, it is not just that there is an *ontological* difference between my being justified in trusting you and your answer's actually being correct, but there is an *epistemological* difference between the sort of justification I have from whatever grounds my trust in you and the (greater) justification I have from checking it out myself—a difference that makes it reasonable to say that my need for trust can, at least in theory, be eliminated. What are the epistemological consequences if the need for trust is not eliminable?

THE INELIMINABILITY OF TRUST

When Descartes urged extreme epistemic autonomy, he did not think that he was thereby narrowing the scope of what he might know. His ambition, to encompass all there was to know about the natural world (including, he thought, ethics) within the limits of his own ability to verify both evidence and reasoning, was not nearly as wild an idea in his time as it appears in ours. It is said that Leibniz was the last person who could have known all there was to know, and the conceptual distance between then and now is immense. That distance is strikingly illustrated in a paper by John Hardwig (1991), in which he draws on examples from physics and mathematics to argue for the epistemological ineliminability of trust in the moral character of others even among experts in a field, who need to rely on the results of collaborators whose work they cannot replicate or, even, in many cases, fully understand. It is not, Hardwig argues, just as lay persons or even as scientists in distant fields that we are required to take the results of science on trust.

What we can do is to put in place practices that we have good reason to believe are effective in certifying the trustworthiness—the competence and integrity—of those on whom we are dependent. Despite our having, even in theory, no independent way of checking on the effectiveness of those practices, we do have ways of playing some of them off against others, of building in redundancies, of constructing overlapping ropes of trust that make our dependency reasonable, not abject. But, as Hardwig points out (1991), such trust-grounding practices are just that: actual practices, engaged in by actual people, and subject to all the vagaries that affect other forms of social interaction. Hardwig's analysis, however, focuses on the importance of individual character and on the role to be played by the teaching of ethics to researchers. He doesn't address my central concern here, namely, the systematically trust-eroding effects of various forms of social, political, and economic injustice. Who, for a start, are the "we" who put in place the mechanisms meant to ensure the integrity of scientific results?

One way of framing the dispute between feminist objectivity theorists and their critics is with the question of whether we ought to understand objectivity (as exemplified by science) in terms of the norms and methods of scientific practice (an internalist account), or whether we can and should go beneath or beyond those norms and methods and the practices that embody them to find critical ground (an externalist account).[26] (To put the dispute in more normative, less naturalized, terms: the question is whether the norms that are meant to yield objectivity are narrowly epistemic or also broadly moral and political.) When the critics take the first, internalist, option, it is in part because the methods and practices of science are supposed to give us reason to believe that the answer to the question Who are "we"? is, *in theory*, All of us, for whom scientists stand in appropriate proxy. Going beneath or beyond the precincts of science is seen as leaving the domain of objectivity, allowing in to the conversation just the sorts of differences in interest and perspective that are seen as damaging to the trustworthiness of science's knowledge claims. Those of us on the outside of science are urged to trust what goes on within its domains not despite but precisely because of our not participating in its innermost practices (as we are, for example, meant to trust the judiciary precisely because of the insulation of judges from public opinion).[27]

Much of the appeal of the internalist account has to do with its rooted-ness in the democratic egalitarianism of modernity (it is not supposed to matter that some of us discover truths for the rest of us to take on trust, because we are all supposed, in all relevant respects, to be interchangeable); and it suffers fatally from the flaws and limits of that egalitarianism. As Shapin's study shows, the actual practices of demonstrating scientific credibility have always been shaped—how could they not be?—by more general practices of judging people as worthy of trust, practices that have not been—how could they be?—immune from the practices that structure and maintain various forms of privilege.[28] It is quite likely that those whose economic exploitation grounded the economic "independence" of gentlemen would not have found a gentlemanly readiness to duel a sign of trustworthiness, or, if they did, it is hard not to see that trust as misplaced. It may well have been reasonable for anyone to conclude that a readi-ness to duel reliably signified some form of honorable behavior among those to whom it applied, but there would have been no good reason for those excluded from that system to think that those guarantees should carry any weight for them. For all they were in a position to conclude (assuming, as seems reasonable, that they were unable independently to verify the claims of gentlemen, hence to form their own judgment about the reliability of those trust-ensuring practices), the whole code of honor might underwrite an attempt to buttress a set of falsehoods supporting the upper-class privileges shared by the gentlemen who gave each other signs of mutual trustworthiness.[29]

I'm not denying (at this point in the argument) that even socially unjust codes of trustworthiness might actually be reliable as "trackers of truth": That's a different question from whether or not someone in particular has good reason to think that they are. And to the extent that such codes are articulated and enforced by, accessible to, and understood by an unjustly privileged elite, those excluded from those privileges have, in fact, little reason to trust them. It does not help to be told that you are included in the "we" in whose name those norms are set and enforced—that you are, in all important respects, the same as those who actually do the setting and enforcing—when what you know is that the chances are minuscule that someone like you (however you understand that) might actually participate in that "we," and, furthermore, that the structures that keep you from participation are the same ones that provide the participants with the means of recognizing each other's trustworthiness. Though scientists no longer have to be gentlemen, there are many people in the world today who are effectively excluded from the ranks of those who set and enforce scientific norms, people for whom identifying with the "we" that does so would be an act of bad faith, hence for whom the only alternative to abject dependency with respect to the claims of science is cynical rejection, an attitude that in fact, to the dismay of scientists, seems increasingly to characterize much of public opinion.[30]

The central problem with the internalist account is thus that it fails to seriously confront the problem of justification as it actually arises. Epistemic dependency means that justification requires rationally grounded trust, and trust needs to be convincingly demonstrated—not just abstractly demonstrable. The world of contemporary science is large and impersonal, and the practices that ground and demonstrate trust are embedded in the workings of institutions such as universities, corporate research departments, government agencies, and academic journals. The trustworthiness of scientific methods derives, in practice, from the effective working of those institutional structures; and justified belief in that trustworthiness derives from the justified belief that those institutions do in practice what they are supposed to do in theory: ground knowledge claims that are acceptable to all of us, not just to those of us with certain forms of privilege, who see the world through certain lenses, from certain biased perspectives. If you believe (as presumably those on the political left *do* believe) that the institutions in question are problematically complicit in society's racism, sexism, classism, heterosexism, and so on, then you ought to be suspicious of the ability of those institutions to ground the trustworthiness of scientific knowledge—even if it seems to you clear that such complicity has no discernible effect on the specific trust-ensuring practices themselves. The important terms there are "seems *to you*" and "discernible" (*by you*): What can you say, and why do you think you should be believed, when those whose experience of those institutions is one of oppression, marginalization, or exclusion ask you why *they* should trust what comes out of them?[31]

The situation is analogous to the one facing the criminal justice system, notably when it comes to seeking convictions for Black defendants.[32] The task of the prosecution is to convince a jury that the prosecution's case demonstrates the defendant's guilt beyond a reasonable doubt. Meeting that epistemic standard is in general impossible without the jury's having a great deal of trust in the competence and integrity of those who are presenting the state's case. To a certain extent what the state (in the person of police, forensic experts, and the prosecuting attorneys themselves) presents can be backed up relatively independently of what those people say, but to a great extent the credibility of testimony rests on the credibility of the testifiers, and, crucially, of the institutions within which they work and that enforce the norms to which they are accountable. When, as arguably in the O. J. Simpson case, the jury is convinced that those institutions are corrupt—that they are, specifically, racist—there does not have to be a story to tell about just how that corruption could have tainted the specific evidence on which the case rests. Rather, all that is necessary for the standard of persuasion beyond a reasonable doubt to be unreachable is that the jury not find the institutions of the state trustworthy.[33]

Many of the discussions in the so-called science wars ignore, as many discussions of the O. J. Simpson case ignored, the specifically epistemological nature of the issues, in particular, the centrality of the notion of justification and the importance of attending to the background context that, for particular believers, either grounds or undermines the trust that is needed for any reasonable standard of justification to be met. The credibility of science suffers, and, importantly, *ought* to suffer—just as the credibility of the prosecution suffers and ought to suffer—when its claims to trustworthiness are grounded in the workings of institutions that are demonstrably unjust—even when those injustices cannot be shown to be responsible for particular lapses in evidence gathering or reasoning. Credibility will suffer especially when the scientists in question, or those to whom they are believed to be close or beholden, are thought to have a stake in what they are reporting, as, for example, in research on racial differences in IQ, on the safety of drugs or food additives, or on the reliability of nuclear reactors. Those who are concerned (as, for example, scientists should be) that the results of science be not just true but justifiably believed to be true by the lay public as well as by other scientists need to be concerned about the systematic complicities with unjust privilege that systematically undermine the trustworthiness of the institutions on which such justified belief depends.

Thus, for example, it ought to be a matter of concern to scientists, if not to internalist philosophers of science, that mainstream medical research on the causes and treatment of AIDS is widely mistrusted in African American communities. According to a survey of African Americans conducted in 1997, 18 percent said they believed HIV was "an engineered microbe" and nearly 10 percent said they believed AIDS was part of a plot to kill Black people. To lay such skepticism about science at the door of the "academic left" is to blame the messenger: Rather than blaming the academic theorists who attempt to understand this mistrust, it makes much more sense to blame the practices in and around science that engender it. The same survey reported that fully 74 percent of African Americans "believed they were very likely or somewhat likely to be used by doctors as guinea pigs without their consent." Surely such a belief has a lot to do with the fact that, to take the most notorious example, in the Tuskegee syphilis experiment African American men *were* so used, and surely such mistrust has a lot to do with the mistrust of what doctors and medical researchers report. As Dr. Alvin Poussaint puts it, "When people don't know science, and most people don't, it's not hard to convince them that something unsavory may be going on. And this becomes a conspiracy to get black people. That's how much they believe that doctors in the system want to kill them" (France 1998, F6).[34] The problem isn't the theories of the academic left: The problem is racism.

As Elizabeth Lloyd puts the point more generally:

> The spectacles of corruption and waste in the manufacture and design of our best military technology, lack of responsiveness within all parts of the health and medical technology professions during the first decade of the AIDS pandemic, and lying and cheating for money and prestige within the top universities and research institutes in the world, and even the waffling on dietary guidelines regarding cholesterol, eggs, and oat bran—all have produced a public mistrust of both the disinterestedness and competence of scientists in general, and thereby of science itself.

Lloyd suggests that the critics of science studies can be seen as "scapegoating" those who are "investigating the possibilities that such things are *built into* the social systems of the sciences as they stand: they might be structural, institutional, and predictable" (Lloyd 1996, 236). The critics' insistence that nonetheless internalist epistemological resources provide the only proper tools for identifying and remedying such trust-destroying activities looks less like the high-minded defense of objectivity than like the defensive warding off of an appropriately democratic demand for accountability.

BEYOND HEURISTICS: IF YOU WANT TRUTH, FIGHT FOR JUSTICE

One might object at this point that, while what I've said might well be true when it comes to the *credibility* of science, it doesn't affect the question of scientific *truth*, provided that science is working as it should, according to its own norms. One might, that is, concede that in the absence of better reasons than are now available for many members of the lay public to trust the institutions of science, their cynicism about what scientists say might well be more justified than their credulity would be. The problem (admittedly a large and important one) would be to find ways of convincing the lay public—especially those among them who are understandably alienated from the institutions of the epistemic establishment—that those institutions are worthy of their trust, or at least that they would be if they lived up to their own, internally justified norms. One could further agree that the solution cannot and should not be seen as a matter of image manipulation: Possibly the only effective but certainly the only proper way of producing such confidence would be to work to make the institutions in question—and, generally, the broader society within which they exist—more genuinely just, more truly worthy of everyone's trust. One could concede all this and still argue that the results of scientific research, conducted according to internal norms, are in fact, objectively, true (or, more reasonably, leading toward the truth), and justifiably believed by anyone who is in a position—as the lay public lamentably is not—to see how it is that the practices of trust-grounding work, despite the injustices of the institutions in which they are housed.

But how *do* those practices work, and why should *anyone* trust them? Why, specifically, do *I* trust them?—because the fact is that, to a very great extent, I do. (To a very great extent, actually, most people do, when it comes to the more settled and well-established fields of science: we cross bridges, go up and down in elevators, use household appliances, fly in airplanes, believe in the solar system, viruses, and electrons, confidently expect eclipses, tides, and comets.) What I want to suggest is that an externalist focus on epistemic dependency and the epistemological centrality of trust enables both better prescriptive accounts of how justification ought to work and better descriptive accounts of how it actually does work, including when its working is apparently accounted for in internalist terms.

Two of the chapters in this volume provide instructive examples of the epistemic role of trust and of the epistemic consequences of its being undermined. Sue Campbell argues against the efforts of the False Memory Syndrome Foundation and its supporters to systematically undermine the confidence of those who experience what they take to be recovered memories of childhood sexual abuse. She compares such efforts to Descartes's evocation of the evil demon: In both cases we are urged to see ourselves as systematically defective, as unable to trust our own faculties, or those of others relevantly like us. As Campbell puts it:

> The FMSF, in effect, argues that the public should support a shift in project that excludes the woman with a troubled past from participating as an epistemic agent in an understanding of her past and in contributing to social knowledge of childhood sexual abuse. . . . Through charging bias and evoking scientific objectivity, the activities of the False Memory Syndrome Foundation instead attempt a skeptical destruction of one of the contexts that allows a woman to understand a troubled and abusive past. But her perspective is critical to any communal project of objective knowledge of sexual harm. (Campbell, this volume, 157)

Specifically, Campbell points to the attempts of the FMSF to present the setting of feminist therapy, one in which the collaborative work of reconstructing a coherent life story goes on, as a systematically distorting one, one that ought not to be trusted. Campbell's point is not that false memories are impossible, or that feminist therapists are always trustworthy: Rather, she argues, the interpretative frame provided by the FMSF undercuts the trust without which even accurate memories cannot be retrieved. "We require," she concludes, "an account of objectivity that can endorse the contexts in which knowledge emerges only through relationships of trust, the influence of imagination, and protection from premature criticism. The cost of supporting these contexts may indeed often be uncertainty about whether our beliefs or commitments are fully justified; the cost of withdrawing our support from these contexts will be the silencing of these perspectives." (this volume, 169)

In Sarah Hoagland's chapter, she raises for feminist philosophers of science extremely challenging questions about the limits of trustworthiness: how ought we think about our commitment—in the name of objectivity—to broadening the critical context within which scientific claims are articulated and evaluated, when some of the women whose voices and perspectives we are bringing into the conversation have good reasons for not wanting their stories told to those whom they do not trust not to misuse them? (this volume, 137–38) Are we, she asks, dangerously naive, in trusting the powerful to hear the stories of the powerless, and in trusting our own ability to tell those stories in ways that will enfranchise, rather than endanger, those who trusted us with them? Hoagland raises these worries in concrete form with the story of a rural Gambian woman, Kaddy Sisay, whose use of birth control was aimed not at reducing the number of children she bore but of maximizing her chances of a successful pregnancy, and of the Western woman anthropologist, Carolyn Bledsoe, who told Sisay's story in a conference setting, as an illustration of the value of attending to "anomalous data."

Hoagland quotes Bledsoe as arguing for the importance of understanding Sisay's use of Depo-Provera on the grounds that "[n]owhere is the need to understand the dynamics of high fertility more obvious than sub-Saharan Africa," to which Hoagland responds: "Why? Whose need? And why the need, exactly?" In a footnote she lists the sources of support for Bledsoe's research, including Gambian governmental agencies and U.S. and British academic institutions and foundations (this volume, 145). Hoagland argues that the ethical obligations of those who would be Kaddy Sisay's trustworthy allies would preclude even inadvertently transmitting her story to those who would use it against her. She characterizes "the scientific move to 'objectivity' [as] an effort to exclude others from meaning-making, deauthorizing all voices it has not trained/tamed" (this volume, 137), arguing that feminist projects to achieve greater objectivity by bringing into the conversation silenced or marginalized voices ignore the ways in which such voices get distorted by the reframing necessary to make them scientifically intelligible, and the ways in which, so distorted, those voices get used against those from whose mouths they come.

Part of Hoagland's point is that it is a mistake to think that dominant discourses have no use for what the nondominant might have to say: The roles of the "native informant" and the research "subject" (i.e., object) are well recognized. That's part of the problem: The voices of the subordinated are all too easy to slot into predetermined places, as producers of "data" the interpretation of which remains in the hands of the dominant. Such placement is facilitated when those voices are transmitted by people with the status of accredited insiders, including feminist philosophers of science—even if we happen to be, to use Patricia Hill Collins's term, "outsiders within" (Collins 1986, 14). Exclusion from meaning-making has never meant that one's life, culture, and body were off limits for "incorporation" by epistemological omnivores, who have always acknowledged that objectivity requires extensive, wide-ranging data collection. In our uneasy (or not uneasy enough) placement *in* universities but not, we think, really *of* them, we (feminist scientists and philosophers of science) pose a real danger to women whose absence from the academy might be as much avoidance as exclusion.

Hoagland's separatism is grounded in her pessimism about the possibilities of trust between the dominant and those they dominate. Specifically *epistemological* separatism follows from her recognition of the epistemic importance of trust. If we accept, as I argue that we should, the conception of objectivity articulated by its feminist friends, then Hoagland poses a deep and serious challenge: We may be barred from pursuing more objective knowledge so long as the conditions of trust are lacking—so long, that is, as some pieces of the perspectival puzzle cannot be added to dominant accounts without betraying those whose perspectives they are.[35] Not only would adding those pieces to *this* puzzle distort them (they are not accurately translatable into dominant terms), but the attempt to do so, to communicate them to those who control the dominant discourse, is a betrayal, a telling of secrets to those who cannot be trusted with them. In the absence of good grounds for trust, the critical work of striving toward objectivity cannot (and *should* not) go on.

OBJECTIVITY, DEPENDENCY, AND INEQUALITY

Return to the democratic ideals that motivated and provided the theoretical underpinnings for the epistemology of modern science. According to those ideals, all knowers are ideally interchangeable, meaning both that individually arrived-at results should be the same for all reasoners and that we can effectively function as each other's surrogate knowers. Our epistemic dependency, that is, is either eliminable or benign. But that assumption—that we are dependent on only our peers who can, as our peers, be trusted—is, in the real world, false, and not only because many of us have been expected to be irrationally dependent on those who have been our oppressors. The dependency of scientists on other scientists—of peers on peers within shared institutional settings—while less obviously irrational, needs also to be called into question in the light of what are widely acknowledged to be the problematic ways in which power and privilege shape the workings of the practices meant to ensure trustworthiness. But there is an additional, deeper problem than those involving the trustworthiness of scientists and of scientific practices. All along, those who have been the authorized knowers have been, in subtle and complex ways, dependent on those whom they would not have acknowledged, except, perhaps, in the most purely theoretical of terms, as their peers; and those forms of dependency have gone unacknowledged and unaccounted for in terms of assessing the trustworthiness of knowledge claims.

The norms of epistemic self-sufficiency and, failing that, dependency on trusted peers, were connected to the individualism of early modernity not just through the ideal of theoretical egalitarianism but also through the picture of persons as essentially competent adults—Hobbes's men sprung up like mushrooms, to take that picture's most striking evocation. If the sort of extreme dependency that characterizes infancy and childhood is acknowledged at all, it is to mark it as something that has, intellectually, to be superseded: The ground that we in fact traversed in our parents' arms has to be retraversed under our own power, in order to prove that the place where we have ended up is one we could and would have reached had we done the entire journey under the direction of our own adult intelligence.[36] Projects of rational reconstruction and the distinction between the realm of discovery and the realm of justification are versions of this project, which has as one of its aims the demonstration that a route to knowledge that in fact crossed over swamps and bogs and very shaky bridges could have been undertaken proceeding solely on firm ground; in other words, that any trusting of those whose trustworthiness cannot be independently verified can be shown to be dispensable.[37] Beyond parents and teachers (those Descartes, for example, charges with having filled his head with unverifiable beliefs before he reached the age of reason), there are those whose unrecognized labor goes into grounding the trustworthiness of scientific endeavors: the workers who make or clean laboratory equipment, for example, or set the type for scientific publications, or, for that matter, the informants who are presumed not to be making up funny stories to tell the various social scientists who pry into their lives.

Annette Baier has been working out the consequences, for moral and political philosophy as well as for epistemology, of starting theory with the universal experiences of infancy and childhood. Such a starting point provides a salutary contrast to the tendentious appeals to the alleged universality of some particular conception of reason that is the starting point of internalist accounts of scientific objectivity. It is, to say the least, odd that something we all do, nontendentiously, have in common—we were born and remained for a considerable time wholly dependent on others not only for our physical survival but for our acquisition of what Baier calls "the essential arts of personhood" (Baier 1985, 84)—should be seen, if it is seen at all, as an *obstacle* to the universality that objectivity aims for, as a site for the acquisition only of limiting, biasing forms of particularity from which we need, as autonomous adults, to wean ourselves. Baier's project has been to rethink adult epistemic, moral, and political competence as an achievement of maturation, involving neither an uncritical acceptance of the lessons and the ties of childhood, nor a fantasy of self-generation. Central to that achievement is the ability to trust when, and only when, it is appropriate to do so.[38]

Thus, to acknowledge the complex webs of dependencies—of lay persons on scientists, of scientists on other scientists, and of scientists on nonscientists—that undergird the workings of objectivity, is to acknowledge the necessity, throughout those webs, for trust to be both psychologically possible and rationally justifiable. If we cannot trust those on whom we are epistemically dependent, we will not believe when we should; and if we ought not to trust them, we risk believing when we should not. Much of what goes into both the psychological possibility and the rational justifiability of trust lies both below and outside of (as well as, in each of our lives, temporally prior to) the explicit norms of scientific practice; and without such grounding, we are powerless to effectively answer the skeptic, who speaks to us from a place of alienation from that ground—whether that alienation be a philosophical conceit or a material reality. As Baier puts it, "the secular equivalent of faith in God (which performs this anti-skeptical role, for example, in Descartes's *Third Meditation*), which we need in morality as well as in science or knowledge acquisition, is faith in the human community and its evolving procedures—in the prospect for many-handed cognitive ambitions and moral hopes" (Baier 1980, 293).

It is the task of the projects I have collectively referred to as "CPR" to argue for the dependence of objectivity on the conditions of social justice that would justify this faith; for the claim that, in the absence of such conditions, objectivity is inevitably compromised; and for the necessity for those who would be objectivity's true friends to struggle for social justice. Such a view of objectivity differs from an internalist account largely in being far more rigorous and demanding: Sandra Harding's term "strong objectivity" is not just a rhetorical ploy (Harding 1993, 69). The internalist provides an account of rational credibility that rests on the suitability of some people to serve as surrogate knowers for the rest of us, who are ineliminably dependent on their expertise, while denying the relevance of many of the questions we might be inclined to ask if we were to take seriously the issue of their trustworthiness. It is, in short, irrational to expect people to place their trust in the results of practices about which they know little and that emerge from institutions—universities, corporations, government agencies—which they know to be inequitable. Even those who are insiders to those institutions have reason to be skeptical about the adequacy of those practices to ensure objectivity, independent of and unchecked by critical scrutiny of the conditions within which they operate. There is, for anyone, little reason to trust that partiality can be adequately dealt with by ruling it out of order or that concrete issues of trust and dependency can be adequately dealt with by systems of rules that pride themselves on studied inattention to the world in which they operate.

Internalist defenses of scientific objectivity are collectivized versions of the methodological solipsism that convinced Descartes that the most stringent criticisms of his arguments were those generated by a figment of his own imagination. Insofar as the practices of science do adequately ensure trustworthiness, it ought to be possible to make that case—actually *make* it, to actual people with actual reasons for being skeptical, importantly including reasons that have to do with the economic and social inequities that underlie the selection and training of experts.[39] Charges of irrationalism are oddly directed at those who point out—correctly, from their perspective—that they do not have good reason to believe what experts say. And it is simply arrogant to be certain that the effort genuinely to engage with those who have been excluded could be of only heuristic value, that all the worthwhile criticisms and advances are generated from within. Objectivity on an externalist account is not an all or nothing matter, settled by rules laid down in advance; it is, rather, a rolling horizon we move toward as we increasingly democratize our epistemic practices.

Hoagland's separatist epistemology is, therefore, a challenge to CPR theorists, who, I want to suggest, can be seen as arguing for a *diasporic* epistemology, one that is sufficiently hopeful about universalist liberatory politics to sustain, and even to encourage less privileged others to sustain, faith in a not-yet-existent human community.[40] That we (feminist academics) might be fools is the least of our worries, Hoagland warns; if our faith is misplaced, we'll be guilty of betrayal. To be a friend of objectivity and simultaneously a friend to those who do not share one's relatively privileged social location is a moral and political risk. I am inclined to think that it is one worth taking, though I urge those of us who take it to also take Hoagland's warnings to heart. What I am certain of is that no defense of objectivity can be made on ground less politically contentious than this.

Those who hold on to internalist conceptions of scientific objectivity do so in part because they believe that a naturalized account of science as a social practice is a wholly different endeavor from a normative account of it as truth producing. Historical and sociological studies such as Shapin's (1994) do typically eschew what is taken to be the central epistemological question: how *ought* we to pursue knowledge? My contention in this chapter has been that it is precisely as a social practice, naturalistically understood, that science needs to be evaluated—especially if what we care about is its objectivity. The normativity that characterizes epistemology can be found not in ahistorical canons of rationality but in the normativity of politics.[41]

NOTES

Over the past few years, a number of graduate students at the University of Minnesota have been working on issues of trust and testimony. I have learned a lot from them: Nancy Nyquist Potter, Heidi Grasswick, Peg O'Connor, Lisa Bergin, Amanda Vizedom, and Jan Binder. I owe a special debt to students, colleagues, and friends in Gothenburg, Örebro, and Helsinki, where I taught short graduate courses in 1997 and 1998, in which I developed these ideas in dialogue; and to the Feminist Studies Department at the University of Gothenburg for a wonderfully congenial work environment. Thanks to Michael Root and Stephen Kellert for comments on earlier drafts.

1. For a recent collection of papers making the case against science studies, see Koertge 1998. It is also noteworthy that all three of the Presidential Addresses to the APA in 1997–98 addressed issues around objectivity. See Fine 1998, Nozick 1998, and Kitcher 1998. Only Fine's address discussed feminist work in this area; the omission is especially striking in Nozick's case. Alison Wylie (2000) points out that Nozick's "third way" between the relativism supposed to follow from the acknowledgment of the role of contextual values in science and an objectivism that denies (the importance of) such a role has been long at the center of, in particular, feminist philosophy of science and science studies—and precisely in the way Nozick claimed in his spoken address, namely in the argument that the interplay of contextual values in science, far from undermining objectivity, serves to secure it. Oddly, the published version drops the discussion of values.

2. For a distillation of these arguments, see Lloyd 1996 and Gross 1998. Objectivity does have self-declared enemies, some feminist theorists among them, but the disputes I want to focus on are those between self-declared friends. In particular, I want to ask why antifeminist "friends" are so convinced that feminist pro-objectivity claims must be either insincere or inconsistent, and, conversely, why feminist "friends" take themselves (correctly, I will argue) to be better, truer friends than those with whom objectivity has usually hung out.

3. Gross and Levitt 1994, 9; quoted in Lloyd 1996, 220; and Gross 1998, 102.

4. My point here is related to Carl Ginet's distinction between interested and disinterested justification. Beliefs, Ginet argues, can reasonably be counted as justified even if their justification is tied to the subject's desire that the belief be true; but *disinterested* justification, which is required for knowledge—that is, belief that anyone at all has reason to accept—cannot so depend. See Ginet 1975, 28–31.

5. For an account of the role of central philosophical theses as in this sense quack remedies, see Scheman, forthcoming.

6. All have published extensively on these topics. Some representative and frequently cited works are: Haraway 1988; Harding 1986 and 1991; Keller 1985; and Longino 1990. Anthologies in feminist philosophy of science include Tuana 1987; Keller and Longino 1996; and Nelson and Nelson 1996.

7. On the connection of critical and contextual values, see Longino 1990.

8. A term used by Lisa Heldke (1988).

9. See Code 1987.

10. See Heldke 1987 for connections between feminist epistemology and John Dewey's, and see Siegfried 1996 on the connections between feminist philosophy and pragmatism generally.

11. On the need to have pluralism from the beginning, in the structure of a theory—not as a footnote at the end—see Lugones 1991.

12. See Haraway 1988.

13. See Heldke and Kellert 1995.

14. The intended scope of "CPR" is illustrated by what I take to be two exemplary texts: Collins 1990 and Dupré 1993. (I've characterized Dupré's position as "Committed Promiscuous Realism.")

15. Sabina Lovibond comes to a similar conclusion at the end of her *Realism and Imagination in Ethics*. Drawing on Gramsci, she argues that the "expressivist view of language" she has been arguing for, both positively and as a reading of Wittgenstein, "commits us . . . to interpreting the idea of an 'absolute conception of reality' not in transcendent, but in immanent terms—not as a conception of reality from which all traces of human perspective would be excluded, but as one in which the individual or local perspectives of all human beings would be able to find harmonious expression" (1983, 218).

16. This appeal to progressive, left politics (along with the citing of leftist credentials), frequently made by the critics of feminist theorists, is unavoidably reminiscent of the Tom Lehrer song, "Love Me; I'm a Liberal"; but it also reflects a serious divide in left politics, going back at least to disputes about scientific/scientistic readings of Marx.

17. In addition to work in feminist epistemology and social epistemology, see Craig 1990.

18. On the failure of much, even explicitly social, epistemology to appreciate the importance of feminist perspectives, see Rooney 1998. Rooney notes the failure even of much of the work in naturalized, social philosophy of science to take feminist work seriously—that is, she argues, to take "naturalizing" or "socializing" seriously. My point is not that seeing knowledge in social and historical terms is sufficient for recognizing the relevance of feminist work, only that is it necessary.

19. Michael Root, following Hume, has argued that, while testimony is epistemologically important, our reliance on it can and should be understood not in terms of trust but as straightforwardly evidential: We ought to believe, on Root's view, when and to the extent that we have good reason to take our informant to be both sincere and relevantly competent (1998). For an argument against a similar position, see Hardwig 1991.

20. This paragraph is a (probably unsuccessful) attempt to answer Michael Root's arguments (1998 and in conversation) that what justifies us in believing another is not such an amorphous sense of trust but, rather, sufficient evidence of the other's credibility, much as we need to check out the reliability of an instrument we are using to collect data.

21. Annette Baier argues against a disembodied, asocial reading of Descartes on the nature of the mind, but she notes that "our genuine theoretical need for a standard of excellence, or correctness, in thought, is met, on Descartes's account, not by fellow finite thinkers, but by that divine mind to which we have direct innate nonmediated access" (1985, 77).

22. It is noteworthy in this regard that when (in the *Discourse on Method* Part VI) Descartes explicitly discusses the role of others in the development of scientific knowledge, he is speaking about the doing of experiments.

23. For a discussion of how to understand the projects of feminist epistemology, see Scheman 1995, and the following critical response by Louise Antony (1995).

24. See Root 1998 for an account of the role played by policing norms in science in underwriting the credibility of scientific reports, and reasons for thinking that such norms work far more effectively among scientists than they do between scientists and the lay public. See Fricker 1998 for an illuminating argument, using Shapin 1994 and Craig 1990, for the need to attend to the ways in which political factors are inevitably—albeit through political change, reparably—implicated in our conceptions of knowledge.

Though the focus of my argument is somewhat different from Fricker's, I found her discussion deeply suggestive, including on the relevance of Shapin's study for these questions.

25. A central point of Fricker 1998 is that we rely on what she calls "working indicator properties," to pick out those to whom we accord credibility. But, insofar as those properties track such things as class, race, and gender, they are unreliable indicators of actual "rational authority"; namely, the "competence" and "trustworthiness" that in fact correlate with reliably having and reporting truths. See also Code 1995a for a discussion of what she calls "incredulity," the refusal to acknowledge another's utterances as credible. Code's principle focus is on how such refusals deny to the subordinated the ability to make (what will count as) truth claims, but she also discusses the use of incredulity (by the subordinated toward the claims of the privileged) as a strategy of resistance.

26. It might seem that, by framing the discussion around the question of the instrumental value of objectivity I am, if not begging the question, at least stacking the deck in favor of the externalists. I do think that such a frame does, if one takes it seriously, support the externalist position, but the frame itself is suggested strongly by the tenor of the critics' attacks on feminist objectivity theories, as well as by their defense of internalism: They emphasize repeatedly that the acceptance of scientific method as the best guarantor of objectivity is something we all benefit from and would suffer from attacks on.

27. See Kellert 1999 for a "situated defense of universalism," an argument specifically from the perspective of Jewish intellectuals for a conception of knowledge that abstracts from the social location of knowers. Building on recent rethinkings of the historical development of logical positivism, Kellert argues that such abstracting—and the articulation of conceptions of knowing and knowers that rendered social location irrelevant—was a politically impassioned counter to the rise of Nazism, and that there are good, situated reasons for valorizing rootless "cosmopolitanism" in the face of calls for the primacy of the pure and the native.

28. For a thoughtful discussion of the resulting "epistemic injustice," see Fricker 1998.

29. Bernard Porter (1999), reviewing David Vincent's *The Culture of Secrecy in Britain 1832–1998*, discusses the "gentlemanly" traits of character and mind, specifically as cultivated by the upper-middle classes, that underlay the extraordinary secrecy of the British secret services. Far from underwriting trust on the part of the British public outside those circles, the class-based exclusiveness of gentlemanly codes of honor fed the mistrust that welled up after grammar-school graduate "outsiders within" blew the whistle.

30. I am writing as though cynicism about the results of science were confined to those who have good reason to feel alienated from mainstream institutions. Clearly, it is not: Many of those in whose interests those institutions work are dismissive of science, especially when—as, of course, happens frequently—particular scientific results do not support their views of the world. My primary interest in this chapter, however, is to explore how "the science question" divides those who are otherwise allied, or might expect to be—why, that is, there is antagonism on the part of many who situate themselves on the political left toward what they characterize as "the academic left." See, for example, Gross and Levitt 1994.

31. As I was doing the final revisions on this chapter, I read Jeremy Waldron's review of John Rawls's *Collected Papers* (Waldron 1999) and was struck by the fact that I seem to be echoing Rawls's insistence that, to be considered just, a social order needs to be justifiable to those who are least well off. On the face of it, an epistemological analogue, such as requiring those with knowledge to justify their claims to those who know least, seems mad: holding expertise hostage to ignorance. But there is, I think, something to be made of pushing the analogy. We can no more simply presume that those who hold disproportionate shares of socially validated epistemic authority do so in ways that are to the benefit of all than we can make the same presumption about those who wield disproportionate shares of political or economic power. And while it is admittedly difficult to specify what it would mean to seriously democratize epistemic accountability, Waldron's discussion makes it clear how far we are from such understanding in the political and economic realms to which Rawls's theory of justice is meant to apply.

32. The parallel with the criminal justice system is noted by the prime minister of Iceland, David Oddsson, in discussing the controversial plan to allow a scientist, Kari Stefansson, the founder of Decode Genetics, to compile and sell a database of genetic and epidemiological information about Icelanders, a uniquely genetically isolated population. Oddsson says about the controversy: "Obviously, this is all about trust. . . . In Iceland, trust is everything. I once saw a documentary about a famous defense attorney. He was asked, 'How do you choose a jury?' He said, 'First, I take out all people who wear bow ties—because they are not likely to be part of a team. Then I get rid of everyone of Northern European descent. They are too trusting and they all believe in authority. When the police testify, Northern Europeans and Scandinavians tend to believe they are telling the truth.' At first I was outraged and considered it a complete stereotype. But I sat there and thought about it for five minutes and I realized he was completely right. I happen to be proud of that quality and think it says something about why we are willing to put ourselves forward and make this database work." The scientific research done on the database is made possible by the trust of Icelanders not only in scientific authorities but in their own health-care providers as well as in the state, which guarantees health care to everyone, making, for example, the problem of the use of genetic information by insurers a nonissue. And all these webs of trust are, as Oddsson recognizes, interwoven in the wider webs of Scandinavian and Northern European attitudes toward authority. This trust is not, however, without its critics: After the authorizing bill passed, "critics compared the database project to the Nazi experiments with racial hygiene and the exploitation of poor blacks in the Tuskegee study" (Specter 1999, 50–51).

33. For discussions of the epistemological issues raised by the Simpson case, see Morrison and Lacour 1997.

34. The survey was conducted by the Institute of Minority Health Research at Emory University's Rollins School of Public Health.

35. It should be clear that it is not just "add women and stir" projects that are threatened: Even the far more critical engagements of more theoretically sophisticated feminist scholars are subject to the same critique. It is dangerously naive, on Hoagland's view, for us to think that we control the terms of the discourse or even to think that the dominant *don't*. She asks: "If feminist scientists are going to study women, I want to know who, and who is the audience? To whose understanding are you attending as you

write? In what frame of reference are you trying to make sense? Who are you trying to represent to whom and why?" (this volume, 139).

36. Making a similar point, Code writes, "As Seyla Benhabib wryly notes, it is a strange world from which this picture of knowledge is derived: a world in which 'individuals are grown up before they have been born; in which boys are men before they have been children; a world where neither mother, nor sister, nor wife exist'" (1995b, 46).

37. Thanks to Jennifer Hornsby for reminding me of this point, that is, of how dependent the most presumptively independent of the early moderns in fact were.

38. Lorraine Code has explored at length the specifically epistemological consequences of Baier's work on trust and on second-personhood. See, especially, Code 1991 and 1995c.

39. Michael Root raises the question of whose skepticism needs to be taken seriously: Do evolutionary biologists need to persuade creationists in order for their accounts to be considered objective? There is, I would argue, no general, formal answer to such questions, nor can we expect answers in particular cases that are prior to or less contentious than the substantive issues under dispute. See footnote 31 and Scheman 1991 for thoughts about parallels between political and epistemic democratic accountability.

40. For a fuller account of what I mean by a "diasporic" epistemology, see Scheman 1997.

41. Here and elsewhere, my indebtedness to Helen Longino will be evident to all who have read her work. To those who haven't: Do.

REFERENCES

Alcoff, Linda, and Elizabeth Potter, eds. 1993. *Feminist epistemologies*. New York: Routledge.

Antony, Louise. 1995. Comment on Naomi Scheman. *Metaphilosophy* 26, 3: 191–98.

Baier, Annette. 1980. Secular faith. *Canadian Journal of Philosophy* 10, 1: 131–48. Reprinted in *Postures of the mind*. See Baier 1985b.

———. 1985a. Cartesian persons. In *Postures of the mind*. See Baier 1985b.

———. 1985b. *Postures of the mind: Essays on mind and morals*. Minneapolis: University of Minnesota Press.

Campbell, Sue. 2001. Memory, suggestibility, and social skepticism. This volume.

Code, Lorraine. 1987. *Epistemic responsibility*. Hanover, N.H.: University Press of New England.

———. 1991. *What can she know? Feminist theory and the construction of knowledge*. Ithaca, N.Y.: Cornell University Press.

———. 1995. Incredulity, experientialism, and the politics of knowledge. In *Rhetorical spaces*. See Code 1995a.

———. 1995a. Must a feminist be a relativist after all? In *Rhetorical spaces*. See Code 1995a.

———. 1995b. *Rhetorical spaces: Essays on gendered location*. New York: Routledge.

———. 1995d. Taking subjectivity into account. In *Rhetorical spaces*. See Code 1995a.

Collins, Patricia Hill. 1986. "Learning from the outsider within: The social significance of Black feminist thought. *Social Problems* 33, 8: 14–32. Reprinted in *Beyond methodology: Feminist scholarship as lived research*, ed. Mary Margaret Fonow and Judith A. Cook. Bloomington: Indiana University Press, 1991.

———. 1990. *Black feminist thought: Knowledge, consciousness, and the politics of empowerment*. Boston: Unwin Hyman.

Craig, Edward. 1990. *Knowledge and the state of nature: An essay in conceptual synthesis*. Oxford: Clarendon.

Dupré, John. 1993. *The disorder of things: Metaphysical foundations of the disunity of science*. Cambridge, Mass.: Harvard University Press.

Fine, Arthur. 1998. The viewpoint of no one in particular. *Proceedings and Addresses of the American Philosophical Association* 72, 2: 9–20.

France, David. 1998. Challenging the conventional stance on AIDS. *New York Times* 22 December: F6.

Fricker, Miranda. 1998. Rational authority and social power: Towards a truly social epistemology. *Proceedings of the Aristotelian Society* 98, 2: 159–77.

Ginet, Carl. 1975. *Knowledge, perception, and memory*. Dordrecht, Holland; Boston: D. Reidel.

Gross, Paul R. 1998. Evidence-free forensics and enemies of objectivity. In *A house built on sand*. See Koertge 1998.

Gross, Paul, and Norman Levitt. 1994. *Higher superstition: The academic left and its quarrels with science*. Baltimore: Johns Hopkins University Press.

Haraway, Donna. 1988. Situated knowledges and the privilege of partial perspective. *Feminist Studies* 14, 3: 575–99. Reprinted in *Feminism and science*. See Keller and Longino 1996.

Harding, Sandra. 1986. *The science question in feminism*. Ithaca, N.Y.: Cornell University Press.

———. 1991. *Whose science? Whose knowledge? Thinking from women's lives*. Ithaca, N.Y.: Cornell University Press.

———. 1993. Rethinking standpoint epistemology. In *Feminist epistemologies*. See Alcoff and Potter 1993.

Hardwig, John. 1991. The role of trust in knowledge. *Journal of Philosophy* 88: 693–70.

Heldke, Lisa. 1987. John Dewey and Evelyn Fox Keller: A shared epistemological tradition. *Hypatia* 2: 129–40.

———. 1988. Recipes for theory-making. *Hypatia* 3: 15–30.

Heldke, Lisa, and Stephen H. Kellert. 1995. Objectivity as responsibility. *Metaphiloso-phy* 26, 4: 360–78.

Hoagland, Sarah Lucia. 2001. Resisting rationality. This volume.

Jones, Karen. 1998. Trust in science and in scientists: A response to Kane. In *NOMOS XL: Integrity and conscience*, ed. Ian Shapiro and Robert Adams. New York: New York University Press.

———. 2000. The politics of credibility. In *A mind of one's own*, 2nd edition, ed. Louise Antony and Charlotte Witt. Boulder, CO: Westview.

Keller, Evelyn Fox. 1985. *Reflections on gender and science*. New Haven, Conn.: Yale University Press.

Keller, Evelyn Fox, and Helen Longino. 1996. *Feminism and science*. Oxford: Oxford University Press.

Kellert, Stephen. 1999. Never coming home: Positivism, ecology, and rootless cosmopolitanism. In *The meaning of being human*, ed. Michelle Stoneburner and Billy Catchings. Indianapolis: University of Indianapolis Press.

Kitcher, Philip. 1998. Truth or consequences. *Proceedings and Addresses of the American Philosophical Association* 72, 2: 49–63.

Koertge, Noretta, ed. 1998. *A house built on sand*. New York: Oxford University Press.

Lloyd, Elisabeth A. 1996. Science and antiscience: Objectivity and its real enemies. In *Feminism, science, and the philosophy of science*. See Nelson and Nelson 1996.

Longino, Helen. 1990. *Science as social knowledge: Values and objectivity in scientific inquiry*. Princeton, N.J.: Princeton University Press.

Lovibond, Sabina. 1983. *Realism and imagination in ethics*. Oxford: Blackwell.

Lugones, María. 1991. On the logic of pluralist feminism. In *Feminist ethics*, ed. Claudia Card. Lawrence: University Press of Kansas.

Morrison, Toni, and Claudia Brodsky Lacour, eds. 1997. *Birth of a nation'hood: Gaze, script, and spectacle in the O. J. Simpson case*. New York: Pantheon.

Nelson, Lynne Hankinson, and Jack Nelson, eds. 1996. *Feminism, science, and the philosophy of science*. Dordrecht; Boston: Kluwer.

Nozick, Robert. 1998. Invariance and objectivity. *Proceedings and Addresses of the American Philosophical Association* 72, 2: 21–48.

Porter, Bernard. 1999. Review of David Vincent, *The culture of secrecy in Britain 1832–1998*. *London Review of Books* 21, 14: 13–15.

Rooney, Phyllis. 1998. Putting naturalized epistemology to work. In *Epistemology: The big questions*, ed. Linda Martín Alcoff. Oxford: Blackwell.

Root, Michael. 1998. How to teach a wise man. In *Pragmatism, reason, and norms*, ed. Kenneth R. Westphal. New York: Fordham University Press.

Scheman, Naomi.1991. Who wants to know? The epistemological value of values. In *(En)gendering knowledge: Feminists in academe*, ed. Joan E. Hartman and Ellen Messer-Davidow. Knoxville: University of Tennessee Press.

———. 1995. Feminist epistemology and Reply to Antony. *Metaphilosophy* 26, 3: 177–90, 199–200.

———. 1997. Forms of life: Mapping the rough ground. In *Cambridge companion to Wittgenstein*, ed. Hans Sluga and David Stern. Cambridge: Cambridge University Press.

———. Forthcoming. Nonnegotiable demands: Metaphysics, politics, and the discourse of needs. In *Future pasts*, ed. Juliet Floyd and Sanford Shieh. Oxford: Oxford University Press.

Seigfried, Charlene Haddock. 1996. *Pragmatism and feminism: Reweaving the social fabric.* Chicago: University of Chicago Press.

Shapin, Steven. 1994. *A social history of truth: Civility and science in seventeenth-century England.* Chicago: University of Chicago Press.

Specter, Michael. 1999. Decoding Iceland. *The New Yorker* 18 January: 50–51.

Tuana, Nancy, ed. 1987. *Feminism and science.* Bloomington: Indiana University Press.

Waldron, Jeremy. 1999. Review of John Rawls, *Collected papers*, ed. Samuel Freeman. *London Review of Books* 21, 14: 3–6.

Wylie, Alison. 2000. Rethinking objectivity: Nozick's neglected third option. *International Studies in the Philosophy of Science* 14, 1: 5–10.

CHAPTER THREE

On Judging Epistemic Credibility: Is Social Identity Relevant?

Linda Martín Alcoff

At the 1998 World Congress of Philosophy hosted by Boston University, John Silber, asked to welcome the participants in the opening ceremonies, provided a very unwelcoming message for feminist philosophers. His complaint, which grouped feminists, Marxists, and postmodernists together, centered on their overtly political agendas. On the one hand, the number of sessions at the World Congress devoted to feminist philosophy indicated this body's recognition of the importance of feminist work in philosophy as a century of historic women's struggles for liberation comes to a close. And conferences like *enGendering Rationalities*, one held in Eugene, Oregon, that attracted scores of feminist scholars from across the country, testify to the vitality of feminist philosophy, and feminist epistemology in particular, as a field of study. On the other hand, feminist philosophy continues to be regularly derided in the profession as inappropriately political in setting its philosophical goals. But this criticism is itself based in a political opposition to feminism rather than in a philosophical argument informed by the history of philosophy.

In a recent work on the history of epistemology, Mary and Jim Tiles provide a useful correction to the revisionist histories of modern epistemology that forgets its open political motivations (Tiles and Tiles 1993). Based on their study, Silber's grouping of politically motivated philosophers would have to be amended to include such figures as Kant, Locke, Russell, and the Vienna Circle, who unashamedly declared and defended the political motivations of their work. Locke's attack on innate ideas in the seventeenth century was motivated by his concern to stem a religious development known as Enthusiasm, which actually gave women a voice in public spaces on the basis of their claim to spiritual insight (Potter 1994). And Kant argued that his critique of reason was necessary in order to defeat a dogmatism that he defined as based in "a conception of objective knowledge as knowledge of objects that exist independently of human beings" (Tiles 1998, 233). Kant believed that such a dogmatism would commit the human species to a Hobbesian state of nature, in which "assertions and claims" can only be established "through *war*" (Kant 1958, A752/B780). He argued that transcendental idealism, in linking knowledge of objects with practices of human reason, affords rational procedures of disputation the *epistemic* ability to decide the truth. Kant then goes on in the same passage to defend his revolutionary contemporaries demands for free speech on the grounds that a public agreement achieved through open discussion is a "criterion by which we distinguish knowledge from belief." Thus, in the midst of philosophical argument Kant takes an interested stand in the ongoing cultural and political revolutionary ferment of his era, and even offered these political considerations as providing reasons in favor of a certain epistemic account. This must surely discredit the claim that philosophies that wear their politics on their sleeve are by that act dishonored.

Tiles and Tiles show this case in more detail than I can recount here, and in regard to other leading modernist philosophers alongside Kant. Most recently, Russell and the members of the Vienna Circle unashamedly explained that their emphasis on logic and empirical verifiability was motivated by a desire to defeat fascism. They put forth logical positivism as a means to discredit totalitarian ideologies that were based in emotive appeals to empirically unsupportable claims about racial superiority and the destinies of specific cultures.

Somehow, later in this century these political agendas were erased from the official histories taught to graduate students, and we now have a generation of philosophers who believe philosophy to be properly apolitical, which is one of the reasons for feminist philosophy's disapprobation. In his underappreciated work *The American Evasion of Philosophy*, Cornel West explains this selective amnesia as the partial result of "cold-war accommodationism" during the 1950s, in which philosophy departments sought refuge from suspicion by immersing themselves in professionalization and apolitical approaches to the study of language and knowledge (1989). Retreating from cultural engagement, philosophy (in the Anglo-American tradition) was rearticulated as a form of logical analysis aided by empirical-based linguistic theory. This might also help to explain the rift between continental philosophy and analytic philosophy, since continental philosophies were associated with the political agendas in Europe of both left and right. In any case, the cold war in the United States created an ideological clampdown that surely explains, at least in part, the sudden uneasiness philosophers felt toward a mix of philosophy and politics. I remember as an undergraduate my favorite Marxist professor recounting to us how he managed to make it into the discipline in the early 1950s by writing a dissertation on etiquette.

In my mind, the conclusions to be drawn from the corrected histories of philosophy we get from West and Tiles and Tiles is not that philosophical truth has been compromised by political motivation, but that the philosophical enterprises we choose to undertake are determined within historically situated contexts of cultural, ideological, and political contestation. Feminist philosophy and feminist epistemology represent a continuation of the tradition in which philosophers openly avow their political aspirations. Like Kant, feminist philosophers are committed to using philosophical methods to clarify and disempower the current dogmatisms that inhibit political advance.

The argument that I will develop in this chapter fits within this rubric by addressing a current political controversy which has epistemic implications. Despite the fact that the issue I will address is seen as a *political* controversy, I would say it is more properly understood as an *epistemological* controversy that has been played out in the political arena. The issue is this: in assessing a claim or judgment, is it relevant to take into account the social identity, (e.g., race or gender), of the person who has made the claim? Does a claim or judgment gain or lose credibility in virtue of the claimants' social identity?

The political debate over this issue has primarily focused on jury diversity: if social identity is epistemically relevant, then it makes sense to require racial and gender diversity in juries (See, e.g., Angel 1996 and 1997; Saunders 1997; Butler 1997; Leipold 1997; Coke 1997; Adams and Lane 1998). If social identity is not epistemically relevant, then diversity is not an issue of concern for jury selection. There may be other reasons given, of course, for diversity in jury selection, such as those involving the *perceived* legitimacy of the jury by diverse communities, or the argument that a jury of one's peers must include a representative sample of one's specific ethnic or racial community, especially if the society at large has had a history of prejudice against this particular group. But I want to set those sorts of arguments aside in order to focus on what is arguably a more defensible reason for jury diversity: that it will increase the likelihood of an epistemically better judgment.

In the U.S. court system, jury selection is driven by the concerns of competing attorneys to win their case, concerns that may only coincidentally conform with establishing the truth. But in the arena of legal theory, debates have ensued over whether random selection of jurors from among registered voters, for example, or from among homeowners, excludes populations that could be important in reaching the best decision of a case given the evidence. In particular, if the poor are systematically excluded by these methods, and yet it is the poor who make up a significant portion of defendants in criminal trials, might it be the case that the *epistemic* adequacy of jury decisions is adversely affected?

This question also taps into a much larger issue of concern within epistemology, that is, the issue of testimonial knowledge. Testimonial knowledge is, in fact, the primary form of knowledge in everyday life, far exceeding its relevance to the courtroom, and there seems to be a small but increasing recognition in epistemology of the important role testimonial knowledge plays in actual belief-forming practices (Lehrer 1987; Sosa 1991; Ross 1975; Price 1969; Hardwig 1985; Elgin 1996; Schmitt 1987). Most of our knowledge is achieved on the basis of testimony from others, whether we hear them give eyewitness reports, make claims of judgment or interpretation, or we read knowledge claims in a less direct encounter. We obtain most of our knowledge by reading or hearing what other persons tell us to be the case in a variety of personal, direct, and indirect media. Despite this obvious fact, for too long it has been the case that epistemology has based its analyses of knowledge on atypical scenarios of direct perception by an individual; whereas, if one is aiming for a *general* account of knowledge one would think the more typical case of belief generation should be taken as the paradigm—that is, knowledge based in one form or another on the testimony of others.[1]

Feminist epistemologists like Lorraine Code (1995) and Lynn Hankinson Nelson (1990) have argued that the importance of testimonial knowledge has implications for the stock issues epistemologists focus on. Such knowledge raises different sorts of epistemological questions than direct perception, questions not about perceptual reliability or perceptual memory but about trust and the basis of interpersonal judgment, credibility, and epistemic reliability. We cannot often directly assess the processes by which the other on whom we are relying has obtained their knowledge; we cannot know with certainty *how* they obtained their knowledge nor do we necessarily have the expertise to know *what a reliable procedure would be* for obtaining certain kinds of knowledge. Therefore, we must assess the other person in a more general way before we can afford them an authority in any epistemic matters.

Thus, knowledge based on the testimony of others requires assessing the epistemic reliability of those offering the testimony. Keith Lehrer argues that epistemic reliability requires epistemic justification:

> When Ms. Oblate tells me that the sun is not round, then I must evaluate . . . whether Ms. Oblate is trustworthy in what she thus conveys. As a result, I am completely justified in believing that the sun is not round only if I am completely justified in accepting that Ms. Oblate is completely trustworthy in what she conveyed. The latter is true only if Ms. Oblate is completely justified in accepting that the sun is not round. The knowledge

we acquire by the transfer of information from others is, therefore, intrinsically dependent on the others being completely justified in accepting what they convey. (Lehrer 1987, 96–97; quoted in Sosa 1991, 216)

Sosa argues, in my view rightly, that this requirement is too strong: "The informant can be trustworthy in the way that a child or a recording device can be trustworthy, which suffices to make the informant a possible source of our own justification" (Sosa 1991, 216). And I would add that Lehrer's account actually gives no guidance about how to assess Ms. Oblate's trustworthiness. If I am required to assess every informant's own justification, then am I not simply achieving direct justification on my own? Lehrer's requirement would in this way invalidate most all of our knowledge gained from testimony, which is most all of our knowledge.

I agree that *I* cannot be said to be justified in a belief simply because it came to me from another person's direct report: my own justification requires that I assess the reliability of the person or source from whom I hear the claim—just as I would distinguish between perceptions in the dark and perceptions in full light—even if it is merely to make a distinction between the *National Enquirer* and the *Washington Post*. I can only rarely assess with any adequacy my source's own epistemic justification. And, as Sosa argues, this is not even a necessary requirement for my own justification in believing the claim. Far more commonly, we make ballpark estimates of our source's trustworthiness: my uncle tells me the family can be traced directly back to Charlemagne, but given the fact that he previously claimed that we were related to Jimmy Carter based on a single name in common—"Smith"—I take this new claim with a grain of salt. My neighbor gives me pruning advice and based on the health of her rosebushes, I take it. But what about the case where one of my students comes to report to me a case of sexual harassment, a case where there are no external witnesses? How am I to assess her trustworthiness?

In cases where my source is direct rather than indirect—that is, from the testimony of an individual rather than some form of news media—special forms of evaluation must be used. One is, in effect, assessing the person. But how does one make such an assessment, and how does one determine what aspects of persons are relevant to take into account?

Gadamer argues that one can make a rational assessment of authority. Against the mistaken Enlightenment belief that giving someone else epistemic authority is "diametrically opposed to reason and freedom," Gadamer argues that authority "properly understood, has nothing to do with blind obedience. . . . Indeed, authority has to do not with obedience but with knowledge." One *grants* authority to another not arbitrarily but because one believes that he or she "has a wider view of things or is better informed. . . . Thus acknowledging authority is always connected with the idea that what the authority says is not irrational and arbitrary but can, in principle, be discovered to be true" (Gadamer 1989, 279–80). In other words, conferring authority is not in contradiction with rational behavior but one form of it.

Lorraine Code argues further that an account of testimonial knowledge will have two specific effects in epistemology: the first is to motivate a reevaluation of the traditional fallacy of the ad hominem argument. Considering the messenger of a claim and not just the claim itself is often epistemically necessary in order to judge the likely viability of the claim (Code 1995, 70–71). But this suggests, secondly, that interpersonal assessments need to be reflective about the moral implications of their assumptions. In other words, epistemological deliberations must be coupled with ethical deliberations. A project of what Code calls " 'everyday' or 'practical' epistemology"—that is, a development and evaluation of normative epistemic principles based not on ideal knowers but on "what real, variously situated knowers actually do"— makes ethical deliberation "*integral* to epistemic discussion" (Code 1995, xi–xii). Like virtue epistemologists, Code holds that a fully developed account of epistemic responsibility must consider the moral issues involved in the production and dissemination of knowledge.

But my focus is this: on what basis should we make an *epistemic* assessment of another's authority to impart knowledge? What features of the other are relevant for such an epistemic assessment? Some obvious and uncontroversial features would be: whether we have known this person in the past to be reliable and trustworthy; whether this person has the necessary perceptual capacities or relevant expertise in regard to the knowledge claim; whether we have any reason to believe that in this particular instance, whatever the past performance has been, this person may be unreliable. In some cases we have no prior experience on which to base our judgment and only the most rudimentary knowledge of the person's cognitive capacities. In cases where we lack any knowledge of these *obviously* relevant features, the question arises as to whether in some cases other features might be legitimate to take into account, such as appearance. Surely this is innocuous and straightforward some of the time. When someone young and muscular assures me that rollerblading is easy to learn, I respond, as we often do, "easy for you to say." Their appearance warns me that their judgments in physical matters may be skewed. Other times, assessing appearance might be more problematic. I was confused by the use of the term "F.L.K.s" by a staff member of a campus rape crisis center some years ago, and I was disturbed to discover that the term meant "funny-looking kids" and was used as a shorthand among some members of the staff to distinguish credible students seeking help from those they thought lacked credibility (based on number of body piercings and the like). Judgments of appearance introduce social practices of interpretation, cultural meanings, and so forth, and may also operate as a covert means to take into account social identity, such as race or sex.

Is social identity epistemically relevant? By social identity, I mean those social markers of identity that our culture employs, which are most importantly race, gender, sexuality, ethnicity, nationality, class, and religion. It is this list that primarily designates, not features of a person, but their identity itself—for example, as Jew or Catholic, Asian or Latino, male or female, working class or middle class, gay or straight, "American" or "foreigner," Black or White. However muddy these categories can be, we are still taught to slot individuals into them, sometimes forcing those who don't quite fit. I would not include the two kinds of categories I mentioned above as categories of social identity—for example, body type or cultural identification as punk, conservative, lowrider, born-again, and so on. Though these subcategories surely affect intersubjective trust and credibility, they are not the principal or fundamental identity categories our society uses, some of them are much more fluid and voluntaristic, and others less historically co-related to epistemic reliability than the main markers of social identity I listed. The issue of age seems to me to warrant a separate analysis altogether, since there is a history of very specific arguments against the epistemic authorization of children in particular, and thus I will not be able to treat it here.

As a means to avoid the potential dangers and unavoidable complications of taking into account social identity, it might seem prima facie best to simply ignore it. This assumes, of course, that we can. But my concern here is not with irremediably unconscious judgments, but those about which we have a degree of control. Although we have little control over noticing the social markers of identity our culture employs, we have some control over whether these should be used in conscious assessments of individual epistemic authority.

There are three sorts of questions that social identity raises for epistemological judgment: first, whether it is *ever* relevant to epistemic assessment, and second, if it is ever relevant, *under what conditions* is it relevant, and third, *how much weight* or significance should any such factors be given. Although these issues are related, such that, for example, the answer to the second question will bear on the first, I would like to hold off as far as possible from approaching the second and especially the third question. I want to address the epistemological question of the relevance of identity without having to then immediately develop an account of its practical implications. In any case, this issue, it seems to me, would be better approached by moral and legal theorists. And I would deny that a yes answer to the first question—the question of relevance—entails any given answer to the third question—the question of weight or significance. Moreover, there may be other considerations that are more critical in answering the third question, such as political considerations.

The first and second questions are less easy to separate: the first (the question of relevance) is probably impossible to answer without providing some answers to the second (under what conditions). But I want to focus on the question of relevance, without having to provide a fully adequate answer to the question of under what precise conditions such relevance may emerge. Often, in my experience, radical social criticisms are cut off at the gate in just this way, by demanding that the claimant provide both the necessary and sufficient conditions for identifying in every case the problem they claim to exist, as well as a fully worked out remedy. And more generally, as epistemologists enter the arena of social interaction, we need to be reflective about the appropriateness of various theoretical standards.

To return to the issue at hand, it is clear that social identity is not a legitimate feature to take into account in every case of assessing epistemic reliability; it would not be germane to a simple perceptual report, for example (unless one is giving a simple perceptual report of a kicking fetus or some other forms of experience specific to certain body types). However, there *are* instances where social identity might well be deemed relevant, such as in determinations of criminal culpability where a relatively small amount of evidence is the only basis for the decision and where social prejudices can play a role in inductive reasoning. In this sort of case, social identities may be taken into account out of a desire to eliminate bias. Even here, the issue is controversial: biases may occur from all quarters and it cannot be assumed that any given group will be free from prejudicial reasoning. But the further question I want to raise is whether social identities are only ever relevant for the purposes of *eliminating* bias. Is there a more positive epistemic role that social identity can play in assessing epistemic reliability?

The case against taking social identity into account is strong. There are at least three main lines of objection. Why should socially prescribed identity categories—often having an arbitrary, culturally variable nature, especially in the case of racial identity—have a bearing on one's epistemic reliability? Social identities like race and sex are not in one's control; they make no reference to agency or subjectivity. Except perhaps for one's status as an adult, what can social identity have to do with perceptual ability, judgment, trustworthiness? These capacities are distributed throughout the population without correlation to social identity. Intellectual capacities of cognition and reasoning are universal across the species and thus not connected in any meaningful way to specific identities.

Moreover, the claim that epistemic reliability *is* correlated to social identity has been a key feature of discrimination. Particular groups have been held to have intrinsic tendencies and limited capacities with epistemic relevance, and have been excluded from juries and many other positions of judgment on that basis. In Blyew vs. U.S., the courts forbid testimony by a Black witness against a White defendant. Through the first part of this century, Black testimony in courts required independent corroboration from White witnesses, much as we often require today in the case of children's testimony (Williams 1997, 47). Stephen Shapin (1994) has provided detailed historical accounts of the ways in which epistemic credibility was correlated with rank and privilege in Europe. Peasants, slaves, women, children, Jews, and many other nonelites were said to be liars or simply incapable of distinguishing justified beliefs from falsehoods. Women were too irrational, peasants too ignorant, children too immature, and Jews too cunning. And slaves, as Aristotle famously argued, were so naturally prone to deceit that they had to be tortured to tell the truth. Surely now, so this objection would go, we must realize that social identity carries no intrinsic epistemic proclivities or necessary limitations on cognitive practice. Such a claim is tantamount to racism and sexism in whatever form it takes.

A third objection targets the very concept of identity itself, arguing that social identities based on racial and ethnic categories and concepts of gender mistakenly homogenize disparate experience. We neither can nor should assume a similarity of experience, outlook, or perspective among those who share only a socially recognized identity category, and in fact to do so is to continue rather than ameliorate oppression. It is true that individuals must interpret and respond to their interpellation within identity categories, and thus that the ways they are identified and grouped are always important features of an individual's life, but there are too many variable responses that individuals can make to their identities for these to serve as useful predictors of individual outlook. Therefore, social identities cannot be taken as relevant aspects for judging epistemic reliability.

Against this last objection, I would concede that identities group together individuals without a common essence or uniform outlook. Even a shared experience is likely to be interpreted in very different ways. Identities are always social constructions of one form or another, attempts to organize the diversity of human experience into categories with some practical relevance. Sociologist Manuel Castells explains identity as a generative source of meaning, necessarily collective rather than wholly individual, and useful not only as a source of agency but also as a meaningful narrative (1997, 7). And Satya Mohanty (1997) makes strong arguments that identity constructions provide narratives that explain the links between group historical memory and individual contemporary experience, that they create unifying frames for rendering experience intelligible, and thus they help to map the social world. To the extent that identities involve *meaning* making, there will always be alternative interpretations of the meanings associated with identity.

Of course, identities can be imposed on people from the outside. But that is more of a brand than a true identity, or more of an ascription than a meaningful characterization of self. Identities, in the sense in which I wish to use the term, must resonate with and unify lived experience, and they must provide a meaning that has some purchase, however partial, on the subject's own daily reality. Anuradha Dingwaney and Lawrence Needham explain that lived experience "signifies affective, even intuitive, ways of being in, or inhabiting, specific cultures. . . . It is perceived as experience that proceeds from identity that is given or inherited . . . but it is also, and more significantly, mediated by what Satya Mohanty calls 'social narratives, paradigms, even ideologies.' " (1996, 21). In other words, although experience is sometimes group related (and thus identity related), its meaning is not unambiguous. Dingwaney and Needham go on to say, following Stuart Hall, that

> what we have are events, interactions, political and other identifications, made available at certain historical conjunctures, that are then *worked through* in the process of constructing, and/or affiliating with, an identity. However, to say that identity is constructed is not to say that it is available to any and every person or group who wishes to inhabit it. The voluntarism that inheres in certain elaborations of the constructedness of identity ignores, as Hall also notes . . . "certain conditions of existence, real histories in the contemporary world, which are not exclusively psychical, not simply journeys of the mind"; thus it is incumbent upon us to recognize that "every identity is placed, positioned, in a culture, a language, a history." It is for this reason that claims about "lived experience" resonate with such force in conflicts over what does or does not constitute an appropriate interpretation of culturally different phenomena. (Dingwaney and Needham 1996, 20–21; emphasis in original; quoting Hall 1987, 44–45)

Dingwaney and Needham emphasize along with Stuart Hall the nonvoluntary character of location and experience because they want to insist that identity makes a difference specifically for knowledges, especially those knowledges involved in cultural interpretation. I agree with this claim, and will argue for it further on, but here I have introduced this account as an example of an account of identity that holds *both* that identity makes an epistemic difference *and* that identity is the product of a complex mediation involving individual agency in which its meaning is produced rather than merely perceived or experienced. In other words, identity is not merely that which is given to an individual or group, but is also a way of inhabiting, interpreting, and working through, both collectively and individually, how it is to be lived. There are many ways in which the identity "woman" can be lived, many interpretations of it as intersected by other types of identity. Yet every woman must construct for herself an identity that grapples with this culturally mediated concept. Even if that grappling takes the form for some women of attempting a complete opposition, this is a struggle those identified as "men" don't need to make. This account, then, answers the third objection insofar as it takes identity to be epistemically salient even while it would reject a notion of identity as a fully determined meaning, uniform across all the individuals of a given identity category. It shows that, despite the interpretive nature of identity, identities also correlate to objective histories and features of the social world which those marked by that identity share.

On a hermeneutic account, identity is understood as constituted by a horizon of foreknowledges within which experience is made meaningful and from which we perceive the world and act within it. Identities are thus not opposed to but incorporate individual agency. Foreknowledges or horizons are not, however, so easily interchangeable, nor are they completely different for every individual. Horizons can be usefully grouped. For example, there is the horizon from which some individuals perceive the United States primarily as a nation that was created through stealing the lands of one's ancestors. There is the horizon from which one's ancestors came here for freedom and economic opportunity. I am picking out historical narratives as key to these horizons, as containing collective memories that provide contexts within which individuals make their lives meaningful.

Thus, I would agree that identities cannot be taken as indications of a uniform outlook or any shared set of beliefs. Rather, identities mark the background for one's outlook, and these backgrounds themselves can be usefully grouped. This should afford at least prima facie grounds for holding that social identities may have epistemic relevance. I have not established that identities produce homogeneous views or outlooks, but that there is something homogeneous between specified identities nonetheless: a relation to a historical narrative, a location on the map of cultural symbols, a figuration in dominant representations as purported threat, and so on.

In regard to the second objection, that holding social identities to be epistemically relevant carries the danger of discrimination, I will not argue that such danger does not exist. But I do maintain that this possibility in itself cannot determine the answer to the question of epistemic relevance. That is, if social identities can be used against individuals, as a means to discriminate or repress, this in itself does not establish whether or not social identity is a relevant consideration in assessing epistemic credibility. It may certainly affect what we decide to do with this information, or with the moral implications of considering social identity in epistemic judgments, but it does not determine the epistemic relevance in and of itself.

Moreover, the danger of discrimination goes both ways. That is, *not* taking social identity into account can also lead to discrimination. I will give an example of such a case that builds off Patricia Williams's work in legal theory

(1991). Williams's writing is particularly abundant with concrete examples of how social identity makes epistemic differences in what is noticed, understood, meant, and, thus, known.

After having discovered Patricia Williams's work, I ask a White male in-law, a civil rights lawyer with whom I often share political agreement, if he has read her work, expecting him to be as excited as I am by it. He is not. "I don't really see why I have to read a description of what she's wearing," he says, evidencing an impatience with the informal, narrative, personal style in which Williams writes legal theory. It is true that her writing is not linear, spare, or "objective." We find out about her family life, her feelings, and, yes, the condition of her bathrobe. My relative finds her writing chatty, cute, indulgent. I find it well organized, scholarly, and intellectually powerful. Her narratives richly portray concrete contexts within which her conclusions then make sense and their plausibility is made clear. Explaining her choice of writing style, Williams writes, "much of what is spoken in so-called objective, unmediated voices is in fact mired in hidden subjectivities and unexamined claims" (1991, 11). The informal style she uses is entirely deliberate, she tells us: since there is no norm for Black women's legal writing—no space, discursive or social, where such a thing has been possible until very recently—she will try to create one, to write fully as herself rather than aiming toward mastering current White male norms. The inclusion of personal information is likewise intellectually motivated: she says "I leave no part of myself out, for that is how much I want readers to connect with me. I want them to wonder about, and to think about some of the things that trouble me" (1991, 92). Like any good teacher, she knows that the most important thing to impart is a sensibility to discern and be engaged by important questions, and not simply the ability to remember the received answers.

All of these arguments might be taken to be beside the point of the topic of social identity's epistemic relevance. That is, Williams's work is a sustained argument toward the redesign of legal education based on her claim that knowledge is not as the current norms in law school understand it to be. Thus, Williams's claim, and her aim, is universal rather than particular. If "much of what is spoken in so-called objective, unmediated voices is in fact mired in hidden subjectivities and unexamined claims," then *no one* escapes the personal or the narrative that her work makes explicit. Her informal style also works to underscore this point: informality in this context is a form of irreverence toward the shibboleths of academic convention. This is not a relativism about procedures of inquiry but an attack against one set of claims and a defense of another. Thus, so one might argue, Williams's work cannot be taken as an argument for the epistemic relevance of social identity but as an argument for a reconfigured account of knowledge and legal judgment, one that can accommodate the ineliminability of context and narrative.

I concede that Patricia Williams is no relativist, gladly. But her arguments strike me as supporting two points: (1) that certain dominant epistemological assumptions in legal theory, those concerning objectivity, transparency of meaning, decontextualized judgment, and so on, are wrong, and will be so in any sphere of discourse; but also (2) that knowledge is dependent on subjectivity, identity, and experience, at least in some important cases. Point (1) is supported directly by point (2), not in contradiction to it. Because knowledge cannot be completely disentangled from social location and experience, the pretension to abstraction only conceals the relevant context, disenabling a productive dialogue between contexts, which is the only means by which true agreement and understanding might emerge.

One of the examples Williams uses related to a recent conversation I had with friends at my own institution. We were sharing experiences of sexism and racism in the classroom, and of the combined sexism and racism some of us experienced from students. Thankfully, most of our students are not problems in this way, though each of us that evening shared a story of a class whose dynamic became difficult because it contained too many such students, a critical mass if not a majority. And for everyone in that conversation, the examples shared were unmistakeable: we *knew* what certain student behavior was about, as clearly as we knew whether it was raining. Students who, when we introduce topics about race or gender identity in the classroom, close their faces up, avert their eyes, and pack their minds away, are just like those who always pack their books up ten minutes before class is over. These are students who have decided that they know why we are introducing such material, what we think about it, and what we want them to think about it, before they have endeavored to study the material or hear what is being said. We also shared stories about students who are inordinately presumptuous, who inquire about our qualifications, who are overly (sometimes way overly) casual and physically impertinent. One White male student in a seminar I taught sat next to me, moving closer and closer during my opening remarks, practically leaning against my shoulder to read the notes I was using. When I asked him what he was doing, he reacted with mock innocence and surprise at the question, but five minutes later was at it again until I had him change his seat. Another student had a habit of prefacing his disagreements with my interpretations with the phrase "What Hegel is *really* saying is that. . . ." I have had other White male students persist in interrupting me in class or making sexual remarks in loud whispers until I had to take disciplinary measures. And I remember so well a nineteen year old telling me how proud she was of my accomplishments, and that I should be proud as well. *Excuse me?* I wanted to say, *Who are you to take pride in my accomplishments, my mother?*

In philosophy classrooms, we provoke student resistance, we rejoice over persistent questioning, and we like, and often learn from, students who share with us and the class their different interpretations or insights. And in my classroom, I encourage a fair amount of informality and democracy. This is not what I am talking about. In the majority of cases, I can tell full well when a student is attempting to be a true philosopher or simply being playful and when they are simply being a pain in the ass. I could not set this out in a set of criteria (e.g. how many questions per class period asked), but I will assert unequivocal knowledge nonetheless, at least in regard to the unambiguous cases of which there are unfortunately too many. My knowledge received confirmation in the conversation that evening from colleagues who have similar identities and had experienced similar treatment, and who understood completely what I was talking about when I began to describe some difficult situation.

This is a problem well known, I would venture, among especially women of color teaching in any White-dominant institution of higher learning today. Equally well known is the absence of assistance or even sympathy we can generally expect from White and/or male colleagues (though, thank goodness, not from all). After raising the issue of racism among her students at a faculty meeting, Williams reports that "I was told by a white professor that 'we' should be able to 'break the anxiety by just laughing about it.' Another nodded in agreement and added that 'the key is not to take this thing too seriously'" (1991, 166). But how can they possibly know just how serious the problem is? If they cannot presume to know the scope of the problem, how can they presume to toss off its (easy) solution? Williams's colleagues counseled her to "not give the voices of racism 'so much power'"(1991, 167). Thus, they blamed her for the degree of power racism had in her classroom, and accorded her the individual, unsupported ability to disempower it. Like Williams, I will not accept that such problems are my fault, or that if I had a better style of teaching I could forestall such problems; I have won teaching awards, I have great teaching relationships with students most of the time, I know I can teach well, and, thus, though I sometimes bungle it, I am not responsible for "giving power" to the problem.

This problem of the inability for almost anyone but women or people of color to recognize the special pedagogical difficulties we sometimes face has much more serious consequences than simply our being misunderstood or not believed. An untenured faculty friend of mine, a Chicana who teaches at a nearby university, was demoted because of this very problem. Her contract was not renewed in the usual way but reduced in length and made contingent on the condition that she prove herself a better teacher. A White male graduate teaching assistant, a new student in the department, had complained about her to the chair just as her third-year review was approaching. My friend believed the student to be groundless in his complaints, and that they were actually based in his discomfort in the position of teaching assistant to a Chicana. Against her account, and without speaking to anyone but the disgruntled student, the department majority formed the opinion that my friend was not a good teacher. This opinion perhaps confirmed their own lack of comfort with her, her "different" style of speaking, interacting, socializing, which she had sensed on many occasions. But this was a young professor who had student evaluations that were numerically consistently *above the average of the college faculty as a whole*. This was a young untenured faculty member who acted as the beloved advisor of the Latina student group, who cooked for her students every semester, who had many great student-teacher relationships, and who had already published one book and received a major grant to write her second. Yet she enjoyed not the slightest presumption of credibility with much of her department when it came to problems of discrimination in the classroom. They assumed that they, a White-only amalgam of faculty, could assess the situation.

Within a year, that same complaining graduate student developed problems with another member of the department, a senior White male. This senior professor then concluded that the student didn't really have a problem with my friend, but with authority in any form. And the rest of her colleagues then changed their view of her and made an effort to reaccept her into the fold. But the real problem was never owned by the department chair or her colleagues. They never considered the possibility that her concern about discrimination could have been accurate, even if the student also had problems with other faculty. She suffered two years of anguish and self-doubt caused by this roadblock in her career. And the institution ultimately lost her to another position.

What should have happened in this situation? The chair should have second-guessed his ability to judge the case, given the fact that he has never himself experienced teaching as a woman of color, nor seen a woman of color alone in a classroom full of White students. Based on this, the chair should have done more consultation, with other students certainly, but also with those at the institution that would be in a better position to evaluate the conflicting claims. I actually spoke to him on the phone before the department meeting at which her contract renewal was decided, urging him to consult with such people, and suggested who they might be. He would have none of it, rejecting out of hand the possibility that cultural difference played any role in this. Although I found this hubris frustrating, I sensed that his motivations were at least partly the desire to treat my friend fairly, but to him this meant treating her as an individual without social identity and resisting the possibility that such facts might be relevant unless *he himself* could see without a doubt that they were so. In my view, his refusal to consider the possibility that social identity might be relevant, that my own motivations, for example, could be based in shared knowledge and not simply in friendship, or that her knowledge of discrimination could be accurate and based on experience, resulted in very unfair treatment. Such is the everyday life of institutional racism and sexism.

This example suggests that *not* taking social identity into account in some cases can lead to discrimination, and thus that the argument that we should ignore social identity, because to do so may often lead to discrimination, is not persuasive. There are certainly dangers on both sides, and serious ones. But it is simply a mistake to continue to hold that social identity cannot be relevant to epistemic judgments because epistemic reliability is equally distributed throughout the population. It has long been accepted that perception is an interpretive exercise; whenever a human being sees something *as* some thing, delimited and identified, that person is bringing specific (and alterable) ontological commitments to bear. Both Kant and Nietzsche believed such commitments to be universal to the human species as such, though Nietzsche believed them to be alterable and Kant did not. The world is a giant Rorschach test, we might imagine, with multiple frames of intelligibility by which a picture can come into relief.

The hypothesis being considered here, however, is that such perceptual framing occurs not only at the species level but also at the level of social identity. The difference between frames in this latter case need not be as drastic as the difference between the epochs that mark human cognitive transformations, and there is likely to be vast agreement with only a small disagreement. Moreover, there is nothing in this hypothesis that commits me to hold that the different perceptions associated with social identity cannot change, or be learned by others, or even disintegrate. These possibilities should, in fact, be considered necessarily the case given that what we are discussing here are *social* identities, subject to all the plasticity and dynamism of the social domain. However, any difference between what we will for now call "frames of intelligibility" will count, as long as it is correlated to social identity and it is relevant to knowledge. But anything having to do with perception is, of course, relevant to knowledge.

Such claims must raise the specter of standpoint epistemologies. Am I then defending a version of a standpoint theory which holds that group identity acts as a standpoint from which knowledge claims are made?

Sandra Harding, the most influential standpoint epistemologist, has held at different times two versions of the standpoint theory. In her early version (1986), standpoints were conceptualized as something like perspectives, yielding fully formed articulations of experience and judgment. This is too easily defeasible by the objection that no such social group is homogeneous enough to have such a shared perspective. The notion of a "woman's standpoint" was either so thin as to be epistemically irrelevant or it was so thick as to be implausibly shared.

Harding then modified her position to hold, following Dorothy Smith, that standpoints yield questions rather than answers (Harding 1991; 1993). In particular, she argued that the social positions of marginalized people give rise to new questions concerning dominant points of view that members of dominant groups are not likely to consider otherwise. If a scientific research community, for example, is homogeneous enough to share common assumptions and methodological approaches, these shared assumptions and approaches may well be invisible, since there are no contrary assumptions present by which they come into relief. Marginalized social groups, then, entering this community, may well not share all of these assumptions, and may find some of them implausible, thus yielding new and potentially fruitful questions for research.

This notion of social identity leading to new questions is a feasible account, in my view, but it leads to fairly narrow conclusions. It counsels us to work for diversity in research communities, but it does not establish any correlation between social identity and epistemic credibility.

Mohanty suggests just such a correlation: "Social locations facilitate or inhibit knowledge by predisposing us to register and interpret information in certain ways. Our relation to social power produces forms of blindness just as it enables degrees of lucidity" (Mohanty 1997, 234). On this account, identity does not determine one's interpretation of the facts, nor does it constitute fully formed perspectives, but it yields more than mere questions. Mohanty's idea strikes me as something like this: identities operate as horizons from which certain aspects or layers of reality can be made visible. In stratified societies, differently identified individuals do not always have the same access to points of view or perceptual planes of observation. Two individuals may participate in the same event, but they may have access to different aspects of that event. Social identity operates then as a rough and fallible but useful indicator of differences in perceptual access.

This argument does not rely on a uniformity of opinion within an identity group but on a claim about what aspects of reality are accessible to an identity group. As such, it does rely on a certain amount of uniformity of experience within an identity group, though only in regard to a more or less small sector of their experience, for example, that sector involving being treated in the society as a certain identity, or having a common relationship to social power. On this account, social identity is relevant to epistemic judgment not because identity determines judgment but because identity can in some instances yield access to perceptual facts that themselves may be relevant to the formulation of various knowledge claims. As Mohanty and others have also argued, social location can be correlated with certain highly specific forms of blindness as well as lucidity. This would make sense if we interpret his account as correlating social identity to a kind of access to perceptual facts: to claim that some perceptual facts are visible from some locations is correlatively to claim that they are invisible to others.

Such an account of the relevance of social identity to epistemic judgment needs to be supported by a theory of perception within which such an account would make sense. Two such accounts of perception present themselves as providing such support, the accounts of perception given by Merleau-Ponty and Foucault, which are accounts not about simple immediate perception but about perception as a historically and culturally variable learned practice and as the foundation of consciousness.

Merleau-Ponty says of perception:

> Perception is not a science of the world, it is not even an act, a deliberate taking up of a position; it is the background from which all acts stand out, and is presupposed by them. The world is not an object such that I have in my possession the law of its making; it is the natural setting of, and field for, all my thoughts and all my explicit perceptions. (Merleau-Ponty 1962, xi)

Merleau-Ponty follows Husserlian phenomenology not in its focus on the immediacy of perception, or in the belief in a reduction whereby meanings can be bracketed off from perceptual experience, but in according a centrality to perceptual experience as the key constitutive feature of human existence. The centrality that Merleau-Ponty accords to perceptual experience in no way leads him toward positivist conclusions. Because the cogito is founded on the percipio, it is both undetachable from bodily experience and *incapable* of achieving absoluteness or permanence. In other words, because knowledge is based in bodily perceptual experience, cognition is incapable of total closure or complete comprehensiveness precisely because of our concrete, situated, and dynamic embodiment. It is only because being is always being in the world, and not apart or over the world, that we can know the world. But it is also because being is always being in the world that our knowledge is forever partial, revisable, incomplete (Merleau-Ponty 1962, xiv). On Merleau-Ponty's view, bringing bodily experience into the center of epistemology has the precise effect of dislodging any hope of certainty or an indubitable foundation.

For Merleau-Ponty, the meaning of an experience is produced within an embodied synthesis of consciousness in the world. Meaning exists in the interworld of history, and thus refers to a world which is always already there before me and yet a world whose meaning is always a meaning for-me (and thus whose meaning necessarily includes values).

> We therefore recognize, around our initiatives and around that strictly individual project which is oneself, a zone of generalized existence and of projects already formed, significances which trail between ourselves and

things and which confer upon us the quality of man, bourgeois or worker. Already generality intervenes, already our presence to ourselves is mediated by it and we cease to be pure consciousness, as soon as the natural or social constellation ceases to be an unformulated *this* and crystallizes into a situation, as soon as it has a meaning—in short, as soon as we exist. (Merleau-Ponty 1962, 450)

The world is not an object at a distance from me nor is it that which I construct or form; "it is the background from which all acts stand out ... the natural setting of, and field for, all my thoughts and all my explicit perceptions" (Merleau-Ponty 1962, xi). As Iris Young explains, for Merleau-Ponty,

> Consciousness has a foundation in perception, the lived body's feeling and moving among things, with an active purposive orientation. Unlike a Cartesian materialist body, the lived body has culture and meaning inscribed in its habits, in its specific forms of perception and comportment. Description of this embodied existence is important because, while laden with culture and significance, the meaning embodied in habit, feeling, and perceptual orientation is usually nondiscursive. (Young 1990, 14)

Thus, experience is never capable of being understood or represented as if prior to specific cultural and historical locations. It is clear today that Merleau-Ponty did not fully grasp all of the implications of this analysis, particularly as these impacted his own "generic" descriptions of bodily comportment, as if such descriptions could be given without taking into account gender and other phenomenologically important differences. Nonetheless, his most general characterizations of experience reiterate their constitutive relationship to the specificity of social location.

If racial and gendered identities, among others, help to structure our contemporary perception, then they help constitute the necessary background from which I know the world. Racial and sexual difference is manifest precisely in bodily comportment, in habit, feeling, and perceptual orientation. These then make up a part of what appears to me as the natural setting of all my thoughts. Perceptual practices are tacit, almost hidden from view, and thus almost immune from critical reflection. Merleau-Ponty says that "perception is, not presumed true, but defined as access to truth" (Merleau-Ponty 1962, xvi). Inside such a system, the specificity of perceptual practices disappears. And moreover, because they are nondiscursive, perceptual backgrounds are incapable of easy description or justification.

Although perception is embodied, it is also learned and capable of variation. The realm of the visible, or what is taken as self-evidently visible (which is how the ideology of social identities naturalizes their specific designations), is argued by Foucault to be the product of a specific form of perceptual practice, rather than the natural result of human sight. Thus he claimed that

> the object [of discourse] does not await in limbo the order that will free it and enable it to become embodied in a visible and prolix objectivity; it does not preexist itself, held back by some obstacle at the first edges of light. It exists under the positive conditions of a complex group of relations. (Foucault 1982, 45)

His central thesis in *The Birth of the Clinic* is that the gaze, though hailed as pure and preconceptual, can only function successfully as a source of cognition when it is connected to a system of understanding that dictates its use and interprets its results.

> What defines the act of medical knowledge in its concrete form is not . . . the encounter between doctor and patient, nor is it the confrontation between a body of knowledge and a perception; it is the systematic intersection of two series of information . . . whose intersection reveals, in its isolable dependence, the *individual* fact. (Foucault 1975, 30)

On this account, which is hardly unique to Foucault, visibility itself cannot serve as the explanatory cause of perceptual outcomes. Thus Foucault shares the view now commonly held by philosophers of science that a "pure" observation is not an observation at all, in the sense that to count as an observation it must be able to serve as a support for a theory or diagnosis. It will not become an observation until and unless it can be deployed within a relevant theoretical context.

> The smallest possible observable segment . . . is the singular impression one receives of a patient, or, rather, of a symptom of that patient; it signifies nothing in itself, but assumes meaning and value and begins to speak if it blends with other elements. (Foucault 1975, 118)

What Merleau-Ponty's and Foucault's work helps us to understand is that perception is not the mere reportage of objects and their features, but serves as an orientation to the world, a background of experience that constitutes one's capacities of discernment and observation.[2] Moreover, it is itself historically situated within particular discursive formations—as Foucault would have it—that structure the possibilities for delimiting objects, concepts, and subject positions or legitimate viewpoints to be taken up by knowing subjects. Foucault famously makes knowing practices—that is, justificatory practices—internal to a discourse, or discursive formation, rather than essentially (or potentially) unchanged across historical and cultural difference.

Identity's epistemic relevance follows not only from its relation to perception, but also to experience. Identity often serves as a shorthand marker for experience. We assume that identities are correlated with particular experiences—of oppression, of privilege, a particular history, and so on—and though this correlation is often more complicated in reality than a shorthand can express, and sometimes in fact the correlation is nonexistent, there persists a utility, however fallible and sometimes misleading, in making a connection between identity and experience. Thus, the utility of identity categories significantly hinges on the issue of the cognitive significance of experience.[3]

In his essay "Identity, Multiculturalism, Justice," Satya Mohanty argues that experience refers to a process in which human beings make sense of information, or stimuli, and that it is through this process that a substantive self is developed (Mohanty 1997, 198–253). This process always involves a kind of mediation or interpretation. That is, an event of which I am a part conveys meaning to me through a mediation I perform. In the phenomenological tradition, starting with Dilthey, experience [erlebnis] is an event involving simultaneously the immediacy of perception *and* a meaning attribution. The meaningfulness of an experience is not understood as attached to the event, after the fact, but as emerging in the event itself. Thus, the conceptual separation between "raw stimuli" and the attributions of meaning are only a useful cognitive division we as theorists make to understand the nature of experience: the separation is not a part of the phenomenology of the experience itself. Hans-Georg Gadamer explains this view as follows:

> Units of experience are themselves units of meaning. . . . The unit of experience is not understood as a piece of the actual flow of experience of an "I," but as an intentional relation. . . . Everything that is experienced is experienced by oneself, and part of its meaning is that it belongs to the unity of this self and thus contains an unmistakable and irreplaceable relation to the whole of this one life. (Gadamer 1989, 65–67)

The intrinsic intentionality of experience is key to understanding its cognitive content. Because experience is an event involving intentionality—the "whole of this one life"—a similar event may be experienced very differently by different persons. The interpretive process itself is both individual and social: the effort to establish meaning is performed by the individual, and subject to modification upon her critical reflectiveness, but it is always also conditioned by the concepts, narratives, values, and meanings that are available in her social and discursive context.

Social identities are relevant variables by which available interpretive processes are grouped and distinguished. This is not of course to say that differently identified individuals live in different worlds, or experience globally different perceptions, but that prevalent narratives and concepts are often correlated to specific social identities.

Charles Mills argues in his essay "Non-Cartesian Sums: Philosophy and the African-American Experience" that the concept of "subpersonhood," or *Untermensch*, is a central way to understand "the defining feature of the African-American experience under conditions of white supremacy (both slavery and its aftermath)" (Mills 1994, 228). By this concept, which he develops through a contrast drawn between the Cartesian sum and Ralph Ellison's invisible man, Mills elucidates the comprehensive ramifications that White racism had on "every sphere of black life—juridical standing, moral status, personal/racial identity, epistemic reliability, existential plight, political inclusion, social metaphysics, sexual relations, aesthetic worth" (Mills 1994, 228).

To be a subperson is not to be a nonperson, or an object without any moral status whatsoever. Rather, Mills explains,

> the peculiar status of a sub-person is that it is an entity which, because of phenotype, seems (from, of course, the perspective of the categorizer) human in some respects but not in others. It is a human (or, if this seems normatively loaded, a humanoid) who, though adult, is not fully a person . . . [and] whose moral status was tugged in different directions by the dehumanizing requirements of slavery on the one hand and the (grudging and sporadic) white recognition of the objective properties blacks possessed on the other, generating an insidious array of cognitive and moral schizophrenias in both blacks and whites. (Mills 1994, 228)

On the basis of this, Mills suggests that the racial identity of philosophers affects the "array of concepts found useful, the set of paradigmatic dilemmas, the range of concerns" with which they each must grapple. He also suggests that the perspective one takes on specific theories and positions will be affected by one's identity, as in the following passage:

> The impatience, or indifference, that I have sometimes detected in black students [taking an ethics course] derives in part, I suggest, from their sense that there is something strange, for example, in spending a whole course describing the logic of different moral ideals without ever talking about how *all of them* were systematically violated for blacks. (Mills 1994, 226)

This results from an understanding that Black lived experience "is not sub-sumed under these philosophical abstractions, despite their putative generality" (Mills 1994, 225). It seems eminently plausible that such a point of view taken in regard to the general ethics curriculum has a strong correlation to social identity. From the perspective of those at the "underside of history" and the underside of European modernism in particular, the modernist debates over moral systems may well appear unintelligibly silent about the simultaneous and systematic patterns of colonialism and enslavement.[4]

Mills develops this argument further in *The Racial Contract*, in which he claims that racist social systems must develop corresponding moral episte-mologies and norms of epistemic judgment. "There is agreement about what counts as a correct, objective interpretation of the world, and for agreeing to this view, one is . . . granted full cognitive standing in the polity, the official epistemic community" (Mills 1997, 18). This merely describes normal science, or any discursive community, but Mills further argues that

> on matters related to race, the Racial Contract prescribed for its signato-ries an inverted epistemology, an epistemology of ignorance, a particular pattern of localized and global cognitive dysfunctions (which are psycho-logically and socially functional), producing the ironic outcome that whites will in general be unable to understand the world they themselves have made. . . .One could say then, as a general rule, that white misunderstand-ing, misrepresentation, evasion, and self-deception on matters related to race are among the most pervasive mental phenomena of the past few hundred years, a cognitive and moral economy psychically required for conquest, colonization, and enslavement. (Mills 1997, 17–19)

These are strong claims. Mills neither naturalizes nor universalizes them; that is, he sees these cognitive dysfunctions as neither natural to Whites nor univer-sal among Whites, and he sees whiteness itself with its concomitant perspec-tive as socially constructed. Nonetheless, if his description of cognition, at least with respect to racial matters, holds true, then there is indeed a strong correla-tion between social identity and epistemic ability, at least in regard to certain kinds of issues.

Social identity matters because experience and perception matter for the possibility of knowledge. No individual is capable of knowing from every expe-riential location, and in our present culture, our social identities are in some cases relevant to our experiential locations, though certainly not the most or only rel-evant feature. The accounts of perception given either in much of contemporary phenomenology or in analyses of the relation between perception and discourse (or theory), as I have related here through the work of Merleau-Ponty and

Foucault, show that perception is a kind of social practice: learned, interpretive, and an index of culture. But the fact that our culture is far from homogeneous must suggest that basic-level perception of events and of people, perception that surmises identity, credibility, salient evidence, probable causal relations, plausible explanations, and other important epistemic judgments, can vary across social identities. This variability pertains not only to factual description but also to evaluation and moral assessment.

Thus, like Code, I would argue that we need to reevaluate the status of ad hominem arguments. Code says that "Prohibitions against appeals to ad hominem evidence derive their persuasiveness from a tacit endorsement of the interchangeableness model of epistemic agency. . . . These prohibitions assume that the truth merely passes . . . through the cognitive (=observational) processes of the knowing subject" (Code 1995, 70). But identity differences can effect interchangeableness. Social identities are differentiated by perceptual orientations, which involves bodily comportments that serve as the background for knowledge, learned practices of perception, and narratives of meaning within which new observations become incorporated into historical experience.

If this account is right, what follows for jury selection or for the judgment of epistemic credibility generally? A mechanistic quota system on juries would seem inadequate to the complexities and constructedness of social identity. But the substantial difficulties in formulating responsible epistemic procedures given the noninterchangeableness of knowers does not justify simply ignoring the epistemic salience of social identity. The correlation between social identity and some types of knowledge does not confer absolute status on anyone's knowledge claims, to authorize or disauthorize merely on the basis of identity. It does not establish a uniformity of knowledge within a specified group, given the active, mediated nature of experience. And it certainly does not establish that social identity is always epistemically relevant in judging credibility (or even most of the time). Identity and experience remain dynamic, complex, never transparent. And yet, to retreat to an epistemic individualism in the face of these complexities is to negate the patterns that can be seen over the long haul, from a wide lens. And it justifies a refusal to even consider whether social identity is possibly relevant in a case of judgment. My argument has been that the question of social identity's relevance needs to remain on the table, to be decided by the context and not proscribed beforehand by a priori argument.

Notes

I would like to thank Leslie Bender, Nancy Tuana, Sandra Morgen, and Pablo De Greiff for their help with this chapter.

1. The *locus classicus* for this argument in feminist epistemology is probably Nelson 1990. In the history of philosophy, there is surprisingly scant discussion of the issue of testimonial knowledge. Sosa cites the following: Leibniz 1981, Bk. IV, ch. xv, sec. 4; Hume 1955; and Reid 1983. But in each of these works, there are only a few pages on questions of testimony. Introductory textbooks on epistemology have little if any discussion of this issue, and none that I have seen devote an entire chapter to it as they do to perception, memory, induction, a priori knowledge, and so on. The burgeoning field of social epistemology is beginning to consider issues involved in testimony, though much of social epistemology works instead on questions related to collective knowing, such as in scientific research teams. The questions involved in assessing testimony are different in important respects from epistemic questions concerning collective processes of knowledge acquisition, which concern, for example, rule-governedness, the justifiability of paradigms, and problems around consensus. Frederick Schmitt (1994) provides an overview of possible positions on testimony but he admits that "we" (meaning Anglo-American philosophers) "do not even have a detailed version of weak individualism, even though it is the historically dominant view of testimony"(17). And it is telling that the view he claims to be dominant, what he names "weak individualism," itself works to reduce the importance of testimony from others, by holding that the only source that can justify testimonial beliefs will be nontestimonial beliefs (5).

2. Similar accounts of perception might have been developed via Kuhn, or Nietzsche, or others, to reach the same conclusions, though I think Merleau-Ponty and Foucault offer more detailed and illuminating descriptions.

3. This explains the interest in "authenticity" especially in terms of racial and ethnic identity. I am not referring here to the existential concept of authenticity, as in accepting one's freedom, but to the more everyday meaning of the term, as in "authentic creole cooking." There have been numerous and compelling criticisms of the concern with authenticity made since the 1960s, that it is used as a test to discredit persons in a reductive manner, where someone's political position may be rejected on the grounds of their purported lack of an authentic identity from which to speak. It also assumes a homogeneity across a specified group and seems to make all-important a criterion that should not be relevant at all in assessing a person's claims. And it sets up a pecking order among the oppressed concerning who is more "street," for example, or who has suffered more, creating divisiveness instead of solidarity. While all of these criticisms have merit, the kernel of truth in the interest in authenticity is rooted in an epistemic concern that reveals the link between identity and experience: is the person's testimony reliable, for example, about the effect that expecting to go to jail has on a boy growing up? This legitimate epistemic concern does not erase all the negative effects of the "authenticity test" as described above, and such construals of authenticity still need to be opposed, but it suggests that we need to acknowledge that the grounds of the concern over authenticity is not (always) mere opportunism or the desire for a simplified evaluative process. In other words, in critiquing the concern for authenticity as reductive, we should also avoid making a reductive characterization of authenticity itself.

4. On this point, see also Dussel 1996; Dussel 1995.

78   Linda Martín Alcoff

Adams, Edward S., and Christian J. Lane. 1998. Constructing a jury that is both impartial and representative: Utilizing cumulative voting in jury selection. *New York University Law Review* (June): 703–65.

Angel, Marina. 1996. Criminal law and women: Giving the abused woman a jury of her peers who appreciate trifles. *American Criminal Law Review* 33 (Winter): 229–000.

———. 1997. Susan Glaspell's trifles and a jury of her peers: Woman abuse in a literary and legal context. *Buffalo Law Review* 45 (Fall): 779–844.

Butler, Paul D. 1997. Race-based jury nullification: Case-in-chief. *John Marshall Law Review* (Summer): 911–22.

Castells, Manuel. 1997. *The power of identity.* Malden, Mass.: Blackwell.

Code, Lorraine. 1995. *Rhetorical spaces: Essays on gendered locations.* New York: Routledge.

Coke, Tanya E. 1994. Lady justice may be blind, but is she a soul sister? Race neutrality and the ideal of representative juries. *New York University Law Review* 69 (May): 327–86.

Dingwaney, Anuradha, and Lawrence Needham. 1996. The difference that difference makes. In *Socialist Review* 26, 3 & 4: 5–47.

Dussel, Enrique. 1995. *The invention of the Americas: Eclipse of "the other" and the myth of modernity*, trans. Michael Barber. New York: Continuum.

———. 1996. *The underside of modernity: Apel, Ricoeur, Rorty, Taylor, and the philosophy of liberation*, trans. and ed. Eduardo Mendieta. Atlantic Highlands, N.J.: Humanities.

Elgin, Catherine. 1996. *Considered judgment.* Princeton, N.J.: Princeton University Press.

Foucault, Michel. 1975. *The birth of the clinic: An archaeology of medical perception*, trans. A. M. Sheridan Smith. New York: Vintage.

———. 1982. *The archaeology of knowledge*, trans. A. M. Sheridan Smith. New York: Pantheon.

Gadamer, Hans-Georg. 1989. *Truth and method*, 2d rev. ed., trans. Joel Weinsheimer and Donald G. Marshall. New York: Crossroad.

Hall, Stuart. 1987. Minimal selves. In *Identity*, ed. Lisa Appignanesi. London: ICA Document 6.

Harding, Sandra. 1986. *The science question in feminism.* Ithaca, N.Y.: Cornell University Press.

———. 1991. *Whose science? Whose knowledge?* Ithaca, N.Y.: Cornell University Press.

———. 1993. Rethinking standpoint epistemology. In *Feminist epistemologies*, ed. Linda Alcoff and Elizabeth Potter. Ithaca, N.Y.: Cornell University Press.

Hardwig, John. 1985. Epistemic dependence. *Journal of Philosophy* 82: 335–50.

Hume, David. 1955. *An inquiry concerning human understanding*, ed. Charles W. Hendel. Indianapolis: Library of Liberal Arts Press.

Kant, Immanuel. 1958. *Critique of pure reason*, trans. Norman Kemp Smith. London: Macmillan.

Lehrer, Keith. 1987. Personal and social knowledge. *Synthese* 73: 87–107.

Leibniz, Gottfried Wilhelm. 1981. *New essays on human understanding*, trans. and ed. P. Remnant and J. Bennett. New York: Cambridge University Press.

Leipold, Andrew D. 1997. Race-based jury nullification: Rebuttal (Part A). *John Marshall Law Review* 30 (Summer): 923–27.

Merleau-Ponty, Maurice. 1962. *The phenomenology of perception*, trans. Colin Smith. New Jersey: Humanities.

Mills, Charles. 1998. *Blackness visible: Essays on philosophy and race*. Ithaca, N.Y.: Cornell University Press.

———. 1994. Non-Cartesian sums: Philosophy and the African-American experience. *Teaching Philosophy* 17, 3 (October): 228–43.

———. 1997. *The racial contract*. Ithaca, N.Y.: Cornell University Press.

Mohanty, Satya. 1997. *Literary theory and the claims of history: Postmodernism, objectivity, multicultural politics*. Ithaca, N.Y.: Cornell University Press.

Nelson, Lynn Hankinson. 1990. *Who knows: From Quine to a feminist empiricism*. Philadelphia: Temple University Press.

Potter, Elizabeth. 1994. Locke's epistemology and women's struggles. In *Modern engendering: critical feminist readings in modern Western philosophy*, ed. Bat-Ami Bar On. Albany: State University of New York Press.

Price, H. H. 1969. *Belief.* New York: Humanities.

Reid, Thomas. 1983. *Inquiry and essays*, ed. R. E. Beanblossom and K. Lehrer. Indianapolis: Hackett.

Ross, James. 1975. Testimonial evidence. In *Analysis and metaphysics: Essays in honor of R. M. Chisholm*, ed. Keith Lehrer. Dordrecht: Reidel.

Saunders, Kurt M. 1997. Race and representation in jury service selection. *Duquesne Law Review* 36, 49 (Fall): 49–77.

Schmitt, Frederick. 1987. Justification, sociality, and autonomy. *Synthese* 73: 43–86.

——— . 1994. *Socializing epistemology: The social dimensions of knowledge*. Lanham, Md.: Rowman and Littlefield.

Shapin, Steven. 1994. *A social history of truth: Civility and science in seventeenth-century England.* Chicago: University of Chicago Press.

Sosa, Ernest. 1991. *Knowledge in perspective: Selected essays in epistemology*. New York: Cambridge University Press.

Tiles, Mary. 1998. Coherence and the jurisdictions of the tribunal of reason. *Social Epistemology* 12, 3 (July–September): 227–39.

Tiles, Mary, and Jim Tiles. 1993. *An introduction to historical epistemology: The authority of knowledge*. Cambridge: Blackwell.

West, Cornel. 1989. *The American evasion of philosophy: A genealogy of pragmatism.* Madison: University of Wisconsin Press.

Williams, Patricia. 1991. *The alchemy of race and rights.* Cambridge, Mass.: Harvard.

———. 1997. *Seeing a color-blind future: The paradox of race.* New York: Noonday.

Young, Iris. 1990. *Throwing like a girl and other essays on feminist philosophy and social theory.* Bloomington: Indiana University Press.

CHAPTER FOUR

How to Be Really Responsible

Lisa Heldke

In this chapter, I explore some connections between a particular notion of objectivity—one that (perhaps surprisingly) defines it as responsibility—and certain forms of realism that (also surprisingly) conceive of reality as constituted through interactions between inquirer and inquired. I argue that, when we define objectivity as responsibility, it functions as both an argument for and a consequence of a realist ontology of the sort suggested by Naomi Scheman and developed by Karen Barad.

In the history of philosophy, objectivity has been understood, variously, as a characteristic of persons, of statements, or of processes. The term has been defined in different, though often interrelated ways. For example, persons have been regarded as objective if they are believed to be dispassionate, detached, or neutral in their dealings with the world. (The objective observer, on these definitions, is the person with no personal investment in the outcome, and no political axes to grind.) Some of these same terms have also been used to describe statements believed to be objective. Statements are also termed objective if they are thought to correspond to an external reality, or to be independent of any particular perspective (the "no eye" view). Processes are regarded as objective if, for example, they are open to criticism, or if they obey well-established rules and principles. I suggest an alternative notion of objectivity, one that, at first blush, may seem odd and even paradoxical (although in fact it has long and important ties to many of the received views of objectivity I've just noted). I define objectivity as responsibility to the context of inquiry. By this, I mean that objectivity is promoted when participants in inquiry work to acknowledge, fulfill, and expand the bonds of responsibility in any given inquiry context. When we define objectivity as responsibility, it functions as both an argument for and a consequence of an ontological position such as Karen Barad's "agential realism," or Naomi Scheman's "contextualism"—positions that understand the world as constituted through the interactions that take place in it.

Before I turn to my two main tasks, however, I pause briefly here in the vestibule, to explain why a feminist would even undertake such a project of constructing definitions. Developing essentialist definitions of Big Concepts like objectivity and reality *is* a useful thing to do—so long as we understand the term "essentialist" in the right spirit.

On the Legitimacy of Essentialist Definitions

In "Rationality and the Politics of Gender Difference," Phyllis Rooney offers an important critique of essentialist definitions of rationality. She writes of theorists who "opt for their favorite ascriptions . . . develop their conception of rationality with respect to that, and . . . subsume (though sometimes with little more than hand-waving) other ascriptions under that 'paradigmatic' one." Such practice, Rooney suggests, often rests on the assumption "that there is a something that the noun 'rationality' refers to" (1995, 25)—that rationality has an essence. But, she points out, one must argue for such an assumption; one cannot simply assert it.

I take Rooney's critique of essentialist definitions of rationality seriously. Her critique can apply to my own definition of objectivity, which could be described as essentialist in just her sense. In a paper entitled "Objectivity as Responsibility," Stephen Kellert and I do exactly what Rooney describes; we ascribe a particular character to objectivity, and then show how other definitions of objectivity are accounted for, reducible to, or dissolved by this definition. How can I justify this sort of essentializing project, given Rooney's apt criticism of essentialism? To answer that question, I'd like to briefly consider another famous essentialist project—the backpacker's list of Ten Essentials.

In the 1930s, a group of outdoor enthusiasts known as The Mountaineers began teaching courses in hiking and mountain climbing. They developed a list of ten items, without which they claimed no climber or wilderness hiker should ever travel.[1] In his book *Backpacking: One Step at a Time*, Harvey Manning explains the "essentialness" of the Ten Essentials thus:

> The rule is absolute for climbers; for hikers there is a sliding scale of necessity. The afternoon walker on a . . . heavily populated trail often can do

without a single Essential. The overnight backpacker . . . may need only several. Those who probe deep into wilderness . . . and especially those who strike off cross-country, must have the full ten.

A further qualification: A family that invariably stays together . . . may need some of the Ten only *as a group*. The more independent the party members the more important it is for *each person* to carry all Ten. (1973, 265)

For Manning, these items are indeed essential—but to describe them thus is only the beginning of the story. He goes on to qualify the context in which each item on the list might be regarded as essential.

One can imagine other qualifications Manning could have added—by addressing the essential needs of small children, hearing-impaired people, dogs accompanying hikers, and so on. One can further imagine that technological advances may actually change the list of essentials—as the compass surely did for earlier travelers. Moving even further into the philosopher's possible worlds, it is obvious that, if Manning were modifying the list for an intelligent life form with radically different physical constitutions from humans', the list would look very different again. If the list were written for a world with geologies, geographies, and atmospheres utterly different from ours, it would necessarily change. The Ten Essentials, in short, are essential for particular kinds of humans operating in particular kinds of environments. They assume, if you will, an "ontology"—or at least a "context of activity" for practitioners.

We might contextualize still further. The context in which *hiking* goes on would be described quite differently from the context in which other sorts of walkers may have traversed the *very same ground*; hiking in the mountains is very different indeed from fleeing one's country by way of the mountains, in fear for one's life. Likewise, hiking in the desert is quite different from going on a vision quest. The features of the land around one are, of course, the same in certain respects, but the purpose of one's activity gives an entirely different significance to each physical aspect, such that it really does make sense to say that hikers, refugees, and vision questers move in different *worlds*.

When we investigate the term "essential" as the Mountaineers employ it, we find a fluid and porous concept. It applies only to certain activities (hiking and climbing); it assumes that one is operating in a world in which certain conditions obtain (abundant oxygen, the presence of sunshine, political stability); and it addresses *people*, whose bodies are constituted in such a way as to make certain needs paramount (the need to eat, the need to minimize loss of blood in the event of an injury).

But for all its fluidity, the list has in fact remained virtually the same since the 1930s, at least in part because some fundamental needs of people have not changed in sixty years, and neither have fundamental features of the world in which people are hiking. The ethics and politics, the equipment and practices of hiking and climbing have changed radically in that time, as has the actual construction of many of the Essentials (synthetic pile and nylon have replaced much wool, rubber, and canvas). But the fact that hikers want to stay warm and well fed has not. So, perhaps the "essentialness" here is best thought of as elastic rather than fluid—it can stretch to accommodate different situations, but it is not infinitely stretchable, infinitely changeable. The term "essential" is still an appropriate one to use here.

Nevertheless, it is also a term that assumes much about the powers, abilities, and resources of hikers. If one inspects the list of ten while contemplating the experiences of Native Americans forced on the Trail of Tears, or refugees from Kosovo fleeing ethnic violence, one is struck by the almost ludicrously privileged perspective from which the list was constructed. *Sunglasses? Extra* food? The list may well speak to needs that humans unquestionably have—needs that actually should be fulfilled, such as the need for food, water, warmth. But to presume that, because such needs should be fulfilled, they are fulfilled, in most cases and for most persons, is to make a very large leap indeed. The level of malnutrition that exists in food-stuffed cities in the United States is all the evidence one needs to show that this presumption is unwarranted. Looking at the Ten Essentials in this light, one is forced to acknowledge that they describe a kind of ideal, privileged world, one in which people actually have the means to meet their needs.

Cautioned by this illustration of the ways in which a seemingly innocuous essentialist system builds in privileged assumptions that must be questioned, I offer here an essentialist definition of objectivity. Like the Ten Essentials, it is a contextually essentialist definition; it is highly elastic, but not infinitely so. I can imagine conditions under which it would be utterly inapplicable, even wrong, but I also believe that those conditions would be quite dramatically different from the sort I considered when developing this definition. Just as hikers would have to stop requiring food before we would be justified in removing it from the list of Ten Essentials, so too would it be necessary to change fundamental features of the world in which inquiry takes place, before this conception of objectivity would cease to obtain.

The Ten Essentials assume that hikers have the privilege not to set out under conditions of deprivation, danger, or other desperation—that they plan on being able to assemble food and warm clothing before setting out, for example. Similarly, my definition of objectivity creates an optimistic, perhaps even idealistic, model of inquiry; I hope for contexts in which inquirers will be able to acquire and utilize the resources they need to pursue their inquiry. I imagine situations in which the conditions that would make for objective inquiry can actually be approached, if not met. If nothing else, such idealism can show us the gap that yawns between the conditions that ought to be in place and the situation that obtains in any given inquiry context. Recognizing the gap, we can then ascertain ways in which a particular scientific study, newspaper investigation, classroom discussion, or other kind of inquiry, builds in conditions that marginalize and subordinate certain participants while privileging others. This conception of objectivity emphasizes not only fulfilling responsibilities clearly acknowledged, but also expanding the number and nature of responsibilities relevant in a given context; this is one way that it addresses the inevitable privileges and power differentials that are built into any inquiry context. (I'll say more about this below.)

Objectivity as Responsibility

In "Objectivity as Responsibility," Kellert and I write that "inquiry is marked by objectivity to the extent that its participants acknowledge, fulfill and expand responsibility to the context of inquiry" (1995, 361). We intentionally define inquiry very broadly, to include "any and all processes of generating, evaluating and communicating knowledge" (1995, 362). We understand participants in inquiry to include not only inquirers (those usually labeled subjects), but also those things/beings into which one inquires (objects), and those to whom the results of inquiry are conveyed (the public) (1995, 362). This means that participants need not be human—and need not even be animate. Obviously nonhuman participants will have very different roles and responsibilities than will human participants—particularly if they are not even animate! But while responsibilities decrease in number the less animate participants are, it is still useful to talk about their participation in terms of responsibility—even if we understand that word only metaphorically. If a gardener trying to understand why her pepper plants are not thriving understands the soil as a participant in that inquiry, she will proceed differently than if she sees the soil as simply an object she employs (or, worse, the background against which she employs objects). It might, for example, make her think about ways she could help the soil to fulfill the responsibilities it has to the plants living in it, and in turn, the responsibilities it has to her and the other eaters dependent on her garden produce. Metaphorical? Undoubtedly—but useful, nevertheless, for drawing our attention to the various players in any given context and the various interactions among them, and *for shaping the ways in which we humans participate in an activity*. Even when we cannot make literal sense of the idea that a participant in inquiry can act on its own, let alone act responsibly, we can still usefully understand that participant as having responsibilities and expectations that must somehow be met. (A book by Wes Jackson, with the evocative title *Meeting the*

Expectations of the Land, discusses how agriculture might be transformed, were we to consider the land a player in the activity—a vital player whose needs and obligations are ignored at our peril.)

Our definition of objectivity specifies three interrelated activities—acknowledging, fulfilling, and expanding responsibility. To acknowledge responsibility is simply to recognize the demands made by others in the inquiry context, whether or not one chooses to respond to them. Fulfilling responsibility goes beyond acknowledging it; it requires meeting the demands made upon one, or otherwise accounting for a decision not to meet them. Expanding responsibility goes even further; it involves transforming existing inquiry projects as a result of identifying and incorporating new areas of concern.[2] To expand responsibility requires actively seeking new arenas into which responsibility extends.

To understand the relationship between acknowledging, fulfilling, and expanding responsibility, consider a familiar inquiry context: a teacher, working with her students to try to understand the origins of a conflict in the classroom. Acknowledging responsibility here would *minimally* require all the participants to note that other participants *do* exist, and that these participants have perspectives that at least *may* be relevant to the task of understanding the conflict. It might mean, for example, recognizing that class differences exist among students, and that such differences will make students view the "same" situation very differently. It does not require that participants listen to each other and take each other's opinions into account; to do so is to begin to fulfill one's responsibilities in the inquiry context.

In fulfilling responsibilities, parties to the conflict listen to others' views, complaints, and frustrations, and recognize their own role in creating those frustrations. In the spirit of resolving the conflict, they may seek ways to change their own actions in order to minimize the ways in which they provoke animosity in others. Alternatively, participants may insist on their right to continue behaving as they have been doing—but they do so by explaining why the complaints of others are unjustified, irrelevant, or otherwise not worthy of their attention. Perhaps they point out how others' complaints simply reproduce the class divisions that have been present among them all along, and thus do nothing to ensure that such conflicts won't arise in the future. (Refusing responsibility can count as fulfilling it too.) Finally, in expanding responsibility, members of the classroom look for connections with others that they have hitherto not even noticed, or have not regarded as relevant to the present situation. Perhaps class members come to see how the conflict in the classroom spills over into their home lives, or into other classes, or into their relations with friends, such that these relationships too must be taken into account—responsibilities extend well beyond the classroom sometimes. Here again, class members must assess the new responsibilities they unearth, to determine whether or not these responsibilities are rightfully theirs, and whether or not they are able to take them on. In any given inquiry context, the number and depth of responsibilities will always exceed the ability of participants to meet them, and some responsibilities will always directly clash with others. Therefore, such assessment is always a necessary part of the acknowledging, fulfilling, and expanding processes.

We suggest that objectivity is, foremost, a characteristic of the process of inquiry, and more derivatively a characteristic of statements and persons. Defining objectivity as responsibility gives participants a valuable tool with which to guide the process of inquiry: "By suggesting that participants reflect on the question, 'how can this inquiry be made more responsible?' [our definition] provides a concrete guide for those struggling with the question of how to be more objective" (1995, 362).

This definition of objectivity produces several important implications, of which I will mention the two most relevant here. First, such a definition makes objectivity an unabashedly moral concept. "Objectivity is generally regarded as a characteristic of good inquiry. . . . In using the term 'good' we embrace the sense of moral rightness as well as of epistemic utility. Making, evaluating, and communicating knowledge is a human activity which invites questions of 'how are we to act?' . . . These are issues of morality and moral epistemology. . . . [O]bjectivity is a value, a virtue, a critical ideal" (1995, 366). In making such an assertion, we called on the work of feminist theorists who have asked, as Sandra Harding did as early as 1977, "Does Objectivity in the Social Sciences Require Value Neutrality?" and who have answered, no! By the mid-1990s, the question of values in science had become more nuanced, so that Phyllis Rooney could entitle an article "On Values in Science: Is the Epistemic/Non-Epistemic Distinction Useful?" The question is no longer, Are values relevant in any way? but has become, Can we distinguish epistemic values from social, cultural, and personal values—and can we still rule out the latter on principle? Rooney argues that the distinction cannot in fact be made successfully. She writes:

> Once we understand how cultural and social values can . . . become encoded into constitutive features of the rationality and objectivity of particular scientific endeavors . . . we are invited to gain greater insight into how that occurs. . . . We get to show how the undermining of an epistemic/non-epistemic divide need not involve dismissing heretofore "epistemic" criteria as hopelessly reductive or relative. (1992, 21)

The second significant implication of defining objectivity as responsibility is that such a definition emphasizes the primacy of relationships. Perhaps it is more accurate to say that this conception of objectivity *presupposes* an under-standing of participants in inquiry as relational beings—not secondarily or su-perficially but essentially. This is true for all participants in inquiry, and not just human inquirers—those often given the honorific title of "subjects." All partic-ipants in inquiry are relational agents, and acknowledging those relations has profound effects on the way in which inquiry—and objectivity—are conceived.

Indeed, understanding objectivity as responsibility requires—or at the very least supports—a radical reconceiving of the roles of "subject," "object," and "public," rendering them more fluid. In order to maximize objectivity, the lines of responsibility must "run" in all directions, among all participants; it is not only the folks who design and carry out the research project who have responsibilities to the objects of their study, and to the public that will receive that study. Those objects have responsibilities too—to the researchers, to themselves and each other, and to the public. The existence of these multiple lines of responsibility necessarily undermines traditional conceptions of subject/object roles. Under-standing that responsibility also runs from so-called objects of inquiry to their subjects, for example, changes the status of objects from passive beings that are acted upon, to active beings who are agents in the inquiry process.

I suggested earlier that responsibilities differ significantly among human, nonhuman animal, and inanimate participants in inquiry, such that the term may have primarily metaphorical meaning for inanimate participants. The point is relevant here as well. To suggest that all participants in inquiry are con-stituted in and through their relations with each other is not to make relations between animate and inanimate beings all of a piece, or to suggest that inani-mate objects can be as active in constituting those relationships as can humans. Another look at the example of the gardener will help to make clearer some of the various ways that participants in inquiry are relational beings, and some of the lines of responsibility that exist as a result of that relationality.

Gardener and soil are beings that are quite literally constituted in and through their interconnections; soil provides nutrients that support plant growth, which, in turn, supports human growth. In the other direction, gar-deners provide nutrients to the soil (in the form of fertilizer, compost, etc.) that strengthen and enrich the soil. The importance of such interconnections is per-haps most evident in the cases in which they are operating poorly. Consider the soil contaminated by toxic runoff from a factory and left unusable for growing food crops for humans; or the soil whose fertility is depleted by repeatedly growing a single crop on it; or the soil treated with chemical pesticides that enter the fiber of the plants grown on it, producing indeterminate effects on the humans who eat those plants. In each case, the actions of the gardener (and other human agencies, like the factory) and the "actions" of the soil affect each other in significant, often measurable ways. A model of inquiry that emphasizes the fact that all participants are essentially and vitally *constituted* through relationships challenges us to take these relationships very seriously. The soil may not, of its own volition, choose how to interact with humans, and enact those choices—but if humans try to "think like dirt" in our interactions with it, we may be more likely to make choices for it that benefit both it and us. (Sometimes, it may even be worthwhile to treat the soil as if it *were* making choices in response to the conditions that affect it. Perhaps I should say that the soil in my garden *refused* to produce pepper plants last summer because it was starving for nitrogen, a condition brought on by my overzealous use of newspaper mulch. While I don't believe that dirt has the power to refuse me, using the language of agency does draw my attention to its needs in a rather striking way.)

The relationality of participants in inquiry also entails that they may play different roles in different inquiry contexts. The anthropologist directing today's study may be the subject of tomorrow's study, when her interview subjects question her about the uses to which her research will be put. Any efforts to maximize objectivity must take these other sorts of relations into account as well. Consider a study investigating the effects of an experimental cancer drug. Participants in the study include not only the scientists and their human subjects, but also the drug companies who may eventually patent the drug (and benefit from or be harmed by it financially), and persons who will use the drug (and benefit from or be harmed by it physiologically). Recognizing that all these participants are interdependent and have mutually constitutive responsibilities to each other leads us to recognize that there is more than one "research agenda" in place—the medical researcher's agenda to develop an anticancer drug is not the only one operative. The subjects of the study have agendas and responsibilities—to themselves, to the scientists conducting the study, to future cancer patients—and these responsibilities may or may not neatly coincide with those of the medical researcher. A context of inquiry in which participants acknowledge each other's interests, agendas, and resulting responsibilities is a complicated and messy context—but it is also likely to be a context that addresses the interests of participants differently situated, with different amounts of power and control in the situation.

Responsibility and Realism: Connections between Objectivity as Responsibility and Feminist Versions of Realism

My epistemological discussion of objectivity has segued into a proto-ontological discussion about the nature of the context of inquiry; to assert that, in inquiry, relations are primary and the roles of inquirer and inquired are thus fluid and

flexible is to make ontological commitments. And indeed, ontology and epistemology are intimately related here. Just as an understanding of objectivity as
responsibility results in certain ontological commitments regarding the context
of inquiry, the reverse is also true; the epistemological argument that objectivity is best defined as responsibility emerges from some understanding of, and
commitment to, an ontological conception of the context of inquiry. In this
section, I flesh out the connections between this concept of objectivity and the
ontological models offered by Naomi Scheman and Karen Barad—models that
meet the requirements that this conception of objectivity sets out.[3]

Scheman

Scheman's model of the world in which inquiry takes place tears down the wall
modern philosophers erected to separate knowers from the reality into which
they inquire. She throws everyone into the same space, and acknowledges that
both inquirers and inquired shape, challenge, and transform each other through
the process of inquiry.

Descartes's method, when properly employed, allows any inquirer working *alone* to arrive at the one true picture of the world as it is—the same picture
at which any other solitary inquirer would arrive, if they applied the method
properly. Scheman's proposal democratizes knowing on a different level. Descartes asserts that anyone can sit in the special chair, wear the special clarifying
glasses (featuring the light of reason attachment), and report on what they see
from that purportedly aperspectival view; Scheman's democracy dispenses with
special chairs. She seeks not the view from nowhere, but *views* from every particular "where," views from a world where everything is or can be a subject and
can "return our gaze" (1993, 100)—whoever "we" are.

In challenging the Cartesian model, Scheman, interestingly, chooses not
to reject its realism, but rather to recreate it. On her view, the world "exists in
complex interdependence with those who know it (who are, of course, also part
of it)." She notes that

> lots of real things are not independent of what we think about them, with-
> out being simply what anyone or any group takes them to be. . . . The in-
> terdependencies are real, as are the entities and structures shaped by them.
> One way we know they are real is precisely that they look different to those
> differently placed in relation to them. (1993, 99)

Knowers and the known inhabit the same "world"; "knowers" are as
much a part of this reality as is "the known." Indeed, these categories shift and

change referent, and Scheman suggests thinking of "subject" and "object" not as "ontological categories, but reciprocal, shifting positions" (1993, 99).

This world is "made up" (in both senses of that expression) by the interdependencies within it, one of which is knowing itself. Having torn down the wall between subject and object, and having established inquiry as one form of interaction *in* the world, the belief that inquiry does not change its participants also falls. Reality is not "out there," is not fixed and unchanging, and is not exclusive of the claims made *in* it. It is constituted through interactions, *including* the interaction we call inquiry.

It is interesting to note that Scheman regards the multiplicity of accounts given by variously situated knowers as *evidence* for the structure of reality, a reality continually constituted by those in it. That is, what is usually taken either as evidence of the unreliability of inquirers' views or as evidence against realism—namely, diversity in claims about the nature of some X—Scheman offers as evidence *for* realism. Scheman draws an analogy to sense experience: one of the ways that I know someone is a real person and not a photograph is that I can look at them from numerous angles. My perceptual experience of the world is perspectival; when I connect my various perspectives together, and when I connect my perspectives to those of someone else, the "composite" is much thicker, much denser than any individual perception. Imitations, mirages, copies, and fakes do not allow for the same rich multiplicity of experiences of them as do "real" things.[4]

Scheman describes her view as a "realism" in part because of its insistence that things are not just "what anyone or any group takes them to be—the economy, for example" (1993, 99). With this move, Scheman separates herself from those who would argue that it is texts (or social constructions, or discourses) all the way down, just as she has separated herself from those who would insist that a realist position requires the existence of a fixed and *independent* reality.[5]

One further characteristic of the real must be noted: this world is not neat, neatly describable, or fully predictable. Scheman borrows from Donna Haraway the notion that "the world as trickster, as protean, is always slipping out from under our best attempts to pin it down. The real world is not the world of our best physics but the world that defeats any physics that would be final" (1993, 100).[6]

I've suggested thinking about Scheman's realism as both a response to the definition of objectivity as responsibility (the descriptive side) and an argument *for* such a definition (the prescriptive). Why is this so? That is, how are the two concepts even related to each other? Scheman suggests one answer to the question, when she observes that understanding selves as bodily, idiosyncratic beings connected to each other in myriad ways "would allow us to be responsible while acknowledging that there is nothing beyond ourselves to be responsible to" (1993, 192)—nothing, that is, beyond a world stuffed with subjects and potential subjects.

Inquiry, I have suggested, becomes more objective as participants expand the number and nature of their responsibilities—the third characteristic of objective inquiry, coming after acknowledging and fulfilling responsibility. To demand that we expand responsibility corresponds to Scheman's call to increase the number and variety of connections among unique, meaning-creating subjects. Inquiry becomes more objective (even as it becomes more complicated, tangled, and incompatible with itself) the more fully we trace out the lines of responsibility that connect us to others, and that bring those others into the inquiry context. (Note that it may become more objective even as it also becomes less "productive" or efficient—perhaps even less "true." Objectivity is one value of inquiry; it is not the only value. Therefore, efforts to increase the objectivity of an inquiry context must always be balanced against efforts to realize those other values. In a well-functioning inquiry context—one in which various participants acknowledge the multiple ways in which they are interrelated—when values clash, participants will negotiate the matter of which values to honor.)

Consider, again, the example of a cancer drug study. Certainly we complicate the study when we insist that there exist multiple research agendas connecting researchers, their research subjects, and members of the general public in myriad ways. But the complexity of that study is one of its virtues. It provides us with the means to understand the consequences of our decisions and actions, given our own locations in the inquiry context; and it makes it possible for us to acknowledge the demands of others, whether and how we choose to honor them. When medical researchers in such a study recognize their research subjects as inquirers in their own right (who bring to the study their own set of interests and demands that may or may not coincide with the scientists'), the researchers must adjust their own agendas to accommodate these others. They must acknowledge that the particular aims that they have as scientists are not the only legitimate aims; patients' interests may be very different from theirs, and must be taken into account as well. Research subjects and interested members of the general public must make the same sorts of acknowledgments and subsequent adjustments of their agendas. When all participants are actively interested in increasing objectivity, power relations shift as participants acknowledge that agendas other than their own exist and have legitimate claims on the course of events. (On the one hand, such a description of inquiry sounds hopelessly idealistic. On the other hand, it could be said to describe the actual kind of process that inquiry often takes—messy, conflictual, contradictory, and anything but idealistic.)

Scheman's realism adds to our account the acknowledgment that there is nothing *other than* the context of inquiry to which we are accountable—no "independent reality" to which our descriptions of the world must be faithful. There is a reality—but we are all in the midst of it, literally and collectively making it up as we go along. We are also responsible to it/us for what we make. But in such a world, it is impossible to *be* fully responsible/fully objective; responsibility is incompletable in principle in a world that changes shape before us and because of us—a world that also literally consists of an infinite number of interconnections among its inhabitants. Given that the world (in which all of this connecting is going on) has its trickster qualities, the goal can never be the production of a Great Chain of Knowing, a single, neat strand of completely consistent ideas. Rather, we must satisfy ourselves with the much more limited, much more "world-appropriate" goal of making (what we consider to be) good decisions about which connections are important, and then forging those connections among participants in inquiry. (It is simply impossible in principle for any one participant to address satisfactorily all the strands of responsibility that involve them. This is true both because of their number and because of the fact that, in any given context, some responsibilities will always conflict with others, such that it is impossible to satisfy all demands, even if one wanted to.) In the language of responsibility, the goal must be to make decisions about those things and beings to which one wants to fulfill one's responsibilities, and then setting out to do so. Such a goal is always revisable in principle, and in any concrete situation it is likely being revised, as new connections that are forged change the shape of the world in which they were forged, making them no longer adequate or appropriate.

Barad

Karen Barad's work, like Scheman's, transforms the realist project from one which conceives of reality as independent of inquiry to one in which inquiry is one fundamental constitutive relation in reality. Barad draws on the work of Niels Bohr to develop a conception of the real in which inquirers and our investigative apparatuses are fully parts of that reality—constituents of it. Her model pushes more deeply than Scheman's in its efforts to crumble the distinction between subject and object. Barad's reality is deeply interactive; in her efforts to describe that interactivity, she invents words to surmount the obstacles to this kind of thinking that are written into our very language.

Barad argues that "there is no unambiguous way to differentiate between the 'object' and the 'agencies of observation'—no inherent/naturally occurring/fixed universal/Cartesian cut exists" (1996, 13). The object and subject "form a nondualistic whole in the sense that it is conceptually incoherent to refer to an inherent distinction between the two." Bohr's term for this "particular instance

of wholeness" is "phenomenon." A phenomenon includes the interaction between the observer (plus the apparatus they have constructed in order to effect
this observation) and the object; the phenomenon is what it is in part because
of the way this interaction is constituted. Indeed, the word "interaction" obfus-
cates the wholeness characterizing the phenomenon, and Barad instead refers to
"intra-actions." It is not that the process of observation links some preexisting
agent and object; rather, in observation, subject and object are constituted, (at
least temporarily) constituted *as distinct* and constituted as *having* the character
of agents and objects.

But although there is no fixed, Cartesian cut between inquirer and inquired, cuts do get constructed between "agencies of observation" and "objects."
These constructed cuts exist where and how they do because of the way that an
observation situation is set up—including the apparatus chosen. The construction of this cut between agent and object just so, this *particular* intra-action involving this particular apparatus, is arbitrary in the sense that it could be
otherwise; the cut could be made differently, and another, different phenomenon would thereby be constituted. (But this doesn't mean that we "make it all
up"; phenomena are always material-discursive complexes. We can't tell a story
powerful enough to make the material do whatever we want it to, or make it
cease to be relevant.)

These phenomena "are constitutive of reality. Reality is not composed of
things-in-themselves or things-behind-phenomena, but things-in-phenomena"
(1996, 22).[7] Barad does not say that observation somehow obscures the an-
tecedent object of inquiry; neither does she advocate the view that it's all interpretation. Rather, she asserts that we are in nature; our observations are
participation within it.

Given this understanding of phenomena, it is clear that, on Barad's ontological schema, we must also attend to the role played by those who are constituted "agents of observation" vis-à-vis any particular "cut." As Barad notes,
"the fact that there can exist mutually exclusive intra-actions . . . reminds us that
descriptive concepts do not refer to an observer-independent reality." The ontological role of observers obviously merits attention. (Scheman similarly notes
that, whereas metaphysical realism speaks to "the ontological status of the objects of knowledge," it is mute about the subjects of knowledge. She argues that
we must be as realist about the knowing subjects as we are about the objects of
their knowledge.) We must attend to the knowers/inquirers/agents of observation because, among other things, they/we construct cuts; and those cuts are
partially constitutive of reality.[8] "Our constructed knowledges have real material consequences" (1996, 32).

This is the point at which I think objectivity as responsibility can be
particularly useful. As I emphasized at the outset, responsibility runs in all di-

rections among all participants in inquiry. However, agents promote objectivity in ways that vary with their "native" abilities and capacities and with their institutionally granted power. Acknowledging, fulfilling, and expanding responsibility often requires challenging the ways in which those power relations are configured, and the ways in which natural capacities are understood and utilized. The cancer patient who uses a development in medical technology will have very different opportunities for increasing the objectivity of the context in which that research was created than will someone who is doing the basic research that leads to that technology (or than the firm that is providing the funding for that research). Researchers typically hold considerable power to define research agendas and to determine how results will be disseminated, but "consumers" of medical technology may not receive all the information they need in order to make an informed choice about whether to use a technology. And when participants in inquiry are inanimate, they are of course regarded as having no power whatsoever (other than the "natural power" to be fertile or infertile, as in the case of soil). Increasing objectivity in such contexts means directly challenging just such a setup, just such a distribution of power, authority, and legitimacy.

All humans probably find ourselves in the position of being the "researchers" sometimes—the ones institutionally given the authority to say how things are going to go. When we have this role, we have considerable power in the inquiry, and this gives our responsibilities a very particular character. We're the ones holding the pens, representing the results of the study to others. On top of that, we are often persons who have particular power or authority because of our race, our class, our gender, or our position in other institutional power systems. These features of our role in any particular inquiry context dictate, in turn, very particular tasks for us, if we intend to work to increase the objectivity of that context. Such an account throws into relief the inherently moral nature of inquiry; agents, whose locations in the world are highly interactive and interactively constituted, are morally responsible for how they/we interact in that world. We cannot sharply separate self from other, or the interests of one agent from the interests of another.[9]

My discussion has once again shifted—this time from ontological concerns back to epistemological ones. This is not unintentional. Ultimately, and in company with Barad, I want to suggest that the interrelationship between these conceptions of objectivity and realism actually point to a more general issue—the mutually constituting relationship between ontology and epistemology. The distinction generally drawn between epistemological questions and ontological ones cannot hold, once we understand "subjects" and "objects" to be part of a nondualistic whole, and once we understand the real to be constituted, in part, by the activity of inquiry. Because the world is such that inquiry transforms its nature, and because inquiry is one of the things that make the world the way it is, we obscure our investigation if we continue to separate questions such as What is there? from questions such as How do we know what there is? The way we take the world to be, when we set out to inquire into it, is one constitutive element of the world.

NOTES

1. The list, for those who are curious, includes extra food and clothing, sunglasses, a knife, fire-starting material, matches, a first-aid kit, a flashlight, a map, and a compass.

2. We assert that this definition of objectivity actually is in sympathy with, or can speak to the motivation behind, many of the received views of objectivity, including objectivity conceived of as correspondence to reality, independence from perspectives, freedom from interpretations, dispassionateness, detachment, obedience to rules, and openness to criticism. I shall not rehearse the arguments for this assertion here.

3. I also find an earlier version of this kind of realism in the work of John Dewey, a point I will not discuss here, but which may be found in my *Coresponsibility* (1987).

4. One can push the analogy with perception only so far, of course; I am wary of getting embroiled in a discussion of the fact that a painting is also "real" and admits of multiple perspectives. Of course it is, *qua* painting. But *qua* horse (or whatever its subject matter), the painting admits of only a couple of perspectives. You'll never see the other side of the horse by flipping over the canvas.

5. The striking resemblance to John Dewey again merits noting. Dewey contends that there is indeed a "real world," but it isn't "out there" at all; he rejects the traditional realist contention that the world has an *independent* existence. The traditional realist wishes to maintain the separateness and fixity of the world, and to sustain the related ontological separation between inquiring subject and inquired-into object. Dewey does away with the separation of observer and observed by placing inquirers squarely in the world, and by making inquiry a species of natural activity.

Dewey adopts this version of realism in part from a desire to acknowledge that knowers are a part of the world they know; they are inquirers in and of it, not external observers to it. Scheman's concern is related; she intends to account for the fact that the world and inquirers are not radically independent of each other, but are mutually constitutive: "Realism ought not to require such independence on the side of the world . . . if by realism we mean the recognition that the world may not be the way anyone . . . thinks it is" (1993, 98). For a further discussion of John Dewey's realism, see Heldke, 1987, chapter 2; for Dewey's own discussion, one source is *Experience and Nature* (1958).

6. Haraway discusses the trickster in her *situated knowledges* (1991). Dewey similarly notes that "the world must actually be such as to generate ignorance and inquiry; doubt and hypothesis; trial and temporal conclusions" (1958, 169).

7. The use of the word "phenomenon" here should not lead us to assume that there must also be a "noumenon" of which it is an "appearance"; this is not a reintroduc-

tion of Kantianism. And here, I think, is another potential source of tension with Scheman, who argues that perspectives presume something of which they *are* perspectives.

8. This is not to say that agents of observation have a different ontological status than those things constituted as objects—which themselves have agency as well. "Nature" (an odd term, I think, in this ontology) "has agency, but it does not speak itself the patient, unobtrusive observer—there is an important asymmetry with respect to agency" (Barad 1996, 29).

9. Elsewhere, I've explored one way that an inquirer who is systematically overprivileged—I look in particular at race privilege—might creatively work to increase responsibility in a particular inquiry context; it requires resisting and transforming their own privilege, and developing what Harding and others call a "traitorous identity." I won't explore this issue here, other than to say that this kind of project—in which agents examine and critique and transform their political, social, historical location in the context of inquiry—seems to me to be one sort of work that is prescribed by this model of objectivity. See my "On Being a Responsible Traitor" (1997).

References

Barad, Karen. 1996. Meeting the universe halfway. Manuscript. Published in *Feminism, science and the philosophy of science: A dialogue,* ed. Lynn Hankinson Nelson and Jack Nelson. Dordrecht: Kluwer.

Dewey, John. 1958. *Experience and nature.* 2d ed. New York: Dover.

Haraway, Donna. 1991. Situated knowledges: The science question in feminism and the privilege of partial perspective. In *Simians, cyborgs and women.* New York: Routledge.

Harding, Sandra. Does objectivity in the social sciences require value neutrality? *Sounding* 60 (1977): 351–56.

Heldke, Lisa. 1997. On being a responsible traitor: A primer. In *Daring to be good: Essays in Feminist ethico-politics,* ed. Bat-Ami Bar On and Ann Ferguson. New York: Routledge.

———. 1987. Coresponsibility: Objectivity from Dewey to feminist epistemology. Doctoral dissertation. Evanston, Ill: Northwestern University.

Heldke, Lisa, and Stephen Kellert. 1995. Objectivity as responsibility. *Metaphilosophy* 22, 26 (4): 360–78.

Jackson, Wes. 1984. *Meeting the expectations of the land: Essays in sustainable agriculture and stewardship.* Berkeley: North Point.

Manning, Harvey. 1973. *Backpacking: One step at a time.* New York: Vintage.

Rooney, Phyllis. 1995. Rationality and the politics of gender difference. *Metaphilosophy* 26 (1&2): 22–45.

———. 1992. On values in science: Is the epistemic/nonepistemic distinction useful? *PSA 1992.* Vol. 1. Philosophy of Science Association.

Scheman, Naomi. 1993. *Engenderings.* New York: Routledge.

CHAPTER FIVE

BEYOND EPISTEMOLOGY: FROM A PRAGMATIST FEMINIST EXPERIENTIAL STANDPOINT

CHARLENE HADDOCK SEIGFRIED

The beginning of a new century provides an opportunity for looking back on decades of feminist criticism of a dominant model of Western rationality that extols detachment as expressed by Descartes's extreme mind/body dualism and a predatory approach to nature as expressed by Roger Bacon's forcing nature to respond to interrogations. The 1997 enGendering Rationalities Conference called for collaborative efforts to continue developing such alternative, multidimensional feminist models of rationality. But instead of a focused inquiry into rationality, the emphasis subtly shifted in some of the suggested topics proposed for the conference to include the thematic of feminist knowledge projects, theories of knowledge, and forms of knowing, thus using rationality and epistemology interchangeably in practice if not in theory. This blurring of the distinction between theories of rationality and theories of knowledge is troubling because I think that the current hegemony of epistemology in philosophical and theoretical discourse, especially in the United States, is itself a direct result of the very model of rationality that feminists have been criticizing.

My reasons for this belief are found in another emancipatory theory inaugurated more than a century ago that also challenged the model of disembodied, detached rationality. In William James's words, it called for understanding rationality as having "at least four dimensions, intellectual, aesthetical, moral, and practical (1977, 55)." Our efforts to "find a world rational to the maximal degree *in all these respects simultaneously* is no easy matter," and the realization of only one or the other dimension still leaves our rational demands unsatisfied (see Seigfried 1992). Rationality, reconstructed according to a pattern of embodiment in the lived world, is an interactive process encompassing perceptual input, conceptual formulation, and active or emotional powers. Satisfying only such cognitive rational demands as consistency and simplicity isolates a part of the process and ignores the fact that unless aesthetic rationality is guided by the emotional and active powers of practical rationality, it cannot provide adequate grounds for decision making. According to this pragmatist model, the abstract phase of rationality is guided by its practical dimension. Ninety years ago, Jane Addams already recognized the feminist potential of this pragmatist interpretation of rationality. After quoting James on the four dimensions of rationality, she laments that it is no easy matter to find a world so ordered and then adds that it is especially difficult if the world one is concerned with is that in which the Hull House settlement works. Addams then explains how the [overwhelmingly female] settlement workers nevertheless strove to accomplish "this fourfold undertaking" (1981, 308) in their efforts to empower the impoverished immigrant community.

But in the philosophical paradigm dominant in the United States since World War II, in which rationality has been deliberately reduced to the one dimension of intellect, it is impossible to simply add back the other dimensions without undermining the model itself, as antifeminist defenses of the standard view point out again and again. It is no accident that both classical American pragmatism and some contemporary versions of feminist theory developed theories of knowledge in the context of theories of science. According to James, because of the influence on philosophy of the intellectualism of Plato and Aristotle, too much emphasis has developed on logical considerations of what "would hold good in all conceivable worlds, worlds of an empirical constitution entirely different from ours. It is as if the actual peculiarities of the world that is were entirely irrelevant to the content of truth. But they cannot be irrelevant; and the philosophy of the future must imitate the sciences in taking them more and more elaborately into account" (1977, 149).

Unlike logical positivists and ordinary language philosophers, the pragmatists recognized the radical implications for philosophy of the Darwinian evolutionary model. It provides strong evidence, for example, that human beings are continuous with nature; have developed over time in a process that is still going on; have no privileged insight into nature, but only ways of interacting with it more or less successfully; and are individuals only through relations to others. In reflecting on the consequences for thinking of this model, the pragmatists rejected the myriad dualisms informing centuries of philosophic speculation and the spectator theory of knowledge that emerged from them. Being in the world not only precedes thinking about it, but our predispositions and intentions shape our transactions with our social and natural environments and are in turn shaped by them. These transactions inform the understandings developed, questioned, acted on, and revised. Knowing as a way of doing replaces the traditional models of knowing as rationally speculative or empirically passive, as abstracting essences, satisfying a priori criteria, and producing certainty. Furthermore, seeking or testing knowledge is not even necessarily the most appropriate or valuable aspect of transactions that are lived through, emotionally, economically, materially, sexually, and so on.

In "The Need for a Recovery of Philosophy" John Dewey (1980b) already warned against developing an epistemology industry preoccupied with answering the skeptic because such a concern assumes a false metaphysics. It is a curiosity of orthodox empiricism that its central theoretical problem is the existence of the external world. Believing that experience is attached to a private subject, it takes the world as external to such experience. This belief is curious "for if anything seems adequately grounded empirically it is the existence of a world which resists the characteristic functions of the subject of experience," which so often "frustrates our hopes and intentions" (Dewey 1980b, 18). The problem is that orthodox empiricism takes the transitory mental state as the only experiential given. This experience yields cognitive certainty because it alone is absolutely and indubitably present. "It alone is *knowledge*. The existence of the past (and of the future), of a decently stable world and of other selves— indeed one's own self—falls outside the datum of experience." Dewey calls this mass of inconsistencies "a doctrine of desperation" and says that criticism is unnecessary because no solution is called for when a basic concept is a fiction (Dewey 1980b, 19).

If it is not true that experience is something developed independently of the world of facts, then the problem of how the mind or subjective consciousness can understand the external world is a meaningless problem. But it is the very problem which forms the core of epistemology. Dewey continues: "The problem of knowledge as conceived in the industry of epistemology is the problem of knowledge *in general*—of the possibility, extent, and validity of knowledge in general. What does this 'in general' mean? In ordinary life there are problems a-plenty of knowledge in particular. . . . But there is no problem of knowledge in general. I do not mean, of course, that general statements cannot be made about knowledge" (1980b, 23). Statements of the conditions conducing to the success or failure of specific instances of inquiry, for example, constitutes logic. Its findings can guide further attempts at knowing. "But this logical problem of knowledge is at the opposite pole from the epistemological. Specific problems are about right conclusions to be reached—which means, in effect, right ways of going about the business of inquiry" (1980b, 23). The relevant distinction is that between knowledge and error arrived at as a consequence of employing "right and wrong methods of inquiry and testing; not a difference between experience and the world" (1980b, 23). Questions concerning knowledge in general arise from assuming that there is a knower in general apart from the world to be known. Unless this assumption is undermined, then the specific contributions that feminists and others make in analyzing the roles of gender, sexuality, class, race, or ethnicity in the production and consumption of knowledge will never be taken as anything other than at best a distraction from, and at worst a distortion of, the epistemological enterprise.

The stakes are high in deciding whether answering the skeptic, which is indeed central to epistemology, should continue to be *the* problem which structures *the* epistemological approach which we should continue to emphasize in philosophy or whether other problems of constructive intelligence are more important. Dewey warned against the pernicious effects of continuing this particular conversation and urged a reconstruction in philosophical outlook and methodology. He said that "a doctrine which exalts thought in name while ignoring its efficacy in fact (that is, its use in bettering life) is a doctrine which cannot be entertained and taught without serious peril. Those who are not concerned with professional philosophy but who are solicitous for intelligence as a factor in the amelioration of actual conditions can but look askance at any doctrine which holds that the entire scheme of things is already, if we but acquire the knack of looking at it aright, fixedly and completely rational." Epistemologists continue to tinker at perfecting a perfectly rational account of knowledge in itself, while ignoring the question of what such knowledge is for, as well as how it arises in experience. Dewey concludes that "to substitute the otiose insight gained by manipulation of a formula for the slow cooperative work of a humanity guided by reflective intelligence is more than a technical blunder of speculative philosophers" (1980b, 20). It is more than technical because insofar as it effectively distracts intellectuals from putting their intelligence in the service of cooperative efforts of alleviating actually oppressive social situations, it becomes one more factor contributing to their persistence.

Pragmatists, including feminist pragmatists, therefore rejected the epistemological turn that eventually became dominant in twentieth-century departments of philosophy in America. They recognized that the Darwinian evolutionary model required a radical break with previous assumptions about the place of human beings in the world. But proponents of logical positivism and linguistic analysis deliberately refused to consider the consequences of Darwinian evolution for reflective thinking, indeed deliberately focused on epistemology and self-referential symbol systems as a way to avoid reflections on the context of thinking, including the body, culture, ethnicity, class, and gender (see Cunningham 1996).[1] The lure of a positivistically defined scientific model that could ignore its own value commitments and which promised to deliver necessary truth was all the stronger in opposition to the competing pragmatist model, which showed the connection of knowledge with values, of understanding with transformation, which argued that the quest for certainty too easily became a means of hegemonic control, and which equated the quest for understanding with resolving problematic situations and overcoming oppressive conditions.

The issue is not, as Lynn Hankinson Nelson seems to think it is, whether the features of much work in contemporary epistemology and philosophy of science, which she grants are incommensurate with feminist analyses of knowledge, are assumptions that are necessary to epistemology and philosophy of science (1995, 37). Just as there is no knower in general, so there is no essential nature of epistemology. Epistemology as a specialty and as a designation for that specialty has been appropriated by a specific tradition of Anglo-American philosophy. It is enough that this particular tradition—as Dewey already pointed out at its inception and as Richard Rorty has pointed out in regard to its mature development—rejects those very assumptions without which feminists could not raise questions about relationships among knowledge, gender, and politics. Rejecting this particular historical variant of a theory of knowledge and its role in experience, which Nelson rightly calls "abandoning epistemology," is not the same thing as abandoning cognitive concerns. It is to place them in a different context.

Because pragmatists argued that philosophers should focus on the oppressive situations in which we find ourselves, individually and socially, and not continue the usual formal examination and refutation of texts deemed classic by the tradition, they found themselves in a battle over the canon. Dewey was on one side, representing members of the earlier pragmatist philosophy department at the University of Chicago, who not only joined psychology with ethics and logic, but engaged in research on the women's movement, racism, and capitalistic oppression of the working classes, and on the other side were Robert Hutchins, president of the university, and his right-hand man, Mortimer Adler and his Great Books program. Hutchins and Adler identified empirical naturalism—not distinguishing between pragmatist and positivist varieties—as the enemy of their own Aristotelian or Thomistic metaphysical absolutism. Dewey countered that "there is implicit in every assertion of fixed and eternal first truths . . . the necessity for some *human* authority to decide, in this world of conflicts, just what these truths are and how they are to be taught," and Hutchins had "completely evaded the problem of who is to determine the definite truths that constitute the hierarchy"[2] (Westbrook 1991, 519).

If pragmatists refused to take the epistemological turn that characterizes so much mainstream twentieth-century philosophy, it does not follow that they developed no theoretical approaches to knowledge. What, then, did they take the business of philosophy, of theory, to be? This takes us back to their radical reconstruction of rationality and consequent emphasis on experience. Philosophy is the intelligent reconstruction of experience according to ends-in-view. Experience is an ongoing process of both undergoing and doing. As a process of undergoing, it is "a process of standing something; of suffering and passion, of affection, in the literal sense of these words. The organism has to endure, to undergo, the consequences of its own actions. Experience is no slipping along in a path fixed by inner consciousness." Just as assertive and aggressive actions are not all action with no passive elements, so too "there is no undergoing which is not on our part also a going on and a going through. Experience, in other words, is a matter of *simultaneous* doings and sufferings. Our undergoings are experiments in varying the course of events; our active tryings are trials and tests of ourselves" (Dewey 1980b, 8–9).

Experience is interpreted through past beliefs and prejudices, which can be uncovered and criticized, and it leads to outcomes, which can be evaluated and redirected. Perception and thinking do not passively register some external object or event; both are interpretive and active.[3] Instead of epistemology, a pragmatic theory of knowledge is construed as inquiry that satisfactorily resolves problematic situations. "Thought or reflection . . . is the discernment of the relation between what we try to do and what happens in consequence" (Dewey 1980a, 151). Jane Addams develops an account of experience from the diversity of women's experiences, her own as well as those of working-class women, ethnically diverse immigrants, the very old and the very young. This link of theory to practice is so important that in Addams's preface to *Twenty Years at Hull-House* she characterizes each of her earlier books as "an attempt to set forth a thesis supported by experience, whereas this volume endeavors to trace the experiences through which various conclusions were forced upon me" (1981, xviii).

It may be of interest to those of us who at the beginning of the twenty-first century are trying to recover the pragmatist reconstruction of philosophy that got stalled early in the twentieth century, to see why professional critics missed the point of its refusal to take the epistemological turn. According to Dewey, professionally trained philosophers, unlike nontechnical readers, interpreted "the doctrine that the meaning and validity of thought are fixed by differences made in consequences and in satisfactoriness" as meaning consequences in personal feelings. They thought that what was being asserted was that "consciousness or mind, in the mere act of looking at things modifies them" (1980b, 42–43). The source of the confusion was their deliberate neglect of temporal considerations. "For the unique epistemological relation [pragmatism] substitutes a practical relation of a familiar type—responsive behavior which changes in time the subject-matter to which it applies. The unique thing

about the responsive behavior which constitutes knowing is the specific difference which marks it off from other modes of response, namely, the part played
in it by anticipation and prediction. Knowing is the act, stimulated by this fore-
sight, of securing and averting consequences" (Dewey 1980b, 43).

Dewey was well aware that in developing his pragmatist theory of knowing as an act of inquiry he was engaged in a paradigm shift, one that thoroughly undermined traditional assumptions and beliefs about knowledge. He
said in 1905: "In short, the point that the critics of pragmatism have missed
with a surprising unanimity, is that in giving a reinterpretation of the nature
and function of knowledge, pragmatism gives necessarily a thoroughgoing
reinterpretation of all the cognitive machinery—sensations, ideas, concepts,
etc." (Dewey 1977, 155). It modifies the traditional conception of experience
and reason in recognition of the practical genesis and purpose of thinking. The
dualistic prejudice that experience only shows how people actually think while
logic shows how they ought to think cannot withstand anthropological, linguistic, rhetorical, and experimental psychological evidence that logic is both
empirical and normative because the norms and regulations of an art of thinking have grown out of the concrete ways that inquiry and testing have proved
efficacious or failed to do so. "If thought or intelligence is the means of intentional reconstruction of experience, then logic, as an account of the procedure
of thought, is not purely formal. It is not confined to laws of formally correct
reasoning apart from truth of subject-matter. . . . If thinking is the way in
which deliberate reorganization of experience is secured, then logic is such a
clarified and systematized formulation of the procedures of thinking as will enable the desired reconstruction to go on more economically and efficiently"
(Dewey 1982b, 157–58).

It takes a while for the proposed shift to sink in. If thinking is literally
the intentional reconstruction of experience, then it is not focused on propositions, judgments, and philosophical models of cognition, to take one set of
current focus. The paradigm shift goes all the way down: for example, concen-
trating on experience rather than cognition, interpretation rather than knowledge, emancipation rather than description, scientific attitude rather than
making scientific contributions, problem solving rather than theory construction, sensitivity to contextual conditions rather than detached analysis, taking
subject matter from contemporary issues rather than from the history of philosophy or from what is currently discussed in professional journals and the
like. Feminist concern to change the actual conditions of women's oppression
becomes a central and not a peripheral issue. The success in preparing persons
to participate in their own emancipation becomes a primary criterion of the
success of philosophical approaches; merely theoretic fluency of analysis
wouldn't be.

The more we explore and reflect on a rationality which has evolved over time as a means of intelligently transforming ourselves and our environment, a rationality which is inevitably informed by our multiple relationships of gender, sexuality, color, nationality, and class, to name a few, the more it seems that feminists would be better off abandoning the misguided epistemological project we've inherited, rather than to continue tinkering with it. Even the fallacies academic epistemologists warn us against reflect their intent to establish an unbridgeable gulf between objective knowledge and subjective apprehension, between formal assertion and experiential context. Recall the ubiquitous warnings against the naturalistic fallacy, the psychologistic fallacy, folk psychology, confusing the logic of validation with the logic of discovery, confusing facts and values or feelings and thought, and cultural relativism. Although in specific instances any of these fallacies may signal a break with valid procedure, in the context of the history of repeated warnings against the recognition of and involvement with culture and embodiment in epistemological analysis, they register the conditions under which epistemology emerged and the limits of its self-understanding. A more radical and productive feminist approach would be to continue developing a transformative model of interested, not disinterested, inquiry into experience; in short, to engage in an unapologetic feminist philosophy of inquiry rather than epistemology. Such an inquiry, sensitive to actual outcomes, requires awareness of diverse contexts, the emotional dimension of understanding, the mutuality of facts and values, the exploration and rejection of pervasive prejudices, recognition of multiple standpoints, cooperative problem solving, and valuing the other in their distinctiveness, the very concerns that the epistemological turn was created to abolish.

It is no accident that Dewey's assertion of the value of women's contributions to philosophy is linked to his refusal to take the epistemological turn. Two places where he explicates this connection are in *Democracy and Education* (Dewey 1980a), where he first developed his pragmatist philosophy as a coherent system, and then a couple of years later in one of his more radical addresses, "Philosophy and Democracy" (Dewey 1982a). In *Democracy and Education* he argues that our theories of knowledge and rationality are still distorted by our Greek philosophical heritage, which originated in a society organized into inferior and superior social classes, and which consequently made sharp distinctions between material and ideal interests and between useful labor and detached contemplation. The mass of people were thought of as fulfilling only vegetative or animal functions and relegated to providing the means of subsistence for the privileged few who could realize their humanity through rational contemplation and living worthily. "Thus by nature, and not merely by social convention, there are those who are slaves—that is, means for the ends of others. . . . Moreover, women are classed with slaves and craftsmen as factors among the animate instrumentalities of production and reproduction of the means for a free or rational life" (Dewey 1980a, 261). By reading these societal hierarchies into nature, the classical Greek philosophers concluded that "the higher the activity the more purely mental it is; the less does it have to do with physical things or with the body. The more purely mental it is, the more independent or self-sufficing is it" (Dewey 1980a, 262). Purely intellectual life was considered fully complete and perfect in itself while administering to the needs of the community, whether by governing or by the more lowly tasks of supplying physical needs, were considered dependent activities because they required other persons to carry them out and were tainted by practice and instrumental doing.

In spite of great social changes, these views still infect and distort theories of knowledge and rationality. In his critique of Aristotle's theory, in particular, Dewey points out that because "the mass of men and all women were regarded as unfree by the very nature of their bodies and minds," there was not necessarily any logical contradiction or moral hypocrisy involved in giving them only training that fitted them for servile labor. Aristotle's statements are false because they confuse social custom with natural necessity. But it is not enough to simply substitute "a different view of the relations of mind and matter, mind and body, intelligence and social service" for Aristotle's if we continue to reproduce many of his assumptions (Dewey 1980a, 265). In our theories, we must reject his belief that there is a natural divorce between theory and practice, between producing goods and rendering service and self-directive thought. More importantly, even such a theoretical revolution is of little use if we tolerate and perpetuate the social state of affairs that generated and sanctioned his hierarchical divisions. More than eighty years ago Dewey asserted that "the revolution is still incomplete" because we have not yet rendered Aristotle's ideas obsolete in fact even though "the increased political and economic emancipation of the 'masses' . . . has destroyed the idea that learning is properly a monopoly of the few who are predestined by nature to govern social affairs" (1980a, 265). At the beginning of the twenty first century, too many people, not least philosophers, still value theory over practice and do not see them as intimately related. They still theorize on the basis of an ontological distinction between inner mental action and outer physical action, of mind and body, and prefer models of truth based on the ideal of a detached spectator over ones that recognize context and the engaged transformations of the experimental method. Autonomy rather than interdependence is still taken to be a more desirable goal.

In "Philosophy and Democracy" Dewey surprisingly denies "that philosophy is in any sense whatever a form of knowledge," calling it instead "a social hope reduced to a working program of action"[4] (1982a, 43). Philosophy is not a science, but as the ancients put it, a love of wisdom, an attitude toward the world and knowledge that seeks a more valuable way of life and that tries to persuade others of the wisdom of this choice. It should employ the known facts of its time and place to support its estimate of the good life. Therefore, it is to be expected that different times and places and different ways of being situated in the world would lead to different philosophical approaches. In fact, one can doubt the sincerity of a generation or group of people if its particular estimate of the good life did not uniquely inform the current social ideal. It is at this point in his argument that Dewey predicts that when women cease being disciples of canonically recognized philosophers and begin developing philosophy themselves, it would be inconceivable "that it will be the same in viewpoint or tenor as that composed from the standpoint of the different masculine experience of things" (1982a, 45).

Insofar as women's and men's experiences are different, they lead to different perspectives on the world and different values, not merely because of their biological differences but because of the way that our sexed bodies enter into, and are modified by, myriad relationships, including power relations, different customs, and institutions.[5] Different philosophies should be interrogated to discover what purposes and cultivated wants inform them, not in the vain hope of gaining insight into the ultimate nature of things or the makeup of reality as such. What is called reality are those selected aspects of the world that support what is thought to be the worthwhile life. "In philosophy, 'reality' is a term of value or choice" (Dewey 1982a, 45). But it is not merely wish fulfillment or vague aspiration. It must clothe itself in the garb of science to carry a conviction that surpasses that of science, because "philosophy is not mere passion but a passion that would exhibit itself as a reasonable persuasion" (Dewey 1982a, 46). New perspectives do not simply disclose new aspects of the lived world, but they open up new tasks.

According to feminist standpoint theory, marginalized persons have not just different but more objective insights into reality, since they not only can understand the dominant view as it understands itself, but can also grasp aspects of the world unavailable to those in power who do not bear the brunt of the decisions and actions they impose on others and thus who are unaffected by them and unaware of their full ramifications. Sandra Harding (1993) has modified her earlier claims that such marginalized standpoints more truly represent the world to the weaker claim that such representations are less false. Pragmatists do not even use this model of a mind representing an external reality. According to a pragmatist account, the reality which standpoint theory assumes is experienced reality, including not only who has the right and power to interpret, validate, and perpetuate their lived experience through popular media and historical records, but also who is empowered to make and assess policy decisions based on their experiences.

How do standard epistemological accounts differ from pragmatist ones? For one thing, according to correspondence or representational accounts of truth, it should make no difference who makes claims about reality. But according to pragmatists, since knowledge is the outcome of inquiry which resolves or fails to resolve a problematic situation, those differently situated will not only experience different outcomes but will also find them more or less satisfactory. And if the problem is the sexual harassment of women in the workplace, or the poverty of Blacks in inner cities, then until it is understood as they understand it and the proposals made are found to have bettered their situation, it has not been resolved. Since what is satisfactory to those in power is not likely to be for those over whom they exercise power, and since both contribute to what makes a problematic situation problematic, then the problem cannot be resolved without substantial interaction, negotiation, acceptance of the worth of each member of society, access to information about contributing factors, willingness to listen to others, consensus building, carrying through action on suggested proposals, and openness to revising the postulated solution in light of actual outcomes. The epistemologist depends on a very different set of criteria to determine whether the truth has been revealed or found. For epistemologists the truth is equally available in every sort of social, political, and economic situation. It just is or obtains. The pragmatist does not speak of truth being revealed or asserted but says that hypotheses are or are not warranted depending on whether the problematic situation has been satisfactorily transformed. Since the value for life of various organizations of experience is the special province of philosophical thinking, according to pragmatists, and the socially problematic situations on which philosophers ought to focus arise from and affect the interactions of multiply constituted members of diverse communities, a democratic society is a precondition for maximal satisfaction. And democracies can succeed in the long run only insofar as the standpoints of their more marginalized and oppressed members are not only heard but taken account of.

Over a century ago, in an article called "The Significance of the Problem of Knowledge," Dewey made a prediction that he based both on the logic of the situation and the signs of the time. He said that philosophical interest would shift from metaphysics and epistemology to psychology and social ethics, including the concrete social sciences insofar as they relate to conduct (1972, 22). By psychology Dewey does not mean a particular empirical science, "below the natural sciences in point of certainty and definiteness, as also far below pure philosophy as to comprehensiveness and ability to deal with fundamental issues" (1972, 22–23). Rather, psychology, understood as "the account of the way in which conscious life is . . . progressively maintained and reorganized," need not succumb to "the occasional supercilious sneers of the epistemologist" (1972 22–23). In psychology "the abstract question of how experience in general is possible [is] translated into the concrete and practical problem of how *this* and *that* experience in particular are possible, and of how they may be actualized" (1972, 22–23). Social ethics, in turn, considers "the values which are necessary to constitute an experience which is worth while" (1972, 22–23).

Dewey's reasoning for the deemphasis of epistemology was that sooner or later we would have enough detailed knowledge and understanding of method that knowledge ceases to be a problem and becomes a tool. The so-called problem of knowledge will either be solved or it is intrinsically meaningless or absurd. "Then the dominating interest becomes the *use* of knowledge; the conditions under which and ways in which it may be most organically and effectively employed in direct conduct." The question of the meaning of the problem of knowledge is part of a larger question "of the relation of knowing to acting, of theory to practice" (1972, 5, 21). When theories of knowledge forget their value in securing methods of action best calculated to solve the problems that generated inquiry in the first place, then their pursuit becomes a useless luxury.

Contrary to Dewey's prediction, it is obvious that metaphysics and, especially, epistemology have neither withered away nor attained their goals. Dewey seriously misread the signs of the times. Why, then, haven't we abandoned them in exasperation or despair? James had an explanation for why formal systems like epistemology are unlikely to be abandoned, despite the fact that they never reach closure. As a purely aesthetic pursuit, the harmonious fitting together of various parts of an epistemological puzzle is inherently pleasing. There will always be persons who particularly enjoy such puzzles and who will continue the game. Such games will not be resolved as long as new questions can be raised concerning them, which is to say, as long as human beings continue to be creative.[6]

All is not lost, however, for those who demand more than aesthetic pleasure from theories of knowledge. Although such purely aesthetic organizations of experience can be endlessly prolonged and multiplied at will, they can also reach a real, if necessarily tentative, closure by being directed toward practical ends. Pragmatists argue, in fact, that it is only by directing knowledge toward such ends, which always express values, that it ceases to be a mere game and fulfills its instrumental promise.[7] Our practical interests are as basic as our aesthetic ones and complement each other unless they are deliberately compartmentalized. Like pragmatists, feminists are among those for whom the use to which knowledge is put is vitally important. Feminists stress psychology, in the sense of valuing, exploring, questioning the origins of, and transforming, the concrete, practical experiences of women. They also emphasize social ethics, which starts from the fact of the subject as already engaged in multiple relationships which are of greater or lesser value, and then examines the conditions of both multiple privileges and oppressions therein disclosed, develops strategies for empowerment, and encourages inclusiveness in the determination of specific ends and in carrying them out. If we take feminist philosophy seriously, then Dewey's prediction that psychology and social ethics would replace emphasis on metaphysics and epistemology has come true after all. He understood the logic of the situation better than he did the signs of the times. Feminists do not have to defend themselves against hostile charges that they are not doing rigorous philosophy, that is, epistemology. They are not doing sloppy epistemology, but have understood that theories of knowledge must continue to develop into theories and practices of inquiry in order to get out of the cul-de-sac in which epistemology has been stuck ever since it went into business for its own sake.

There are two reasons that it matters to distinguish between epistemology and concrete theories of knowing or theories of inquiry (Dewey prefers the phrase "the logic of inquiry"). First, I think that the revisions that Phyllis Rooney, Lorraine Code, Helen Longino, Lynn Nelson, and many other feminist epistemologists and philosophers of science rightly want to make will never be accepted *as* revisions just because they more radically undermine the epistemology industry than they seem to realize. The continued ignorance that mainstream analytic philosophers exhibit toward feminist epistemological writings is more than ignorance: they do not want to recognize that we are playing the same game, since we call into question the founding assumptions of twentieth-century epistemology. Ironically, early last century Mary Whiton Calkins made the same point in regard to pragmatism. Calkins said: "I cannot too unequivocally state my conviction that Dewey here proposes not the reconstruction, but the abandonment of philosophy" (1930, 200). But in her case, the essential core of philosophy that Dewey is accused of abandoning is not epistemology but metaphysics, or the study of the ultimately real. In a perverse way I think both analytic philosophers and Calkins are right; if they were to accede to the changes feminists and pragmatists require, then epistemology as well as metaphysics as we have known them will no longer exist. Secondly, as long as we continue the old conversation, new directions in philosophy will not proliferate and succeed. I am thinking especially of a paradigm shift from theories of knowledge to theories of praxis or the intentional reconstruction of experience as the core of philosophical activity.

I have been using "epistemology" in the same narrow sense that Lynn Hankinson Nelson (1995) says that both Susan Haack and Lorraine Code do, the former as a defender of its purity against feminist assault, and the latter as a defender of feminist theoretical autonomy. I do so not only to locate it historically within a philosophical perspective that has become dominant in America over the course of last century, but also to highlight its hegemonic claims in order to refuse allegiance to them. As Nelson points out, many other alternative philosophical perspectives, aside from pragmatism and feminism, have also challenged its hegemony over the course of the last century, from existentialism and critical theory to postmodernism. The conclusion she draws is that diverse feminist approaches to epistemology have as much right to criticize, correct, and develop new formulations of epistemological subject matter and methodology as does the dominant approach, which is not all that monological, in any case. But Nelson also recognizes that the incorporation of feminist interests "is deeply incommensurate with the view of epistemology (or philosophy more broadly) as something like a 'first knowledge': an enterprise which identifies first (i.e., foundational and universal) principles and starting points, and which need not concern itself with the actual circumstances within which knowledge is generated" (1995, 44). I have been arguing that analytic epistemology was historically developed precisely to limit the scope of legitimately grounded knowledge in just this way and that it has continued this commitment, based on faulty positivist and psychological assumptions, throughout its various permutations.

Where Nelson and I disagree is over whether adopting alternative approaches or perspectives, or making assumptions such as the value-ladenness of knowledge-claims, means abandoning epistemology or only abandoning a particular version of epistemology. I have deliberately restricted the term "epistemology" to the version(s) developed within a dominant philosophical tradition that continues to resist feminist inroads because of the epistemological turn this form of philosophy took early in the century and which continues to shape it as an historical entity. Other approaches, which define themselves through other central concerns, may incorporate theories of knowledge into their outlooks, but they are not epistemological in the strong sense which defines the epistemology-centered version.

Nelson fears that abandoning the epistemological industry is too high a price to pay because it will render feminist epistemological projects irrelevant to mainstream epistemology, which will therefore continue to promulgate a distorted view of knowledge. It will also lessen feminism's cognitive authority in academic disciplines and make it plausible for mainstream epistemologists and philosophers of science to ignore feminist insights (1995, 40–41). But from my perspective, it is mainstream epistemology that is irrelevant to feminist theories of knowledge, which have for some time challenged its distorted view of knowledge. Both Code and Nelson explain what contemporary epistemological theories lack that could be supplied by feminist theorists. But the failure of epistemologists to appreciate what is offered is itself a result of these very same deficiencies. Feminist theories have been ignored or derided in mainstream epistemological circles because these mainstream views are "abstract, nonempirical, universalist, and elitist," because they resist efforts to historicize knowledge claims, and because they claim epistemological authority on the grounds that their analyses are not influenced by concrete circumstances that distort everyday knowledge, such as historically specific references and political, gender, class, or racial relations. The point is not that someone doing philosophy in this epistemological vein could not recognize the error of their ways, but that doing so entails abandoning epistemology as it has been construed and doing something else. Feminist efforts to explain the theoretical shortcomings of epistemology will hardly be accepted as relevant criticism when it requires abandoning the very assumptions that underpin this epistemological perspective.[8]

Nelson argues that mainstream epistemology, not feminist epistemology, has abandoned a viable account of evidential warrant because it does not recognize the situatedness of cognitive agents and it does not take account of the material and cultural circumstances of cognitive agents (1995, 42). According to her own criteria, she has better grounds for accusing them of not really doing epistemology than they do for excluding feminist versions. I am making this *tu quoque* argument to show that the question of whether feminism is a legitimate theoretical enterprise does not depend on whether those working within the established paradigm of epistemology recognize feminist criticisms as internally cogent. Therefore, Nelson's argument for staying in the game of epistemology so as not to be stigmatized as failing to be doing philosophy "proper" (1995, 44) does not hold. Radical, not piecemeal, change is required in order for feminist reconstructions of knowledge to get a hearing, take hold, and thrive. That is already happening despite, and not because of, acceptance by epistemology-centered philosophy. It is not accidental that feminist analyses have thrived in alternative philosophical perspectives, such as postmodernism, queer theory, and critical theory.

Nelson voices one strategic response to the ghettoizing of feminist epistemology; namely, to continue to insist that we want to join the big boys at the table and—somehow—force them to pay attention to us. Being accepted is certainly attractive professionally, and wanting to steer epistemological discussions into feminist areas of interest is a worthwhile project, but I fear that the price for sitting at this particular table is too high. For one thing, the Anglo-American epistemological table has grown so large that it has obscured or shoved out of sight other tables that reflect on issues of knowledge differently. For another, it seduces us into patterns of thinking that are less than helpful for feminist theory. We don't have *epistemic* identities, for example, or *cognitive* crises, but are multiply located and related as persons active in the world who are at a disadvantage insofar as the world is ordered and valued from a masculinist or racist or homophobic or colonialist perspective. The disparity between conventionally distorted societal perspectives and one's own lived experience causes problems that can escalate into crises. When these problematic, oppressive situations cannot be resolved in the normal course of affairs, we ought to engage in inquiry, shared with others, to intelligently deal with them by transforming them into emancipatory ones. Prefacing or describing every issue with "epistemological" or "cognitive" should strike us as an odd use of language. The fact that it doesn't is itself odd and indicates a thorough professional indoctrination.

It is evidence that philosophers have succumbed to what Dewey called the intellectualistic fallacy; that is, a deliberate forgetfulness of the limits of context and purpose and illicit extension of knowledge to being or existence in general. It manifests itself in the egocentric predicament. "From the intellectualistic point of view, the self that is implicated in every knowledge event has to be conceived as a term of the knowledge relation; the intellectual function being final and inclusive, there is no other way of disposing of it" (1978, 88–90). The self or ego is therefore conceived of as a mind or consciousness, one constituent of the knowledge relation of which the other is the object known. From this swarmed "the whole brood of 'epistemological' problems." Dewey appeals instead to the facts of the empirical situation in which agents are seen to undertake and are responsible for cognitive events. "The relation in question is that of an agent to its act, not that of one of the two terms of knowledge to the other term" (1978, 88–90). The concrete questions that then concern us are how knowledge functions to resolve the particular conflicts that bother us and undermine a just and compassionate social order.

I am therefore advocating a different strategy from Nelson's, since the epistemological standpoint restricts our options rather than expanding them. It is one also articulated by Code—namely, to continue playing at another table, at another game, which someday, some nonfeminist epistemologists will probably wander over to, anyway. The advantage is that we get to continue to do really exciting work on our own terms, move in creative new directions, and not keep looking over our shoulders to see if it meets someone else's (or some other theory's) criteria. But the more I hear from others, even beginners in philosophy, the more discouraged I become about the absolute hegemony of epistemological thinking, the result of many generations of one-sided graduate education. Some, like Nelson, fear a loss of cognitive authority if feminists too overtly abandon the epistemological mainstream, since they might not then be hired or asked to help select APA papers or be able to train graduate students. Putting aside the oddity of a self-proclaimed feminist revolution that after only a few decades worries more about fitting into the mainstream than of subverting it, I can only reiterate what has already been said.

Feminist power consists precisely in our ability and determination to point out those aspects of our inherited beliefs, customs, institutions, and practices that disadvantage, demean, or otherwise oppress women and other discriminated groups; to propose and help enact emancipatory alternatives; and to contribute to the development and sustaining of an alternative, woman-affirming, inclusive set of beliefs and practices. I have been arguing that the epistemology industry, as it has developed over time and as it is presently practiced, incorporates assumptions harmful to women and minorities that must continue to be pointed out and criticized and that in order to do so effectively an alternative approach to knowledge and understanding—which I have been calling a "method of inquiry"—has already been developed by pragmatists and feminists. What is still lacking is the courage of our convictions and the recognition that those aspects of a theory of knowledge that feminists have painstakingly developed have outgrown the dominant paradigm of twentieth-century Anglo-American epistemology. I have in mind alternative, nonepistemological but nonetheless legitimate versions of a theory of knowledge that deal with issues of knowledge in a broader social-political context and as instrumental to transformations of the life-world. If such an approach disenfranchises feminists in political exercises of power involving hiring, committee selections, and fellowships in philosophy, then our response should not be to downplay our opposition to the epistemological paradigm as such, but to join with others whose nonepistemic, emancipatory traditions have been marginalized in philosophy and help bring about the changes required in the profession if power is ever to be more widely and fairly held. Anything less is to acquiesce in our own co-optation.

Nelson's aversion to subsuming philosophy of science under the rubric of epistemology (1995, 46 n1) is well founded and has the potential for reconciling our differences, but only if she is willing to follow through on the implied criticism such a stance contains, one that the pragmatists made explicit. The reason Nelson has difficulty including Quine as an exemplar of analytic philosophy (1995, 47 n16) is precisely because of his view "that a theory of knowledge should be pursued as an empirical science." But what does it mean to pursue it as an empirical science? It means not to investigate knowledge as though it were an independent discipline, as it was taken to be earlier in the last century by neo-Kantians, language philosophers, and members of the Vienna School of logical positivism, and as it continues to be in the dominant analytic paradigm. It means rejecting the epistemological turn and instead investigating how we find ourselves always already situated in an already interpreted, already structured world of unequally positioned persons. It means questioning how it came to be structured as one means of emancipating ourselves and others from entrapment in contingent situations masquerading as necessary or inevitable ones. It means beginning with concrete conditions and developing the tools necessary for resolving problematic situations, as science does. Unlike the scientific approach dominant today, however, it includes questioning the power relations that are intrinsic to situations and contesting the informing values. Knowledge in this alternative paradigm is not epistemological, but an instrument for intelligently guiding action, a cognitive ability which has evolved over time.[9]

The fact that late twentieth-century versions of naturalist epistemology keep epistemology in touch with science, particularly with cognitive science, is not enough to satisfy Dewey's prediction that philosophical interest would shift to psychology. Naturalized epistemology, in the sense of the scientific study of perception, is very different from what Dewey advocates. He argues that we will only be doing philosophy when we move from scientific description to evaluation (Dewey 1984). Rather than developing a scientific version of cognition, Dewey took the task of philosophy to be "to interpret the conclusions of science with respect to their consequences for our beliefs about purposes and values in all phases of life" (1988, 250). But this does not mean either taking over the results of the sciences uncritically or becoming a specialist in some domain of the sciences.

Pragmatist philosophy is scientific not in subject matter but in its attitude of antidogmatic experimentation. It takes for its subject matter aspects of everyday experience that are available to and can be observed by everyone, not just trained philosophers or scientists. Both "the starting point and the ultimate test of philosophy is . . . gross or macroscopic experience." Instead of taking the issues that dominate naturalized epistemology, either as they originate in the theories of psychology or of philosophy of mind, pragmatism is only concerned with those aspects of the sciences that have relevance to everyday experience, either in regard to issues that grow out of everyday experience or as they are reabsorbed back into it. Dewey's critique of the growing dominance of scientifically technical philosophy is as cogent today as when he said it in 1932: "Much of present-day philosophy that claims to be ultra-scientific seems to be wandering in a wilderness because . . . it tries to build upon the results of the special sciences in independence of, and in opposition to, coarse everyday experience" (1985, 276–77).

Dewey is hardly antiscientific, but he does criticize the context in which science is often practiced and the values that too often distort it. He anticipated, for example, the current widespread distrust of science and technology as evidence of the harms that accrue when science is made to serve the private accumulation of wealth or the political goals of domination. But he also criticized the denigration of science and technology as being intrinsically dangerous and necessarily harmful. Such blanket condemnation is yet another proof of the survival into present times of the assumptions that shaped Aristotelian aristocratic culture. To call for radical changes in society so that all can share fully in its goods—social, educational, and moral, as well as economic ones—without developing the necessary means to such ends, is sheer wish fulfillment. Our power to deliberately control our "own affairs depends upon ability to direct natural energies to use: an ability which is in turn dependent upon insight into nature's processes" (Dewey 1980a, 236). It cannot therefore be antiscientific or antitechnological without losing the most effective means to such ends.

Dewey does not want philosophers to become scientists or to turn philosophy into a science for the production of knowledge. Such endeavors over the past century have led to the increasingly specialized and technical jargon and to the growing chasm between philosophical—especially epistemological—research and the problems of everyday life. Philosophy can learn from science the value of experimentation as a method of transforming rather than recording already given reality. And it can acquire from its various branches some knowledge of the conditions of human action. But its purpose in doing so is socially democratic, that is, urging the dignity and worth of every person, developing the means necessary for ensuring that everyone learns the abilities needed for participating in their own growth and development while contributing to society, and promoting the growth of social sympathies, that is, the identification of one's own good with that of others.

Dewey urges us not to follow science in its ever-increasing specialization and arcane, technical vocabularies and interests, but to direct our attention in the opposite direction, back to where the experimental method originated; namely, to ordinary experience. In fact, on his view, the scientific method of observation, reflection, and testing is the formalization of the method of experience itself. The formality of science, whether in the sciences proper or in the increasingly technical epistemological theory constructions, creates an unnecessary stumbling block to the nonexpert. Dewey said that what is needed is less emphasis on a technical body of knowledge and procedures and more on "learning the scientific way of treating the familiar material of ordinary experience" so that more of us can gain "independent power to deal with material within [our] range" (1980a, 228). The situation has, if anything, only gotten worse. According to Ellen Messer-Davidow intellectual skirmishes between foundationalist philosophers and their critics over theories of truth "have distracted scholars from impacting experience, so that the social consequences of the humanities are negligible" (1991, 288).

Philosophy differs from science because of its intimate connection with an outlook on life. Such conceptions as generality, totality, and ultimateness do not literally apply to the subject matter of knowledge because completeness and finality are out of the question in a world of process where experience is ongoing and ever changing. Science, however, can isolate aspects of experience, circumscribe particular means and ends, and effect closure. The philosophic attitude, by contrast, "is averse to taking anything as isolated; it tries to place an act in its context—which constitutes its significance" (Dewey 1980a, 335–36). Dewey then makes a distinction that can help to explicate his puzzling claim, made earlier, that philosophy is not a form of knowledge. What he has in mind is a distinction between knowledge and thinking, a contrast he calls, in other places, that between knowledge and understanding. The form of validated knowledge that is the province of science "represents objects which have been settled, ordered, disposed of rationally. Thinking, on the other hand, is prospective in reference. It is occasioned by an *un*settlement and it aims at overcoming a disturbance" (Dewey 1980a, 336). Therefore, feminist reflection, which begins with the disturbing situations in which we as women in all our various identities find ourselves, in all the ways women suffer or are disadvantaged by more privileged genders, ethnicities, "races," sexualities, and so on, and which has in view the overcoming of such oppressive situations, is centered, not marginalized, in pragmatism. For Dewey, "philosophy is thinking what the known demands of us—what responsive attitude it exacts. It is an idea of what is possible, not a record of accomplished fact. Hence it is hypothetical like all thinking" (Dewey 1980a, 336). Philosophy is not primarily concerned with reflection on being or with solving epistemological puzzles. "It presents an assignment of something to be done—something to be tried." But philosophers have no privileged basis on which to solve problematic or oppressive situations for others: "Its value lies not in furnishing solutions (which can be achieved only in action) but in defining difficulties and suggesting methods for dealing with them" (Dewey 1980a, 336).

Notes

1. Fifty years earlier Herbert Schneider had pointed out that "the more recent movement of logical positivism, imported from abroad . . . has attempted to promote a greater 'unity of science' than the pragmatists ever dreamed of and has shifted the emphasis of scientific logic from factual experimentation to verbal or semantic manipulation." As a result, the empiricism has become "too logical to be 'radical'" (1963, 477).

2. It is not accidental that when pragmatists at the beginning of the twentieth century developed a contextual, problem-based theory of inquiry as an alternative to the mass of inconsistencies that inform the epistemological model, they found themselves in a battle over the canon and responded by charging the upholders of the epistemological view with evading the issue of who has the power to legislate truth. The fact that feminists toward the end of the same century, despite their different focus on the oppression of women, also challenged the by-now standard epistemological view and found themselves embroiled in battles over the canon and made similar responses to their critics should arouse suspicion about the viability of that model.

3. In contrast to the pragmatist position that the human situation falls wholly within nature, epistemological perspectives isolate the subjective from natural existence and draw a sharp line of demarcation between belief and knowledge because "they assign to knowledge alone valid reference to existence. Desires, beliefs, 'practical' activity, values are attributed exclusively to the human subject," and are relegated to the realm of the merely private and arbitrary (Dewey 1981, 315–16).

4. Surely, this is hyperbolic exaggeration for the sake of effect. One way that it might be true to say that philosophy is not a form of knowledge is that—once its purely speculative theories are rejected—it seems to be the case that the function of philosophy is not to engage in primary research like the sciences do, but to reflect more generally on the meaning and purpose of life and how to obtain a better state of affairs than the one in which we find ourselves. But this would mean that it is not the particular form of knowledge engaged in by the empirical sciences, not that it is in no sense whatever a form of knowledge. But see also the concluding paragraph of this chapter regarding the distinction between knowledge and thinking.

5. In response to Nelson's qualms about feminist standpoint epistemologists, empiricists, and pragmatists assuming "gender-specific ways of knowing" (1995, 36), the explication of the experiential perspective in this chapter should show that pragmatists in the tradition of James, George Herbert Mead, Dewey, and Addams, at least, are not confused about whether gender as it enters into their theory of knowledge requires essentialist views of self or gender. It does not. Nor is it an open issue for pragmatists whether the loci of knowledge are individuals. Knowledge is not a state of inner consciousness, but the outcome of a method of inquiry (see note 3). They do not wonder what the content and role of experience is as it is related to knowledge. This relationship constitutes the core of pragmatist philosophy.

6. For a fuller discussion of the aesthetic and practical dimensions of rationality, see Seigfried 1990, 29–38 and 117–38.

7. For the pragmatist radical reconstruction of instrumental reasoning, see chapter 8 of Seigfried 1996.

8. Code puts it this way: "It would not be possible to develop a feminist theory of knowledge that retained allegiance to the pivotal ideas around which epistemology—for all its variations—has defined itself" (1991, 314).

9. Pursuing a theory of knowledge as an empirical science does not have its roots in Quine's proposal that epistemology be naturalized, as Nelson says, but in pragmatism. However, there is a significant difference between the two. Following Quine's recommendations leads to naturalized epistemology, which is still limited by positivist assumptions about science and by a misguided attempt to *be* a science; following pragmatist recommendations leads to a radical reconstruction of philosophy in which knowledge is an instrument of emancipation of concretely situated persons who transform themselves by transforming their social and natural environments. This pragmatist perspective seems close to Nelson's position that theories of knowledge "are tools to organize, explain, and reconstruct our present and past experiences, and to be used in the service of our efforts to develop better knowledge and epistemic practices" (Nelson 1995, 45).

REFERENCES

Addams, Jane. 1981. *Twenty years at Hull-House* (orig. 1910). New York: Signet Classic.

Calkins, Mary Whiton. 1930. The philosophical *credo* of an absolutistic personalist. In *Contemporary American philosophers*, vol. 1, ed. George P. Adams and William Peperell Montague. New York: Macmillan.

Code, Lorraine. 1991. *What can she know? Feminist theory and the construction of knowledge.* Ithaca, N.Y.: Cornell University Press.

Cunningham, Suzanne. 1996. *Philosophy and the Darwinian legacy.* Rochester, N.Y.: University of Rochester Press.

Dewey, John. 1972. The significance of the problem of knowledge. In *John Dewey, the early works, vol. 5: 1895–1898*. Carbondale and Edwardsville: Southern Illinois University Press.

———. 1977. The realism of pragmatism. In *John Dewey, the middle works, vol. 3: 1903–1906*, ed. Jo Ann Boydston. Carbondale and Edwardsville: Southern Illinois University Press.

———. 1978. Some implications of anti-intellectualism. In *John Dewey, the middle works, vol. 6: 1910–1911*, ed. Jo Ann Boydston. Carbondale and Edwardsville: Southern Illinois University Press.

———. 1980a. Democracy and education. In *John Dewey, the middle works, vol. 9: 1916*, ed. Jo Ann Boydston. Carbondale and Edwardsville: Southern Illinois University Press.

———. 1980b. The need for a recovery of philosophy. In *John Dewey, the middle works, vol. 10: 1916–1917*, ed. Jo Ann Boydston. Carbondale and Edwardsville: Southern Illinois University Press.

———. 1981. *Experience and nature.* In *John Dewey, the later works, vol. 1: 1925*, ed. Jo Ann Boydston. Carbondale and Edwardsville: Southern Illinois University Press.

———. 1982a. Philosophy and democracy. In *John Dewey, the middle works, vol. 11: 1918–1919*, ed. Jo Ann Boydston. Carbondale and Edwardsville: Southern Illinois University Press.

———. 1982b. Reconstruction in philosophy. In *John Dewey, the middle works, vol. 12: 1920*, ed. Jo Ann Boydston. Carbondale and Edwardsville: Southern Illinois University Press.

———. 1984. Philosophy. In *John Dewey, the later works, vol. 5: 1929–1930*, ed. JoAnn Boydston. Carbondale and Edwardsville: Southern Illinois University Press.

———. 1985. Review of *collected papers of Charles Sanders Peirce, vol. 1.* In *John Dewey, the later works, vol. 6: 1931–1932*, ed. Jo Ann Boydston. Carbondale and Edwardsville: Southern Illinois University Press.

———. 1988. *The quest for certainty.* In *John Dewey, the later works, vol. 4: 1929*, ed. Jo Ann Boydston. Carbondale and Edwardsville: Southern Illinois University Press.

Harding, Sandra. 1993. Rethinking standpoint epistemology: "What is strong objectivity?" In *Feminist epistemologies*, ed. Linda Alcoff and Elizabeth Potter. New York: Routledge.

James, William. 1977. *A pluralistic universe*. Cambridge: Harvard University Press.

Messer-Davidow, Ellen. 1991. Know-how. In *(En)gendering knowledge: Feminists in academe*, ed. Joan E. Hartman and Ellen Messer-Davidow. Knoxville: University of Tennessee Press.

Nelson, Lynn Hankinson. 1995. The very idea of feminist epistemology. *Hypatia* 10. 3: 31–49.

Schneider, Herbert. 1963. *A history of American philosophy*, 2d ed. (1st ed., 1946). New York: Columbia University Press.

Seigfried, Charlene Haddock. 1990. *William James's radical reconstruction of philosophy*. Albany: State University of New York Press.

———. 1992. William James's concrete analysis of experience. *Monist* 75, 4: 543–45.

———. 1996. *Pragmatism and feminism*. Chicago: University of Chicago Press.

Westbrook, Robert B. 1991. *John Dewey and American democracy*. Ithaca and London: Cornell University Press.

Part II

Unveiling Rationality

CHAPTER SIX

RESISTING RATIONALITY

SARAH LUCIA HOAGLAND

They asked her to feel sorry for their plight. They told her how it was hard for them to cry, how dominance had been expected of them. They said that they knew no other life than the one that they were taught. That hence they were not responsible for what they did or said. They said that such changes as she was requiring of them were impossible. That their bodies could not be otherwise. That one could not change overnight. That these matters she spoke of so bluntly were subtle and complex. That she must be more patient. That she made them feel guilty. That guilt kept them from moving. She was bringing them to tears, they said: "Pity us." Couldn't she see that they had tried. Couldn't she see she was asking too much of them? Be fair: "You are unreasonable," they told her. But she answered them, "You have called me unreasonable before."

And she said she was tired of this old dialogue. Whenever she heard that cry, she said, of guilt, whenever she heard them moan for patience, her jaw closed. She could feel her face redden, and the back of her spine was rigid. She was certain she would explode. Yes, she said, she had grown unreasonable. "And I don't want to hear," she barked, "any more of your reasons." She had been patient, she growled, too long. "Do you know what the cost of this patience has been?" she yelled. This dialogue is over.

—Susan Griffin, *Women and Nature*

Introduction

I return to conceptual coercion. To pursue conceptual separatism, and resistance.

I began looking at conceptual coercion involved in scientific description/ explanation in the early 1970s when I ran into a wall trying to argue against those who argued with scientific confidence that women's natural place was subordinate to men, and that women, with the exception of a few crazed suffragists and feminists, were content with their lot. I argued that pronouncements on women were not empirical or factual, but rather prescriptive. An empirical proposition is one it makes sense to deny, yet counterexamples to claims about femininity were not countenanced, and claims that women accepted subordination were not falsified by the existence of Lesbians and the many women who did not fit the official description. Instead we were discounted as not-real-women. Using some of my work on Wittgenstein, I argued that studies like Sandra Bem's, designed to discover the nature of "femininity," merely served to solidify and hold the concepts in place, like an axis. The male-constructed concept of "femininity" erases female resistance to male domination: a woman who resists male domination is mad, insane. I also argued that some version of the feminine model has been applied to other oppressed peoples and is used to portray resistance to domination as a mental aberration, for example, slave resistance was equally scripted insane (Hoagland 1977; 1978; 1980a; 1980b; 1982; 1988).

Moving away from science's self-description as strictly empirical, and offering another approach to the type of conceptual coercion that engaged me, Thomas Kuhn argues that scientists do not treat anomalies as counterinstances, that "no process yet disclosed by the historical study of scientific development at all resembles the methodological stereotype of falsification by direct comparison with nature" (Kuhn 1962, 77). Exploring the task of the historian of science, he argues that scientific knowledge is not incremental; change in science happens by revolution not by evolution, by paradigm shift and not through falsification by means of counterexamples.

This story about science, combined with my work on Wittgenstein, helped make my struggle with empiricism coherent: Sense, meaning, emerges within a paradigm, holding a foundation, in this case male supremacy, in place, like an axis.[1]

A number of feminist theorists of science have also been struggling with science's treatment of women, and many with science's treatment of people of color. Sandra Harding categorized and clarified different feminist projects, showing us how theorists had been moving from the "woman question in science to the science question in feminism," that is, from a masculinist to a feminist focus (Harding 1986). Nancy Tuana, in particular, has documented the long tradition of Western misogyny dispatched from religion to science. Science retains the religious tradition of condemning women to a subordinate position. The inferiority of women is an *assumption* of scientists rather than an hypothesis open to investigation (Tuana 1993, 18). The patriarchal paradigm of misogyny was not affected by the scientific revolution.[2]

This suggests that change by shift in paradigm that Thomas Kuhn suggests is not a total change. While significant developments in knowledge happen by means of paradigm shift, they are revolutions or paradigm shifts only with respect to certain aspects of the previous paradigm. While I would agree that there have been a number of paradigm shifts, the Copernican revolution being one, to the scholar of the patriarchal naming of women in the 2500-or-so-year tradition that flows from ancient Greece through Christianity, colonial conquest and science, to capitalism, no significant change in the dominant, patriarchal naming of women, either evolutionary or revolutionary, leaps to mind.

Still, not everyone lives in acquiescence to that paradigmatic naming. And so I continued exploring ways of breaking from the dominant logic, from the embedded meaning in the hegemonic paradigm or conceptual framework. I have been particularly interested in resistance in the form of separatist political strategies: Black separatism, Jewish separatism, Lesbian separatism. What interests me has been the creation of distinct (in some respects incommensurable) conceptual contexts which do not hold the same values as the dominant frame—contestatory frameworks disrupting the seamless rationality of the dominant frame. This is apparent in the logic of what Wittgenstein calls the "language-games" that make up a framework; in Lesbian space, for example, female inferiority is as meaningless as male inferiority is in the dominant frame.

However, such spaces have often also retained dominant logic, usually about other groups: racism among White Lesbians, sexism among Black men. While we could, through consciousness raising, come to reinterpret our own experience and that of those we identify with (seeing resistance where dominant rationality paints insanity, criminality, perversion, nonsense, or nothing at all), few successfully reinterpreted dominant logic about experiences and practices of those we didn't identify with and so most remained lodged one way or another in the dominant paradigm about Others (whoever Others were, relative to us). (Note Lugones, forthcoming.) This was not just a failure of will. Those working to preserve the sense of a dominant paradigm employ an array of strategies to appropriate, coopt, and erase distinct worlds of sense. Conceptual coercion.

Postmodern understanding stresses our embeddedness in a system of meaning. Gadamer, for example, presents a compelling case against Enlightenment dogma of liberating reason from tradition. We are located in a culture without having an external view of it, in fact the idea of such a view makes no sense. And thus it would seem any attempt to separate from the existing world of sense is futile and self-delusional. Further, Foucault's proposal that the subject is constituted by disciplinary procedures and professional discourses raises serious problems about the possibility of resistance not already inscribed by and ultimately beneficial to these discourses: deviants and delinquents are used to reinforce the prescription of normalcy—the naming—for the majority.[3] And in response to Mary Daly's charge that men have stolen the power of naming from women comes the answer from academic men that they can't help this, for they were also named: the system is larger than their intentions, and we must have patience as they try to sort all this out—a move which itself reinforces patriarchy. This paradigm is, among other things, a system of penis reference. And the language I use to challenge it becomes like quicksand: each step I take embeds me deeper.

It is to resist such sinking entrapment that I work to reaffirm separatism. I am interested in ways to disrupt conceptual coercion from within the belly of the beast. I am interested in disrupting the language-game of female inferiority and penis reference. I know this is unreasonable.

What is scientific rationality? The discourse of the human sciences is the disciplinary procedures that organize, differentiate, and hierarchalize subjects (Foucault 1979). The authority of science obscures the way it is produced (Bunkle 1993, 296). The sciences of difference and inequality were constructed through the exclusion of critical writing by those who were marginalized (Stepan and Gilman 1993, 171). And seen from the experiences of many Third World women, the modes of thinking used in science to legitimate progress are male, Western projects, both historically and ideologically (Shiva 1993, 305).

Must we seek common ground within such a tradition, with such practice, in order to be intelligible, to engage in speech or enter the realm of meaning, to make sense, to be reasonable? What does it mean to be reasonable, rational? Rationality involves making sense of the world. But to make sense, must one enter an existing framework in order to be understood, accepting, thereby, its unquestioned values?

It made sense to bomb Hiroshima. It made sense to murder Jews.[4] Robert Proctor argues that many scientists and physicians in nazi Germany were attracted to the nazi appeal to biology to solve social "problems" (Proctor 1993, 350). Nazi racial policy emerged from within the scientific community, it was not imposed (1993, 355).

It makes sense to lay off thousands of workers and "downsize" and claim the economy is strong. Slavery made sense. Animal husbandry makes sense. These things make or have made sense; in fact they have been pursued by rational agents, in part because the frame of reference within which these things make sense excludes ideas that would show them to be ludicrous. So I pursue forms of conceptual separatism as a means of resisting the conceptual coercion of dominant rationalities.

Philosophically, there are at least two ways to challenge a statement: we can argue it false or we can render it nonsense. Rendering it nonsense disrupts its logic, treating it as unintelligible. Arguing it is false, on the other hand, may bring satisfaction, but it is nevertheless to agree that the statement in question is intelligible, indeed possibly true—that it is worth debating. Thus at a deeper level we validate it. When one continues to respond to the dominant discourse, one continues to reinscribe it. To withdraw from a system or a particular situation is a different kind of challenge. To withdraw or separate is to resist acting according to the system's rules and framework and thereby to work against validating its underlying values (note Hoagland 2000).

Keep in mind there is a difference between separatism and purism. What I have in mind is not a transcendent stance, nor is it a doctrine of rules. It is in part an activity of refusal and disruption, it is a practice of disloyalty, noting vested interests and resisting coercive constructions. It is also a creative project, embodying shifts in language-games, shifts in logic which make new ways of engaging possible.

FEMINIST PHILOSOPHY OF SCIENCE: KNOWLEDGE AND KNOWERS ARE SITUATED

In moving from the woman question in science to the science question in feminism, feminist philosophers of science have been struggling with conceptual challenges that science presents us. Science research is often portrayed as a systematic investigation called the "scientific method," developed to eliminate bias and prejudice from research, to maintain objectivity and impartiality. Yet as has been well documented, much scientific work has been sexist and racist. This raises the question of whether the science done was bad science—after all, much of it was done following established scientific methods—or whether sexist and racist science is merely "business as usual." Some argue that science has not been about the *discovery* of race and gender so much as it has been about the *construction* of race and gender. Further, politically motivated (feminist) research has been able to expose biases in research whose explicit goal is value-neutrality. So we have the paradoxical situation that overtly politically motivated research can be more "objective" than purportedly value-neutral research. The questions raised by feminists and feminist philosophers of science over the last three decades have led to reevaluations of scientific objectivity.

Feminist empiricists work to mediate between enlightenment positivism and Kuhnian incommensurability, between a strict distinction between reality and our perception of it on the one hand, and social construction and relativity on the other. Lynn Hankinson Nelson argues that both positivists, such as Hemple or Nagel, and constructionists like Kuhn, share certain assumptions about the nature of science, for example, that science communities are autonomous and fundamentally self-regulating (Nelson 1990, 80). Emphasizing, on the contrary, the fundamentally communal nature of evidence, she argues that while the world constrains us, our experience is social. Individual knowledge is derivative upon communities that construct and acquire knowledge (Nelson 1993).

This resistance to a strict positivist division between reality and our grasp of it was nourished by Quine, who exposed dogmas of empiricism. What interests me here is the idea that observation statements are not value-free. For example, some philosophers argue that we don't see desks, we see color and shape, or rather sensory data. Desks are, after all, enduring bodies, and what our eyes take in is temporary, lasting only as long as our eyes are so focused. Yet if we were to describe only sensory data, for example, when trying to describe a desk we wanted someone to fetch something out of in the next room, they would not know what we were talking about. *Desk* is a theoretical construct, but desks are what we see. That is, our processes of seeing are partly theoretical. Lynn Hankinson Nelson offers an excellent in-depth discussion and analysis of Quine's arguments indicating the theory-dependence of observation: "Part of his argument for the primacy of physical-object ontology is the view that . . . physical-object ontology, which we learn as we learn language, is what permits coherent experience" (Nelson 1990, 101; note pp. 100–17). What we ordinarily see are physical objects, but *physical object* is a theoretical concept; our observations are value-laden. Interestingly, Quine remains unable to follow the consequences of this, perceiving science as removed from everyday intercourse.

Leading Quine, feminist empiricists like Nancy Tuana and Lynn Hankinson Nelson argue we must recognize the value-ladenness of science beyond a physical-object ontology and reconsider the question of value-neutrality in science. In fact rather than avoid value, we must embrace value in science— democratic values—seeking the input of many viewpoints or standpoints. There is a very interesting shift, a paradigm shift, in the development of this distinct sense of objectivity. Shifting from the logic, the language-game of Descartes's disembodied observer, it involves developing our understanding of rationality by embodying knowers, locating us, and seeking an ever-widening circle of embodied discussants whose experiences are located, contextualized.

While I admire this work of negotiating the terrain, articulating how rationality develops in a conceptual framework and developing a new concept of objectivity, my sensibilities run counter to the holism, for it doesn't address power relations: contest and conquest and resistance. I see no reason to believe that if scientists open their work to a discussion of values, justice values will be embraced. Nor do I believe that if establishment scientists were persuaded to let go their disbelief about the value-ladenness of observation, they would rush to embrace pluralist values. My experience leads me, rather, to expect many of them to jockey themselves into positions whereby they can openly impose those values they think important (such as misogyny simpliciter, or perhaps coded as respect).[5] And I am dissatisfied with the feminist focus on value-neutrality. Originally, the question concerned sexism in science. The debate has moved to the more abstract question of whether value-neutrality is an oxymoron, and so our focus is one step removed from acknowledging and directly addressing oppression (and resistance) in science.

Further, as a result of her focus on the communal nature of evidence, Lynn Hankinson Nelson maintains that racist and sexist science of the nineteenth and early twentieth centuries, while oppressive, was nonetheless good science because the work cohered with received theories of the day, albeit theories that clearly need revision[6] (Nelson 1993). I just can't rest with this. Scientists stood there and dismissed counterexamples to their theories—dismissed skulls directly in front of them which to them might indicate female superiority or the superiority of people of color. They would not countenance them; indeed when a given criterion turned out not to support their beliefs in their own superiority, they dumped that criterion and went in search of another one (note Gould, Marshall, e.g.). Still, I do know in my own experience that it is difficult at times to tell whether something before you is an anomaly or a serious challenge to something you have previously believed; for example when someone you trust has done something that hurts you. And Nancy Tuana offers a very important argument: "Craniologists' belief in female inferiority should . . . not be dismissed as an unwarranted assumption, but rather understood as a reasonable inference from currently accepted theories. . . . The belief in women's inferiority was for the vast majority of nineteenth-century scientists not a hypothesis open to refutation, but a 'metaphysical' commitment whose truth was a given. Contradictory evidence was thus seen as proof of a flaw somewhere in the experiment" (Tuana 1995, 445). I suspect this is quite accurate, for some, at least. My discontent lies in remaining focused on hegemonic, oppressive discourse, attending to the practices of men or Whites who can't help themselves, and not shifting to disruptive, resistant practices.

Again, part of the way hegemony maintains itself is in rendering resistance invisible, rendering meaningless practices that challenge it by framing them as stupid, insane, criminal, perverse, or nonsense. A slave breaking a tool would be seen as clumsy, leaving those challenging racism to argue in the dominant discourse that slaves really weren't inferior, just downtrodden and needing help to come up to (White) standard. And the (incommensurable) conceptual frame disappears in which slaves breaking tools could be known by such observers as saboteurs.

So I remain interested in separatism, incommensurability, even relativity.

Sharing an interest with feminist empiricists both in objectivity and embodied knowledge, feminist postmodernist Donna Haraway argues that feminist objectivity means situated knowledges. "There is no unmediated photograph or passive camera obscura in scientific accounts of bodies and machines; there are only highly specific visual possibilities, each with a wonderfully detailed, active, partial way of organizing worlds. Feminist objectivity involves understanding how these visual systems work" (Haraway 1991, 190). She argues in favor of working from subjugated standpoints because they appear to offer both more objective accounts of the world and more transforming ones. But she rejects appeals to holism and calls for a power-sensitive, not a pluralist, conversation, arguing that we seek partiality for the connections and unexpected openings situated knowledges make possible (Haraway 1991, 192–96).

Arguing for a practice of objectivity that privileges contestation, she nevertheless rejects relativism because it involves being nowhere while claiming to be everywhere (thereby resisting responsibility and critical inquiry): To pretend not to be able to judge between two competing ideologies is simply to allow the dominant ideology to reign uncontested. Point well taken. In fact we do judge (even in just observing), and in so doing we are located in a framework. This is particularly significant for feminist theorists located in a context of colonial cum global capitalist practice. My interest in relativity, however, is different and stems from a strategic move Wittgenstein made in response to commonsense realist G. E. Moore's efforts to defeat skepticism.

Wittgenstein appealed to Einstein's relativity in addressing both the skeptic and Moore, who tried to refute the skeptic by claiming to know the propositions of common sense: "Here once more is needed a step like the one taken in relativity theory." That step is a strategic move with regard to absolute claims—showing an absolute claim is nonsense, makes no sense, rather than attempting to prove it false. In unpacking the language-game of knowing, Wittgenstein investigates conditions under which one makes knowledge claims, professes certainty, claims doubt, ascribes mistake. Moore's strategy was to declare the skeptic mistaken. Wittgenstein invoked the strategic move in relativity theory in order to suggest that Moore's strategy of proving the skeptic mistaken was itself mistaken; such absolute claims as flew between the skeptic and realists like Moore are not false but rather are nonsense because context-less[7] (Hoagland forthcoming; 1975).

Disputing Einstein's take on relativity because it posits an independent world, physicist Karen Barad draws on the work of Niels Bohr to dispense with the strict division between us and the world. Concepts obtain meaning by reference to a particular apparatus marking the placement of a constructed boundary between the "object" and the "agencies of observation" or tools to measure, pinpoint, the "object." What we study and measure—phenomena—are the meeting place between the universe and our inquiring, measuring, categorizing minds, the result of "intra-action." There is no unambiguous way to differentiate between the object and the agencies or tools of observation. Hence observations don't refer to objects of an independent reality. But nor are they simply a matter of social construction—they are embodied. The conceptual, linguistic material we use to make sense of the world involves the cut we make, how we slice to measure. And we could make other cuts (Barad 1997). For example, the human cut.[8] Karen Barad introduces the concept of agential realism to bring attention to our agency: we're not describing material objects out there, we're describing "our participation *within* nature" (Barad 1997, 176).

Objectivity thus refers not to properties of independent objects; to say something is objective is to say that no explicit reference is made to any individual observer.[9] And realism is not the representation of an independent reality "but about the real consequences, interventions, creative possibilities, and responsibilities of intra-acting in the world" (Barad 1997, 188). Consequences such as domination, exploitation, oppression.

This theorizing by feminist philosophers of science and feminist scientists about objectivity and the embodied nature of knowledge is making conceptual room for contesting the seamless rationality of the dominant paradigm that has legitimized oppression: reason is not transcendent but embedded. Observation is value-laden, and descriptive concepts are context dependent. Knowledge and knowers are situated.

Still, I question feminist philosophers of science's discomfort with incommensurability, even relativity, and especially conceptual separatism. In one respect, *objectivity* and *relativity* are concepts of classical physics, and without the one, you don't have the other. But acknowledging that observation is value-laden and that knowledge and knowers are situated has little to do with classical objectivity. I'd like to see a willingness among feminist philosophers of science to explore relativity in an equally complex way.[10]

In developing a Latin American postcoloniality that dates the emergence of Modernity not with the European Enlightenment but with the European Conquest/colonization/occupation of "the new world," Walter Mignolo argues that cultural relativism is an important step in understanding cultural difference. However, the idea is not to tell stories from different points of view but rather to develop analyses within the context of power, including domination and occupation,[11] as well as the struggle for resistance, adaptation, and transformation. What is at stake is not a diversity of representations but "the politics of enacting and constructing loci of enunciation," not "cultural relativity or multiculturalism, but the social and human interests in the act of telling a story as political intervention" (Mignolo 1998, 15, 331–34). Contrasting cognition as representation with cognition as enactment, he notes challenges for human science including "the positionality and politicization of the understanding subject and his or her drive to know or understand" (Mignolo 1998, 24–25). Observation is value-laden in that it is embedded in our activity, and understanding epistemology as enacting something rather than representing something else will help us in our encounters with difference and our desires for difference.

He develops what he calls a "pluritopic hermeneutics" not to more accurately represent the Other but for the possibility of creating new meaning: "Instead of looking at marginal societies from the perspective of academic centers," his pluritopic hermeneutics "proposes to look at cultural and political centers from the academic margins. Loci of enunciation are only partially related to the physical domiciles and academic affiliation of speaking and writing subjects. They are constructed by *both joining and detaching oneself from previous performances*" (Mignolo 1998, 312; emphasis added). Even within the belly of the beast, we have choices. Suggesting the possibility of new worlds of sense even for academics, he writes: "When the scholar-scientist (and writer) as observer is placed in a space in between, the space in which the universality of Western reason encounters different rationalities, then cultural relativism becomes transformed: from relative conceptual frameworks that could be compared and analyzed, to hybrid conceptual frameworks from which new ways of knowing emerge. At this point the question is no longer how to use the enlightening guidance of Western notions of rationality in order to understand colonial, postcolonial, and Third World experiences but, rather, how to think from hybrid conceptual frameworks and spaces in between" (1998, 331).

This suggests the possibility of practicing agential reality and resonates with what I have in mind by conceptual separatism—spaces that operate with a logic distinct from (in some respects, incommensurable with) the dominant paradigm, frame, context. And it is in my desire and efforts to move in conceptual spaces not (fully) colonized by Anglo-European scientific practice that I find useful Wittgenstein's strategic use of relativity theory in addressing the epistemology of Anglo-European classical realism.

But perhaps I can more concretely articulate my thoughts. I am trying to encourage questions about where we focus our attention, about the agenda of the frame of those locations as well as of those located therein, about the seemingly postmodern belief that the dominant logic is ultimately the authority to which we must refer for meaning, and about the belief among many of us located in Western colonial capitalist culture that it is self-delusional to believe we can inhabit or animate different logics, that we can separate from dominant reason, that there are other sources of meaning.

Specifically, I will here address two questions: (1) If, as Donna Haraway suggests, we pursue partiality for the connections and openings situated knowledges make possible, for whom are we pursuing this, and why? What is the purpose of any knowledge project and who is it addressed to? Most importantly, who will benefit from this knowledge? (2) Given all the work by feminist philosophers of science and feminist scientists on observation, knowledge, and objectivity, must we still only see our capacity to make sense, meaning, as embedded in the dominant tradition? Feminist philosophers of science have argued that the knower and knowledge are not transcendent. I want to stress that neither is reason's logic nor the audience feminist epistemologists and scientists address, those by whom we seek to be recognized and understood.

Situated Audiences

First, what is the purpose of any given knowledge project? Again, if we pursue partiality for the connections and openings situated knowledges make possible, for whom are we pursuing this, and why? A while ago I attended a paper presentation by anthropologist Caroline Bledsoe in which she reports on her investigation of women's use of birth control in Gambia. Her work is significant because rather than ignore a "statistically insignificant" anomaly, as Kuhn argues scientists working within a paradigm have done, instead she investigated it. She concerned herself with the situation of Kaddy Sisay in rural Gambia who was trying to get pregnant. After numerous tries Kaddy Sisay divorced one husband, remarried, and finally gave birth only to have the infant die at seventeen months. She then went on birth control (using Depo-Provera). In a nation where bearing many children is highly valued, her actions appeared crazy to this Western researcher. Nevertheless Caroline Bledsoe chose to investigate the anomaly.

In the process she discovered that rural Gambian women understood (apparently without the help of Western biology) that their bodies could stand only so many births, and were using birth control not to restrict the number of babies they had but instead to better have babies. Caroline Bledsoe came to realize that the women used what she called a "health model," not a "demographic model"—they were concerned with having strong bodies (capable of bearing children well) not with having as many children as possible.

Having shown by example that understanding an anomaly can restructure our understanding of the norm, one of Caroline Bledsoe's final comments mentioned a question for policymakers (admittedly not her area of expertise) about whether "we" want to continue funding birth control to Third World nations if it is not going to be used to limit births.

Having gotten the women she researched to "open" to her and "make connections" for her, as Donna Haraway suggests, what did she do with these connections? For whom was she writing? With whom did she engage in conversation? I address my questions to feminist epistemologists, feminist philosophers of science, and feminist scientists. She says, for example, "Nowhere is the need to understand the dynamics of high fertility more obvious than sub-Saharan Africa" (Bledsoe 1997, ms. p. 3). Why? Whose need?[12] What is the need, exactly?[13] Cognition as enactment.

Discussing China as a spectacle for the West through U.S. media representation in the events of Tiananmen Square, Rey Chow argues that our technology does much more than enable us to see: "Extraterritoriality—the exemption from local jurisdiction—becomes itself exempted from the history of its own role, not in the promotion of freedom and rights but in the subjugation of other peoples in the course of colonial conquests. . . . Nowadays, instead of guns, the most effective instruments that aid in the production of the 'Third World' are the technologies of the media . . . the 'reality' that is broadcast in the U.S. and then 'faxed' back to China" (Chow 1991, 86).

The sense of access to observe Others is an imperial sense, part of the way children are trained in an imperialist culture. Analyzing the novel *Kim*, Satya Mohanty argues that Rudyard Kipling creates children who embody values and skills essential for white colonial rule. The story of Kim is not simply the magic of innocence and childhood. "The crucial difference is that Kipling's hero is a white boy who can discard his color at will or whim" (Satya Mohanty 1991, 319). Satya Mohanty connects this literature with the practice of scientific knowledge of India, the consolidation of colonial rule, and the training of White boys developed by Lord Baden-Powell in forming the Boy Scouts.

I am not simply reiterating the point that knowers are situated, I am raising questions about the purpose a knower, especially a feminist knower situated in the U.S. academy, has for engaging in her project and for whom, and questions about the openings we are offered when we pursue knowledge of Others. What are we enacting and what is our need? And by stressing that this is about Others,[14] I am trying to keep in focus questions about what is deemed to stand in need of explanation and to whom.

Again, the sense of access, of entitlement to access, to observe Others is an imperial sense that leads us away from assessing our purpose, what we are enacting. It is also a way we avoid contest, avoid local jurisdiction. That this sense carries the mantle of scientific knowledge, of research, is one way our observations avoid being contested by those observed. We learn from Bakhtin that meaning is made in conversation. The scientific move to nonengaged, detached observation is an effort to exclude others from meaning-making, deauthorizing all voices the academy has not trained/tamed. As Jo Trigilio argues, "Ordinary individuals with the capacity to make rational, consistent, 'socially' verifiable observations are not, in practice, sanctioned empirical knowers. Groups of mothers who have observed environmental illness in their children are not empirical knowers. Only when a scientific study performed by institutionally sanctioned researchers verifies their subjective testimony, do their observations become knowledge" (Trigilio, ms. p. 6). In her study of the "debate" over Depo-Provera, Phillida Bunkle documents the dismissal of women's experience with the drug (Bunkle 1993).

Caroline Bledsoe is not in dialogue with Kaddy Sisay. She reported that she never even met her. Instead, she is moving in her world without being touched by it, the imperialist training of *Kim*. Instead, she is in dialogue with anthropologists about the fact that new worlds of sense can open when a scientist does not ignore "statistically insignificant anomalies." And this is significant in one sense. In another, it is simply a matter of understanding that if you see what you take to be strange behavior, consider your own limitations and try getting to know the person's world, particularly when they move in a world without your assumptions.

But, by looking at Kaddy Sisay and searching out her secrets, her sense, Caroline Bledsoe is also carrying information to U.S. policymakers, admittedly not her field, policymakers moving in the tradition of policymakers who allowed Depo-Provera to be marketed in Gambia in the first place. This is not about representation, it's about enactment.

I do not see that such science researchers differ significantly from the U.S. media in their mission to represent others or their exemption from local jurisdiction, certainly not in their exemption from the history of their role in imperial progress. Jack Stauder argues that anthropologists are the scouts of imperial forces; those in power must understand dominated people in order to resist attempts to overthrow the system. Significantly, most anthropologists don't study the ruling class or allied elites abroad, they study people oppressed by imperialism, facilitating colonial rule or its child, multinational exploitation (Stauder 1993).

Rather than study the "statistical anomaly" of Kaddy Sisay, in a rural area that depends on children for agricultural work and family survival, to dis/cover how women were using birth control to subvert U.S. and Gambian governmental plans to limit births for the benefit of U.S. policymakers, Caroline Bledsoe might have investigated the "statistical anomaly" of corporate executives, in this case Upjohn, who provide Depo-Provera to Gambia, a drug the F.D.A. once rejected in the United States because of its effects, to dis/cover and explain how the U.S. practices imperialism, for the benefit of women like Kaddy Sisay.[15]

Feminist scientists and philosophers of science are arguing that the knower is not transcendent. My point is that neither is the audience of our work. Even when we seek in friendship the openings and unexpected connections that situated knowledges make possible, we can be dangerous. To whom are we addressing ourselves, to whom are we offering information, and why? What are the limits and consequences of our practice in context?

Raising the question of who we can (logically) be friends with, Sherley Anne Williams writes about a slave woman, Dessa Rose, who with others, escaped a coffle.[16] She was recaptured but not hanged immediately because she was pregnant. Before she gives birth and is hanged, friends rescue her, and she winds up on the plantation of a White mistress, Ruth, who is fairly clueless about the world around her, and whose husband is never there. In order to move on to freedom, Dessa Rose's friends hatch a plot involving Ruth. The developing relationship between Dessa Rose and Ruth is complex. Eventually Ruth comes to recognize that slaves are humans capable of making considered choices, much as Caroline Bledsoe came to recognize Kaddy Sisay, and her first instinct is to tell everyone (the Whites) around her the "truth."

It is at this point that she becomes most dangerous to Dessa Rose. As Dessa tells it: "Miz Lady didn't believe most white folks was mean. She thought that if white folks knew slaves as she knew us, wouldn't be no slavery" (Williams 1986, 231). Later, Dessa Rose reports that Ruth confesses, "'I don't want to live round slavery no more; I don't think I could without speaking up,' she say then, looking down at her hands like she couldn't look at me. But it was funny, cause that was the thing I had come to fear most from her by the end of that journey, that she would speak out against the way we seen some of the peoples was treated and draw tention to us. And what she was talking now would sho enough make peoples note us" (1986, 239).

In coming to know and then befriend Dessa Rose, Ruth became dangerous to her in part because her newfound empathy involved what Vicky Spelman calls boomerang perception—Ruth looked at Dessa Rose and came right back to herself, and so she could not see White people as they constructed themselves in relation to Dessa Rose, as they appeared and behaved toward her. Having opened to Dessa Rose and seen her past her own framing of Blacks, Ruth had not yet shifted to Dessa Rose's framework. Ruth saw those in power as being as clueless as she—there had simply been a grand oversight. Had Ruth attempted to represent Dessa Rose to the White folk around them as Dessa Rose now made sense to Ruth, Ruth would have done irreparable harm to Dessa Rose.

I want feminist scientists and philosophers of science, myself—I want myself to not be dangerous to women, to Lesbians, to women of color, to myself. Given that knowers are situated and our knowledge partial, we need to assess the power relations and projects that construct that partiality. If feminist scientists are going to study women, I want to know who is the audience? Who are you trying to represent to whom, and why? To whose understanding are you attending as you write? In what frame of reference are you working to make sense? What interests are you enacting? And my separatist instincts course like whitewater.

LOGIC AND RESISTANCE

The understanding of those we address will affect the logic we use in characterizing and explaining what we report—what is called into question and what needs no explanation. Which takes me to the second question I raised. Must we see our capacity to make sense, meaning, as only embedded in the dominant tradition? It's too easy to say we are all part of a system of meaning, seeing it as a comprehensive whole such that any development must refer back to it, and hence believe it doesn't matter who we address ourselves to, for it will all come out the same truth anyway, or believe we don't really address ourselves to anyone but a neutral audience.

The dominant frame has its own agenda. And we can be trapped within a framework which limits us. Recently an HBO production aired on television about the Tuskegee Syphilis Experiment, *Miss Evers' Boys* (1997). In this portrayal, while the funding for the experiment and thereby its directives came from White congressmen and scientists involved in the U.S. Public Health Service, the scientist immediately involved in the experiment was a Black doctor. The drama of this representation surrounds his choices and the choices of a Black nurse who got the men to come and remain in the project, Miss Evers (Miss Rivers in the literature). The rationale from the power structure for the experiment was to observe the course of development of syphilis, even though an 1891 to 1910 study of Norwegian men dying of syphilis had already been conducted (James Jones 1993). The doctor and nurse began the work having been told that once discoveries were made about how to cure syphilis, the men would receive treatment. When it became clear that there was to be no treatment forthcoming as promised, the doctor did not let go of the project, nor did the nurse tell the men the truth. His reason was that this was a chance to prove that Black and White men did not differ biologically—the study, continued until the men's deaths, would show Black men deteriorated the same as White men.

Exploring this portrayal for the moment, I try to imagine what it was like for a Black man who struggled to become a doctor in the United States. In the

1930s. Lodged in the positivist scientific paradigm, his options of resistance as a doctor/scientist were severely limited.[17] Had he simply walked away from the White funders and the study, he would have been "proving" to them that Black men aren't rational, can't do science. He had become a scientist in part because he believed it would lead to truth and so he saw it a tool to resist racism. And he was embedded in positivist portrayals of science and reason. I'm not sure how far removed I would have been at that time either. Nevertheless some were, like Zora Neale Hurston.

To simply say we are all in language, in a system of meaning, presupposes the overall system is logical and coherent. And in a sense it is. But the logic is not transcendent any more than reason is, they emerge from practice.[18] And the coherence comes in part from science's ability to dismiss other modes of sense as irrational or nonsense, meaningless.[19] I question feminist scientific or epistemological projects that dialogue with those comfortable in the dominant frame, particularly with those comfortably located there.

In doing so, I am teasing out two implications of knowers being situated, embodied: knowers are enacting something, and knowers are trying to be understood by someone in particular. I've argued that the audience is not transcendent, different audiences will have different agendas, and writing as if to a generic professional audience continues the Enlightenment practice of narcissistic responsibility. I am arguing now, in answer to my first question, that the logic of the conceptual framework is also not transcendent. If rationality arises within a conceptual framework, then the logic/grammar of what is rational also emerges within a conceptual framework. In other words, rationality is not a neutral, mental tool, but a practice—a practice located in a world of domination, exploitation, and oppression. The logic of the dominant conceptual framework is partial and particular . . . and contested.

So rather than dialogue with those comfortably ensconced in the dominant logic, I want to suggest instead a double operation: (1) finding resistant logics, and (2) resisting the logic/language-games of hegemonic medical, legal, and scientific models, exploring how those at the center keep the center by rendering the resistance of others invisible as resistance. This includes dis/covering resistant worlds of sense outside the dominant Realm, but not in order to report back to the Realm's apologists. The project I'm suggesting involves exploring what is rendered irrational and invisible by exposing patriarchal racist heterosexist rationality, and instead engaging the logic which operates in these sites of resistance.[20] I am interested in strategies of resisting rationality both in the sense of resisting (dominant) rationality and also of finding nondominant resisting rationalities. The resisting rationality I seek is embedded in what the dominant society renders irrational or criminal, or perverse, or invisible. (Investigating a subjugated standpoint, Caroline Bledsoe dis/covered such a resisting rationality, but like Ruth at the stage in her developing awareness where she is most dangerous to Dessa Rose, Caroline Bledsoe exercises boomerang perception.)

So I'm suggesting a direction for a feminist knowledge project. It involves understanding that lies outside the bounds of dominant sense, a rationality that is unreasonable, including your own. To pursue objectivity is to adopt the project of taming other worlds of sense. Cease trying to explain yourself and other feminists to those who frame you as in need of explanation. And learn from that to enter new worlds and see resistance where the dominant rationality has erased the local context and so paints quite a different story. This, of necessity, also involves seeing yourself as a player, subject to local jurisdiction including for what purpose you want to know. It involves being clear about whom you are talking to and why, even realizing that in some cases it may not be appropriate for you to know. It involves seeing yourself as embedded and situated as the knowledge project you take up. It involves seeking out what Walter Mignolo calls "the places in between." And all this will change you.

Lorraine Code has argued that we should think of knowledge on the model of knowing persons, not of knowing things, an ongoing process whereby we are able over time to give or withhold trust.[21] Further, we can recognize different levels: "I can know Alice is clever and not know her very well at all in a thicker sense." This knowing is open to negotiation "where the subject and object positions are in principle interchangeable. Neither self-conception nor knower-conception can claim absolute authority" (Code 1993). Under this model, we are no longer simply taking the removed stance of a scientist.[22] Such knowledge of the subject will change our self-knowledge, our subjectivity, especially our sense of ourselves as scientists and theorists, as participants in the world.

It is precisely because of this effect on the knowing subject that, as one of my students, Nereasa Bello, remarked, many do try to know many people in the manner we know objects: the way many White people "know" Black people, for example, or many Blacks and Latinos in Chicago "know" each other. By characterizing and fixing a static object rather than engaging what we approach, our subjectivity does not have to change as a result of the encounter.

Lorraine Code's suggestion invites a different logic. You are no longer an expert, immune to challenge and study. And your program is no longer removed from the agendas of those you seek to know, no longer simply a matter of furthering objective knowledge. When a researcher engages another, she can find herself directly challenged by those she interacts with, changed by the one she seeks to know. What if Caroline Bledsoe sought her ground of meaning in conversation with Kaddy Sisay and not in conversation with anthropologists who maintain the illusion of neutral observer/informer for U.S. policymakers?

The logic of how we come to understand/engage those we perceive as different from ourselves is distinct from the logic of (dominant) rationality; it holds the possibility of intra-acting subjects. It is the logic of what María Lugones calls "playful" world travel. By traveling to the world of another who is quite different from me without trying to destroy it or them, I can work to "understand *what it is to be them and what it is to be [me] in their eyes*" (Lugones 1987, 17). In this way, our subjectivity changes and we become subject to local jurisdiction, affected by and cognizant of consequences of our engagement.[23] We can both see ourselves as colonizers and also cease to acquiesce in the process of colonization.

But the point of all this is not to then tell White folks about how wrong they are about slavery in the midst of it. For what I'm suggesting now lies outside the official practice, beyond the bounds of sense. And if it is represented within the official discourse, made commensurable with it, it will be reconfigured to promote dominant logic, rationality, often by being characterized as perverse, criminal, or irrational.[24] For this reason I pursue conceptual separatism.

For example, in her groundbreaking book on women who kill, Ann Jones notes that when men's violence against their wives finally broke through to dominant consciousness, the newspapers initially were supportive of women who resisted, who fought back against abusive husbands. However, the media quickly began portraying them as getting away with murder. Concomitantly the courts shifted, and lawyers defending such women were forced to enter a plea of insanity instead of self-defense, erasing resistance. As a result, dominant social perception of the feminine was reestablished: a feminine being is someone who is subordinate such that if someone designated feminine fights back, she must be mad. Ann Jones's work is a study of the logic of the social reaction to women who kill (Ann Jones 1980). Overt resistance, when it became visible, was reinscribed by dominant rationality as criminal or insane.[25]

I find ways hegemonic discourse appropriates, coopts, or renders resistant discourse nonsense, fascinating. And even if I can maintain a grasp on my own resistant logic as the forces of mystification grind onward, what of others' resistant logics? You may be quite adept at recognizing your own counterlogic, but if you do not engage in world travel, you will have only the dominant frame of reference/sense with which to interpret and understand other counterhegemonic practices (Lugones forthcoming).

If while I understand only my own resistant logic, I nevertheless try to make sense in, be understood within, the dominant frame of reference, then I'll read slaves breaking tools, Lesbian alcoholism, teen's pregnancies, gang economies, women's recovered memories, teen's drug use, guide dogs running their people into poles, old women in nursing homes being "troublemakers," annubis female baboons' "antisocial" behavior, the existence of "maiden aunts," gangsta rap, women killing abusive men, all through dominant logic which renders them nonsense as choices and renders invisible their oppositional (and potentially liberatory) nature. Seeing other resistant logics and searching for resistance to domination is to reject holism; there is no "we" here of common sense, no "we" of Upjohn and Kaddy Sisay.

I want to see the work of feminist epistemologists undermine hegemonic discourses by helping to establish among ourselves and those we engage with counterdiscourses, thereby shifting not only the ground of epistemic sense but also the center of our attention, those for whom we try to appear reasonable, those with whom we are open to dialogue, conversation.

Separatist practice facilitates this project for me. That's the point of the separatism, to emerge from the mystification of dominant discourse and search out places in between, worlds that are (at least partly) incommensurable with White capitalist patriarchy, worlds made commensurable only through the erasure of resistance and the taming of voice. Critics argue we can never separate from culture, that to think so is to deceive ourselves. Of course we are never outside language or culture. But it does not follow that we can never move in spaces that do not carry dominant Anglo-European White phallic cultural logic, that there is no sense apart from what makes sense in that discourse.[26] A more significant criticism is that often dominant values make their way into separatist spaces, White gentile Lesbians carrying unaddressed racist values, for example, or Christian values. On the one hand, the belief that we can just walk away from what we have learned is naive. But on the other hand, it is colonial arrogance to declare all meaning limited to dominant (phallic) logic.

There are worlds of sense not countenanced by White Western patriarchal dominant discourse. It is not the job of feminist epistemologists to find those worlds and tame them for dominant men, making them commensurable, bringing them into the dominant realm of rationality, but something else altogether. For me, separatism is not about purism, it is about the creation or affirmation or maintenance of meaning and value distinct from what passes as common sense in an imperial society, strategies and tactics for disrupting and resisting hegemony; strategies that include recognizing multiple resistant logics. Going back to my work in the seventies, that which is scripted insane or nonsense by the dominant logic is the breeding ground of resisting rationalities precisely because in those places our attention is not riveted on the logic of the dominant, dominating drama. I seek illicit conversations, resisting rationality.

NOTES

This chapter emerged from my work at the 1996 NEH Summer Seminar on Feminist Epistemologies run by Nancy Tuana. Her encouragement of feminist philosophers and support of feminist philosophy in all its guises is virtually unparalleled in my experience.

Geologist Karen Bartels joined me last year in teaching my course on Feminism and the Philosophy of Science and we played, scientist and philosopher, with these ideas, especially with implications of Karen Barad's work. My students, as always, are a main source of my continuing education. Thanks also to Teddy Bofman and Laura Sanders for reading and commenting on the manuscript. Anne Throop Leighton has contributed to this effort and to my capacity to work in so many ways.

1. Addressing the "foundations" of empirical knowledge in his later work *On Certainty,* Ludwig Wittgenstein suggests that foundations are like an axis, held in place by all that surrounds it (e.g., 1969, 152). In other words, foundations are not grounds/building blocks supporting and thereby justifying what we know; rather foundations are what never get questioned and so are held in place by our activity, from everyday interactions to specialized research. Grounds are different than foundations in my work. Grounds are something that support something else, much as science holds. But foundations are not the bottommost ground that ultimately supports and justifies human knowledge. Again, foundations are that which is taken for granted by such knowledge and are thereby unchallengeable by it (Hoagland 1975; forthcoming).

Note that the metaphor of an axis contests the Modernist metaphor of a building block by focusing on the unquestioned center; the metaphor of a frame focuses on the edges, the bounds of sense, and/or the shaping and highlighting of what moves within the frame. Another epistemological metaphor to play with is Quine and Julian's metaphor of a web.

2. Linda Alcoff notes Donald Davidson and Alasdair MacIntyre's arguments that all interpretation and translation require some ground, some commensurability. Well, a good portion of the common ground sustaining the scientific revolution is sexism and ethnocentrism.

3. For example, the forms of rebellion for teenage girls articulated by the dominant logic include doing drugs and getting pregnant. Those girls who do so rebel are then used as "object lessons" by officials to threaten other girls into staying "in line." Ultimately, as Foucault points out, such deviants benefit the state and those in power, justifying further repression in the name of protection. What Foucault sees as resistance develops when such deviants are not just written about, but actually talk back, for example homosexuals. But while it is obvious that those named and framed by the dominant logic do present a threat to the seamlessness of hegemony, for Foucault their resistance is lodged within the dominant logic. They are still, ultimately, named by the professionals. I am interested in finding spaces for the imagination that are not constructed by the professional class of the state.

4. Actually, Sartre argues this was a self-contradictory project (Sartre 1965).

5. Not that this doesn't happen now, it's just that they could be open about their enforcement of masculinism, much like White supremists are open in the light of moves toward multiculturalism.

6. On this view, of course some of the science of the day was patently bad science. But this was because it did not follow scientific standards, not because its conclusions were racist and sexist, or even because its premises were.

7. To the extent that they were not nonsense, they were no longer absolute claims, but quite particular claims in particular contexts and hence could not perform the job Moore and the skeptic had in mind for them.

8. It is interesting to study the sorts of claims made by those focused on the cut between human and animal in contrast to claims made by those focused on the cut between human and machine, because often things rejected by those focused on the one cut are appealed to by those focused on the other. Other cuts: human and divine, human and female, and human and non-White.

9. While Moore is a realist who does posit an independent reality, his analysis of an external object (an object external to our minds) is interesting: to say X is external to our minds is to say that the proposition "X exists and no one perceives it" is not a contradiction.

10. It is interesting to investigate exactly what individual feminist philosophers of science are rejecting when they reject relativity. For example, some are concerned with wanting to prove men mistaken about sexist findings. Elsewhere I argue that strategically, such a move is a mistake (Hoagland forthcoming).

11. Note also Sandra Harding's work, *Is Science Multicultural?* particularly her discussion of the relation of the European science project to the Conquest/Occupation.

12. One hint: she acknowledges support from the Medical and Health Department of the Gambian Ministry of Health, the Gambian Central Statistics Department, the Gambian National Population Commission, the British Medical Research Council, the University of Chicago, Northwestern University, Harvard University, and the Mellon and Rockefeller Foundations. (Note Chandra Mohanty 1991a, 6.)

13. Noting that the myth of overpopulation is pervasive, Betsy Hartman examines the thesis that population growth poses one of the biggest threats to the global environment and explores various governmental efforts to control women. She shows how population-control programs have sacrificed women's health and safety. And she notes that high birth rates are linked to a number of factors, including the economic subordination of women (Hartman 1995). The problems designated the consequence of "over population" are significantly reduced when organizations work to directly improve women's impoverished economic situation. And ecological feminist Chris Cuomo exposes sexism and racism involved in the Deep Ecology Movement, including their use of family planning (Cuomo 1995).

14. When we talk about ourselves or those we feel identified with, we tend to be more circumspect. When speaking of Others, the myth of contextless observation leads us to be less cautious.

15. Phillida Bunkle gives a short history of Depo-Provera and documents corporate construction and control of knowledge (Bunkle 1993). There have been subsequent experts who have insisted that Depo-Provera, while having some side effects, is safe enough (WHO nd; Thomas and Ray 1992; Stanford and Thomas 1991; FDA, e.g.), and they make the same assumptions that Bunkle initially exposed. (I thank Peter Grossman for doing the research and providing me with this information.) And Depo-Provera is now being distributed in the United States mostly in communities of color.

16. A coffle is a group of slaves chained together and herded, often to market.

17. Nancy Leys Stepan and Sander Gilman categorize strategies of resistance literature to scientific racism between 1870 and 1920.

18. Sandra Harding notes that scientists' logic and methodology is not immune from social influences, what is logical and rational is context dependent (Harding 1986, 38, 182).

19. As Michel de Certeau puts it: "Rational organization must repress all the physical, mental, and political pollutions that would compromise it" (Certeau 1988, 94).

20. Exploring tactics of marginalization of Western rationality, Michel de Certeau addresses Foucault's disciplinary matrix and argues that while he has foregrounded certain practices, numerous practices persist unnoticed (Certeau 1988, 47–48).

21. While Lorraine Code notes that there are obvious disanalogies—the idea is not to get knowers to be friends with chemicals, particles, etc.—I wouldn't be so quick to dismiss the idea of applying a model of knowing persons to our understanding of objects. After all, if we regarded knowing objects as something that takes time and is a process, we might find our physical-object ontology shifting from objects as static to a more process-oriented perception of the world. After all, physical object ontology has certain features that go against experience, such as stasis and permanence. And as Benjamin Lee Whorf notes, what counts as an object as opposed to an event is a matter of grammatical categories in English. For example, why is *fist* a noun (object) and not a verb (event) in English? It is, after all, a temporary event like *strike, turn, run*, which are verbs (Whorf 1956, 215). What makes a tree an object and not an event?

22. Of course while the stance may be removed or detached from one context, it is certainly located in another.

23. Mainstream scientists are both serious (not playful) in their methods and purification rituals, and not serious (cavalier) in their acknowledgment of the effects of the logic of their work on those they seek to know.

24. Someone could perhaps do a study of the times by studying the drugs prescribed for women. My acupuncturist, Pam Mills, noted that during the political unrest of the seventies, the physicians' drug of choice for women was Valium, a downer. Now that the movement phase of political resistance has passed, their drug of choice is Prozac, an upper.

25. Evaluating strategies of feminist work on recovered memory is absolutely crucial in this regard.

26. If we use another metaphor, not Lacan's phallus but, for example, Wittgenstein's game, and someone were to argue I cannot get out of the game of White male sense/reference, then I am enormously interested in cheating and breaking the rules. Besides, it is the nature of games that there is a point beyond which one is not breaking rules but no longer playing the game.

REFERENCES

Alcoff, Linda. 1996. *Real knowing*. Ithaca, N.Y.: Cornell University Press.

Alcoff, Linda, and Libby Potter, eds. 1993. *Feminist epistemologies*. New York: Routledge.

Bakhtin, M. M. 1981. *The dialogic imagination*. Austin: University of Texas Press.

Barad, Karen. 1997. Meeting the universe halfway: Realism and social constructivism, without contradiction. In *Feminism, science, and the philosophy of science*, ed. Lynn Hankinson Nelson and Jack Nelson. Boston: Kluwer Academic Publishers.

Bem, Sandra L. 1976. Probing the promise of androgyny. In *Beyond sex-role stereotypes: Readings toward a psychology of androgyny*, ed. Alexandra Kaplan and Joan P. Bean. Boston: Little Brown.

Bledsoe, Caroline, Fatou Banja, and Allan G. Hill. 1997. Reproductive mishaps and western contraception: Tiny numbers, far-reaching challenges to Western theories of fertility and aging. Paper presented at Northeastern Illinois University. This material appears in two papers: Caroline Bledsoe, Fatoumatta Banja, and Allan G. Hill. 1998. Reproductive mishaps and Western contraception: An Africa challenge to reproductive theory. *Population and Development Review* 24, 1 (March): 15–17; and Caroline H. Bledsoe, Allan G. Hill, and Umberto D'Alessandro. 1994. Constructing natural fertility: The use of Western contraceptive technologies in rural Gambia. *Population and Development Review* 20 (March): 81–113.

Bunkle. Phillida. 1993. Calling the shots? The international politics of Depo-Provera. In *The racial economy of science*, ed. Sandra Harding. Bloomington: Indiana University Press.

Certeau, Michel de. 1988. *The practice of everyday life*. Berkeley: University of California Press.

Chow, Rey. 1991. Violence in the other country: China as crisis, spectacle, and woman. In *Third World women and the politics of feminism*, ed. Chandra Talpade Mohanty et al. Bloomington: Indiana University Press.

Code, Lorraine. 1993. Taking subjectivity into account. In *Feminist epistemologies*, ed. Linda Alcoff and Libby Potter. New York: Routledge.

Cuomo, Christine J. 1995. Ecofeminism, deep ecology, and human population. In *Ecological feminism*, ed. Karen J. Warren. New York: Routledge.

Daly, Mary. 1978. *Gyn/Ecology*. Boston: Beacon.

Einstein, Albert. 1907. *Relativity: The special and the general theory*. London: Methuen.

Foucault, Michel. 1979. *Discipline and punish*. New York: Vintage.

———. 1980. *The history of sexuality*, vol. I. New York: Vintage.

Gadamer, Hans Georg. 1996. *Truth and method*. New York: Continuum.

Gould, Stephen Jay. 1993. American polygeny and craniometry before Darwin. In *The racial economy of science*, ed. Sandra Harding. Bloomington: Indiana University Press.

Griffin, Susan. 1978. *Women and nature*. San Francisco: Harper and Row.

Haraway, Donna. 1991. Situated knowledges. In *Simians, cyborgs, and women*, ed. Donna J. Haraway. New York: Routledge.

148 SARAH LUCIA HOAGLAND

Harding, Sandra. 1986. *The science question in feminism*. Ithaca, N.Y.: Cornell University Press.

———, ed. 1993. *The racial economy of science*. Bloomington: Indiana University Press.

———. 1998. *Is science multicultural? Postcolonialisms, feminisms, and epistemologies*. Bloomington: Indiana University Press.

Hartman, Betsy. 1995. *Reproductive rights and wrongs: The global politics of population control*. Boston: South End.

Hoagland, Sarah Lucia. 1975. The status of common sense, G. E. Moore and L. Wittgenstein: A comparative study. Ph.D. Dissertation, University of Cincinnati.

———. 1977. On the status of the concepts of masculinity and femininity. *Proceedings of the Nebraska Academy of Sciences* 4, (August): 169–72.

———. 1978. Coercive consensus. *Sinister Wisdom* 6 (Summer).

———. 1980a. Androcentric rhetoric in sociobiology. *Women's Studies International Quarterly* 3 (2/3): 285–93.

———. 1980b. Naming, describing, explaining: Deception and science. *ERIC* (Spring).

———. 1982, 1985. "Femininity," resistance and sabotage. In *"Femininity," "masculinity," and "androgyny": A modern philosophical discussion*, ed. Mary Vetterling-Braggin. Totowa, N.J.: Littlefield, Adams; reprinted in *Women and values: Readings in recent feminist philosophy*, ed. Marilyn Pearsall. Belmont, Calif.: Wadsworth.

———. 1988. *Lesbian ethics: Toward new value*. Chicago: Institute of Lesbian Studies, PO Box 25568. Chicago, IL: 60625.

———. 2000. Separatism. Entry in *Encyclopedia of feminist theories*, ed. Lorraine Code. London: Routledge.

———. forthcoming. Moving toward uncertainty. In *Rereading the canon: Feminist interpretations of Wittgenstein*, ed. Naomi Scheman. State College, Penn.: Penn State Press.

Jones, Ann. 1980. *Women who kill*. New York: Holt, Rinehart and Winston.

Jones, James. 1993 The Tuskegee syphilis experiment. In *The racial economy of science*, ed. Sandra Harding. Bloomington: Indiana University Press.

Kuhn, Thomas. 1962. *The structure of scientific revolution*. Chicago: University of Chicago Press.

Lugones, María. 1987. Playfulness, "world"-travelling, and loving perception *Hypatia* 2, 2: 3–19.

———. forthcoming. Boomerang perception and the colonizing gaze. In *Pilgrimages/peregrinajes: Essays in pluralist feminism*.

Marshall, Gloria A. 1993. Racial classifications: Popular and scientific. In *The racial economy of science*, ed. Sandra Harding. Bloomington: Indiana University Press.

Mignolo, Walter D. 1998. *The darker side of the Renaissance*. Ann Arbor: University of Michigan Press.

Mohanty, Chandra Talpade. 1991a. Introduction: Cartographies of struggle: Third World women and the politics of feminism. In *Third World women and the politics of feminism*, ed.Chandra Talpade Mohanty et al. Bloomington: Indiana University Press.

———. 1991b. Under Western eyes: Feminist scholarship and colonial discourses. In *Third World women and the politics of feminism*, ed.Chandra Talpade Mohanty et al. Bloomington: Indiana University Press.

Mohanty, Chandra Talpade, et al., eds. 1991. *Third World women and the politics of feminism*. Bloomington: Indiana University Press.

Mohanty, Satya P. 1991. Drawing the color line: Kipling and the culture of colonial rule. In *The bounds of race: Perspectives on hegemony and resistance*, ed. Dominick La Capra. Ithaca, N.Y.: Cornell University Press.

Moore, G. E. 1966. *Philosophical papers*. New York: Collier.

Nelson, Lynn Hankinson. 1990. *Who knows*. Philadelphia: Temple University Press.

———. 1993. Epistemological communities. In *Feminist epistemologies*, ed. Linda Alcoff and Libby Potter. New York: Routledge.

Nelson, Lynn Hankinson, and Jack Nelson. 1997. *Feminism, science, and the philosophy of science*. Boston: Kluwer Academic Publishers.

Proctor, Robert. 1993. Nazi medicine and the politics of knowledge. In *The racial economy of science*, ed. Sandra Harding. Bloomington: Indiana University Press.

Quine, Willard Van Orwin. 1963. *From a logical point of view*. New York: Harper and Row.

Quine, Willard Van Orwin, and J. S. Julian. 1975. *The web of belief*. New York: McGraw Hill.

Sartre, Jean Paul. 1965. *Antisemite and Jew*. New York: Schocken.

Shiva, Vandana. 1993. Colonialism and the evolution of masculinist forestry. In *The racial economy of science*, ed. Sandra Harding. Bloomington: Indiana University Press.

Spelman, Elizabeth. 1988. *Inessential woman*. Boston: Beacon.

Stanford, J. L., and D. B. Thomas. 1991. Depot-Medroxyprogesterone Acetate (DMPA) and risk of epithelial ovarian cancer. *International Journal of Cancer* 49 (2) [Sep 9]: 191–95

Stauder, Jack. 1993. The "relevance" of anthropology to colonialism and imperialism. In *The racial economy of science*, ed. Sandra Harding. Bloomington: Indiana University Press.

Stepan, Nancy Leys, and Sander L. Gilman. 1993. Appropriating the idioms of science: The rejection of scientific racism. In *The racial economy of science*, ed. Sandra Harding. Bloomington: Indiana University Press.

Thomas, D. B., and R. M. Ray. 1992. Depot-Medroxyprogesterone Acetate (DMPA) and risk of invasive squamous cell cervical cancer. *Contraception* 45 (4) [April]: 299–312.

Trigilio, Jo. nd. Cyborgs, nomads, and experts: In search of the ordinary knower in feminist epistemology. Unpublished manuscript.

Tuana, Nancy. 1993. *The less noble sex: Scientific, religious, and philosophical conceptions of woman's nature*. Bloomington: Indiana University Press.

———. 1995. The values of science: Empiricism from a feminist perspective. *Synthese* 104: 441–61.

U.S. Department of Health and Human Services, Food and Drug Administration (FDA). 1992. Press Release. June 19.

WHO (World Health Organization) Task Force on Long-Acting Systemic Agents for Fertility Regulation, Special Program of Research, Development and Research Training in Human Reproduction. nd. Multinational comparative clinical trial of long-acting injectable contraceptives: Norethisterone Enanthate given in two dosage regimens and Depot-Medroxyprogesterone Acetate. Final report.

Whorf, Benjamin Lee. 1956. *Language, thought and reality*. Cambridge, Mass: M.I.T.

Williams, Sherley Anne. 1986 *Dessa Rose*. New York: Berkeley Books.

Wittgenstein, Ludwig. 1967. *Remarks on the foundations of mathematics*. Oxford: Basil Blackwell.

———. 1969. *On certainty*. Oxford: Basil Blackwell.

CHAPTER SEVEN

MEMORY, SUGGESTIBILITY, AND SOCIAL SKEPTICISM

SUE CAMPBELL

I study memory and I am a skeptic.
—Elizabeth Loftus, *The Myth of Repressed Memory:*
False Memories and Allegations of Sexual Abuse

HOW MUCH SKEPTICISM?

The explicit intent of the writings and activities of the False Memory Syndrome Foundation (FMSF), founded in 1992 as a lobby for parents whose adult children have accused them of abuse, has been to challenge the public to be far more skeptical about women's claims of abuse when these women have reevaluated their pasts in the "suggestible" context of therapy or when they have had any delayed recall of the abuse.[1] The FMSF claims that a certain phenomenon is epidemic: the practice among therapists and feminist authors of inappropriately suggesting to women that they may have been abused as children and yet may fail to remember the abuse. These women, under the influence of therapists, come to falsely believe that they have been abused, and spend years of their lives enacting what the FMSF believes is the now socially validated role of abuse victim, destroying their families through false accusations.

In a short period of time, and due in no small part to the authority of its Scientific and Professional Advisory Board, the FMSF has ignited public distrust of women's recall of abuse. Foundation and advisory board members have reanimated stereotypes of women as easily influenced, narcissistic, and vindictive, they have cast doubt on the competence of women therapists and counselors, and they have reinforced a public perception of feminists as zealots with little concern for evidence or fair procedures.

The institutional response to the FMSF has been widespread and profound. In a skeptical relay, the media has shifted from reporting on the harm of childhood sexual abuse to a nearly exclusive reporting on alleged parent victims of false accusations. Professional associations of psychologists and psychiatrists have expressed formal concern about recovered memory and suggestive therapy and have legitimated the activities of the FMSF. The courts have moved to disallow uncorroborated recovered memory testimony and to open possibilities for third-party negligence suits against therapists while accepting expert testimony from foundation advisors and supporters about false memory syndrome. These responses are in accord with the FMSF's objectives of shifting attention from the narratives of survivors to the narratives of those who have been accused of abuse, and in working to eliminate the contexts in which survivors can narrate abuse.[2]

Moreover, skepticism about women's recall has not been and will not be contained in those situations where women recover memories of abuse while undergoing therapy. Sara Scott writes that false memory syndrome "is fast becoming a free floating explanation, bobbing up in 'ordinary' conversation, providing a mechanism by which child sexual abuse can be transformed into errors and overreactions" (1997, 33). The widespread suspicion that women have not been telling the truth about past abuse creates elastic possibilities for now contesting their claims. For example, Harold Merskey, a foundation advisory board member, recently "sounded a warning note" that "complainants . . . have reacted to legal skepticism . . . by disguising the purported origin of their recollections . . . [portraying] these memories as having been there all along" (*Toronto Globe and Mail*, May 8, 1998, A8). Nor can we assume that skepticism about abuse will be limited to the group of women initially targeted by the FMSF. For example, a 1995 Supreme Court of Canada ruling allowed limited defense access to rape complainant's confidential therapeutic files if there was a suspicion that therapy had "influenced the complainant's memory of alleged events" (Kristiansen et al. 1997, 42). The ruling (since modified) was in response to a case involving the alleged abuse of Native Canadian children by a bishop at a residential school.[3]

Despite our recognition that the FMSF is engaged in a serious and successful multitargeting of women's competence and epistemic authority, feminists have been cautious in their response to foundation activities and claims, and it is the restraint of our response that directs my concern in this chapter. While feminists have encouraged and defended the contexts in which women can testify to their experience of harm, we have accepted much of the way the FMSF frames the dangers of therapeutic contexts.

Feminist critics of therapy have suggested that feminism has moved from public activism to private healing, making room for the FMSF's claim that women seek the status of victim.[4] Feminist therapists, in reconsidering their practice, have been sensitive to charges of depoliticizing abuse, but have also become preoccupied with the problem of suggestibility.[5] Finally, some feminists have adopted the FMSF's characterization of the debate as a polarized conflict between scientific skeptics and naive believers. They have suggested that we should transform this bipolarity by, to some extent, bracketing the conservative profamily and antifeminist rhetoric of the FMSF and seeking a middle ground in a judicious caution about the malleability of memory, especially in therapeutic contexts. Shelley Park writes, for example: "It is too facile and ultimately unpersuasive to denounce or deconstruct these views. Despite the conservative rhetoric of the false memory movement, empirical evidence suggests that pseudo-memories (including memories of limited trauma) can be created when subjects are exposed to misinformation by a trusted authority figure. . . . The malleability of human memory raises serious philosophical questions with which feminists must be prepared to grapple" (1997, 10). Feminists have, on the whole, tried to be responsive to foundation concerns while maintaining their commitment to the reality of childhood sexual abuse, to the welfare of women affected by abuse, and to the necessity of feminist political engagement. Sara Scott argues, however, that recent feminist caution about women's abuse narratives amounts to a political paralysis and that we have failed to respond effectively to the "discourse of disbelief" promoted by the FMSF (1997, 33).

The "false" memory debate is a deep and troubling context for examining questions of influence in a social epistemology. The FMSF's writings and activities and the institutional, public, and feminist responses to the FMSF raise serious ethical/epistemological questions about the appropriate role of skepticism in inquiry, and about the appropriate degree and kind of our epistemic reliance on others. In this chapter, I investigate the interdependence of these issues in the false memory debate by examining the link between skepticism and suggestibility in foundation writings. Like Scott, I am concerned with how responsive we can be to foundation charges while maintaining our commitment to women who have been abused.[6]

I first describe the difference between feminist and foundation projects and argue that the intent of a skeptical discourse is often to effect a shift in project. Specifically, the FMSF means to promote a shift away from the practical project of women trying to understand and make clear past harm (often in association with other women and with therapists) in favor of the project of waiting for science to discover the truth of the mind. I then examine a key imagining used by the FMSF to effect the shift in project; namely, that we are the victims of suggestive therapy. This imagining has a surprising precedent in Descartes's *Meditations on First Philosophy* and seeks to motivate a shift in epistemic project through promoting skepticism about our faculties.[7] However, invoking this level of skepticism creates a dilemma for the FMSF as it can also work to undermine the faith in science that the FMSF promotes. Thus, in the final section, I examine the FMSF's use of the discourse of suggestibility to target therapists and limit our skepticism to women's memories of abuse.

My intent is to lift concerns about influence from their home in FMSF skeptical strategies and to subject them to a self-reflective feminist examination. How might we have been influenced by the foundation's strategies? In focusing on the thought experiments that guide our skepticism, I am particularly concerned to explore the role of imagination in shifting relations of epistemic dependence. That we become dependent on those with whom we share imaginings is the FMSF's accusation: to encourage our dependence through shared imaginings is also its objective.

SKEPTICISM AND OUR PROJECTS

A striking feature of the FMSF writings is their explicit endorsement of the language of skepticism. The scientific advisors to the FMSF associate skepticism positively with the commitment to a scientific method characterized by impartiality and the demand for fully evidenced claims. That the FMSF links skepticism with the avoidance of bias and the search for objective truth should first direct feminists toward assessing the charges of bias in relation to our projects and their underlying values. The aim of a skeptical discourse that depends, in part, on accusations of bias can be to disallow the values that undergird certain practices by claiming that the practices themselves cannot be pursued in ways that would allow for epistemic norms of objectivity.

Here is a common example of the kind of deflection that concerns me. When students sometimes accuse my marking of bias, they may be urging me to greater fairness in my evaluations. In this context, my having biases may mean that I fail to show an appropriate fidelity to some set of norms or standards for a particular evaluative practice, where my failure manifests itself in treating one set of cases quite differently from a relevantly similar set of cases. If I accept this charge of bias, I am obliged to exercise more caution in my procedures or to find better procedures that reduce or eliminate the possibility of unfairness. I can accept the charge of bias while continuing to endorse the practice of grading.

I sometimes suspect, however, that there are no procedures that would exonerate me from a student's charge of bias. I thus sometimes suspect that students are trying to get me to concede that I should not be evaluating their work. Such students may either doubt that grading can ever be objective, or may object to the values that underlie the practice. They may object, for example, to the institutional power that gives me the authority to judge their work. For these latter groups of students, an invocation of objectivity through the charge of bias is the strategy and disguise of a skepticism about the practice of grading. Thus the charge of bias can challenge the adequacies of procedures within a practice, or, more seriously or extravagantly, can challenge the practice itself.

Since its inception, the primary stated activity of the FMSF has been to publicize the prevalence of false memory syndrome and the conditions that cause it—namely, therapeutic practices, self-help literature, survivor support groups, and broader social influences including feminist activism. The FMSF has identified therapists who both believe and express in their practice that childhood sexual abuse is widespread and an ongoing source of trauma for those victimized, as those people most directly responsible for the spread of false memory syndrome.[8] As feminist therapists clearly fall into this category, I will understand the FMSF's critique of therapy as directed at feminist therapists. Because feminist therapists are committed to providing a context in which women who have been abused can explore and articulate their experience, I will assume for this chapter that feminists have an interest in supporting responsible feminist therapy.[9]

The FMSF has accused feminist therapists of not paying adequate attention to science, particularly to work on the malleability of memory, the unreliability of testimony, and the inability to test for repression under laboratory conditions. Rather, the FMSF charges that feminist therapists have an ideological bias toward childhood sexual abuse as an explanation for the unhappiness of their clients. Therapists manifest this bias in too easily accepting the claims of clients who say they were abused, and in encouraging clients to search for abuse in their pasts. They exert harmful and careless influence over vulnerable clients through suggestive therapeutic techniques ranging from hypnosis to simply asking clients if they have been abused. The ideologically driven commitment of these therapists to prefer and suggest certain explanations over others that might be equally compatible with the evidence is said to lead to great social harm—the accusation of innocent parents and the "brutalization of patients in therapy" (Ofshe and Watters 1994, 13).

Sociologist Richard Ofshe, a member of the FMSF's academic advisory board, accuses many therapists of having "slipped the ties that bind their professions to science research and sound method" (Ofshe and Watters 1994, 5).

Psychologist Elizabeth Loftus, memory researcher and foundation advisor, dedicates *The Myth of Repressed Memory: False Memories and Allegations of Sexual Abuse* "to the principles of science which demand that any claim to 'truth' be accompanied by proof" (Loftus and Ketchum 1994, v).[10] Loftus identifies the important epistemic project as the scientific understanding of the malleability of memory and divides the public into Skeptics, on the one hand, and True Believers on the other. True Believers accept the existence of repression. Skeptics recognize that the notion of repression "is essentially untestable" and talk of "proof, corroboration, and scientific truth seeking" (1994, 32, 31).[11] So the FMSF charges that feminist therapeutic practices display bias, both partiality that causes us to ignore alternative compelling explanations for women's unhappiness and problems with evidence. Unlike my students, who can offer no alternative to grading, foundation advisors offer a different and familiar locus of objectivity in the scientific study of memory and offer the public an option of perspectives—science-minded skeptic or true believer.

I do not believe the FMSF charge of bias can be read as an injunction to exercise caution within the project of a type of therapy that would allow a narrative about past abuse; the FMSF's work is more reasonably interpreted as committed to destroying this context. Foundation advisors explicitly campaign against therapy that involves attention to a client's past and against therapy that regards childhood sexual abuse as sufficiently serious and widespread that the possibility of such abuse might be raised as a hypothesis for a woman's distress. Richard Ofshe proposes that all mental health disorders be treated either by biomedical therapy or by "rehabilitative psychotherapy," which concentrates on "identifying troubling behaviors and coping patterns" and requires "no assumptions . . . about the etiology of disorders" (1994, 297–98). Hollinda Wakefield and Ralph Underwager favor "cognitive behavioral therapy" that "pays minimal attention to the feelings of the client" since its intent is to change behavior and "maladaptive thinking." Because "it is assumed that the person's cognitions are . . . in error . . . an important part of the therapy is challenging the beliefs of the client." The authors mention, in particular, beliefs about causality that lack "credible scientific support" (1994, 362–63).

Foundation members and advisors have also widely endorsed third-party negligence suits against therapists that would hold therapists accountable for "foreseeable harm" including emotional distress to the families of clients. The likely effect of such suits is that therapists will be less willing to treat those women who struggle to understand abusive pasts (Bowman and Mertz 1996). Foundation supporters have campaigned for consumer mental health protection acts on a state and federal level that would limit access to the types of therapy that support disclosures of childhood sexual abuse and acknowledge the problems survivors face with recall of the abuse. A call for funding to develop model legislation for New Hampshire in 1994 stressed the necessity of developing a rationale that would include an explanation of "why the 'scientific community' should police therapy methods and procedures," and of developing "a legal analysis comparing fraudulent and politicized psychotherapists to drunk drivers" (National Association for Consumer Protection in Mental Health Practices 1994, 7–8). The legislation would ideally involve rules of ethical conduct for all therapy professionals "eliminating political 'psychology' theories" (1994, 8). Clearly, such proposed legislation targets feminist therapists.[12]

Moreover, the division between skeptics and true believers argues for a replacement of psychotherapy by science and not a collaboration of the two. Foundation skeptics do not support research designed to lend credence to women's experience of problems in recalling abuse. They are emphatic in contending that repression is untestable and that its investigation is not a part of scientific truthseeking.[13] Moreover, Ofshe warns that science is distorted when influenced by social movements. Nevertheless, foundation skeptics explicitly support a science of the malleability of memory whose effect is to challenge psychotherapy as a site of suggestibility and memory distortion.[14]

The FMSF, in effect, argues that the public should support a shift in project that excludes the woman with a troubled past from participating as an epistemic agent in an understanding of her past and in contributing to social knowledge of childhood sexual abuse. She is not a participant in the scientific project of understanding memory and her coming to understand her own past has no place in this inquiry. Through charging bias and evoking scientific objectivity, the activities of the False Memory Syndrome Foundation instead attempt a skeptical destruction of one of the contexts that allows a woman to understand a troubled and abusive past. But her perspective is critical to any communal project of objective knowledge of sexual harm.

The Argument from Misdesign

I believe that there is a disturbing philosophical story about this shift from her project to their project, the attendant obliteration of the possibility of her perspective, and the degree of public skepticism the FMSF has ignited. There are obviously many factors at work in the success of the FMSF. My interest here is in one FMSF strategy that has its prototype in the least discussed and most powerful of Descartes's skeptical arguments in the Meditations, which I shall call the argument from misdesign.[15] I discuss this argument in order to show that, in attempting to move us from support of therapy and survivor narrative through an appeal to scientific objectivity, the FMSF invites us into a shared imagining about the malleability of memory. This imagining is meant to promote both a shift in epistemic project and in relations of epistemic reliance, but, in fact, promotes a metaphysical skepticism that leaves knowledge unavailable.

In the Meditations, Descartes wishes to undertake the project of establishing a certain foundation for his beliefs. To do so he must withdraw assent from the opinions he has as the result of habit, education, and other prejudice. This shift in project away from practical activity and the epistemology of the trusting believer is difficult. It requires the proof of real errors to engage doubt, which doubt must then become sufficiently powerful to allow for the complete suspension of trusting belief. There is an antiskeptical momentum, however, to our ability to identify errors within a practice, for these identifications suggest we can develop our procedures and refine our practices to prevent future error. Descartes needs to find a ground for doubt that cannot be answered by the ordinary practical precautions we might take in circumstances where we know that making a certain kind of mistake is a possibility. Descartes begins with the argument from illusion where the grounds for doubt can be lessened by appropriate attention to perceptual circumstances (if things far away always look deceptively small to me, I should get closer before judging their size). He moves to reasons for doubting that cannot be resolved by pointing to the possibility of precautions against error: the argument from dreaming, which is meant to make us wonder whether we can be sure about the source of our perceptual ideas, and the argument from misdesign.

The argument from misdesign, the final skeptical argument of the Meditations, is meant to bring all of Descartes's beliefs—even those which, like mathematical truths, are one by one indubitable—within the scope of a doubt that will lead to Descartes's withholding assent from all the ideas he has previously acquired. The argument from misdesign is developed by Descartes precisely in order to make his doubt as intense as possible by bringing into question the adequacy of his reason to withhold assent from what has not yet been proven certain. Descartes needs to become sufficiently skeptical about the worth of his ideas to compel a lasting shift of attention away from practical concerns and toward an examination of his faculties. As he seeks, so he says, not action but knowledge, he believes he cannot yield too much to distrust.

In making the argument from misdesign, Descartes notes that he has observed that others are sometimes in error even about that of which they think they have perfect knowledge. This leads him to contemplate that God, through imperfection or malice may have made him, Descartes, such that constitutionally, he is subject to deception and error even about matters of which he is certain: "How do I know that he has not brought it about that there is no earth, no sky, no extended thing, no shape, no size, no place, while at the same time ensuring that all these things appear to me to exist just as they do now?" (CSM II,

14). The argument is summarized in the sixth meditation as follows: "Since I did not know the author of my being (or at least was pretending not to), I saw nothing to rule out the possibility that my natural constitution made me prone to error even in matters which seemed to me most true" (CSM II, 53).

Descartes concludes from the argument from misdesign that "there is not one of my former beliefs about which a doubt may not be properly raised. . . . So in the future I must withhold my assent from these former beliefs just as carefully as I would from obvious falsehoods" (CSM II, 14–15). He then takes care to keep the doubt in his mind by setting for himself the project of imagining that some malignant demon, at once exceedingly potent and deceitful, has employed all his artifice to keep deceptive presentations before Descartes's mind. "It will be a good plan to turn my will in completely the opposite direction and deceive myself, by pretending for a time that these former opinions are utterly false and imaginary. . . . I will suppose therefore that not God, who is supremely good and the source of truth, but rather some malicious demon of the utmost power and cunning has employed all his energies in order to deceive me" (CSM II, 15).

The argument from misdesign is a form of skeptical argument specifically oriented to motivating a shift in our projects, away from the possibility of taking precautions in certain circumstances in which we might err. The shift is effected by postulating an internal mechanism that is unreliable, which may cause us to be in error and not know it. Because the problem is one of an internal mechanism, potential error in judgment cannot be guarded against by attention to circumstances that form the settings of our projects. We must move away from these projects to an examination of the problematic faculty.

"Shirley Ann Souza was a mother's dream" (Loftus and Ketchum 1994, 1). "Christine, who was twenty-six the year that she began therapy, had known all her life that she had not come from a perfect family" (Ofshe and Watters 1994, 16). These narratives begin Loftus's and Ofshe's accounts of suggestive therapy involving "false" memories of abuse and the destruction of decent families. Foundation advisors make liberal use of narrative to make vivid the dangers of therapy, and these narratives have a single theme: a therapist could persuade any one of us that we are a victim of childhood sexual abuse. I regard these narratives as invitations to our imagination. In making this point, I want to allow that some are probably fairly accurate representations of irresponsible therapy. I follow Alan White in the view that to imagine something "is to think of it as possibly so. It is usually also to think of it in a certain way" (White 1990, 184). The activity of imagining is independent of the truth or falsity of the content of the imagining.

My concern is that our imaginative participation in these stories, which we are meant to take as representative of feminist psychotherapy, follows the form of an argument from misdesign. Here is a very explicit example from Richard Ofshe and Ethan Watters: *Making Monsters: False Memories, Psychotherapy and Sexual Hysteria* (1994). Ofshe is the one of the most vocal board members of the FMSF and its specialist on questions of suggestibility and social influence:

> Picture an elephant. Imagine an apple. Now spend a moment visualizing an image of being sexually abused by a parent. It is often a distressing trick of the mind that will create any event regardless of our desire to visualize the event. What separates an imagined image from a memory image is not a simple matter, for even imagined images are themselves largely built from memory. . . . To create this image, we might use recollections of our parents' physical appearance and of ourselves as children. We might place the scene in the memory of our childhood room. To create the action of the scene, we might use memories of other people's descriptions of sexual assaults or of abuse scenes depicted in books or movie dramas. In the end, all the pieces of the imagined event would have something of the weight of real memory. . . . Our innate ability to distinguish between memory and imagination is a precarious and, at best, an imperfect mechanism. (107)

The content of the shared imagining that we are to undertake as readers is here supplied by Ofshe. However the text that surrounds the quoted passage makes clear that what we are meant to imagine in thinking about this passage is that we are asked to produce a visualization of abuse during therapy. We are to engage in this imagining supposing the visualization is suggested to us by a therapist.

I am not concerned with whether, as a thought experiment, the proposed visualization produces, for any reader, an imagining, let alone one that seems like a memory. It need not succeed at doing this. If it does not succeed, we are then to further imagine that the therapist accuses us of denial and subjects us to further techniques of influence. We are to hold this therapist in our mind. The type of therapist we are asked to imagine, labeled a "recovered memory therapist," is described by Ofshe as "poorly trained, overzealous, or ideologically driven." Recovered memory therapists "without an understanding of the damage they have caused . . . have employed methods that blur the already perilously thin line that separates memory from imagination" (Ofshe and Watters 1994, 5). In the passage following the imagining, we are told that such therapists can "destroy the patient's ability" to distinguish between memory and imagination (1994, 108).

We are first, then, asked to imagine that we are not well designed, that we may be prone to damaging error that we cannot detect as error. Our sometimes inability to distinguish a memory image from a visualization is characterized as being the result of a precarious and imperfect psychic mechanism. Secondly, we are asked to concentrate on the figure of a therapist as potential deceiver. We are asked to imagine that she supplies the content of the visualizations by which we are misled and will use all her power to persuade us that the visualizations before our mind are memories. To hold in mind the presence of the therapist as a potential deceiver is to keep the possibility of misdesign concrete and vivid. She is the device that we use in this thought experiment to remind ourselves of our vulnerability to false memories. As the figure that supplies our visualizations, her presence, like the demon's, also works to define the project, which we must abandon. Finally, that we should take ourselves to be deceived also serves to keep us hopeful by reminding us there is a truth to be discovered about memory.[16] Ofshe believes that our understanding of memory and our cultural ability to deal with major mental health disorders "awaits the painstaking, expensive and time-consuming application of science" (Ofshe and Watters 1994, 298).

I believe the argument from misdesign is particularly suited to the FMSF's objective of turning us from feminist therapy as a kind of project within which we could take reasonable precautions against suggestions of abuse, and of casting doubt wholesale on the abuse memories of women who seek therapy. Motivating our participation in a misdesign imagining does not depend on getting us to recognize our own serious errors, but uses our own confidence or credulity against us by pointing to confident or credulous others who have been in serious error. Only a few serious and suspect cases involving perception, judgment, or memory are needed to motivate the argument and these suspect cases do not need to come from our own experience. Most foundation writings recycle the same cases, some now notorious, of dubious recovered memory while engaging the reader, often explicitly, in thought experiments about the possibility of her own misdesign.

Secondly, a misdesign imagining may be raised on the suspicion that a number of our or others' beliefs or memories are false, but the argument bypasses questions of whether individual beliefs and memories are, in fact, false. It is meant to raise skepticism about whole categories of thought.[17] We can be alarmed by the potential for confident, unwitting error without adequately pausing to consider whether particular traumatic rememberings might be accurate, and whether dependence on a therapist might not sometimes be wise.

A willingness to doubt women's memories with no attention to whether the memories are true or whether the abuse happened is evident in some of the most disturbing legal and political affirmations of the FMSF's work. In 1994, when Gary Ramona successfully sued his daughter's (Holly Ramona) therapists for negligence, the jury was asked to decide whether Holly's therapists had inappropriately reinforced Holly's false memories without being asked to reach a determination as to whether the memories were, in fact, false or whether the abuse had taken place.[18] The Justice Department in Canada recently affirmed it will consider reviewing all cases involving recovered memory testimony in which men have been convicted. Alan Gold, the lawyer responsible for the initiative, argues that "Real or not, such alleged memories are too readily confused with the results of suggestion and confabulation to have any degree of reliability" (*Ottawa Citizen*, May 4, 1998). The appeal to misdesign renders ineffectual the reasonable position that cases of recovered memory should be individually assessed.

Finally, we need to grasp what is both tempting and problematic for feminists in being responsive to the FMSF's doubts while affirming the widespread reality of childhood sexual abuse. The FMSF does not ask us to disbelieve women's narratives but advises caution about them, and this may seem like an appealing middle ground. However, the misdesign imagining replaces the focus on belief with a focus on assent or acceptance, and can be read as encouraging an even deeper shift in epistemic commitment than the withdrawal of support for survivor therapy.

For Descartes, to withhold assent from an idea is to treat it as false for the purposes of inquiry. Modern epistemologists are more likely to distinguish between belief and acceptance of a hypothesis, where, according to Bas Van Frassen, acceptance is "a commitment to the further confrontation of new phenomena within the framework of that theory, a commitment to a research programme, and a wager that all relevant phenomena can be accounted for without giving up that theory" (1980, 88).[19] Although we often believe and accept the same hypothesis, we may accept a hypothesis for the purpose of inquiring without thinking it is true; alternatively, we may think a hypothesis is true, but inadequate to direct inquiry. Feminists historically have not only believed women's testimony of abuse but have accepted this testimony as the foundation of our research and activism. It is this commitment that has allowed recognition of child sexual abuse as a widespread and serious reality for women. The FMSF offers the option of continuing to think that most women are probably telling the truth about their experiences of abuse while rejecting this testimony as adequate to direct our projects.

There is, however, an obvious difficulty for the FMSF in utilizing misdesign imaginings to promote reliance on science as a substitute for projects that rely on memory testimony. The intent of a misdesign imagining is to move our attention from projects that depend on the use of our faculties toward an examination of these faculties. However, if the problem of misdesign cannot be solved by our caution within certain projects, then neither can it be resolved by abandoning these projects for other projects that rely on the faculties of those who are similarly misdesigned. The figure of the therapist in foundation arguments, like the demon in Descartes, acts to delimit circumstances that remain epistemically unsafe. The demon reminds Descartes of the unreliability of sense perception and its deficiency as a source of knowledge. The figure of the therapist reminds us of the unreliability of memory testimony and its deficiencies as a source of knowledge. Descartes can, perhaps, investigate reason avoiding problematic uses of perception. We cannot, however, in our pursuit of the sciences of memory, avoid reliance on memory. Memory scientists rely not only on their own memories, but rely extensively on the testimony of their experimental subjects.

Metaphysical skepticism is the view that there is some subject matter (the external world, other minds, the past), knowledge of which transcends our powers. There is no way of improving our position for knowing the truth, and the reason for this has to do with the alleged fact that the truth transcends our faculties and methods. The distinctively metaphysical skeptic has to widen the gap between reality and our faculties and methods to ensure that even the most persistent and cautious use of our faculties/methods could not in principle close this gap. In offering the argument from misdesign, Descartes is a metaphysical skeptic. In offering the argument from misdesign, so too are foundation authors metaphysical skeptics. Descartes moves back from metaphysical skepticism. Recognizing that he is not epistemically self-sufficient, he resolves his doubts about reason partly through trust in the goodness and power of the cause that produced him. When memory is the faculty devalued in a misdesign imagining, faith in science and scientists is, quite obviously, no remedy.

SUGGESTIBILITY

In the third meditation, Descartes characterizes the doubt raised by the argument from misdesign as slight. A benevolent God would not have left us prone to undetectable error; moreover, the imagined demon is a device to aid withdrawal of assent, but is no real deceiver. My students, however, find more power in Descartes's description of the demon than he might have anticipated. They frequently ignore Descartes's claim that the demon is only a device, thus activating the real possibility of their own deception. Their reading converts the argument from misdesign into an imagining about suggestibility.

The power of the FMSF's misdesign imagining depends on our actual concerns about suggestibility in therapeutic contexts. Although the therapist is a figure in the imagining, she is meant to differ from the demon in being a real threat. In this final section, I examine the sorts of worries expressed through an alarm about suggestibility. I want to question, perhaps tendentiously, whether suggestibility is the appropriate language in which to express concerns about influence in therapy, and argue, at least, that we need more precision about the nature of these concerns.

The charge of suggestibility is the heart of the FMSF attack on therapy, but what suggestibility is is not at all clear. Michael Yabko, author of *Suggestions of Abuse*, defines suggestibility as "people's responsiveness to other's beliefs, perceptions, ideas, behaviors, feelings, attitudes and values" (1994, 96). Since we are all responsive to others' beliefs, perceptions, ideas, values and necessarily so, this kind of definition of suggestibility is unhelpful in coming to understand what it means to raise a social alarm about suggestibility.

Suggestibility is clearly a worry about influence: that in some specifiable set of circumstances, some people are inappropriately influencing others. When we analyze suggestibility, we need to keep clear that it is raised as a worry; we are not being offered the option that the influence in question is a good thing.[20] Suggestibility not only involves a claim about influence but a judgment about the quality of the influence. I also take it in what follows that suggestibility as a particular configuration of worries about influence derives from its association with hypnosis. Discussions of hypnosis are where the concept has taken shape, and it is the sometime use of hypnosis in therapy that has legitimated the language of suggestibility in foundation writings.

According to Nicholas Spanos: "Hypnotic susceptibility (or suggestibility) refers to the subject's level of responsiveness to test suggestions. Test suggestions do not instruct subjects to enact an overt behavior. Instead their wordings describe a 'make-believe' or counterfactual situation. This wording further implies that the make-believe situation is to be treated by subjects as if it were really happening and is to lead to the occurrence of a congruent overt response. . . . In short, suggestions implicitly invite subjects to suspend the tacit rules usually employed to differentiate imagined events from actual events, to define the ongoing situation in terms of imagined events and to enact behaviors implied by those imagined events" (1986, 90). Spanos thus describes the situation of suggestibility as one of a shared project of imagination where what is to be imagined is under the control or given by one of the parties, to others. These others then enact the imagining.[21] For reasons, which will become clear, it is not my intention to endorse the concept of suggestibility as ideal for understanding problematic influence. I do wish to understand the force of the concept as an expression of social worry. I believe there are at least three possibilities for what might be ethically worrying in situations of influence that we describe as cases of suggestibility.

The first concern that might characterize a situation of suggestibility is a concern about truth. The implication of Spanos's contrast between the imagined and the actual might look to be that what is to be imagined is not true— "your arm is so heavy that you can't lift it." The subject of a suggestion may come to believe what is not true and act as if it were true, for example, that she has been abused.

Worrisome influence, however, can take place in shared imaginings where the subject does not come to believe something that is false, and, moreover, such imaginings can have, as their objective, discovering something about the world. In such cases, there may still be a concern about precipitous and unwise action. A case in point: my grade-six science teacher and school principal, Mr. Duckworth, vigorously explaining resistance to our class by bouncing his wooden yard stick off a linoleum floor added, as an aside, that were Randy to run headfirst into the wall he too would bounce off. Whereupon Randy, caught up in the spirit of demonstration, stood up and running the length of the classroom took himself headfirst into the wall.

This second concern about precipitous and unwise action is a concern that some feature (or features) of the circumstances of the suggestion encourage the person suggested to, to act congruently with what is to be imagined, while this same feature(s) of the circumstances renders that person in a deficient position to evaluate whether they should so act. Further, their actions are unwise. Mr. Duckworth's authority encouraged Randy to act and to act without thinking, and Randy hurt his head. When social workers are instructed to be careful in speculating about a client's situation when that client is in crisis, to avoid saying, for example, "What would happen if you were to confront him about his abuse," the worry is that the need to take some action may be so great that the client is rendered less able by this same feature of the circumstances to evaluate the consequences of acting; moreover, that it would likely be unwise for her to so act. I take the concern about unwise action to be central to suggestibility as a worry. It is the type of action that women sometimes take on coming to believe they have been abused—namely, accusing a parent—that has motivated the FMSF's concern with suggestibility.

The third concern that might determine a worry about suggestibility is a concern about autonomy. What was perhaps most alarming about Randy's behavior was his willingness or eagerness to be a prop in a grade-six science demonstration. This third concern, again inherited from the association of suggestibility with hypnosis, is that the self-presentation of the subject is not under the subject's control. However hypnosis works, the subject seems to be involved in a project of presenting the self where a defining feature of the project is that the self is presented as under the control of another. This form of self-presentation violates deeply held cultural commitments about autonomy as self-governance. According to Ofshe "patients [in therapy] receive encouragement . . . to surrender their will" (Ofshe and Watters 1994, 120). These patients are, in fact, "blank canvasses on which the therapists paint" (Ofshe and Watters 1993, 9).

The foregoing analysis is meant to indicate that to adequately evaluate a specific worry about suggestibility we must come to a complex understanding of the projects of shared imagining in which the inappropriate influence is suspected, and we must carefully disentangle a number of different kinds of concerns. When framed through the model of hypnotic suggestibility, worries about influence are easy to activate, mutually provoke each other, and are difficult to contain. By understanding psychotherapy on a model of hypnotic suggestibility, the FMSF has raised a picture of women in therapy as deluded about their pasts, as acting unwisely, and as lacking autonomy.[22] I want to emphasize three interrelated points in calling on feminists to deconstruct the manipulation of the model in foundation writings.

First, to raise an alarm about suggestibility is not just to advance the concern that through participating in imaginings we come to believe what is false. It is a more complex grouping of concerns about who we become and what actions we take through our associations with others and their influence on us. Women who explore their pasts in therapy or with the support of other women may come to identify as survivors, perhaps undertaking a radical change in self-presentation. They may act in ways that the FMSF was established to counteract. They may confront their families and even sue those they hold responsible for abuse. The change in women from dutiful daughters to the critics of patriarchal families has occasioned deep distress, and suggestibility must be engaged with as political criticism.

Secondly, the specter of suggestibility, made vivid in the misdesign imaginings, works on an added level to promote a shift in our projects toward a science of the malleability of the memory, and I have argued we should resist this shift. A key strategy of the FMSF's replacement of testimonial contexts for survivors with scientific experiments about memories has been to raise fears about suggestibility, and then reabsorb the analysis of suggestibility into a body of preexisting psychology research on the inaccuracy of recall, particularly the studies of eyewitness testimony devised by foundation advisor Elizabeth Loftus. There has been a growing sophistication of the FMSF's organization of suggestibility as a problem for memory science, more recently involving experiments designed to have subjects develop pseudo-memories for traumalike events when given posthypnotic suggestions or when prompted by a trusted individual (Loftus and Ketchum 1994, ch.7).

Finally, in the previous section, I noted that the argument from misdesign is intended to raise skepticism about a whole category of beliefs on grounds that we may be in error and not know it. Incorporating fears of suggestibility adds to the rationale for rejecting the memory claims en masse when women have had therapy. When suggestibility is scientifically framed as the malleability of memory, there is an especially acute conflation of the issue of false belief with other effects of influence. In a typical memory experiment, a subject is first shown a series of slides of a scene and then tested on her recall. Test questions incorporate false information, for example "Did the car go through the stop sign?" when the slide showed a yield sign. The subject's answering yes will be taken as evidence that memory is malleable for details. In other words, suggestibility is operationalized by scientists as "the susceptibility to error when given false information or asked questions designed to elicit false information" (Fivush 1996, 152). As scientific tests for suggestibility are tests for false information, they easily lead to the conclusion that insofar as we are influenced in our beliefs, we come to believe what is false.

In looking at the scientific treatment of suggestibility, we have some explanation for how the fact of therapist influence on clients has been used to organize a widespread fear of false belief. The FMSF has frequently made use of the results of a survey by Poole et al. (1995), which claims that up to 25 percent of therapists are using suggestive techniques in therapy. The study has been widely quoted as evidence for the potentially epidemic nature of "false" memory. The study did not, however, distinguish between techniques when they incorporate misleading information, and these same techniques when they do not include misleading information. Nor did the researchers show that the techniques enumerated "are differentially associated with supplying false or misleading information about child abuse" (Pope 1997, 1000). The study only supports a concern about "false" memory if the targeted techniques lead to false belief and this reading uses the notion of suggestibility operationalized in memory science.[23] More deeply, if these techniques do not tend to contribute toward false belief, precipitous and unwise action, or lack of autonomy in self-presentation, I do not see the grounds for regarding them as suggestive techniques.

Even vigorous feminist critics of the FMSF have accepted that suggestibility is a problem amenable to scientific analysis. Laura Brown, for example, identifies two levels to the false memory debate: the level of science—what we can know and how we know it—and a political level of who owns the history of the family and childhood. Her discussion of suggestibility takes place under the heading of science (Brown 1996a). At the same time, Brown wants to concede that "the charge of suggestibility cannot be avoided when the therapeutic task is recognized as one of the joint construction of meaning" (Brown and Burman 1997, 13). Because suggestibility is a complex of easily confused worries about inappropriate influence, we must lift the analysis of suggestibility from under the jurisdiction of science. At the same time, while it is appropriate and essential for therapists to realistically assess the influence they have on individual clients, there is no reason to accept suggestibility as a description of this influence. What seems to unify suggestibility worries is the denial of

168 SUE CAMPBELL

agency to the client, hence her susceptibility to false belief, unwise action and nonautonomous self-presentation. To adopt suggestibility as a description of influence imports ideas of harmful influence and the absence of client agency.

The FMSF invites us into an imagining about suggestibility as a strategy of influence, and I initially set the question of how we might have been influenced by the foundation's skepticism. It may seem tempting and tidy to conclude from my analysis that through a bombardment of "false" memory imaginings, the FMSF has succeeded in suggesting we are suggestible, and that as a public we are unwisely enacting our role in this shared imagining. I do not accept this reading of FSMF influence. I do not believe, in particular, that feminists have come to believe what is false, are acting in ways that are precipitous and unwise, or have given over our autonomy to the FMSF. Nor do I believe that members of the public lack epistemic agency in relation to the FMSF. I do believe that the FMSF uses relatively powerful rhetorical strategies to shift our support from women who have been abused. I have argued that the use of imaginings in the "false" memory debate is to influence the direction of inquiry and to configure relations of epistemic reliance. When we read the testimonials of incest survivors, and when we read "false" memory writings, we are, in both cases, engaged in shared imaginings where what is to be imagined is under the control of the authors of the texts. The imaginings to which we commit our assent will determine different kinds of epistemic projects. One is a political project of supporting the contexts in which women can explore and articulate their experience of harm and of taking their testimony as fundamental to our own understanding of childhood sexual harm. The other is an equally political project of supporting the FMSF's science of a malleability of memory.

I have argued that the two projects are not compatible and that the FMSF seeks to shift our support from the first to the second. The FMSF project, however, is an invitation to uncontained skepticism; moreover, when a science of the malleability of memory is offered as an investigation of suggestibility, such a science encourages an ungrounded fear of widespread false belief. Finally, when we confront the doubts raised by an alarm of suggestibility, we need to address concerns about the appropriate degree and kind of our epistemic and practical reliance on others. It is important to realize that what is appropriate here does depend on our projects.

CONCLUSION

I believe that the context of therapy will remain problematic for feminists to assess, and that the current debate directs us to incorporate a study of interpretive contexts like therapy more fully into our epistemologies. We need first an understanding of the influence of shared imaginings in a positive epistemology. Our ability to participate in shared imaginings is crucial to our response to art and to our moral ability to empathize with others. Susan Babbitt (1996) has argued that committed action on the basis of imagined possibilities is also necessary to bring about the social conditions that make possible objective knowledge. She acknowledges that commitment in advance of knowledge is always a risk, but is often an epistemically necessary one.

Secondly, and relatedly, feminists who are committed to defending objective knowledge must critically evaluate the demands for transformative criticism in our current feminist accounts of objectivity.[24] Helen Longino (1994) and Naomi Scheman (1996) are among feminists who have argued for a view of objective knowledge as the tentative product of "the critical workings of a sufficiently democratic epistemic community" (Scheman, 231). Scheman's account stresses that sufficiently democratic is to be understood partly in that community's encouragement of marginalized or outlaw perspectives that challenge how privilege can be naturalized and justified. Facilitating the articulation of these perspectives requires "the cultivation of relationships of trust" and an understanding of "how we create possibilities for meaningfulness in each other's lives" (233, 234). We require an account of objectivity that can endorse the contexts in which knowledge emerges only through relationships of trust, the influence of imagination, and protection from premature criticism. The cost of supporting these contexts may indeed often be uncertainty about whether our beliefs or commitments are fully justified; the cost of withdrawing our support from these contexts will be the silencing of these perspectives.

NOTES

I am very grateful to Jan Sutherland and Rockney Jacobsen for discussion and encouragement, to Angela Failler for research assistance, and to Sue Dwyer for encouragement and many helpful comments on framing. Reading K. Brad Wray's dissertation, "The Role of Community in Inquiry," was an opportunity to think about the issues in this chapter. Ancestors of this chapter were presented to the Canadian Society for Women and Philosophy, the Canadian Philosophical Association, and the enGendering Rationalities conference at the University of Oregon. I thank the audiences for their comments, and especially thank Susan Babbitt and Richmond Campbell, whose copresentations on the two latter occasions influenced the direction of this chapter.

1. I consider as writings of the False Memory Syndrome Foundation both writings by its members, primarily the FMSF Newsletter, and those writings by members of its advisory board specifically directed toward raising public awareness/alarm about the creation of "false" or pseudo-memories of incest. For an argument against adopting the terminology "false memory," see Campbell (1997).

2. For the media turnabout, see Stanton (1997). Kirk Makin, justice reporter for the *Globe and Mail* (Toronto) reports that seven professional associations have expressed formal caution about recovered memory (May 8, 1998, A8). Moreover, the American Psychological Association has approved FMSF as a sponsor of continuing education programs (Pope 1996). For a discussion of legal decisions, see Bowman and Mertz (1996) and Kristiansen et al. (1997). For an eloquent presentation of the importance of survivor narrative, see Culbertson (1995).

3. See Kristiansen et al. (1997) for a discussion of Canadian cases influenced by the debate.

4. See Armstrong (1994), Brown (1996b), Brown and Burman (1997), Enns et al. (1995), Haaken (1996), Kitzenger (1993), and Tavris (1993), both for various expressions and for discussions of these concerns. Haaken's criticism of trauma-based models of feminist therapy seems to me particularly insightful. Enns et al. warn against confusing the incest survivor's movement with the recovery movement.

5. See, especially, Enns et al. (1995), Brown (1996a), and Brown and Burman (1997).

6. In this chapter, I deliberately do not respond to the content of FMSF skepticism about women's recall. This may make some readers uncomfortable, and I hope it will seem justified by the project of the chapter: investigating FMSF strategies for promoting skepticism.

7. All references to the works of Descartes are by volume and page number to John Cottingham, Robert Shoothoof, and Dugald Murdoch, eds. *The Philosophical Writings of Descartes, Vol. 1 and 2* (1989), abbreviated as CSM.

8. Information on the FMSF can be obtained through their web page, their brochures, and their newsletters. Information is available online at http://advicom.~fitz/fmsf or can be obtained from the foundation's office at 3401 Market Street, Suite 130, Philadelphia, PA, 19104. Feminist overviews of the FMSF are provided in Enns et al. (183–86), and in Park (1997). Ofshe and Watters (1994), Loftus and Ketchum (1994), and Wakefield and Underwager (1994), all books with one advisor to the FMSF as a co-author, systematically list and analyze purported causes of "false" memory.

9. For my understanding of responsible feminist therapy, see Brown 1996b.

10. Ofshe and Loftus appear to be the primary authors of these books.

11. As Loftus makes clear in a footnote, she regards the problems of delayed recall that incest survivors may face as a commitment to repression, no matter what term therapists use (1994, 141).

12. R. Christopher Barden, who directed this initiative, has recently written to the Judiciary Committee of the United States House of Representatives to press for federal control on innovative psychotherapy (letter of Jan. 5, 1998 reprinted on ADAADC@aol.com, April 14, 1998). A number of prominent psychologists have signed the letter.

13. For a research program designed to positively investigate survivor's problems with recall, see Freyd (1996).

14. Feminists, among others, have vigorously criticized the type of extreme positivism that is manifest in foundation writings: a demand for falsifiable hypotheses, a commitment to the neutrality of the context of justification, and little recognition of the role of social interests in the setting of scientific agendas.

15. In my reading of this argument, I follow Jacobsen (nd.). There has been much discussion about what the third level of skeptical doubt is in the Meditations. Jacobsen notes that only a few commentators have treated the argument from misdesign as importantly distinct from the use of the demon as a device.

16. I owe this point to Jan Sutherland.

17. In a persuasive questioning of the evidence for FMSF claims about the nature of false memory syndrome and its alleged epidemic status, Kenneth Pope (1996) has challenged the FMSF and its Scientific and Professional Advisory Board to "report any available scientific data about the ability to diagnose false memory syndrome without meeting the person alleged to have the disorder" (962). Pope notes "that it remains unclear whether the protocol of any research purporting to validate the false memory syndrome diagnosis in large numbers of people used any criterion other than the decision rule that all recovered memories of abuse are inherently false" (959). The use of misdesign imaginings is the rhetorical strategy that supports this decision procedure. Disturbingly, to point out that there is no evidence for false memory syndrome has seemed somehow beside the point in this debate, a weak technicality that does not address the ground of the skepticism.

18. See Bowman and Mertz (1996) for a feminist analysis of the Ramona case.

19. I am grateful to K. Brad Wray (1997) for drawing my attention to this article.

20. In Western-Anglo culture, we have very few positive models of influence. See, however, Babbitt (1996).

21. Walton (1990) informs my understanding of suggestibility in terms of shared imagining.

22. There is no general feminist support for the use of hypnosis in therapy with survivors. See Enns et al. (1995, 184, 210-11).

23. See, as well, Enns et al. (1995) discussion of the scientific research for a feminist concern about suggestibility that is insufficiently wary of the conflation of falsity and influence.

24. The description of transformative criticism is in Longino (1994).

References

Armstrong, Louise. 1994. *Rocking the cradle of sexual politics.* New York: Addison-Wesley.

Babbitt, Susan. 1996. *Impossible dreams: Rationality, integrity, and moral imagination.* Boulder, Colo.: Westview.

Campbell, Sue. 1997. Women, 'false' memory and personal identity. *Hypatia: A Journal of Feminist Philosophy* 12, 2: 51–82.

Bowman, Cynthia Grant, and Elizabeth Mertz. 1996. A dangerous direction: Legal intervention in sexual abuse survivor therapy. *Harvard Law Review* 109, 3: 551–639.

Brown, Laura S. 1996a. On the construction of truth and falsity: Whose memory, whose history? In *The recovered memory/false memory debate*, ed. K. Pezdek and W. Banks. San Diego: Academic.

———. 1996b. Politics of memory, politics of incest: Doing therapy and politics that really matter. *Women and Therapy* 19, 1: 5–18.

Brown, Laura S., and Erica Burman. 1997. Editors' introduction. The delayed memory debate: Why feminist voices matter. Feminist responses to the 'false' memory debate. *Feminism and Psychology* 7, 1: 7–16.

Culbertson, Roberta. 1995. Embodied memory, transcendence and telling: Recounting trauma, reestablishing the self. *New Literary History* 26: 169–95.

Descartes, René. 1984. Meditations on first philosophy. In *The philosophical writings of Descartes*, vol. 2, trans. John Cottingham, Robert Shoothoof, and Dugald Murdoch. Cambridge: Cambridge University Press.

Enns, Carolyn Zerbe, Cheryl L. McNeilly, Julie Madison Corkery, and Mary S. Gilbert. 1995. The debate about delayed memories of childhood sexual abuse: A feminist perspective. *The Counselling Psychologist* 23, 2: 181–279.

Fivush, Robyn. 1996. Young children's event recall: Are memories constructed through discourse? In *The recovered memory/false memory debate*, ed. K. Pezdek and W. Banks. San Diego: Academic.

Haaken, Janice. 1996. The recovery of memory, fantasy, and desire: Feminist approaches to sexual abuse and psychic trauma. *Signs: Journal of Women in Culture and Society* 21, 4: 1069–94.

Freyd, Jennifer. 1996. *Betrayal trauma theory: The logic of forgetting abuse.* Cambridge, Mass.: Harvard University Press.

Jacobsen, Rockney. Unpublished paper. Descartes on the misdesign of the mind.

Kitzenger, Celia. 1993. Depoliticizing the personal: A feminist slogan in feminist therapy. *Women's Studies International Forum* 16: 487–96.

Kristiansen, Connie M., Susan J. Haslip, and Katharine D. Kelly. 1997. Scientific and judicial illusions of objectivity in the recovered memory debate: Feminist responses to the "false" memory debate. *Feminism and Psychology* 7, 1: 39–45.

Lindsey, D. S., and J. D.Read. 1994. Psychotherapy and memories of childhood sexual abuse: A cognitive perspective. *Applied Cognitive Psychology* 8: 281–338.

Loftus, Dr. Elizabeth, and Katherine Ketchum. 1994. *The myth of repressed memory: False memories and allegations of sexual abuse.* New York: St. Martin's.

Longino, Helen. 1994. The fate of knowledge in social theories of science. *Socializing epistemology: The social dimensions of knowledge*, ed. F. Schmitt. Lanham, MD: Rowman and Littlefield Publishers, Inc.

National Association for Consumer Protection in Mental Health Practices. 1994. A proposal to finance preparation of model legislation titled "mental health consumer protection act."

Ofshe, Richard, and Ethan Watters. 1993. Making monsters. *Society* (March/April): 4–16.

———. 1994. *Making monsters: False memories, psychotherapy, and sexual hysteria.* New York: Charles Scribner's Sons.

Park, Shelley M. 1997. False memory syndrome: A feminist philosophical perspective. *Hypatia: A Journal of Feminist Philosophy* 12, 2: 1–50.

Pezdek, Kathy, and William P. Banks. 1996. *The recovered memory/false memory debate.* San Diego: Academic.

Poole, Debra A., D. Stephen Lindsay, Amina Memon, and Ray Bull. 1995. Psychotherapy and the recovery of memories of childhood sexual abuse: U.S. and British practitioners' opinions, practices, and experiences. *Journal of Consulting and Clinical Psychology* 63: 426–37.

Pope, Kenneth S. 1996. Memory, abuse, and science: Questioning claims about the false memory syndrome epidemic. *American Psychologist* 51, 9: 957–74.

———. 1997. Science as careful questioning: Are claims of a false memory syndrome epidemic based on empirical evidence? *American Psychologist* 52, 9: 997–1006.

Scott, Sara E. 1997. Feminists and false memories: A case of postmodern amnesia. Feminist responses to the "false" memory debate. *Feminism and Psychology* 7, 1: 33–38.

Scheman, Naomi. 1996. Feeling our way towards moral objectivity. In *Mind and morals: essays on cognitive science and ethics*, ed. Larry May, Marilyn Friedman, and Andy Clark. Cambridge, Mass.: MIT.

Spanos, Nicholos P. 1986. Hypnosis and the modification of hypnotic suggestibility: a social psychological perspective. In *What is hypnosis?* ed. Peter L. N. Naish. Philadelphia: Open University Press.

Stanton, Mike. 1997. U-turn on memory lane. *Columbia Journalism Review* (July/August): 44–49.

Tavris, Carol. 1993. Beware the incest survivor machine. *New York Times Book Review* (Jan. 3).

Wakefield, Hollinda, and Ralph Underwager. 1994. *Return of the furies: An investigation into recovered memory therapy.* Chicago: Open Court.

Van Fraassen, Bas. 1980. *The scientific image.* Oxford: Clarendon.

Walton, Kendall. 1990. *Mimesis as make-believe: The foundation of the representational arts.* Cambridge: Harvard University Press.

White, Alan R. 1990. *The language of imagination.* Oxford: Basil Blackwell.

Wray, K. Brad. 1997. The role of community in inquiry: A philosophical study. Doctoral Dissertation. University of Western Ontario.

Yabko, Michael. 1994. *Suggestions of abuse: True and false memories of childhood sexual abuse.* New York: Simon and Schuster.

CHAPTER EIGHT

RELATIVISM AND FEMINIST
SCIENCE SCHOLARSHIP

LYNN HANKINSON NELSON

Whenever the enemy keeps lobbing bombs into areas you consider
unrelated to your defense, it's always worth investigating.
> —Ti-Grace Atkinson (Lloyd 1996, 217)

INTRODUCTION

Elisabeth Lloyd describes Ti-Grace Atkinson's advice, quoted above, as "political savvy" that feminist science scholars "would do well to emulate" in the context of the so-called science wars (Lloyd 1996, 217). I concur. The specific charge I investigate here—that of relativism—is a recurring theme in challenges to the rationale of feminist science scholarship, to its status as legitimate inquiry and to the integrity of those engaged in it. I construe these challenges broadly to include charges leveled by prominent philosophers Susan Haack and John Searle that feminist science scholars are "in the propaganda," rather than the "truth-seeking business" (Haack 1993, 37–38; cf. Searle 1993), and charges leveled by scientists, mathematicians, and philosophers that "science studies" in general constitute a threat to objectivity and rationality.[1]

Atkinson's advice is relevant, of course, because relativism is a charge many feminist science scholars take to be unrelated to our defense. There is good reason for this. The critiques feminist scientists have offered of specific research programs and theories are replete with appeals to counterevidence, and with arguments that specific methodologies are flawed, specific interpretations of research results are unwarranted, and so forth—hardly the kinds of argument relativists could or would offer. Similarly, feminists who have explored the implications of these critiques for general theories about science, such as those developed in the philosophy of science, rarely advocate relativism.[2] To the contrary, most are engaged in efforts to develop nonrelativist epistemologies that are able to accommodate the findings and development of feminist science scholarship.

Given that these themes are pervasive in feminist theorizing within and about science, it might seem plausible to view the charges of relativism as deliberate misrepresentations, unworthy of investigation.[3] I don't deny that some of these misrepresentations are deliberate, and that those which are, are not worth responding to. But I also believe there is a line of reasoning at work in the major lines of argument advancing this charge that feminist science scholars have not always recognized or addressed as explicitly as we could. I undertake a sustained investigation of this reasoning, not to identify ways to convince critics of feminist science scholarship that "we really aren't relativists." I am concerned, instead, with how we understand our own work and the future directions our research takes on this basis. I introduce the line of reasoning on which I will focus through an exploration of issues more obviously at stake in the debate over science studies.

COGNITIVE AUTHORITY AND SCIENCE STUDIES

Clearly, cognitive authority is at stake. The efforts to undermine science studies (if not shut them down) both support the feminist argument that science's cognitive authority is a consequential feature of our social landscape and afford an unusual opportunity to study the social, institutional, and conceptual mechanisms that sustain it (cf. Addelson 1983). To be sure, this authority is being claimed and defended less subtly in the present context than it is when there are no perceived threats to it. But these current claims are carefully constructed to link science's cognitive authority to what is assumed to be its special claim to rationality and objectivity, which is to say they make use of assumptions that sustain science's authority in quieter ways and times.

It would be ironic, for example, in a purported defense of the core values of science, rationality and democracy, and of their interrelationships, to claim that science is *outside* the realm of practices subject to critical scrutiny. It would be no less ironic to argue that approaches to studying science that one does not like should be, on *this* ground, shut down. But one can ask if anyone other than scientists does or could understand science well enough to produce analyses of scientific practice of any consequence. If one answers this question in the negative, and ignores the fact that many of those engaged in science studies—and certainly many engaged in feminist science scholarship—*are* scientists, one can ask whether the NSF or universities should fund or in other ways support science studies. So put, the argument against science studies appears to be about qualifications (cf. Lloyd 1996).

Yet reflection suggests that there must be more to this argument than is apparent, for it entails consequences its proponents do not embrace. As Lloyd notes, it would seem to follow that Norman Levitt, a professor of mathematics who maintains that biologist Anne Fausto-Sterling's claims about sex differences are "scientifically indefensible" (Gross and Levitt 1994, 125), is hardly in a position to claim more cognitive authority than she concerning research and theories in biology (Lloyd 1996, 245–46). And, in its bald form, the qualifications argument would also undermine the vigorous defenses of science "against science studies" offered by philosophers Haack and Searle.

At the same time, the qualifications argument *would* grant cognitive authority to anthropologists and sociologists of science, *qua* scientists—although some in these disciplines are among those critics of science studies want most to discredit. It is open, of course, to critics of anthropology and sociology of science to appeal to the prestige of the natural sciences over the social sciences. But explicitly acknowledging such prestige hierarchies would compromise the critic's claim that science's objectivity is secured by its inherently democratic nature. Alternatively, critics of science studies might appeal to specialization—to maintain, for example, that anthropologists are not in a position to understand or evaluate research in biology. But appeals to specialization not only undermine the defenses of science offered by nonscientists Haack, Levitt, and Searle; they suggest that research projects and theories in specific sciences are unable to be understood and assessed even by other *scientists*.

What I am suggesting is a familiar observation. There is no small amount of tension between the efforts to restrict those deemed capable of understanding science and the longstanding assumption that "the 'rationality' of science . . . lies in the fact that scientific understanding is the most open to criticism of *all* understanding" (Addelson 1983, 166).

EXPLANATORY PRINCIPLES AND RELATIVISM

There is, I suggest, a second, more subtle line of argument against science studies which functions to resolve the tensions just noted and also explains (or so I will argue) the persistent charge that feminist science scholars embrace relativism, despite substantial evidence to the contrary. This is the argument that the *explanatory principles* used by science studies scholars, including feminists, only produce and *can* only produce pseudo-explanations of science. Critics of science studies sometimes explicitly argue, but more typically simply assume or declare, that explanatory principles that invoke "social factors"—such as social processes that characterize or impact on scientific practice, and nonepistemic values—*necessarily* minimize or deny the role of evidence and epistemic standards in scientific practice. Given that evidence and epistemic standards are at the heart of scientific practice, this argument continues, explanations invoking social factors not only fail to reveal anything significant about science, but actually "block" adequate understandings of it (e.g., Wolpert 1992, 103–17; Perutz 1995, 54; Gross and Levitt 1994, 11).

As Miriam Solomon and others argue, the lack of attention to "social factors" in traditional explanations of science reflects a commitment to construing rationality in individualistic terms, and most social factors as inherently compromising of it (Solomon 1994; cf. Longino 1990 and Nelson 1990). This commitment is perhaps most obvious in claims, such as that made by philosopher Larry Laudan, that "The sociology of knowledge may step in to explain beliefs if and only if those beliefs cannot be explained in terms of their *rational* merits" (Laudan 1977, 202; emphasis added). But it is also implicit in philosophical theories that presuppose that the discernment and evaluation of evidential relations is, in principle, a solitary undertaking driven largely by logical relationships. Add to this commitment the modernist skepticism about the objectivity of values (at least "nonepistemic" values), and it is not difficult to see what motivates the critic's assumption that the kinds of social factor feminists cite in their explanations of science do not concern evidence.

As I noted earlier, I believe that the distinction critics allege between explanations that invoke social factors and explanations that invoke evidence and epistemic standards, is the lynch pin of major lines of argument that feminist science scholars embrace relativism. I think it serves as the grounds on which critics dismiss analyses of research programs and theories offered by feminist scientists, despite their credentials and appeals to evidence. I think it also explains why "traditional" philosophers of science, such as Karl Popper and Haack, who limit the kinds of social factor that impact on science to those scientists recognize (for example, peer review), are credited with "understanding science" and their feminist colleagues are not. This is a line of reasoning that I don't think we often address as explicitly or straightforwardly as we can.

One exception is an argument offered by Elisabeth Lloyd in defense of anthropology and sociology of science (Lloyd 1996). The bottom line of Lloyd's argument is that critics of these research programs fundamentally misunderstand their core research questions and goals. Invoking a view of anthropology and sociology of science she attributes to Bruno Latour, Lloyd argues that the explanations of science generated in these disciplines constitute fundamentally different kinds of explanation from those traditionally offered by scientists. As much to the point, Lloyd maintains that such explanations contribute "perfectly complementary" pieces of a "full and complete" account of science (1996, 228).

Lloyd uses an analogy to explicate the distinction she wants to draw, contrasting the explanation of a religious ritual that would be offered by a theologian with that offered by an anthropologist. The theologian's explanation would be, so to speak, an "in house" or internal explanation—one which "include[s] the theories and assumptions about the ways the world works and the way the world is" presupposed by the ritual (1996, 228). In contrast, Lloyd argues, the anthropologist is agnostic toward such theories and assumptions, and uses the methods and theories of her own discipline in framing an explanation of the ritual.

Lloyd maintains there is "an exact parallel" to the present case, in which scientists (and I would add traditional philosophers and historians of science) have a role akin to that of the theologian, and anthropologists and sociologists of science a role akin to that of the anthropologist (1996, 228). According to Lloyd, the explanation of an episode of, say, theory adoption that invokes social factors constitutes a *genuine* explanation that can and should function *alongside* the explanation invoking evidence offered by scientists. Further, Lloyd maintains, the standards to be used in evaluating explanations generated in science studies come from *within* these disciplines where research into other complex human activities reveals "the complexities of human self-understanding" (1996, 231). Against the background of this research, Lloyd argues, it is clear that "giving *unquestioned and exclusive authority* to scientists' own descriptions of their actions and motives . . . is an impoverished and silly way to understand scientific activities" (1996, 231; emphasis in original).

An obvious strength of Lloyd's argument is its appeal to the methodological assumptions, research questions, and goals of anthropology and sociology of science. Challenging these would seem to require critics of science studies to take on the rationality of entire scientific disciplines, a position in apparent conflict with the qualifications argument. In addition, the "methodological relativism" to which researchers in anthropology and sociology of science claim to subscribe bears a strong resemblance to the "disinterested stance" critics of science studies attribute to scientists and associate with "objectivity" and "(legitimate) inquiry."[4] It is open to critics to grant that methodological relativism is appropriate to cross-cultural research, but not to investigations of science. But this immediately prompts the question Why not?—and it is not clear that there is an answer to this question that does not beg it.

Should the model of science studies invoked in Lloyd's argument be extended to feminist science scholarship? I suggest not.[5] In contrast to the research on which Lloyd is focusing, attention to evidence, and to the nature and scope of the evidence drawn on by scientists, are integral aspects of the critiques feminist scientists have offered, and of the general analyses of science offered by feminist science scholars. Relatedly, most feminist scientists and science scholars intend their explanations to *critically engage* traditional explanations and explanatory principles, not function alongside them.[6]

Consider, for example, why Lloyd's analogy breaks down when we consider feminist scientists. It is true that these scientists bring hypotheses, categories, and questions to bear on science that many of their colleagues do not, and that these have emerged within feminist scholarship. In this sense, feminist scientists are like Lloyd's anthropologist: they work with and appeal to experiences and knowledge different from their colleagues. But feminist scientists are simultaneously *in house*: they draw on their expertise as scientists in their critiques of research hypotheses and methods, often appealing to research results in the same disciplines as the research and theories they criticize.

Moreover, it is not clear that, even as a defense of anthropology and sociology of science, Lloyd's argument adequately responds to a crucial premise in the critic's argument: that the division of labor she claims is only apparent. To the critic of science studies, to continue the analogy, the explanation provided by the "anthropologist" *undermines* that of the "theologian"—and, in the case of science, gets things *wrong*. This is because the critic of science studies shares Lloyd's view that explanations of science that invoke social factors are distinguishable from those that invoke evidence—but sees the former as competing, not complementary, explanations.

In any event, I suggest that feminist science scholars should not grant the distinction between kinds of explanation that critics of science studies maintain, but challenge the distinction head on. The argument that needs to be made is that the critiques feminist scientists and science scholars offer of social factors that characterize and impact on science are *simultaneously* critiques of *the bodies of evidence* available to, and drawn upon by, scientists.[7] I construe evidence broadly here, to include not only data and observation, but the broader bodies of accepted theory that also provide evidential warrant for particular hypotheses and theories.[8]

Consider, for example, the numerous cases in which androcentric assumptions have shaped research questions, categories, observations, and hypotheses. Such cases indicate that divisions in experience and cognitive authority along the lines of gender can have, and often have had, an impact on the directions and content of scientific research.[9] Unless we assume that generations of scientists deliberately ignored or skewed evidence, or that feminist scientists are for some reason more capable scientists, it is reasonable to conclude that a complex set of social arrangements limited and shaped the evidence available to earlier scientists. Or, consider the amount of research devoted to finding a biological basis for alleged sex differences in cognitive abilities, despite extensive research in the social sciences demonstrating the substantial role of social factors. Such cases suggest that differences in prestige, and/or the demands of specialization, can also have an impact on the evidence available to and considered by scientists. As a final example, consider Kathryn Pyne Addelson's investigation of the impact of divisions in cognitive authority within a scientific specialty. That "only some of the many people who work within a research specialty have epistemological authority within it," Addelson argues, raises an important question.

> [This] is not whether top scientists in most fields produce some very good work, but rather the more important question of whether other good work, even work critical of the top scientists, is not taken seriously because its proponents are not members of the same powerful networks and so cannot exercise the same cognitive authority. The question is made particularly difficult because, by disregarding or downgrading competing research, the "top scientists" cut off the resources necessary for their competition to develop really good work. In most fields, it is next to impossible to do research without free time, aid from research assistants, secretaries, craftsmen, custodians, and in many cases, access to equipment. (Addelson 1983, 178)

In each of these cases, the questions feminists raise about specific social factors impacting on or characterizing science are simultaneously questions about the bodies of evidence available to, and drawn upon by, scientists.

There are significant benefits to challenging the distinction maintained by critics of science studies and by anthropologists of science. For one thing, this approach aptly locates feminist science scholarship in relation to the charges made by its critics. Critics are correct that, as they function in feminist science scholarship, explanatory principles invoking social factors *compete* with traditional explanatory principles—but *wrong* that a concern with evidence is not an integral aspect of them (cf. Wylie 1996). This approach also makes it clear that the assumption that good science and democratic social processes are related is not the invention of critics of science studies. The examples just cited indicate that the assumption that such relationships obtain has motivated, and continues to motivate, feminist theorizing about science. The difference is, of course, that feminists do not assume that recognizing such relationships entails that science is *now* as democratic as it might be, or that the research and theories generated to date are the *best* that they might have been.

Finally, consider how the distinction alleged between explanations that invoke "social factors" and those that invoke evidence underwrites a line of argument specifically aimed at discrediting feminist science scholarship: that it cannot constitute (legitimate) inquiry because it is politically motivated. Definitions carry the weight of most such arguments. Susan Haack begins by defining inquiry as "aim[ing] at the truth," defines feminists as those who would "politicize" inquiry, and concludes that feminists *cannot* be in "the truth-seeking business" (Haack 1993, 37–38). Clifford Geertz worries that "the autonomy of science, its freedom, vigor, authority, and effectiveness will be undermined by the subjection of it to a moral and political program—the social empowerment of women—external to its purposes" (quoted in Lloyd 1996, 217). Norman Levitt and Paul Gross dismiss Anne Fausto-Sterling's painstaking analyses of research and theories in the biological sciences in *Myths of Gender* as "polemical," and apparently feel no obligation to engage her analysis once it is so categorized (Gross and Levitt 1994, 125). And John Searle proclaims that feminist scholars cannot meet the ideal of the inquirer because this inquirer *just is* "disinterested" (Searle 1993). Not one of these conclusions is based on *evidence*—on an analysis of specific critiques feminists have offered, evidence they have appealed to, alternative models they have advocated, and so on (cf. Lloyd 1996). Each presupposes that a concern with social and political processes is necessarily distinct from, and undermining of, a concern with evidence and epistemic standards.

Note how effectively this specific line of argument resolves a problem in the qualifications argument earlier noted. Given traditional prestige hierarchies, Ruth Bleier, Anne Fausto-Sterling, and Evelyn Fox Keller have far better credentials in terms of understanding and evaluating research in biology than do their critics in mathematics, philosophy, and sociology. Moreover, their critiques often focus on the very sciences in which they are trained, have published research, and so on. But if their critiques are not scientific by definition, they are safely ignored.

FEMINIST SCIENCE SCHOLARSHIP AND FEMINIST VALUES

I have suggested that a distinction between explanations of scientific practice that invoke social factors, and explanations that invoke evidence and epistemic standards, underlies charges that feminist science scholars embrace relativism.[10] In this section, I express concern about the growing consensus among feminist science scholars that what distinguishes our practice, as scientists and as science scholars, is "feminist values." To anticipate, I am concerned that the ways in which feminist values are described (or not described) can obscure the significant insight that there are relationships between the empirical adequacy of hypotheses and theories generated in science, and social processes that characterize and impact on it.

Some qualifications are in order. The first is that I offer the arguments of this section somewhat tentatively. Although I don't think the fact/value distinction is tenable, I have yet to find a way to talk about values and evidence that doesn't seem to presuppose echoes of it. In addition, the analyses that I suggest "overemphasize" the political nature of the values that motivate and inform feminist science scholarship occur in work in which a concern with evidence is central. My suggestion is that the emphasis on feminist political values can overshadow, mute, or disguise feminists' concern with evidence and empirical adequacy. If my arguments miss subtleties that others find significant, perhaps they can be interpreted as suggesting the need for further clarification in analyses of the relationships between feminist science scholarship and "feminist values."

The first example I will cite comes from my own work. In the introduction to a book published in 1990, I offered a description of the science that feminist science scholarship suggested we should work to bring about. Although the book as a whole constituted a sustained argument for feminist empiricism and emphasized the role of evidence in feminist science critiques, there was no reference to evidence in my descriptions of the practice of feminist scientists and the future science I took these to foreshadow.

> Unlike the science community's present conception of science, [the science that feminist scholarship suggests that we should bring about] will incorporate values. Unlike much of the present practice of science in which values *are* incorporated and we simply deny that they are, the incorporation and infusion of values will be self-conscious and subject to critical scrutiny. . . . [Thus, the science we should work to bring about] is foreshadowed in what feminist science critics and scientists are currently doing. (Nelson 1990, 5)

What are the "values" referred to here? What is the content of the claim that values are "incorporated" in science? And what role, if any, does evidence have in science—in the practice of feminist scientists and more generally?

Today I would say that nonepistemic values can do more than motivate research questions and methods (something the critic of feminist science scholarship need not deny). Nonepistemic values can be *integrated* in research questions, methods, and theories that, with the obvious exception of value-neutrality, meet discipline-specific and general standards for "good science."

184   LYNN HANKINSON NELSON

Consider, for example, Fausto-Sterling's analysis of the commitment to sexual dimorphism informing research questions, methods, observations, and hypotheses in a number of specialties in biology. Her analysis suggests that the assumption that there are two, and only two, sexes is not a "value-free fact." It is, of course, tied to the definitions of males as sperm-producing organisms and of females as egg-producing organisms, tied as well to the centrality of reproduction to biological theory. But it does bifurcate organisms that actually lie on what is a continuum in terms of physiological, chromosomal, and hormonal traits. This bifurcation in turn entails the classification of hermaphrodites and two types of pseudo-hermaphrodites as "intersexed" (rather than distinct sexes) and permits their development to be classified as "abnormalities" (Fausto-Sterling 1993). Moreover, Fausto-Sterling argues, the assumption of sexual dimorphism in the biological and medical sciences not only reflects deep-seated cultural interests, but also reinforces them. There is enormous pressure on parents of intersexed individuals to engage in medical procedures to "correct" the perceived abnormalities.

Less subtle examples of how nonepistemic values have been integrated in scientific categories, methods, and assumptions concern the attribution of gender (complete with social connotations) on other species and objects that are not sexed. Feminist scientists have shown that associations of male with "activity" and "presence," and of females with "passivity" and "absence," have been imposed on laboratory animals, explanations of fetal development, androgens and estrogen—even the nucleus and cytoplasm of cells, and bacteria (Fausto-Sterling 1985; L. H. Nelson 1996; and Spanier 1995).

I will later argue that the critiques feminist scientists have offered of the assumptions just outlined are not aptly characterized as simply aimed at replacing one set of political values with another. They are demonstrably concerned with the empirical adequacy of models and theories in which such assumptions are integrated. But it is by now probably clear that this was not at all obvious in the passage I have quoted.

Perhaps the most important source of the current emphasis on feminist values in the practice of feminist scientists are several articles by Helen E. Longino, which consider the questions "What does it mean to do science as a feminist?" and "Are the cognitive or theoretical virtues that guide scientific practice [for example, simplicity] purely cognitive?" (Longino 1989; 1994; 1996). One significant contribution of Longino's work is that it has focused attention on the practice of feminist scientists, on what it means "to do science as a feminist," rather than on the "content" of "feminist science." In the article on which I will focus, "In Search of Feminist Epistemology," Longino posed the question, "What does it mean to do science as a feminist?" She answered it by identifying a list of values that she found to guide the practices of feminist scientists—that is, to guide their assessments of specific hypotheses and theories, and linked to feminist political commitments and goals (Longino 1994).[11]

The most traditional of these values is empirical adequacy, which Longino defines as "agreement of the observational claims of a theory or model with observational and experimental data, present, retrospective, or predictive" (Longino 1994, 476). Additional values "come into play" in the assessment of theories, hypotheses, and models, Longino argues, because "empirical adequacy is an insufficient criterion of theory and hypothesis choice" (1994, 477). Those Longino identified as guiding the practice of feminist scientists are ontological heterogeneity, complexity of relationships, diffusion of power, applicability to current human needs, and novelty (1994, 477–79).

I focus on two of these values. "Ontological heterogeneity," according to Longino, "permits equal standing for different types, and mandates investigation of such difference" (1994, 477). "Complexity of relationships" Longino describes as "taking complex interaction as a fundamental principle of explanation," and valuing models in which "no factor can be described as dominant or controlling and that describe processes in which all active factors influence the others" (1994, 478). In response to the question, "What is specifically feminist or gendered about these standards?" Longino maintained that "one of the effects they all have in one way or another is to prevent gender from being disappeared." Each makes gender "a relevant axis of investigation" and this feature gives each "its status as feminist" (1994, 481). Longino describes "the non-disappearance of gender" as "a bottom line requirement of feminist knowers," its intent "to reveal or prevent the disappearing of the experience and activities of women and/or to prevent the disappearing of gender" (1994, 481).

In this article, Longino explored the relationships between these standards and feminist political values. She explicated how they reflect "the rejection of theories of inferiority" (1994, 477), function to "make visible the role of gender in the social structure of social institutions" (1994, 478), and, in these ways, reflect the requirement that "gender not be disappeared." Longino also distinguished these values from "empirical adequacy"—for, as I earlier noted, she maintains that, like the traditional values of simplicity and generality of scope, these values come into play because empirical adequacy is not itself sufficient to guide the choice of research programs and theories (1994, 474, 482).

Longino's identification of these commitments in the practice of feminist scientists, and her initial definitions of them, seem both insightful and correct. I also agree that "ontological heterogeneity," "complexity of relationships," and "the non-disappearance of gender" have what Longino later refers to as "political valence" for feminist scientists and science scholars (Longino 1996). But I submit that this political valence does not *exhaust* their rationale or force for the scientists who subscribe to them. As they function in the critiques

Longino cites, all three values function as *epistemic* values, the rationale of which lies in the value feminist scientists attribute to empirical adequacy, explanatory power, and generality of scope.[12]

Consider, for example, the critiques of linear, hierarchical models of gene action offered by Ruth Bleier, Ruth Hubbard, and Evelyn Fox Keller that reflect a commitment to the value Longino calls "complexity of relationships." Although these critiques are concerned with the political implications of linear, hierarchical models of biological processes, they are simultaneously concerned with the empirical adequacy of models of gene action and of theories that incorporate these models. Bleier, Hubbard, and Keller argued that unidirectional models of gene action—models that posit discrete effects of discrete genes in, say, cellular protein synthesis—*oversimplify*, and hence *distort or obscure*, complex biological processes. On this basis, each called for models characterized by what Longino calls "complexity."[13]

> Not only can a complex behavior pattern or a characteristic not be linked to a gene or a gene cluster, there is not even any single cause and effect relationship between a particular gene and a particular anatomical feature. ... Any gene's action or expression is affected, first of all, by its interactions with many other genes ... [and] occurs only within an environmental milieu and [is] affected by it. (Bleier 1984, 43)

> Genes (DNA) impart specificity, but so do other molecules (e.g., RNA, proteins, and even carbohydrates and lipids), and so do many *processes* that occur within organisms and in the interactions in which organisms engage with their environments. (Hubbard 1982, 65; emphasis in original)

Similarly, Keller's argument that "order" should replace science's traditional emphasis on "lawlike" relationships, while obviously related to feminist concerns with dominance and hierarchies, is made within the context of a sustained argument that the search for linear, hierarchical relationships focuses attention on *a subset* of natural relations and precludes attention to others. Her argument, like those of feminists critical of the emphasis on dominance hierarchies in research in primatology, appeals to the norms of empirical adequacy and generality of scope:

> The concept of order, wider than law and free from its coercive, hierarchical, and centralizing implications, has the potential to expand our conception of science. Order is a category comprising patterns of organization that can be spontaneous, self-generated, *or* externally imposed; it is a larger category than law precisely to the extent that law implies exter-

nal constraint. Conversely, the kinds of order generated or generable by law comprise only a subset of a larger category of observable or apprehensible regularities, rhythms, and patterns. (Keller 1985, 131–32; cf. Keller 1983)

There are parallels with the ways in which "ontological heterogeneity" and "the non-disappearance of gender" function in the practice of feminist scientists.[14] Consider, for example, the case made by feminist biologists against hypotheses positing an organizing function for prenatal testosterone in the development of male fetal brains, and the further hypothesis that this explains sex differences in cognitive abilities (e.g., Bleier 1994; Fausto-Sterling 1985; and Hubbard 1982). This case is not exhausted by the political implications of these hypotheses, or of theories of female inferiority more generally. The *full* case involves critiques that appeal to empirical adequacy, explanatory power, and generality of scope. It includes critiques of the lumping together of such disparate behavior as rat maze-negotiating behavior and mathematical problem solving; criticism of the assumption that gender is a sufficient variable in research devoted to establishing human sex differences; criticism of the emphasis on male hormones, and arguments that conclusions cannot be drawn from studies apparently establishing their effects until a similar amount of research is devoted to the effects of estrogen; critiques of the labeling of androgens and estrogens, and lines of fetal development, as "male" and "female," in turn based on the complexity of the relevant biological entities and processes; critiques of the assumption that the "female" line of development is "the default" line and of the relative lack of attention to its mechanisms; and experimental results that indicate complex interactions between cells, and between cells and the maternal and external environments, during every stage of fetal development.

The reasoning is that, were the criterion of heterogeneity at work, the assumption consistently made of strong analogies between rat brains and human brains, and between rat and human behavior, might have been recognized as in need of substantive articulation as well as substantial qualification. Were the "non-disappearance of gender" criterion at work, presumably less androcentric research hypotheses and investigations—and, hence, hypotheses that enjoyed more empirical adequacy, explanatory power, and generality of scope—would have resulted. In these cases, and they are representative, the argument is that more heterogeneity, and attention to the role of gender in shaping research questions, would have resulted in *better* research questions and experiments, where "better" has *epistemic* content.

Seen this way, the values Longino identified in 1994 as guiding the practice of feminist scientists are not illegitimately imposed *on* science. They are taken to be, and given their relationship to empirical adequacy, generality of scope, and explanatory power, appropriately taken to be, *epistemic values:* criteria of good *science* (cf. Lloyd 1996; Nelson and Nelson 1994; and Wylie 1995 and 1996).

In subsequent articles, Longino has gone on to question the traditional distinction between "epistemic" and "nonepistemic" values, analyzing ways in which contextual values (submerged or explicit) can be a factor in the weighing of and judgments of adherence to values assumed to be simply epistemic (see, e.g., Longino 1996).[15] One premise underlying Longino's argument is the view, articulated by Kuhn two decades ago, that the epistemic virtues traditionally attributed to knowledge claims are heterogeneous and (usually) incapable of being satisfied simultaneously. Kuhn argued that, although "accuracy, consistency, scope, simplicity, and fruitfulness . . . are all standard criteria for evaluating the adequacy of a theory,

> two sorts of difficulties are regularly encountered by men [sic] who must use these criteria in choosing [between theories]. . . . Individually, the criteria are imprecise: Individuals may legitimately differ about their application to concrete cases. In addition, when deployed together, they repeatedly prove to conflict with one another; accuracy may, for example, dictate the choice of one theory, scope the choice of its competitor. (Kuhn 1977, 31)

Thus, Kuhn maintained, there are inevitable trade-offs between the various epistemic values. To Kuhn's arguments, Longino adds the significant insight that contextual (i.e., nonepistemic) values can play a role in these trade-offs and judgments (Longino 1996). If this is the case, can the traditional distinction between "epistemic" and "nonepistemic" values continue to be maintained? I suggest that it can and should be.

Consider, again, the critiques leveled by feminist biologists of the accounts of embryonic sexual differentiation offered in the 1970s and early 1980s. Building on Longino's arguments, Alison Wylie and I recently argued that the critiques offered by Ruth Bleier and Anne Fausto-Sterling illuminated trade-offs between simplicity and generality of scope in *one* sense (applicability to males in a variety of mammalian species)—and empirical adequacy and generality of scope in *another* sense (citing the lack of explanation of female sexual differentiation, and of the role of hormones and entities, e.g., the fetal ovary, designated "female"). We also argued that these critiques demonstrated that androcentrism contributed to the privileging of simplicity and generality of scope in terms of applicability to males, and we credited feminist contextual values with leading to the recognition of these trade-offs and the costs in terms of empirical adequacy. But, as the foregoing makes clear, our argument that research questions informed by feminist contextual values represented *advances*, appealed to the *epistemic* standards of empirical adequacy and generality of scope (Nelson and Wylie 1998).

CONCLUSION

The empirical hypothesis that guides feminist science scholarship is that gender and other social relations have had implications for the directions of scientific research and the content of scientific theories, a hypothesis for which there is now an abundance of evidence. I am suggesting that we reemphasize it. The goal of science is, after all, empirically adequate theories, not enlightened social policy.[16] But one of the more significant implications of feminist science scholarship is that there are *relationships* between these things—that Geertz is wrong that "the social empowerment of women" is *external* to science's purposes. Identifying the relationships between empirically adequate theories, and social policies and processes, requires that we can still make sense of each category.

Moreover, important empirical questions emerge when we emphasize the relationships between social factors and evidence.[17] These include general questions concerning whether the social processes that now characterize science— for example, those involving the recruitment and education of scientists, peer review mechanisms, and differences in prestige that separate specialties and sciences—do or do not contribute to the development of empirically adequate theories. Do current mechanisms for peer review insure that the most promising research is published and/or funded, or are they such that very good research, if it challenges entrenched models or powerful networks, will not receive funding? That science has achieved substantial empirical success does not entail that the theories and research programs it has generated are the best that might be generated.

As we turn to individual cases, our questions about the social processes that characterize science can be expected to take on more specific content. For example, the analyses feminist scientists have undertaken of various research programs in the biological sciences suggest that we need to explore whether the processes that characterize science education and recruitment, or the current makeup of science communities, are likely to foster awareness among scientists of the social values and beliefs integrated in the research questions and theories they inherit. Does science education as currently organized make it reasonable to expect scientists to be in a position to assess the impact of their highly-specialized endeavors on the broader social community, and vice versa? How does specialization impact on the directions of research? Does it contribute to cases in which a substantial body of research in the social sciences relevant to the existence and explanation of sex difference is not considered by scientists exploring a biological basis for these?

I want to be clear here. I have argued that these questions concerning social processes are simultaneously questions about the bodies of evidence available to and drawn upon by scientists, and demonstrably concern the empirical adequacy of hypotheses and theories that rely on them. At the same time, there are important *political* reasons to emphasize the epistemic values that motivate and inform feminist science scholarship. As Alison Wylie argues,

> An acute sense of determining "how things are" with as much empirical accuracy and explanatory power as they can muster is characteristic of feminists' work in and about the sciences. This is crucial not only in achieving the internally defined goals of empirical research, but also in choosing effective courses of action under conditions that are frequently hostile to women and to feminists. (Nelson and Wylie 1998)

NOTES

Earlier versions of this chapter were presented at the enGendering Rationality Conference at the University of Oregon and at a meeting of the Eastern division of the Society for Women in Philosophy. I am grateful to members of these audiences, and to Sandra Morgen and Nancy Tuana, for helpful suggestions and constructive criticism.

1. I am speaking, of course, of books such as Gerald Holton's *Science and Anti-Science*, Paul Gross and Norman Levitt's *Higher Superstition*, and Lewis Wolpert's *The Unnatural Nature of Science*, as well as the three-day conference "Flight from Reason and Objectivity," held in June 1995 and funded by the New York Academy of Sciences. In terms of this conference, see Gross and Levitt 1996; *The New York Times*, June 6, 1995; and *Nature* 375, June 8, 1995.

2. See, e.g., Alcoff and Potter 1993; Bleier 1984; Fausto-Sterling 1985; Keller 1985; Keller and Longino 1996; Lloyd 1996; Nelson and Nelson 1996; Potter 1995; *Synthese* 104 (3); Tuana 1995; and Wylie 1996 and 1998.

3. Indeed, this was the reaction of some subscribers to the "Feminism and Science" listserve to the "Flight from Reason and Objectivity" conference organized by Gross and Levitt in 1995.

4. I add that anthropologists and sociologists of science "claim" to begin from a position of methodological relativism because I am not convinced such a position is possible.

5. Nor do I think Lloyd takes this argument to be applicable to feminist science scholarship. The arguments she offers in defense of the latter are more in keeping with those I advance below.

6. Put another way, these scientists and science scholars not only don't claim "methodological relativism" as their starting position, their analyses are simply incompatible with it.

7. I have offered sustained arguments for the claims made in this and the preceding paragraph in L. H. Nelson 1996. See, also, the articles included in a special issue of *Synthese* devoted to feminism and science [*Synthese* 104 (3), 1995].

8. I explicate and defend this holistic view of evidential warrant in L. H. Nelson 1996.

9. Contrary to critics' claims (e.g., those offered in Haack 1993), recognizing such relationships is not the same as claiming that women and men, *qua* females and males, differ in how they do science. The relationships feminists propose are more subtle and defensible. See, e.g., works cited in n. 2, this chapter.

10. There are exceptions. See, especially, Lloyd 1996; Tuana 1995; and Wylie 1996.

11. In response to the second question, Longino 1996 uses the juxtaposition of the values she identifies in the practice of feminist scientists with traditional epistemic values (for example, simplicity) to argue that the latter are also not "purely" cognitive but carry "political valence." Longino builds on this argument to challenge the distinction between epistemic and nonepistemic values that I argue below needs to be maintained.

12. The next several pages closely parallel arguments offered in Nelson and Nelson 1994.

13. See, also, Keller 1983, 170–85.

14. See, also, Nelson and Nelson 1994.

15. Longino uses the terms "cognitive" and "non-cognitive."

16. But see Longino 1996 and Jack Nelson 1996 for arguments (albeit, different arguments) that raise questions about privileging empirical adequacy as the goal of science over other needs of the broader social communities within which science is practiced.

17. The next paragraphs closely parallel Nelson 1996, 112–13.

References

Addelson, Kathryn Pyne. 1983. The man of professional wisdom. In *Discovering reality*, ed. Sandra Harding and Merrill Hintikka. Dordrecht: Kluwer.

Alcoff, Linda Martín, and Elizabeth Potter, eds. 1993. *Feminist epistemologies.* New York and London: Routledge.

Bleier, Ruth. 1984. *Science and gender: A critique of biology and its theories on women.* New York: Pergamon.

Fausto-Sterling, Anne. 1985. *Myths of gender: Biological theories about women and men.* New York: Basic.

Gross, Paul, and Norman Levitt. 1994. *Higher superstition: The academic left and its quarrels with science.* Baltimore: Johns Hopkins University Press.

———, eds. 1996. The flight from reason and science. *Annals of the New York Academy of Sciences* 775.

Haack, Susan. 1993. Epistemological reflections of an old feminist. *Reason Papers* 18: 31–44.

Holton, Gerald. 1993. *Science and anti-science*. Cambridge, Mass.: Harvard University Press.

Hubbard, Ruth. 1982. Have only men evolved? In *Biological woman: The convenient myth*, ed. Ruth Hubbard et al. Cambridge, Mass.: Schenkman.

Keller, Evelyn Fox. 1983. *A feeling for the organism*. New York: W. H. Freeman.

———. 1985. *Reflections on gender and science*. New Haven, Conn.: Yale University Press.

Kuhn, Thomas. 1977. *The essential tension: Selected studies in scientific tradition and change*. Chicago: University of Chicago Press.

Longino, Helen E. 1989. Can there be a feminist science? In *Women, knowledge and reality*, ed. Ann Garry and M. Pearsall. Boston: Allen Hyman.

———. 1990. *Science as social knowledge*. Princeton, N.J.: Princeton University Press.

———. 1994. In search of feminist epistemology. *Monist* 77, 4: 472–85.

———. 1996. Cognitive and non-cognitive values in science: Rethinking the dichotomy. In *Feminism, science, and the philosophy of science*, ed. Lynn Hankinson Nelson and Jack Nelson. Dordrecht; Boston: Kluwer.

Lloyd, Elisabeth. 1996. Science and anti-science: Objectivity and its real enemies. In *Feminism, science, and the philosophy of science*, ed. Lynn Hankinson Nelson and Jack Nelson. Dordrecht; Boston: Kluwer.

Nelson, Jack. 1996. The last dogma of empiricism? In *Feminism, science, and the philosophy of science*, ed. Lynn Hankinson Nelson and Jack Nelson. Dordrecht; Boston: Kluwer.

Nelson, Lynn Hankinson. 1990. *Who knows: From Quine to a feminist empiricism*. Philadelphia: Temple University Press.

———. 1996. Empiricism without dogmas. In *Feminism, science, and the philosophy of science*, ed. Lynn Hankinson Nelson and Jack Nelson. Dordrecht; Boston: Kluwer.

Nelson, Lynn Hankinson, and Jack Nelson. 1995. Feminist values and cognitive virtues. *Proceedings of the Philosophy of Science Association*, 2: 120–33.

———, and Jack Nelson, eds. 1996. *Feminism, science, and the philosophy of science*. Dordrecht; Boston: Kluwer.

Nelson, Lynn Hankinson, and Alison Wylie. 1998. Coming to terms with the value(s) of science: Insights from feminist science scholarship. Presented at the Workshop "Values in Scientific Research," University of Pittsburgh, October 1998.

Perutz, M. F. 1995. The pioneer defended. Review of G. L. Geison, *The private science of Louis Pasteur*. In *New York Review of Books* 42, 20.

Potter, Elizabeth. 1995. Good science and good philosophy of science. *Synthese* 104, 3: 423–39.

Searle, John. 1993. Rationality and realism: What is at stake? *Daedalus* 122, 4: 55–84.

Spanier, Bonnie B. 1995. *Im/partial science: Gender ideology in molecular biology.* Bloomington and Indianapolis: Indiana University Press.

Solomon, Miriam. 1994. Social empiricism. *Nous* 28: 325–43.

Tuana, Nancy. 1995. The values of science: Empiricism from a feminist perspective. *Synthese* 104, 3: 441–61.

Wolpert, Lewis. 1992. *The unnatural nature of science: Why science does not make (common) sense.* Cambridge, Mass.: Harvard University Press.

Wylie, Alison. 1995. Doing philosophy as a feminist: Longino on the search for a feminist epistemology. *Philosophical Topics* 23, 2: 345–58.

———. 1996. The constitution of archeological evidence: Gender politics and science. In *The disunity of science: Boundaries, contexts, and power,* ed. Peter Galison and David J. Stump. Stanford: Stanford University Press.

CHAPTER NINE

THE BIAS PARADOX
IN FEMINIST EPISTEMOLOGY

RICHMOND CAMPBELL

———————————

A central issue in feminist epistemology is how to understand *bias*. Louise Antony has called attention to a paradox that lies at the heart of this issue (Antony 1993). Feminist critics of traditional approaches to epistemology generally believe that the ideal of impartiality for intellectual inquiry is flawed because in many contexts its application gives gender-biased results. Feminist standpoint theorists, for example, argue that the ideal of value-neutrality or freedom from any partiality serves to suppress nonstandard values and interests while leaving the dominant, largely invisible biases in place (Harding 1995). Since gender bias tends to be a pervasive force in our culture, the ideal of impartiality thus has the effect of reinforcing rather than eliminating it. The problem is that this criticism appears to imply that the ideal of impartiality should be rejected because it is itself not *impartial*. Paradoxically, the criticism of impartiality appears to reject and at the same time to accept the same ideal.

Can this contradiction be avoided? We need to explain what is flawed about the ideal of impartiality but in a manner that does not presuppose the same ideal. One way we might achieve this aim is to distinguish somehow between good biases and bad biases, counting gender bias as an example of bad bias. We might then argue that the ideal of impartiality is doubly flawed. First, it is flawed because the ideal is impossible to achieve; partiality of some form or other is inevitable in any intellectual inquiry. But, second and more importantly, attempts to apply the impartiality ideal can filter out some valuable or good biases as well as some bad ones, like bias against women. Notice that impartiality is not presupposed as the basic value behind the criticism. We thus avoid the contradictory position of both endorsing and rejecting the same ideal. The ideal we endorse is the elimination of bad biases; the ideal we reject is the elimination of all bias.

This solution is the one Antony proposes, but she recognizes that it is viable only if we can make the distinction between good and bad biases in a way that isn't arbitrary and question-begging. Feminist epistemologists cannot reasonably say, for example, that gender bias in science is objectionable just on the ground that it conflicts with their biases. Some way needs to be found to distinguish good biases from bad that doesn't simply assume that the biases of feminist epistemologists are good ones. We might be tempted even to say that what is needed is some "impartial" basis for the distinction, except that this path returns us immediately to the original paradox. We need a way to give the distinction a nonarbitrary basis without invoking the ideal of impartiality.

Antony's own suggestion is that good biases are good because unlike bad biases they are conducive to the truth (Antony 1993, 215). On this view there is nothing intrinsic to biases as such that makes them good or bad. We cannot, therefore, discover what makes them so by a priori reflection; we must investigate empirically how they operate in the contexts of actual inquiry to determine whether or not certain ones promote true conclusions in their specific contexts. Antony defends this suggestion as part of a naturalized epistemology in which our capacity for knowledge and even the norms that guide the search for knowledge must be evaluated on the basis of empirical investigation.

> We know that human knowledge requires biases; we also know that we have no possibility of getting *a priori* guarantees that our biases incline us in the right direction. What all this means is that the "biasedness" of biases drops out as a parameter of epistemic evaluation. There's only one thing to do, and it's the course always counseled by a naturalized approach: *We must treat the goodness or badness of particular biases as an empirical question.* (1993, 215)

Though I find this conclusion plausible, its viability depends heavily on the plausibility of naturalized epistemology. Is the latter an acceptable approach to theory of knowledge in light of feminist concerns about the practice of science? Elsewhere I have defended a positive answer (Campbell 1998), but here I want to resolve some problems for Antony's distinction between good and bad biases without invoking the (admittedly) controversial general epistemology that she and I find so attractive.

Her proposed solution faces, first of all, the following *Problem of Circularity*. How do we explain how to access the truth in order to discover good biases? We are supposed to do it empirically, but how? It appears that Antony would have to say that access to the truth depends on having the *right* biases, but then isn't her suggestion viciously circular and as puzzling as the original paradox? If her appeal to truth to explain how to distinguish good biases from bad presupposes that we already know how to distinguish them, we are no further ahead in understanding the distinction or in resolving the paradox along the lines just sketched. If, on the other hand, her solution implies that access to the truth does *not* depend on having the right biases, then it would appear to be based (covertly) on the ideal of impartiality, which she rejects, and thus to be only a more complex version of the bias paradox.

A second problem is to explain how good biases are relevant to good evidence. Call this the *Problem of Relevance*. Suppose that biases that favor a hypothesis run counter to the weight of evidence. Is it possible that those biases might still be good even though they are unsupported by the evidence? If biases can be good even if they do not accord with the weight of evidence, it seems that it can be irrational to follow good biases. Moreover, if we accept Antony's solution, we have the further paradox that believing according to the weight of evidence in such cases is *not* conducive to believing the truth. If, on the other hand, biases are good only when they have evidential support, it appears that they have no independent epistemic role to play. Even worse, insofar as belief based on the weight of evidence goes hand in hand with belief based on an impartial consideration of evidence, we appear to be led back once more to the original paradox.

Should we therefore reject Antony's suggestion that good biases are conducive to the truth? Despite these problems of circularity and relevance, I find Antony's proposal promising, though much more needs to be said before we can be said to have resolved the paradox. In particular, we need to find a way to overcome the problems of circularity and relevance. To this end, I begin by distinguishing two concepts of objectivity (making explicit a distinction that Antony clearly implies). I then apply the distinction to a familiar example of gender bias found in science to show how to meet the problem of circularity. Next I construct a conception of objective justification to show how to dissolve the dilemma posed by the problem of relevance. I contend that we can avoid the charges of circularity and irrelevance by relying on a realist understanding of truth and objective justification and still avoid the trap of supposing that one can learn the truth and gather evidential support independently of any kind of bias. Finally, I address four deep-seated feminist worries about coping with the bias paradox by appeal to a realist understanding of truth and objective justification. They are: (1) that a realist interpretation of evidential support rests ultimately on the impartiality ideal and hence is apt to mask gender bias when it is the norm; (2) that the epistemic ideal of reflexivity, implicit, for example, in

Sandra Harding's concept of strong objectivity, is incompatible with realist objectivity; (3) that this objectivity presupposes that there is an all-encompassing, single truth about reality rather than multiple, equally accurate or true perspectives; and (4) that a realist perspective undermines the feminist component of feminist epistemology, rendering such epistemology incoherent.

Two Concepts of Objectivity

Compare two fundamentally different ways of thinking about objectivity in the context of scientific inquiry. In one interpretation, to be objective in inquiry is to be uninfluenced by any concerns or values beyond those of reaching true conclusions and perhaps following the canons of good scientific practice. I shall call this the concept of *value-free objectivity*.[1] In the post–Kuhnian era the applicability of this concept is no longer taken for granted. Still, this is the concept that people commonly associate with the idea of objective inquiry. Indeed, when people assert that it is *not* possible to be truly objective, what they usually mean is that it isn't possible to avoid being influenced by some concerns beyond reaching true conclusions or following good scientific practice. They mean, in other words, that value-free objectivity isn't possible.

In another, less common interpretation, to be objective is just to pursue an inquiry in a way that is conducive to finding out the truth about the subject of the inquiry. Here what is true is to be understood as being true regardless of how the truth is pursued or who pursues it or whether it is ever discovered. It is this *realist* reading of "true" that defines the sense in which inquiry conducive to learning the truth is supposed to be objective. The inquiry is objective, not because of its intrinsic character, but because it is likely to lead to a conclusion that is true in this realist sense of the term. I shall call this second concept *truth–conducive objectivity*.

Obviously the two concepts are closely related. One might suppose that the best method for reaching true conclusions in the realist sense is to pursue an inquiry that is neutral with respect to values other than truth and good scientific practice. The two concepts are, nonetheless, logically distinct. It is at least possible (and, as I shall argue, often the case) that an inquiry that is truth-conducive is not value-free. In fact, it can happen—as in examples that give rise to the bias paradox—that inquiry aiming at value-free objectivity fails for that reason to be objective in the sense of being conducive to truth. Before it is possible to explain in any detail why this happens, however, we need to be clearer about the basic distinction.

It will be helpful to anchor the distinction by applying it to a real case.[2] Consider the often cited example of gender-biased studies in coronary heart disease. Although this disease is the single most frequent cause of death among women, just as it is among men, the main studies until very recently have been done exclusively on men. One such study, known as Mr. Fit, tracked 12,866 high-risk men between the ages of 35 and 57. Another was a controlled study of 22,071 male physicians to determine whether low-dose aspirin reduces the risk of myocardial infarction. When studies were eventually done on women, researchers found that men and women manifest the disease differently. For example, the first manifestation of the disease in women is usually angina pectoris (chest pain due to reduced coronary blood supply); whereas, in men the most common initial manifestation is myocardial infarction (a death of some of the muscular tissue of the heart due to blockage of blood supply). Indeed, myocardial infarction is rare in women under age 65. On the other hand, since the rate of coronary heart disease increases gradually in postmenopausal women until the rate of myocardial infarction is the same as for men and since more women than men are over the age of 65, more women than men have coronary heart disease in this age group. These and other facts about how the disease differs in men and women are now widely accepted, yet for a long time they were not known, and consequently the research on coronary heart disease was not conducive to learning facts about it that are important to women's health. The exclusively male studies, for example, had no means of testing the effects of estrogen in women. In such respects the research was not conducive to learning how women ought to be treated differently from men and was thus biased against women.

Notice how the two concepts of objective inquiry would apply in this context. We can say that the inquiry into coronary heart disease was not objective in the respects cited, since the inquiry was not conducive to revealing facts about the disease especially relevant to women's health. It failed to be objective in the truth-conducive sense, and in this sense the inquiry showed an unacceptable *bias*. It would be a mistake, however, to infer that researchers who conducted the massive studies of males were deliberately trying to avoid learning facts relevant to women's coronary health. It is entirely possible (and, short of detailed historical analysis, we may charitably assume) that the researchers were aiming at the truth about coronary heart disease and trying to avoid being influenced by factors they would identify as bias. They could have been trying, that is, to conduct an inquiry that is objective in the other sense of being value-free. Moreover, insofar as they regarded study of males as representative for humans generally and would have seen a woman-centered study as biased, it is possible that the studies failed to be conducive to revealing the truths in question, in some part, because they were based on the false ideal of impartiality.

The relevance of the example to the bias paradox should now be plain. We asked how it is possible to criticize the ideal of impartiality without presupposing it. If one claims that the earlier studies failed to be designed to reveal information especially relevant to women's health because the studies were based on this untenable ideal, one invokes the ideal of truth-conducive objectivity and *not* that of value-free objectivity (the ideal of impartiality). Since the two concepts are manifestly distinct, to invoke one in criticism of the other occasions no contradiction. It is possible to go even further and suppose without contradiction that it was an interest in, or, as we might also say, a "bias" toward, learning about women's health that led to a more objective inquiry regarding it. The right bias in this case makes the inquiry in one important sense more objective.

TRUTH AND CIRCULARITY

Although Antony does not explicitly consider a conception of objectivity as truth-conducive, she explicitly rejects the conception of objectivity "as neutrality" and proposes instead to distinguish good biases from bad on the basis of whether they are conducive to discovering the truth, interpreted realistically. Since this move is tantamount to making the distinction that I am advocating, the above result is, I believe, Antony's solution, applied to an actual case and restated with the distinction made explicit. Have we now succeeded in resolving the dilemma regarding circularity raised earlier? In particular, does the concept of truth-conducive objectivity explain the difference between good and bad biases without presupposing that we already understand the difference? We can answer these questions in the affirmative, I will now argue, provided that we bear in mind the *realist* interpretation of truth that is built into the concept of truth-conducive objectivity.

Consider the example at hand. Circularity threatens when there appears to be no independent determinant of what should count as true. Does there appear to be none for the various facts cited about the differences between men and women in the manifestation of coronary heart disease? Clearly not. They obtain independently of whether any of the researchers have feminist values. It would be preposterous to suppose, for example, that myocardial infarction is not commonly experienced by women under the age of 65 but that this is true only from the perspective of those who have feminist values or care about the health of women. While it seems plain that this perspective is conducive to bringing such facts to light, it is hardly true that these facts obtain or can be specified only in relation to feminist interests or that someone who does not share those interests wouldn't be making a mistake in denying that these facts about women's health have any reality. Seen within this specific context of inquiry, where a realist interpretation of the facts is almost irresistible, the problem of circularity simply dissolves. We can say without any fear of circularity that in this instance some biases are better than others because they afford a less distorted view of the truth.[3]

A committed antirealist can, of course, resist this realist interpretation of the facts cited, but that would miss the point. The example is offered not to prove the credibility of realism but to show that, *given a realist interpretation of the facts*, the problem of circularity has no force. If we allow ourselves to think of these facts realistically, which is surely the more straightforward way to think of them, then we have a nonarbitrary and noncircular demarcation between good and bad biases that is easily generalized to other examples. Needless to say, the demarcation provides no recipe or algorithm for sorting the good biases from the bad. Antony, though, does not offer her proposal as a practical guide for truth seekers. She offers it rather to give a nonarbitrary (hence noncircular) meaning to the idea that impartiality can be itself biased. She succeeds, I am insisting, provided that we are prepared to interpret realistically her distinction between good and bad biases.

Suppose, however, that we were to give an *epistemic* interpretation to truth (e.g., Alcoff 1996). Let truth be the conclusion we will reach ideally on the basis of following "the right methods," leaving unspecified for the moment what the right methods consist of. I contend that the problem of circularity in this case would be severe and ultimately unresolvable. The right biases in Antony's proposal would have been on this interpretation just those biases that are conducive to reaching conclusions that would be reached ideally by following the right methods. But what could those methods be, given the theoretical context of the bias paradox?

We might formulate the methods by using one or other of the theories of justified belief found in mainstream epistemology or by using contemporary accounts of rational scientific practice. The difficulty is that the bias paradox arises in the context of seeing such theories and accounts as being inadequate to block gender-biased conclusions. If we are to take the bias paradox seriously in the first place, then we have to be skeptical that such methods, unsupplemented by feminist values, can yield unbiased results. The problem is not simply that any such method is apt to rely on the ideal of impartiality, but that feminist values have a central and ineliminable role to play in uncovering the sources of gender bias. Given this theoretical context, we need in our construction of the methods to appeal to the right biases in order to avoid gender bias, but then we are left with no noncircular explanation of the difference between good and bad biases. Good biases will be the ones conducive to getting true conclusions, that is, ones that are guided by the right methods, namely, those that are guided in part by good biases.

Alternatively, we might begin afresh to construct methods not derived from mainstream epistemology or philosophy of science. Some feminist theorists have tried this path, and their proposals constitute important suggestions for how society might be transformed in a feminist image (Longino 1990). For example, the methods might be embedded in the democratic processes of inquiry in a nonhierarchically structured research community in which the lines of communication are not blocked by power differentials based on such factors as gender, race, and class. Nevertheless, I remain skeptical if the proposal is to be interpreted as definitive of truth. The reason is again the theoretical context of the bias paradox in which gender bias (among other kinds) is seen as deeply entrenched. Although the proposals in question may be the best we can imagine as global strategies for avoiding bias, it would be a mistake to take them as simply definitive of truth, since it would not be impossible for the wrong kind of bias to occur in such ideal settings (given the pervasive character of bias as now conceived). Imagine, for example, most women and men in a democratically structured research community being persuaded on the basis of evidence (then) available that it is not necessary to test for differences between men and women regarding heart disease. Such bias would be *by definition* the right kind on the hypothesis being considered, rendering Antony's distinction between good and bad bias incoherent. This result seems inevitable, unless we stipulate that the community will be structured in ways that eliminate the wrong kind of bias, but in the latter case we render the explanation of the distinction circular.

Relevance and Objective Justification

It may be objected that the example I have chosen is unfair because it takes for granted certain factual claims about women's health, creating the illusion that the concept of truth-conducive objectivity is unproblematic. Suppose that the facts are in dispute and that the weight of evidence appears to support a hypothesis that feminists think reflects a systemic bias against women. (This bias, feminists might claim, explains why the evidence appears as it does, as in the case of the current drive to locate biologically based gender differences.) In this context, it may be argued, a realist interpretation of objective inquiry tends to go hand in hand with the ideal of impartiality, for what will seem to most people to be impartial *and* conducive to finding out the truth is to favor the hypothesis that currently has the strongest evidential support. But then Antony's way of distinguishing good biases from bad gives exactly the wrong result. Feminist leaning in this case appears to be bias that is likely to lead away from the truth.

    This kind of case, where systemic bias weights the evidence in the wrong direction, presents the bias paradox in a trenchant form. Not only do the usual reasons exist to say it is contradictory to regard impartiality as a source of bias, but Antony's way of resolving the paradox by appeal to truth-conducive bias faces the following problem of relevance. On the one hand, it will appear arbitrary and unwarranted, even irrational, to be biased in favor of a hypothesis that has weak evidential support. If, on the other hand, the idea of truth-conducive bias is aligned with the idea of good evidential support, then, without further elucidation, the concept appears irrelevant to uncovering systemic bias, since such bias affects what is to count as good evidence and weights the evidence in the wrong direction.

To address the problem of relevance, we need to consider in schematic terms a situation in which some evidence E weighs clearly in favor of a theoretical hypothesis H. This is a situation in which the appeal of impartiality and hence the bias paradox is acute. Suppose that E is the outcome of an experimental setup or empirical survey designed to test H. Under what conditions should E count as positive evidence in favor of H? It is sometimes assumed that if the truth of H would explain E within the theoretical context in which the survey or experiment is conducted, then E should count as at least some degree of evidence in favor of accepting the truth of H. But is this a reasonable assumption? There is good reason to think not. If some alternative hypothesis H* exists that explains E equally well (within the present theoretical context), E should give no reason whatsoever to accept H rather than H*. In other words, when H explains E, the experimental outcome E gives us a reason to accept H as true only if no alternative H* explains E just as well.

Recall our example of studies in coronary heart disease. Let H be the hypothesis that no fundamental differences exist between men and women in the manifestation of the disease, and let E be the results of an empirical survey showing the mortality rate for men and women suffering from the disease to be roughly the same. Does E constitute some positive evidence for H? Notice that if H were true, this fact would explain E. On some accounts, if the truth of a hypothesis would explain the evidence or even make it likely, the evidence supports the truth of the hypothesis. But there is good reason to believe that this consideration is not enough for E to count as positive evidence for H. In the theoretical context in which the hypothesis is being considered, there exists a plausible, although more complex, alternative hypothesis H* about the different ways the disease develops in men and women that would explain E just as well as H. In short, the existence of this credible alternative explanation completely undermines the suggestion that E gives us some reason to believe H. Since the point does not depend on the details of the example, I want to say in general that a necessary condition for evidence E supporting a hypothesis H is *that there is no credible alternative hypothesis H* that explains E just as well as H.*

While the requirement that there be no credible alternative explanation has in my view considerable immediate plausibility, I realize that not everyone will agree.[4] Since I have defended it more fully elsewhere (1994; 1998) and there is not space to pursue the issue, I simply will assume it in the following to develop a resolution of the problem of relevance and hope that readers will be interested enough to continue reading. An important ambiguity exists, however, in the way that I have formulated the requirement. Both strong and weak interpretations are possible. The requirement says that no alternative hypothesis exists that explains the evidence just as well. What exactly does it mean to speak of there existing no alternative hypothesis? On a weak interpretation what is required is that no alternative hypothesis is being actively considered in the research community or would be actively considered if it were proposed there. This interpretation makes the requirement much less stringent than it might be. For example, suppose that the alternative hypothesis regarding coronary heart disease had been suggested by some people in the community at a time when those with more authority would have dismissed it out of hand as having insufficient initial credibility to be taken seriously. On the weak interpretation the requirement could still be met, since the alternative hypothesis in question would not be actively considered. (Those with less authority may not command the resources needed to pursue it.) Applied to the situation at hand, the understanding of evidential support when it is weakly interpreted would yield the conclusion that the similar mortality rate for heart disease is positive evidence for there not being fundamental differences in the manifestation of the disease among men and women.

It is possible, however, to interpret the requirement much more stringently so that for the requirement to be met there can be no alternative hypothesis that could be actively considered by the research community, *given appropriate experiences, imagination, and reasoning,* that (in combination with plausible auxiliary assumptions) would explain the evidence just as well as the original hypothesis does. Obviously, on this interpretation, an alternative explanation existed for the similarity in mortality rate even before the research community was ready to take it seriously. Thus, the requirement is not met at the earlier time, although then E may have appeared to most people to support H. It is in this respect a realist interpretation of evidential support, since whether the support obtains turns on truths about alternative explanations that no person in the research community may be aware of now (or at any other time). Let us say that evidence provides some degree of *objective justification* for a hypothesis only if the requirement is satisfied in its realist interpretation. We can then say, in these terms, that the similarity in mortality rate never provided objective justification for the first hypothesis, however it may have appeared when the main studies focused exclusively on men.

I now want to argue that the concept of systemic bias, interpreted along the lines of Antony's proposal for understanding bad bias, provides good reason to favor the realist interpretation of the requirement. The term "systemic bias" could be used to speak of bias that is systemic and good, but I will use it here in the context of testing hypotheses against the evidence to refer to the way that the generation of hypotheses and evidence in a research community can systematically *obscure* the truth. In the case of gender bias in the generation of hypotheses and evidence, research is structured so that alternative hypotheses that can better explain the evidence, as well as evidence that is better explained by them, tend not to be available or, if they are, tend not to get actively considered. As a consequence truths about women that are relevant to their well-being and to opposing women's subordination to men are not readily established through research.

Another example may help to bring this point home. A gender stereotype is that women are by nature passive and men by nature active. This stereotype is reflected in various ways that researchers (men and women) have thought about reproduction. In particular, contemporary textbooks in biology have represented eggs as passive and sperm as active. With reference to the first edition of a well-known textbook on molecular cell biology, Bonnie B. Spanier writes:

> Just as scientists have inaccurately credited the ejaculation of sperm and the motility created by the sperm's tail with the power that propels the sperm to the egg, ignoring the critical role of vaginal contractions and sweeping waves of cilia lining the fallopian tubes, the textbook describes the sperm as the active agent in fertilization. The sperm "penetrates" and is "explosive"; in contrast, the egg membrane "fuses with sperm membrane," with a "depolarization of the egg plasma membrane," and a "rapid release of calcium." (Spanier 1995, 59–60)

It is now accepted that this picture of the sperm doing all the work is false. The activation of the sperm's enzymes to effect a fusion with the egg is caused by secretions from the female reproductive tract and in some cases by the protrusion from the egg's surface of microvilli that draw the sperm into the egg (a process shown by microcinematography). Why weren't these facts known earlier? Was the relevant evidence accessible only through advanced technology? In fact, as Spanier notes (1995, 60), an eminent embryologist documented the egg's cone of microvilli in 1895, yet this evidence along with the hypothesis that the egg is active rather than passive was ignored until very recently. It appears that the truth was not known, at least not generally, because the research community was biased toward thinking of sperm as active and eggs as passive. Research was so structured that a less sexist hypothesis that can better explain the evidence, as well as evidence that is better explained by it, tended not to be available or were ignored. Not only is a harmful gender stereotype perpetuated as a result, but until recently research on fertilization focused primarily on the properties of sperm.

Many examples of systemic bias are noted in the literature (Fausto-Sterling 1985; Keller 1985; Spanier 1995). I take it that there is ample evidence that such bias can exist and will just assume this much as a premise of my argument. Given this premise, we ought on some occasions to be able to say meaningfully that because of systemic gender bias the weight of evidence appears to support a hypothesis that is not really justified on the evidence. Such an assertion makes sense, however, only on a realist interpretation of evidential support. If the question of justification were to be relativized just to hypotheses that are currently deemed worthwhile, as in the weak interpretation, we would have to assert that the evidence *justifies* our believing a hypothesis in a case where we believe that the appearance of evidential support is purely an artifact of systemic bias. We would have to say, for example, that the evidence gathered from studies solely of men justifies the hypothesis that there are no significant gender differences in coronary heart disease, or that until recently all the evidence that was worthy of consideration justifies the conclusion that sperm are the significant active agents in fertilization. These assertions are extremely paradoxical if we accept the existence of systemic bias. Only with the concept of objective justification, it seems, can we avoid such conclusions and render intelligible some basic normative claims that we want to make about evidence under conditions of systemic gender bias.

How Good Bias is Relevant to Evidence

We are now in a position to propose a resolution of the problem of relevance. Recall that the problem is to explain how good bias is relevant to good evidence in a context where the weight of evidence appears to favor a hypothesis that reflects systemic bias. Bias favoring the weight of evidence seems irrelevant to uncovering systemic bias, yet bias that runs contrary to the weight of evidence seems irrational. How can we resolve this dilemma? With the concept of objective justification in hand, we can argue that good bias can run contrary to the weight of evidence as it is currently structured within a research community and yet be conducive to objective justification. In the context of systemic bias, good bias is to be aligned, not with the weight of evidence so structured, but with what is objectively justified by this and other evidence. Thus interpreted, good bias is conducive to discovering the truth in the particular respect of being conducive to learning relevant truths about objective evidential support. As long as the suspicion of systemic bias can have a rational basis, and I have assumed this much as a premise, good bias can play a rational role in uncovering systemic bias and discovering objective grounds for belief.

Let me illustrate this resolution with a further example, this time from the research on sex differences (Fausto-Sterling 1985, 28–29). The case is simple and just one among many that fit a particular pattern. Some researchers accepted the hypothesis H, that boys are on average superior in reasoning skills to girls at the same stage of development, on the evidence E, that boys performed better on average than girls who were a few years younger on tests measuring reasoning skills. Of course, the truth of H would explain E only given a theoretical context in which it is considered plausible to assume that the younger girls are at the *same* stage of development as the older boys. This assumption was made, since it was generally accepted that girls mature faster than boys physically and that mental and physical development tend to go together. Given this theoretical background, the alternative hypothesis H*, that boys and girls are roughly equal in reasoning skills, does not fit with the evidence E. Within this simple framework, it appears that E supports H rather than H*.

In this example I am focusing on the background assumptions to illustrate how good and bad bias can operate in shaping the theoretical context in which evidential support is evaluated. A feminist researcher may suspect that an unacceptable bias has helped to shape the theoretical context and wish to question the assumption that mental development is closely tied to physical development, but we can suppose that without further evidence most people working in the field feel no need to question this auxiliary hypothesis. Her skepticism regarding H may, however, incline her to search for a way to alter the theoretical context. Fausto-Sterling describes a researcher testing a different sample of girls and boys, ones who were older than sixteen years, at an age past puberty when boys are supposed to have caught up with girls in physical development. Given the theoretical background at the time, there was no reason to assume that in this group boys and girls of the same age were at a different stage of mental development. The new evidence E* was that the boys did *not* perform better on average than the girls in some forty studies done on these subjects. Note that now H* explains E* better than H does and is consistent with the previous evidence, except for the unsupported assumption that the rates of mental development are different prior to puberty. Dropping this assumption, we find that H* better explains both E and E*. In sum, the feminist bias of the skeptical researcher leads to a change in the theoretical and evidential context, making H* better supported than H.

Though the example is dated and somewhat idealized, it suitably illustrates how to understand the distinction between good and bad bias in a way that resolves the problem of relevance. Bias is good when it leads to the discovery of new hypotheses and evidence relevant to constructing objective justification of hypotheses on the evidence; bias is bad when it leads in the opposite direction. When bias is bad and sufficiently entrenched, the weight of evidence, *as this bias has structured it in the research community*, may appear to support hypotheses that are not objectively justified. The relevance of good bias is that it can change the evidential and theoretical context in such cases and thereby lead to a more objective basis for belief.

Does Realism Imply Impartiality?

This resolution implies a realist interpretation of objective justification. Many feminist theorists, however, are suspicious of realism. One worry is that the concept of realism tacitly relies on the discredited ideal of impartiality. The realist will say that when the conditions for objective justification are truly satisfied, the hypothesis is justified on the evidence, *whatever anyone might believe to be the case*, but this view appears to imply that truth can be recognized independently of any particular point of view. It appears, in other words, that realism implies the possibility of a "God's eye" or completely impartial viewpoint. I wish to argue, on the contrary, that just the opposite is true and indeed that the realist concept of objective justification explains just how the ideal of impartiality can give biased results.

That a certain hypothesis H is objectively justified on evidence E is one thing; persons coming to think that E objectively justifies H is another. The latter is a defeasible process on the realist interpretation defended here. The community may come to think that there is no better alternative explanation of the evidence when there is, and they may come to see this when some of them are moved to present such an alternative. From whence do these alternatives come? They arise from various local historical conditions, such as the training, experiences, dreams, even political motivations of those who are in a position to propose alternatives and have them taken seriously. They arise, in effect, from various partialities contained in what used to be called "the context of discovery." Inevitably, the supposition that a hypothesis is objectively justified arises from the contingent partialities or biases that are contained in that context.

Notice that, unlike the positivist's separation of the contexts of justification and discovery, the two contexts are interwoven on the present realist interpretation of how evidence can be taken to give objective support to a hypothesis. Whether it does depends on whether there is any alternative explanation of the evidence, and whether anyone thinks that there is depends on the contingencies of the context of discovery as noted. The upshot is that, contrary to the objection that realism implies a God's eye or completely impartial point of view regarding evidence, realism of the kind defended here implies that this point of view is a myth based on a misunderstanding of the nature of evidential support.

Nevertheless, it is easy to create an illusion of impartiality by simply ignoring the ways in which the context of discovery is incorporated into the context of justification. Let us imagine that the theoretical background in a certain context of inquiry is fairly stable, with the auxiliary assumptions that a researcher might acceptably draw on to explain the outcome of an experiment being A1, A2, . . . , AN and the alternative hypotheses considered at all plausible in the research community being H1, H2, . . . , HN. Of course, the theoretical context is never completely stable, but allowing a certain range of variation in this regard won't affect the points to follow. In this context it may be possible for a researcher to adopt a neutral attitude to these alternative hypotheses. If the outcome of the experiment is E, it may be clear to anyone who is competent in the field that only H2, taken together with the acceptable auxiliary assumptions, explains E. A researcher may acknowledge this, even if the researcher would like some other hypothesis (either in or lying outside the plausible set) to be true. In this sense the researcher can be "unbiased" in assessing the implications of the evidence. Never mind that it is partly in virtue of specific interests within the community that this particular theoretical background is in place. The point is that, taking it as given, one can adopt a neutral attitude (relative to it) at least for the purpose of designing an experiment that might discriminate among the given alternative hypotheses and assessing the implications of the outcome. The argument advanced thus far does not deny that this state of mind is psychologically possible or even that unusual.

It should be clear, however, that this attitude of neutrality or impartiality may not be conducive to uncovering the truth in a situation in which there is systemic bias of the kind described earlier. If the theoretical background has been generated in a way that systematically ignores certain relevant alternatives and/or makes difficult the production of evidence needed to question the current set of acceptable auxiliary assumptions, then the self-conscious espousal of impartiality will tend to leave the theoretical background more or less undisturbed and thus not be conducive to discovering which hypotheses can be objectively justified on the evidence. The realist understanding of objective justification is thus able to explain just how the mindset of impartiality can give biased results. Indeed, the latter concept of objectivity, as long as it is realistically conceived, is compatible with encouraging certain biases and hence giving up the attitude of impartiality (which is, after all, only a pretense of neutrality, since it takes as given the theoretical background as it has evolved in the context of discovery).

Reflexivity and Objectivity

A second worry about realism on the part of feminist theorists is that it directs attention away from reflection on the historical contexts in which our epistemic practices evolve. (Truth is truth, however it is discovered, whoever knows it, whether it is known or not.) By now it should be amply clear that, where questions of evidence arise, the present conception of objective justification encourages a reflexive consideration of how the evidence is generated and, in particular, whether the biases generating evidential support are good or bad. Sandra Harding has championed the idea that we need to examine the sociological and economic contexts of our reasoning, not only in the cases where we reason badly, but also in those where we reason well (Harding 1991, 138–63). Strong objectivity, as she calls it, demands that our knowledge of these contexts and how they have influenced our reasoning be applied reflexively to see whether our claims to understanding our world are thereby strengthened or undermined. I take objective justification, as conceived here, to support this reflexive perspective.

Suppose that a hypothesis is claimed to be objectively justified by the evidence in the above sense. Different words may be used, but the basic idea is that there exists, in the strong sense, no better way to explain all the relevant evidence. The claim is defeasible, of course. A better explanation may turn up. How then might one proceed to guard against that possibility? An important strategy for contexts in which one is worried about systemic bias is for a research community to study the mechanisms through which new hypotheses and evidence are generated in the community. One explanation of why the evidence agrees with the favored hypothesis is that the hypothesis is in fact true. But a possible competing explanation is that the mechanisms by which the hypothesis and evidence are generated tend to create a fit between the two independently of whether the hypothesis is true. Unless the explanation that the fit between evidence and hypothesis is ad hoc can be reasonably eliminated, the claim of objective justification is undermined.

Likely examples are the "just so" stories concocted to explain certain gender stereotypes on the basis of natural selection. Sociobiologists claim that the greater sexual aggressiveness in males and their lesser tendency toward sexual fidelity are best explained by the greater biological investment that females have made upon fertilization (Barash 1977, 147). Given this investment, natural selection favors, they suppose, more sexual aggression and less fidelity in males. A general difficulty with all such stories is the need to postulate an adapted mechanism that accounts for the behavioral patterns noted. The fit between such stories and the evidence (assuming, for the sake of argument, that we take as given the behavioral patterns cited as evidence) can be explained either by the existence of this mechanism or *merely* by the fact that it was made up to fit the gender stereotypes. If the latter explanation is equally good—and it will be in the absence of good independent reasons to think that the story is true or any attempt to rule out alternative explanations of the evidence—the original evidence does not provide objective justification for the natural selection story. Sociobiologists may reply that differential investment itself provides such an independent ground, but this claim can be challenged (Fausto-Sterling 1985, 183–89). Moreover, there still must be a sustained effort to investigate alternative explanations of the evidence. Suppose, however, that reflection on the way the research program is structured reveals that neither the main hypotheses nor alternative explanations are being thoroughly investigated. Then the evidence does not likely give objective justification, even when the evidence in question is accepted as given.

Because it is always possible that systemic bias as yet uncovered skews the consideration of relevant alternative explanations, reflection on the forces that shape the context of justification is an important means to discovering whether a claim of objective justification is itself objectively justified. Notice that this strategy arises naturally from considering the nature of objective justification on its realist interpretation. The realist conception calls for this kind of reflexive activity. Moreover, in keeping with Harding's insight, the examination is as appropriate for seeing the merit of good biases as it is for locating bad biases. Good biases as much as bad are the products of contingent forces (social, political, economic, etc.) at work in the generation of evidence and hypotheses. In the case of good biases, however, an examination of this context should not undermine the claim to objectivity (though there can never be a guarantee that evidence there will not mislead). If feminist biases are generally good biases, we expect that generally they will not be undermined by understanding their origins but rather will be sustained by new evidence, as in the example of a bias favoring an active role for the ovum in fertilization.

How far can this reflexive procedure be pushed? Is it appropriate, for example, to question the concept of objective justification itself, or is its status immune to this kind of critical reflection? To be consistent, I have to say that it is not immune, but this is a result that I welcome. A feminist worry is that realism is ultimately motivated by a foundational approach to knowledge found in traditional epistemology and is therefore deeply at odds with the idea of "situated" knowledge that has played a major role in the development of feminist philosophy. Elsewhere I have responded to this worry by developing a feminist naturalized epistemology which is both nonfoundational and realist (1998). This is not the place to rehearse the reasons given there for realism, but it is worth noting that the argument offered in this chapter in favor of the realist interpretation of objective justification begins with reflecting on the situatedness of knowledge claims and thus the possibility of systemic bias. It is such reflection that calls for a realist interpretation of objectivity. I do not exclude the possibility that the appeal to realism might, even so, be itself the product of systemic bias. My point is rather that the appeal of realism seems to arise from taking seriously the very phenomenon that calls for reflexivity in thinking about our limits. On my view, then, it is entirely appropriate to try to understand why the epistemic standard of objective justification is being advanced. If its apparent appeal is best explained by the existence of systemic (bad) bias, it would be defeated on its own terms. No a priori method exists to preclude this possibility.

<h2 style="text-align:center">REALISM WITHOUT TRUTH</h2>

The concept of truth contained in realism occasions two further worries. First, realism appears to imply that there exists a single all-encompassing truth transcending any individual point of view rather than a set of multiple, equally accurate or true perspectives. Such a concept of truth is problematic, because it lends credibility to elitist and hierarchical modes of knowledge acquisition and thereby contributes to subordination of women and others who are not in positions of power and authority. Second, since truth is a property of propositions (or sets of sentences), the realist concept of knowledge seems limited to what has propositional form. But it is reasonable to think, as some feminist theorists have argued, that many important kinds of knowledge, for example, emotional knowledge and narrative forms of moral knowledge, are not best understood as directed toward the truth of propositions. The price of the realist resolution of the bias paradox may be too high if it has these unfortunate implications.

Up until now I have couched the realist proposal in the traditional terms of truth. It is possible, however, to formulate realism without reference to truth and not sacrifice the power of the realist resolution. What realism requires is a separation of representation and reality. The core thesis is that reality, however it or some part of it is constituted, is as it is, independently of how we, individually or collectively, might try to represent it. This will be so whether we are thinking of a particular physical structure, social relations, contents of our minds, or whatever. It is not required, at least not as I am understanding realism, that the representation be sentential or propositional. Though reality has often been thought of as comprised of facts or states of affairs corresponding to true propositions, nothing in the core thesis of realism requires this. Nor need we think of what is known as having propositional structure in order to advance a realist conception of knowledge.

What form might a representation take if not propositional? A proposal that has appealed to some feminist philosophers writing about science is that a theory in science is a model of a system in nature (Gorham 1995). A model presents a particular nonpropositional structure that may or may not be similar to the system studied. The model could be an abstract entity, say a mathematical or set-theoretical structure, or a physical entity, for example, Watson's cardboard model of DNA. As such, the model is neither true nor false, yet it can be used to represent the structure of something else. It will be a good model provided that it is sufficiently similar in the relevant respects to the system that it represents. Some models will represent the system in question more accurately than others, and we can test how similar they are to what they present by making predictions based on their supposed similarity. Thus, the earlier talk about evidence supporting the truth of one hypothesis as opposed to some alternative hypothesis will correspond in all relevant respects to talk about evidence supporting the accuracy of model over some alternative.

The difference at first blush may appear to be trivial, but its consequences are significant, since they allow us (among many other advantages) to meet the objections raised a moment ago. First, there will not be much sense speaking of a single all-inclusive model of reality, since indefinitely many distinct models can be in different respects equally similar to the system under study. Consider maps of a certain terrain (Giere 1993). These are models in the relevant sense; they are nonpropositional representations of the independently existing terrain. There can be indefinitely many distinct but equally accurate maps of the same terrain: street maps, elevation maps, geological maps, population density maps, and so on. Such models can sometimes be usefully combined, but only up to a point. Postulation of a single "complete" map is neither helpful nor theoretically necessary. Yet some maps may be woefully inaccurate, and we can discover this even if we are mapping a distant terrain that we can never directly observe. We can, therefore, be realists about the accuracy of maps (allowing the existence of mistakes and even gross misrepresentations), and at the same time suppose that there are indefinitely many equally accurate, partial representations of the reality we are interested in. We could even speak of a map as being "true," meaning completely reliable for our purposes, without any temptation to think of the map as a sentence or propositional entity. These points hold for models generally and undercut the charge that realism is incompatible with democratic pluralism regarding the multitude of equally accurate and reliable perspectives on the same reality.

Second, since the mode of representation is not propositional, it is possible to give a realist understanding of emotional knowledge, even on the (plausible) assumption that emotions need not be understood as propositional in their structure. Emotions can present a structure that accurately represents relevant aspects of a situation and also moves one to respond to them appropriately without its being the case that emotions comprise true or false judgments. Led to think that I am not being unfair, I may assert sincerely that nothing is wrong but, because I am being unfair, feel uneasy to such an extent that I change behavior and come later to believe that I was unfair. It is possible that I first know my unfairness in my feelings of unease, long before I accept any proposition that I was unfair. Similarly, a form of human relationship depicted in a narrative may accurately represent a moral reality without being itself true or false. Elsewhere I have developed these points regarding emotional and moral knowledge at length (1998), but perhaps enough has been said already to suggest that a realist construal of such knowledge need not imply that its object is always truth.

While this realism is pluralistic, it does not imply that anything goes. It allows that most current models (for example, all current models of women's cognitive powers or of who should be responsible for child care) give systematically distorted representations. We can still say, as before, that certain biases—toward creating new models or devising experiments to call in question old models—are good. They would be good in the sense of being conducive toward coming up with more adequate models (say, of women's cognitive powers or men's responsibilities) and toward devising an objective justification of their adequacy. Moreover, there would be, as before, no temptation to say that the accuracy of a model must be defined by the goodness of the biases that promote it. In effect, the resolutions of the problems of relevance and circularity are untouched by giving up truth.

IS IT REALLY FEMINIST?

A charge sometimes leveled at feminist philosophy is that it isn't really *philosophy*, because it begins from premises partial to women (e.g., that the subordination of women is wrong) and hence not from first principles. The criticism can be disarmed in part by calling attention to the problematic nature of the impartiality ideal, but then one must address the bias paradox. This I have done by appealing to realism to draw a nonarbitrary distinction between good and bad biases. But now it might be asked: How is this philosophy really *feminist*? After all, there is nothing inherently feminist about realism per se or about the distinction made here between good and bad biases. The combination of charges comprise a dilemma often posed to feminist philosophers: Either make your philosophy inherently feminist, so that it is no longer legitimately philosophy; or else make it fully philosophical so that it is no longer feminist. You can't have both!

Might our resolution of the bias paradox also resolve this dilemma? Let us examine closely its second horn, that our treatment of the bias paradox isn't really feminist. Why in particular might the present proposal, with its realist distinction between good and bad biases, seem not feminist? The explanation is that good biases are not tied in any essential way to feminist values. Good biases, as they are conceived in this chapter, can include many other kinds of resistance to oppression. Resistance to bias against racial minorities could count as good bias, as could resistance to bias against gays, and so on. There is nothing uniquely feminist about such a distinction. The distinction itself, it could be objected, is no more intrinsically feminist than the distinction between justice and injustice.

The premise of this criticism is well taken. The distinction between good and bad biases is not defined by reference to feminist values. This is by design, since otherwise it could be objected, as we noted at the beginning, that feminists are unable to explain how there could be a basis for the distinction that does not beg the question whether feminist biases are good. Nevertheless, the distinction is offered within a perspective that is itself motivated and defined by feminist values. It is such values that underlie the rejection of the impartiality ideal when it is shown to perpetuate the subordination of women to men. The proposal explains how this perspective, which is intrinsically feminist, is consistent with a realist interpretation of the difference between good and bad biases and thus avoids, in a philosophically satisfying way, the apparent contradiction in rejecting the impartiality ideal because it is biased against women. The philosophical theory in which the distinction is offered is, therefore, as much feminist as it is philosophical.

Still, some feminist philosophers may object that, once the distinction is granted, the appeal to feminist values will be redundant, implying we can get on with the pursuit of unbiased science on the basis of the realist understanding of objective justification *alone*. They may urge this objection as a *reductio ad absurdum* of the hybrid perspective. Ironically, the objection rests on the assumption that it is possible to pursue objective inquiry apart from specific biases. It rests, in short, on accepting the ideal of impartiality, whose rejection gave rise to the bias paradox in the first place. If we have good reason to reject this ideal, we have good reason not to be taken in by the objection. Moreover, if we accept the proposed resolution of the paradox, then we know, from the above analysis of objective justification, that it cannot exist apart from a context structured by various biases. The ideal of objective justification itself defuses the objection. The only reason to give up a feminist bias, according to this ideal, would be the discovery that it is not a good bias. The ideal gives no credence to the thought that one might learn the truth without any bias whatsoever or that striving to achieve that state would be a good thing.

CONCLUSION

In feminist epistemology the ideal of impartiality is often rejected for the reason that its application gives gender-biased results. This chapter attempts to develop a theory of evidential support that avoids the contradiction implicit in rejecting the ideal of impartiality while at the same time endorsing it. In defense of Antony's proposal that the contradiction can be avoided by distinguishing between good biases and bad on the basis of their being conducive or not to finding out the truth, I address two serious philosophical problems that threaten to nullify this line of reasoning. One is that her solution seems circular, since we appear not to be able to understand what is true apart from already knowing how to make the distinction in question. The other is that we need an understanding of how the concept of a good bias is relevant to that of good evidence that does not undermine the intelligibility of the distinction or make it redundant. These problems are solved by appeal to a realist conception of objective justification that explains how feminist biases can be effective guides to the truth in a context of systemic gender bias. In the later sections of the chapter I outline answers to four feminist worries about relying on realism to resolve the bias paradox in feminist epistemology.

NOTES

I gratefully acknowledge the helpful comments made on an earlier draft by Gordon McOuat, Sue Sherwin, and the editors of this volume.

1. This concept corresponds to what Antony calls "the conception of neutrality as objectivity" (e.g., 1993, 208).

2. The information below regarding sex differences in the manifestation of coronary heart disease is drawn from the Committee on the Ethical and Legal Issues Relating to the Inclusion of Women in Clinical Studies 1994, 64–66.

3. In the preceding paragraphs I have assumed that facts obtain just in case there are truths and thus have not distinguished between talk of truths and talk of facts. For my purposes these modes of speaking are interchangeable. Later I discuss how realism need not rely on the category of truth (or fact).

4. Many philosophers believe that the observation of a black raven offers some reason, however little, to believe that all ravens are black, since the latter hypothesis would explain why the raven observed is black. But, depending on the theoretical context, seeing a black raven can give one reason to believe instead that not all ravens are black. Suppose that it is plausible to believe that ravens have either of two kinds of genetic make-ups relevant to their coloration: G and G*. If ravens have G, then quite possibly all are black, but there may be good reason to think that ravens with G would not survive in the environment in which the raven in question is observed. On the other

hand, ravens with G* would do fine in the present environment, but in this case one can expect a few albino ravens.

REFERENCES

Alcoff, Linda Martín. 1996. *Real knowing: New versions of the coherence theory.* Ithaca, N.Y.: Cornell University Press.

Antony, Louise. 1993. Quine as feminist: The radical import of naturalized epistemology. In *A mind of one's own: Feminist essays on reason and objectivity,* ed. Louise Antony and Charlotte Witt. Boulder, Colo.: Westview.

Barash, David. 1977. *Sociobiology and behavior.* New York: Elsevier.

Campbell, Richmond. 1994. The virtues of feminist empiricism. *Hypatia* 9, 1: 90–115.

———. 1998. *Illusions of paradox: A feminist epistemology naturalized.* Lanham, Md.: Rowman and Littlefield.

Committee on the ethical and legal issues relating to the inclusion of women in clinical studies. 1994. In *Women and health research,* vol. 1: *Ethical and legal issues of including women in clinical studies,* ed. Anna C. Mastroianni, Ruth Faden, and Daniel Bederman. Washington, D.C.: National Academy.

Fausto-Sterling, Anne. 1985. *Myths of gender: Biological theories about women and men.* New York: Basic.

Giere, Ronald. 1993. Underdetermination, relativism, and perspective realism. Presented as an Austin and Hempel Lecture, Dalhousie University, Halifax, Nova Scotia on August 5.

Gorham, Geoffrey. 1995. The concept of truth in feminist sciences. *Hypatia* 10, 3: 99–116.

Harding, Sandra. 1991. *Whose science? Whose knowledge?* Ithaca, N.Y.: Cornell University Press.

———. 1995. "Strong objectivity": A response to the new objectivity question. *Synthese* 104, 3: 331–49.

Keller, Evelyn Fox. 1985. *Reflections on gender and science.* New Haven, Conn.: Yale University Press.

Longino, Helen. 1990. *Science as social knowledge.* Princeton, N.J.: Princeton University Press.

Spanier, Bonnie B. 1995. *Im/partial science: Gender ideology in molecular biology.* Bloomington: Indiana University Press.

Part III

On the Matter of Knowing

CHAPTER TEN

MATERIAL LOCATIONS:
AN INTERACTIONIST ALTERNATIVE
TO REALISM/SOCIAL CONSTRUCTIVISM

NANCY TUANA

I locate my analysis in the midst of an ongoing debate, a debate where even the terms are contested. Some refer to it as "Realism vs. Social Constructivism," others refer to it as "Realism vs. Antirealism."[1] Although there is much at stake in this controversy, I locate my interests around assumptions concerning material locations, for I believe that this is a productive site for unraveling a serious limitation in the way these debates are framed. It is my contention that feminist work in epistemology and science studies has begun to identify the need for a close and nuanced examination of the complexities of materiality, including the cognitive impact of embodiment and the relationships between human materiality and the materiality of the more-than-human world. Our investigations are beginning to raise serious concerns regarding the adequacy of the metaphysical assumptions of realist positions. But our inquiries are also undermining the natural/cultural distinction posited or implied by social constructivist accounts.

To clarify the debates, let me briefly discuss the players. There is an abundant array of theories located on both sides of the realist/constructivist divide. For reasons of space, I cannot here provide a comprehensive analysis of either side, but I will offer a brief overview of the types of claims made by such theorists. Realism emerges out of the commonsense viewpoint that a fixed and human-independent world exists and that our best theories, for the most part, tell us what the world is like. There is currently a broad array of philosophical theories of realism, from Boyd's convergent realism to Horwich's semantic realism to Ihde's instrumental realism to Putnam's internal realism, to name just a few.[2] Contemporary realisms were developed in response to the wellspring of support for the Kuhnian revolution in science studies that advanced the perceptual model of interpretation linking ways of seeing with changes in the world.

> Examining the record of past research from the vantage of contemporary historiography, the historian of science may be tempted to exclaim that when paradigms change, *the world itself changes with them*. Led by a new paradigm, scientists adopt new instruments and look in new places. Even more important, during revolutions *scientists see new and different things* when looking with familiar instruments in places they have looked before. . . . In so far as their only recourse to that world is through what they see and do, we may want to say that *after a revolution scientists are responding to a different world*. (Kuhn 1962, 111; emphasis added)

Unwilling to allow that Kuhn's "world change" could refer to anything more than a change in what humans perceive, modified realisms developed concerning just how and how much human perceptual activities influence knowledge.

To provide a working definition of realism, I will briefly outline three tenets concerning ontology, truth, and epistemology common to many versions of realism.

1. *Ontology: What exists is wholly independent of any person's perceptual act.* In the commonsense terms of John Searle's *The Construction of Social Reality*, external realism is the position that "the world (or alternatively, reality or the universe) exists independently of our representations of it" (Searle 1995, 150). On such an account, what exists, or at least a significant portion of what exists, are mind-, culture-, language-, perception-independent entities. Hence, what exists is seen as existing prior to and independent of human interactions.

2. *Truth: A theory or statement's truth is determined by the way the world is.* What makes a statement true is that it represents things as they really are, independent of human actions or cognitions. Thus the practices by which we determine the truth of a statement or theory in no way affect the reality that it represents. In the words of William Alston, "the truth *maker* is something that is objective vis-à-vis the truth *bearer* . . . truth has to do with the relations of a potential truth bearer to a REALITY beyond itself" (Alston 1996, 7–8).

3. *Epistemological: Our best theories (scientific theories), for the most part, tell us what the world is like.* According to Richard Boyd (1983), arguments to the best explanation lead to the conclusion that successful theories in "mature" sciences are approximately true and their terms refer to mind-independent natural kinds.

Social constructivism is often juxtaposed to realism in an either/or relationship. But there are perhaps as many meanings to the term "constructed" as there are uses of the label "realism." Though hardly the first use of the term "constructive" in reference to knowledge, Bas van Fraassen's use is revealing for my purposes. Van Fraassen states: "I use the adjective 'constructive' to indicate my view that scientific activity is one of construction rather than discovery: construction of models that must be adequate to the phenomena, not discovery of truth concerning the unobservable" (van Fraassen 1980, 5). My intent here is not to examine van Fraassen's theory of constructive empiricism for merits or problems, but to focus for a moment on his notion of "construction."[3] The metaphor of construction is here being used to refer to a kind of "making" or even "fabrication." Construction work in the work-a-day world involves relatively natural materials—wood, cement, steel—being refashioned by human labor and design. The metaphor of "construction" connotes something built or put together systematically—bridges or apartment complexes or cyclotron facilities. "Socially constructed" is often opposed to "natural." What is constructed is not found in nature or occurring naturally but is the result of the impact of human actions on natural phenomena or consists of an event or object that emerges simply out of social practices. And—like the tenement housing or the Nestlé baby formula or the silicone breast implants—social meanings, needs, and human labor reconstruct the material of the natural world to craft or fabricate new phenomena, be they social, like gender and race, or material, like androids.

I will argue that this mechanistic metaphor of "construction" is inadequate to the complex relations of materiality being posited in contemporary feminist scholarship in the areas of epistemology and metaphysics. My position is that the either/or of realism/social construction must be avoided, for I contend that neither account provides an adequate view of the complex interrelations between humans and the more-than-human world. I call my position an "interactionist" account. I use the term "interactionism" in an effort to reject the sharp world/representation and "in here"/"out there" assumptions of realism, as well as to transform the emphasis on discovery versus fabrication of realism/social constructivism to that of *emergent interplay.*[4] This term is additionally designed to engender a departure from the connotations of building and manufacture of the construction metaphor and to invoke the linked meanings of communication, connection, and interchange connoted by the term "interaction."

THE CONSTRUCTIONS OF SOCIAL CONSTRUCTIVISM

Since an interactionist account has important similarities to contemporary constructivist accounts, I will frame this chapter around the potential as well as the limitations of constructivist accounts in order to provide an understanding of what I mean by an interactionist account.[5] To this end, it will be fruitful to look at the types of things that theorists have claimed to be socially constructed and the processes of these constructions. There are four basic categories of constructed entities: (1) Social phenomena/institutions/practices; (2) emotions; (3) knowledge about the world; and (4) what exists. Although I'll briefly mention the first two, I will focus my analysis on the latter two.

Social Phenomena/Institutions/Practices

Five examples of social phenomena, institutions, and practices that are socially constructed and to which much scholarly attention has been devoted are gender, sexism, race, racism, and cognitive authority.[6] To say that these phenomena or practices have been constructed is not to deny their reality. They are phenomena that we must deal with regularly in our daily practices and that have clear economic, social, and psychological effects. Gender structures, for example, create restraints and resources, to which individuals and social groups must respond, and have psychological effects. Treating people as gendered creates gendered people. The "constructions" of gender structures, what counts as feminine/masculine or which roles are identified as female or male, is evidenced in part by their amazing variability across cultures and between historical periods. Or consider institutions of cognitive authority that determine who will be listened to and who will not, whose interests will frame research programs and whose will be ignored. These are phenomena that do not exist independently of the institutions, theories, and power relations that bring them into effect.

Emotions

Some social constructivists have argued that while there may be a material basis to emotions and affective states, the particularities of their expressions, both phenomenological and intersubjective, are at least partially socially constructed. David Halperin, for example, argues that sexuality as a distinct and unified psychophysical entity is a modern invention. "Far from reflecting a purely natural and uninterpreted recognition of some familiar facts about us, sexuality represents a peculiar turn in conceptualizing, experiencing, and institutionalizing human nature" (Halperin 1990, 25). Naomi Scheman in "Anger and the Politics of Naming" argues that "feelings don't bear their meanings on their faces: we need to learn socially what they add up to" (Scheman 1993, 33). Warning that the idea that one can simply "get in touch with their feelings" is a dangerous myth, Scheman argues that not only experiencing an emotion like anger *as anger*, but indeed even the phenomenon of *being angry* is something that emerges out of particular social contexts, beliefs, and behaviors. "I want to suggest that someone who felt like a woman who is unstraightforwardly angry today [about sexism] would not previously have been considered to be, and *would not have been*, angry (Scheman 1993, 33).

I will focus on the epistemological and ontological aspects of the constructivist move away from realist conceptions for it is here that the promise and need for interactionism is the most obvious. These aspects of constructivist theories are what fuels the current realism/social constructivism debates, but they are also, as I will argue, the point at which a new model is emerging.

Knowledge of the World

Realists often articulate a particular theory of perception and representation in which our concepts, although admittedly conventional in their format, are realist in reference. That is, the term we use to refer to an entity is a convention, but it will be a useful term in a successful theory only if it refers to a natural kind; that is, a way the world is, independently of our ways of knowing the world. For social constructivists, the world we have knowledge of is a world mediated by our ways of representing and knowing. Constructivists often reject the realist posit of a correspondence between our representations and the world, focusing instead on the social processes that are constitutive of the production and acceptance of knowledge claims, including the manufacture of facts.

> Rather than considering scientific products as somehow capturing what is, we will consider them as selectively carved out, transformed and constructed from whatever is. (Knorr-Cetina 1977, 672–73)

> "Reality" cannot be used to explain why a statement becomes a fact, since it is only after it has become a fact that the effect of reality is obtained. . . . We do not wish to say that facts do not exist or that there is

> no such thing as reality. . . . Our point is that 'out-there-ness' is the *con-sequence* of scientific work rather than its *cause*. (Latour and Woolgar 1986, 180–82)

Since on a constructivist account our conceptual framework emerges out of and is structured by human interests, constructivists abandon the representational theory of meaning and truth typically embraced by realists.

Lynn Hankinson Nelson's feminist transformation of the work of Quine is a good example of the move away from a simple realist account of theories as representing facts about the world. Interestingly, Quine's "bridge-building" metaphor—that is, that science is a conceptual bridge of our own making that enables us to make connections both across our various theories and between our theories and our experiences—is a good example of a "construction" metaphor. Gone is the sway of a representationalist account of "knowing" as seeing things as they really are, and in its place is a more pragmatist concern with constructing theories that best account for the evidence, where "best" is relative to our needs and interests rather than defined by "representing" reality the way that it is independently of our models or uses of it. Though Quine himself never embraced the label, his work was one element in the explosion of constructivist accounts in the late seventies and eighties.

Hankinson Nelson provides a different account of the relationship between theories and the world than is found in typical realist accounts that embrace a representational view of knowledge.

> But holism and the demise of foundationalism change the nature of the connection observation sentences can provide between experience and theory. . . . We are certainly not demanding of a theory that it "correspond" to "the world." We are trying to see if what a theory implies in the way of observation coheres with our experiences, with the understanding that observation, and experience generally, are shaped by a going body of theory. (1990, 112–13)

For Hankinson Nelson, as for Quine, experience is not neutral, theory-free contact with the world, but is informed by the interactions between communities, theories, and the world as experienced. A representational theory of truth or of meaning where successful theories and concepts provide a model or representation of the way the world is, gives way to a coherence theory of evidence and a theory of meaning as practice that undermines the belief that our knowledge of the world could be, even in principle, separable from social features of our communities.

In "Epistemological Communities," Hankinson Nelson embraces a construction metaphor concerning knowledge, but hints at the more interactive model I argue for.

> What lies behind my earlier statement that "communities construct and acquire knowledge" has emerged, and with it some features of an alternative to objectivism and relativism. The term *construct* reflects the view that knowledge, standards of evidence, and methodologies are, "of our own making" rather than pieces passively discovered and added incrementally to a unique, true theory of nature and that these are constructed in the contexts of our various projects and practices and evolve in response to the latter and experience. . . . But the term *acquire* is equally deliberate, reflecting the fact that there are *constraints* on knowledge. The standards of evidence, ontologies, and methodologies we adopt and the knowledge we build are communal, interconnected, interdependent, and relative to larger blocks of things known and projects undertaken: *beliefs and knowledge claims are constrained by these things and experience.* (1993, 141; emphasis added)

Hankinson Nelson's enriched Quinean perspective suggests a complex interaction that goes beyond what we know and how our experiences of the world are shaped and hints at the centrality of material interactions.

To fully understand the import of material interactions we must shift from epistemological to ontological concerns. While only a few constructivists explicitly acknowledge ontological dimensions of construction, it is through the lens of ontology that we can best undermine the current realist/constructivist stalemate. Although my own work on this subject has been influenced by the work of constructivists like Knorr-Cetina, Latour, and Woolgar, I will argue that their accounts ultimately fall short.

What Is

The strongest ontological component of constructivist accounts is the recognition that science often measures phenomena that are "artificial"—that is, are produced in the lab. When we run a complex scientific experiment, our theories are compared to phenomena produced/created by the apparatus in the laboratory and are measured by instruments that we have engineered. Knorr-Cetina argues that

> In the laboratory scientists operate upon (and within) a highly preconstructed artificial reality . . . but the source materials with which scientists

work are also preconstructed. Plant and assay rats are specially grown and selectively bred. Most of the substances and chemicals used are purified and are obtained from the industry which services the science, or from other labs . . . in short, nowhere in the laboratory do we find the "nature" or "reality" which is so crucial to the descriptivist interpretation of inquiry: The laboratory displays itself as a site of action from which "nature" is as much as possible excluded rather than included. (Knorr-Cetina 1981, n. 3, 119)

Similarly Latour and Woolgar in *Laboratory Life* assert:

The central importance of this material arrangement is that none of the phenomena "about which" participants talk could exist without it. . . . It is not simply that phenomena depend on certain material instrumentation; rather, the phenomena are thoroughly constituted by the material setting of the laboratory. (Latour and Woolgar 1979, 64)

According to Knorr-Cetina and Latour and Woolgar, our theories and the world fit together so snugly less because we have found out how the world is than because we have tailored each to the other. Theories are not checked by comparison with a passive world. Scientists inhabit a world in which both the social and many of the material realities they encounter are constructed. We have, on such an account, not a coherence theory of truth, but *a coherence of interpretation, practice, phenomena, and materials*. One can grant, à la Searle, the preexistence of an unknown material world—prior to hominid development or after our extinction there will be a material world. No constructivist I know denies that. What they do deny is "the pre-existence of specific objects before they have been delimited by science in precisely the way that they are delimited by science" (Knorr-Cetina 1992, 557). What we count as a natural kind, be it oxygen or phlogiston, humors or blood circulation, changes with changes in science. The existence of a scientifically delimited world and the particular entities of that world is a variable over time. Specific ontologies, and with them views about natural objects, emerge from cultural practices, science being just one of these practices. "Thus specific scientific entities like subatomic particles began to 'pre-exist' precisely when science has made up its mind about them and succeeds in bringing them forth in the laboratory" (Knorr-Cetina 1993, 558).

Although I see this aspect of constructivism as a crucial component of the enriched account that I am calling "interactionism," I also see it falling short for two reasons. First, constructivist accounts have a tendency to omit or downplay human embodiment and the complex interactions of human materiality and the materiality of the more-than-human world. Second, constructivists too often frame the relationship between materiality and human practices as additive: a mixing of human labor and natural materials, the framing of a pre-existing reality by the conceptual framework of science. It is my contention that interactionism builds on the strengths of what Knorr-Cetina calls "strong constructivism," by embracing the centrality of material relations. Indeed, I hope to demonstrate that an awareness of materiality reveals an alternate conception of ontology and epistemology that avoids the problems of an additive model of culture/nature. In addition, a move to an interactionist position dissolves many of the debates concerning realism/social constructivism by transforming the terms of the debate.

What I believe must be added to strong constructivism is an enriched version of an embodiment hypothesis—the tenet that human ways of knowing, our concepts, meanings of terms, and modes of reasoning are grounded in patterns of bodily being. At an epistemological level the embodiment hypothesis is the belief that our concepts emerge from and are in part formed by the particularities of our bodies and of our bodily interactions with the physical world. At a metaphysical level the embodiment hypothesis involves a recognition of the always present complex interactions of material-social.[7]

What I am proposing in this chapter can only be suggestive, partial, fragmented—a plea for a new metaphysic.[8] But to provide an initial description, I will employ a few illustrations, selected, for the most part, from ordinary, everyday examples that model the complexity of interrelationships I refer to as an "interactionist account."

THE INTERACTIONIST ALTERNATIVE

Walking in Oregon

It doesn't take me long to find the turnoff I've been looking for. One of those lush Oregon waterfall paths carpeted with ferns, rhododendrons, early summer wildflowers, and canopied by towering trees. I grew up in Northern California camping in Yosemite and the Northern redwood forests. The lushness of the Western Oregon footpaths dazzle me, reminding me of the redwood forests of my childhood. Majestic trees soaring overhead, the ground at my feet a patchwork of colors and shapes of the different plants. I haven't yet traveled to the Eastern part of the state. I'm not really attracted to the "beauty" of the high desert.

My desire to walk to the top of the waterfall is converted to a pattern of muscle activity. There is an activation of the lower neural centers, which subsequently establish the sequence of muscle activation patterns. The muscles, when activated, develop tension, which in turn generates forces at and movements across the synovial joints. The joint forces and movements cause the rigid skeletal links, the thigh, calf, foot, etc., to move and exert forces on the ground beneath my feet. The various planes of resistance of the ground provide complex sensory feedback to and from muscles, joints, and other receptors that modifies the movement to address the incline of the path and the roughness of the ground.[9]

I came here to regain a sense of balance. To forget the various tensions of my every day life, now accelerated by new commitments. I walk hard at first, hoping the physical exertion will push the Hypatia *issue deadline, the career change my partner is considering, the series manuscripts, the meeting with my youngest son's kindergarten teacher concerning his alleged "behavior problems," the book manuscript left too often untouched, and my aging parent's illnesses out of consciousness. To provide me space to breathe.*

I would like to suggest three ways material interactions are central both to what we know and to what there is—that is to both epistemology and ontology.

1. The particularities of human material configurations are epistemically significant, but it is important to see these as neither fixed nor as developed in the same ways in all communities.[10]

2. The types of material interactions we engage in with the human and more-than-human world are materially shaped by our interests and our particular materiality; and the material agency of the more-than-human world in turn shapes our particular materiality and our interests.[11]

3. Our best theories, including but not limited to science, indicate that the world is a flexible fabric of interconnections, where many, but certainly not all nor all the most important interconnections involve humans. This realization demands a new ontology that renders any type of "out there/in here" "nature/culture" dichotomy nonsense, and carries a recognition that we (all we's) are of and in the world, or, to speak more poetically, that worlding is always part of our relationality.

Human Material Configurations

First on my list is what I call "human material configurations," by which I focus attention on human embodiment. I have in previous publications argued that attending to embodiment reveals the specificity and partiality of human knowledge, as well as reminding us of the importance of acknowledging the body, and its variations, in the knowledge process.

There are many ways to remember the significance of the situatedness of vision and thereby inhibit the tendency to use visual metaphors to construct allegedly generic images of reason. One of these is to reflect upon the significance of the specificities of human vision. A frog's visual cortex is different from ours. Neural response is linked to small objects in rapid, erratic motion. Objects at rest elicit little neural response and large objects evoke a qualitatively different response than small ones. (Tuana 1996b, 28)

I go on to develop an argument of Katherine Hayles that a frog processes information in such a different way than do humans that Newton's first laws of motion, while obvious from a human point of view given the ways we process information, would be almost unthinkable for a frog since it is size and variation of motion rather than continuation of motion that is important for frogs. The point is that bodily differences in perceptual organs and neural patterns organize perception in highly specific—in this case species specific—ways. Far from being the neutral receptor or static mirroring of the visual metaphors informing traditional accounts of knowledge, observation and all of our material interactions are dynamic processes of organization in which our bodily being plays a central role.

The beginning of the path is level and I progress quickly. I'm soon walking up one of those steep switchback paths as I begin my ascent. Total carbon dioxide eliminated and oxygen consumed increases with the lift of the grade. I find myself becoming conscious of my breathing as my respiration rate increases and slow down the pace to adjust to the increasing demands on my somewhat out of shape body. When I began the walk I had pulled my jacket tight around me, chilled by the early morning air, but now I'm feeling warm and think about removing it altogether. The energy needs of walking up such a grade increases metabolic demands, increasing my caloric consumption and raising the amount of heat output.

In a simple act of walking I am in a series of complex relationships with the world that includes me. My absolute dependence on the world that I am both of and in is illustrated in my dependency upon that so-called world-out-there for oxygen, which I in turn replace with carbon dioxide. But how much oxygen I consume, make part of the "in here" rather than the "out there," is dependent on my age (my children will have a higher oxygen uptake due to their smaller step length and higher step rate at the same pace and the higher maximum oxygen uptake for children than for adolescents and adult), my aerobic capacity, my overall body weight, the weight of the backpack I am carrying (for people whose lifestyle does not include constantly carrying heavy loads, women and men alike, carrying a load of 20 percent of their body weight causes their metabolic rate to increase by at least 13 percent; but for women or men who regularly carry heavy loads, such as women in the East African communities of Luo and Kikuyu, metabolic rates stay constant when carrying such loads [Maloiy 1986]), the incline of the path, my walking speed, and the length of my stride. Additionally, my energy expenditure will depend on the surface of the path, increasing approximately 10 percent if I walk on grassland rather than black- top and a surprising 80 percent if I walk on loose sand rather than a hard surface.[12]

Material Interactions

Lest we slip at this point into a generic materiality that is epistemically signif- icant, it is important to remember that human embodiment, like all embodi- ment, is emergent. It is shaped by and in turn shapes our material locations and our interests. Hence, point 2, the material conditions of our environments, whether they be our lab instruments or the configurations of retirement com- munities or those so-called natural spaces called national parks, are materially shaped by our interests and our particular materiality *and* the material agency of these environments in turn shapes our materiality. This "and" is the impor- tant addition of an interactionist account, but it is crucial not to make it *addi- tive*. The constructivist metaphor focuses attention on the ways human practices shape material or social environments, but neglects the press of the more-than-human world on human materiality and social practices.[13]

Let me walk into the scientific lab to make this point. An example pro- vided by Karin Knorr-Cetina concerns the method of gel electrophoresis in molecular genetics for separating and determining the length of DNA and RNA fragments. Part of the measuring instrument—in this case x-ray imaging—is such that good resolution is obtained only in the middle of the matrix and not at the bottom or top of the film. But since scientists do not know the length of the fragments in advance, it is difficult to determine where to stop the gel run to get an image with good resolution. The solution to this problem emerges from the interaction between the measuring instruments and the researchers. We too often forget that humans are measuring instruments too and our materiality is shaped by our interactions, in this case with the ma- teriality of this particular lab instrument:

> Individual scientists develop a sense for a reasonable strategy in response to the challenge. Scientists are expected to make a good guess about what procedure might work best and to thereby optimize procedures holistically and locally. The required sense of successful procedure draws heavily upon an individual's experience: upon the prognostic knowledge which individ- uals must somehow synthesize from features of their previous experience, and which remains implicit, embodied, and encapsulated within the per- son. It is a knowledge that draws upon scientists' *bodies* rather than their minds. (Knorr-Cetina 1992, 121)

Materiality is emergent, not fixed. Not only are the entities that we study in the lab produced by our complex interactions with the materiality of the more-than-human world, but human materiality itself is formed in interaction with the materiality of this world.

Science, and knowledge practices in general, are not representational practices. Inquiry, whether in the lab or in the kitchen, is an interaction between agents, in this case human agents and material agents, in which *both* are shaped. It is in this sense that we go astray in thinking of the world as filled with preexisting and independent entities rather than a world of events or phenomena. We deal every day with material agency, whether it be the limits of x-ray technology changing our tacit embodiment, the push back of the earth beneath our feet that modifies our muscle activation patterns, or the physiological effects of the foods we eat.

It is important to note that the material interactions I refer to here are not just those interactions between humans and human-constructed places like science labs. One important interaction too often overlooked in constructivist accounts is between people and places.[14] To fully understand the multiple effects of my hike up an Oregon waterfall path, or the Chumash experience of living in the shadow of Mt. Shasta, a sacred site, or the impact of plantation practices upon the peoples of Hawai'i and their knowledge practices, we must richly acknowledge the interactions between people and places.[15] To hint at the richness of this interaction, I turn to the work of Sandra Harding, whose recent book *Is Science Multicultural?* addresses the importance of place in our epistemological and ontological musings.

In her efforts to develop her tenet that modern sciences and technologies are not just influenced by local resources, but deeply and completely constituted by them, Harding introduces a category she calls "locating cultures in heterogeneous nature's order." Harding reminds us that nature is not uniformly organized.

> The very survival of societies depends upon their ability to interact effectively with their own, local share of nature's regularities—even when that local share is spread through their travel from Genoa to the Caribbean or from Cape Canaveral to the moon and beyond. Some cultures daily interact with high altitudes and others not; some with mountainous terrains, deserts, oceanic islands, rain forests, or rivers; some interact with extremely cold and others with extremely hot climates; some with one range of diseases and health hazards, and others with quite a different range. People in each culture need to be able to protect themselves from the natural patterns peculiar to those particular climates, land formations, plants, animals, and diseases that surround them as they move about, and to figure out how to gain access to the potential resources for food, clothing, shelter, travel, exchange, and other needs that their part of nature offers. (Harding 1998, 62)

Harding acknowledges the dialectical relationship between human materiality and that of the more-than-human world. "Moreover, biological differences—dark skins or light, immunity or not to malaria, and so on—create different interactions with surrounding environments" (1998, 62). She argues that not only will a culture's research projects emerge out of the specificities of their interactions with particular places, but even notions of "reasonability" will be affected. "Theories that appear plausible in one environment may not appear so in another. For example, cultures living on the edges of continental plates might well find the geology of plate tectonics more plausible (and 'interesting'!) than do cultures with little experience of earthquakes, volcanoes, and other phenomena characteristic of plate-juncture environments" (1998, 64).

It isn't a very difficult path, it has a moderate grade, and it is only three miles to the top. But it provides a good outlet from my normal desk sitting. Though it is a warm sunny summer day, there are few travelers along this path. Indeed so far the only other people I've met were two women and two men descending. The men were dressed in the typical jeans, t-shirt, and Nike uniform found so often in Oregon. But both women wore tight clothes; one had on shorts, the other a short skirt. Both were slipping and walking in short, mincing steps. When I looked at their feet, the cause became obvious. One was wearing slip-on sandals that were living up to their name. The other wore the platform sneakers so popular now, with three-inch soles and an extra two inches at the heel.

People who wear high-heeled shoes demonstrate an increase in the plantar flexion of the ankles that leads to compensatory knee flexion, pelvic tilt and other postural changes. The center of gravity doesn't change significantly, indicating the existence of anatomical compensations that take place at the knee and lumbar areas.[16] *The prolonged pressure on the foot caused by narrow-toed, high heels often aggravates or causes the emergence of bunions and can cause neuroma and degenerative arthritis.*

Social constructivism is particularly good at identifying the role of interactions and relationships between communities and cultures in shaping the questions considered epistemologically relevant, determining standards of evidence, and so on. And this is a crucial part of the picture. It isn't, after all, the shape of our feet that accounts for women's propensity to wear high-heeled shoes. But we cannot neglect the agency of the more-than-human world in these material interactions. Human communities and human interests, both embodied and social, select the materiality to be the subject of investigation and construct enhanced modes of material interaction: x-ray machines, space shuttles, internet technology, chemotherapy. But in these material interactions agency is not limited to human agency. The material agency of the more-than-human world impacts human embodiment, not just the other way around. What is too often missing in constructivist accounts is that not all the actors in this play of interaction are human and not all that is "constructed" is semiotic.

The material-semiotic linkages that Donna Haraway has been urging on us pushes us toward a recognition of the limitations of a realist metaphysic that posits the world as static, preformed, and independent. Hence, my third point, the need for a new ontology.

The Metaphysic of Interactionism

The realist/social constructivist debates often focus on existence. Realists, in the spirit of Samuel Johnson, return to the solidity of kicking a rock, insisting that there is a world that preexists human interactions, intending this truth to undermine social construction. Others grant that there are realms of existence that are social—gender, money—but return to the preexisting independent world to ground scientific truth. Social constructivists all too often embrace this same metaphysical divide between nature and culture, wanting to retain a realist ontology while embracing the *epistemic* significance of social practices. To provide just one example, David Demeritt advocates what he labels "artifactual constructivism." Arguing that this type of constructivism is developed in the work of theorists like Ian Hacking and Bruno Latour, who argue that artifacts and phenomena are constructed through the material interventions and interactions of the scientific lab, Demeritt cautions that this type of constructivism

> does not deny the ontological existence of the world, only that its apparent reality is never pre-given; it is an emergent property that "depends upon the configurations of practices within which [it] becomes manifest" (Rouse 1987: 160–61). This Heideggerian insight is a difficult one. It is easy to slip from artifactual constructivism that is ontologically realist about entities but epistemologically anti-realist about theories (the things we call electrons are real objects, but our ideas about them are constructed) into a much stronger use of the construction metaphor that is anti-realist about both theories and entities (electrons have no objective existence; our belief in them as social objects is what gives them their apparent "reality"). (Demeritt 1998, 178)

While denying a representational theory of meaning and truth, Demeritt retains the firm solidity of a realist ontology. The world exists and is independent of humans. It is only the world's *"apparent reality"*—how it appears to us, the categories we employ to know it—that is affected by human interactions. Electrons and rocks remain real objects; it is just our ideas about them that are constructed. The noumena/phenomena, natural/cultural divide runs deep even in constructivist theories.

We can find in the work of feminist theorists an alternative to this divide between nature and culture, a metaphysical alternative that promises to transform our ways of being in the world.

Knowledge arises from the flesh—that intertwining of my body and the world, and my interactions with others. The world and I reciprocate one another; the sun breaks through as I reach the top of the waterfall and its rays lighten the weight of my body with their reverse gravity and I am caught by the beauty of the world shimmering around me. My perception is always fragmentary for I cannot see everything all at once and each thing is itself emergent, an entity shifting and changing in time, though the rhythms of changes may be quicker or slower than my own. Each presence presents some facet that catches my eye while the rest of it lies hidden behind the horizon of my current position, each one inviting me to focus my senses upon it, to let the other objects fall into the background as I enter into its particular depth. When my body responds to the solicitation of another being, that being responds in turn, disclosing to my senses some new aspect or dimension that in turn invites further exploration. By this process my sensing body gradually attunes itself to the style of this other presence—to the way of this stone, or tree, or table. In this way a thing comes to take its place more deeply in my world, and may become a world for me.

I find the complex interchange I am calling "interactionism" best illustrated in the work of Donna Haraway.[17] I do not have the space to do justice to her views, but let me hint very quickly at the richness of her account.

Haraway's material locations revolve around technoscientific practices. One, in particular, OncoMouse™, provides a tangible, albeit haunting example of the complex interactions of the material-social. OncoMouse™ is a culturally constructed natural being. OncoMouse™ is a living, breathing, fleshed mouse, kin of those we desperately try to keep out of our houses unless they arrive in the fancy tubular cages designed more for the entertainment of our children than for the needs of the mice. S/he is a living animal, a natural kind, who has been artificially constructed. S/he is a living invention. Her/his materiality, along with those of other transgenic research mice, has been materially refigured by technology. S/he contains an oncogene, a transplanted, human tumor-producing gene, the gene that produces breast cancer. S/he is the first patented animal in the world. OncoMouse™ is constituted by a series of complex interactions. To list just a few of those discussed by Haraway, s/he is "a scientific instrument for sale"; "an animal model for a disease, breast cancer, that women in the United States have a one in eight chance of getting"; s/he "inhabit[s] the multibillion-dollar quest narrative of the search for the 'cure for cancer'"; s/he is "a living animal"; "the pollution of natural kinds"; "produced by mixing labor and nature" (1997, 80–81). Her/his patent was issued to her two inventors, Philip Leder and Timothy Stewart, who assigned it to the president and trustees of Harvard College, who in turn licensed it to Du Pont, who contracted with Charles River Laboratories to market OncoMouse™.

The genes and marketed flesh of OncoMouse™ exist because of complex interactions between material-social processes: oncogenes, venture capital, biochemistry, the bodies of mice, the breasts and lives of the women Onco-Mouse™ lives and dies to save, the politics of intellectual property and the patenting of life, and the quest for profit in a market economy, to name just a few. There are many points at which one can, and Haraway does, enter into an exploration of the complex meanings of this one, not-so-simple interaction.

> Who lives and dies—human, nonhuman, and cyborg—and how, because OncoMouse™ exists? What does OncoMouse™ offer when, between 1980 and 1991, death rates in the United States for African American women from breast cancer increased 21 percent, while death rates for white women remained the same. Both groups showed a slight increase in incidence of the disease. Who fits the standard that OncoMouse™ and her successors embody? Does s/he contribute to deeper equality, keener appreciation of heterogeneous multiplicity, and stronger accountability for livable worlds? Is s/he a promising figure, this utterly artifactual, self-moving organism? Is the suffering caused to the research organisms balanced by the relief of human suffering? What would such balance mean, and how should the question inflect practices in the machine-tool industry of science—that is, designing research protocols? (Haraway 1997, 113)

With one twitch of her/his mousy tail, OncoMouse™ dissolves the divide between nature and culture and provides a different ontology than what we typically find in either realist or social constructivist accounts. Organisms like OncoMouse™, as well as entities like genes, are neither "out-there," to be "discovered," preexisting human interactions, nor are they constructed in the sense of "made up" by human interactions.

> Technoscientific bodies, such as the biomedical organism, are the nodes that congeal from interactions where all the actors are not human, not self-identical, not "us." The world takes shape in specific ways and cannot take shape in just any way; corporealization is deeply contingent, physical, semiotic, tropic, historical, international. Corporealization involves institutions, narratives, legal structures, power-differentiated human labor, technical practice, analytic apparatus, and much more. The processes "inside" bodies—such as the cascades of action that constitute an organism or that constitute the play of genes and other entities that go to make up a cell—are interactions, not frozen things. (Haraway 1997, 142)

But OncoMouse™, for all her/his uniqueness, is hardly unusual. Though the interactions out of which her/his being emerge are perhaps more newsworthy than yours or mine, they are hardly different in kind. Though OncoMouse™ serves as a better symbol for the inadequacies of a realist/constructivist divide, my being, or yours, will do as well. My body is defined by its relations with objects that both delimit my physical possibilities and provide the potential for new forms of embodiment. I do not interact with the material world as an isolated individual, but as a member of various communities for whom certain material instantiations are cultivated and from which the various meanings of corporealization emerge, bestowing self and object with sense and form, providing a structure, organization, and ground within which objects are to be situated and against which the body-subject is located.

We live in and through the ongoing interchange between our bodies and the world that we are of and in. We are immersed in a rich dialogue of the flesh, much of which unfolds far below our verbal awareness. As I turn and begin my descent, the muscles of my body, especially those of my legs, respond to the subtle tactile and visual cues provided by the waterfall path. The trip down involves numerous interactions, fluid movements of flesh, some of which I attend to—the call of my first sighting of Indian Pipe—others that occur at a preconscious level—the constant muscle adjustments that keep me balanced. As I walk my thoughts turn to the problems that weighted me down at the beginning of the day and I find them somehow lighter, more manageable.

We are not just bodies existing independently from the external world; we are subjects committed to the world. Material locations are shaped by many forces, including physical, social, linguistic, political, economic, historical. And all of these forces, including the physical, are not fixed, but emergent. The world that we are of and in is, in the words of Haraway, a "multifaceted set of interactions" between human and material agency (Haraway 1997, 142). Neither the materiality of the more-than-human world nor human materiality is an unchanging given. What exists is emergent, issuing from complex interactions between our embodiment and the world.

Conclusion

My position then, what I am calling "interactionism," is neither antirealist nor is it an embrace of realism. It is similarly neither anticonstructivist nor a modified constructivism. The point of an interactionist alternative is to restructure our working metaphysic as well as our understandings of epistemology in ways that will undermine the divide that makes an either/or out of realism/ social constructivism. The world is neither "fabricated" in the sense of created out of human cultural practices, nor is its existence independent of human interactions of a multitude of forms, including cultural, at least as long as humans exist. My theory of interactionism posits a world of complex phenomena in dynamic relationality.

It is important to point out that in my own work, as well as in the work of theorists who embrace realism and social constructivism, the interrelations emphasized are often those between humans and the more-than-human world. Though this is an interaction that is of paramount interest to many of us who work in the area of science studies or epistemology, human interactions are only one of the many types of interactions that make up the emergent interplay of the world. As I have elsewhere argued, *all* organisms and their environments are always dynamically interrelated in phenomena, a relationship I represented symbolically by linking organism-environment, rather than the dichotomy of organism/environment. Organisms and environments co-evolve and the organism actively participates in its own development. We often forget that our "nature" is another entity's "culture."

> The environment does not pre-exist organisms, but is constructed by those beings as the organisms *determine what is relevant*, "the bark of trees is part of the woodpecker's environment, but the stones at the base of the tree, even though physically present, are not," *make their own climate*, "the temperature and moisture within a few inches of the soil in a field is different from the conditions on a forest floor or at the top of the forest canopy," and *alter their environment*, "grazing animals actually increase the rate of production of forage, both by fertilizing the ground with their droppings and by stimulating plant growth by cropping."[18] (Tuana 1996a)

An interactionist account of the type emerging from the work of feminist science studies theorists will transform the current stalemate between realism versus social constructivism into a far more productive dialogue about the roles of materiality *and* cognition in human knowledge practices. It also holds the promise of providing a more adequate model of the complexities of interactions between human knowledge projects and the more-than-human that can serve as the basis for encouraging greater epistemic responsibility.[19]

NOTES

An earlier version of this chapter was written for a session on feminist epistemology arranged by Chris Cuomo at the University of Cincinnati. The other participants in the session were Lorraine Code, Sandra Harding, and Lynn Hankinson Nelson. I want to thank Chris Cuomo for the opportunity to participate in such an exciting dialogue and to thank Code, Harding, and Nelson both for the way their work has influenced my account of interactionalism and for their feedback on my position. I also give particular thanks to Sandi Morgen for her insightful comments and her enduring friendship.

1. For a preview of some of the realism/antirealism debates in philosophy see *Realism/Antirealism and Epistemology* (Kulp 1997), which contains essays by William P. Alston, Roderick M. Chisholm, Donald Davidson, Gilbert Harman, Richard Rorty, and John R. Searle. Three texts that are representative of social constructivist positions are Peter Berger and Thomas Luckmann's *The Social Construction of Reality*, Bruno Latour and Steve Woolgar's *Laboratory Life: The Social Construction of Scientific Facts*, and Karin Knorr-Cetina's *The Manufacture of Knowledge : An Essay on the Constructivist and Contextual Nature of Science*. To add another layer of contestation to the debates, Latour and Woolgar in their later addition of *Laboratory Life* deleted the term "social" from the subtitle, to reflect their later position that such a demarcation creates a false dichotomy between social and technical factors. Knorr-Cetina has consistently referred to her work as a "constructivist interpretation."

2. Boyd 1983; Horwich 1990; Ihde 1991; Putnam 1978.

3. My analysis here is indebted to the insights of Tim Adamson and his unpublished manuscript concerning the metaphor of construction.

4. In using the term "interaction" I also hope to create a bridge to the pragmatist tradition of John Dewey, for the notion of interaction was a central tenet of his thesis that logic is naturalistic, not in the sense of being *reducible* to natural objects, but as emergent from the interactions of intraorganic and extraorganic energies, where no sharp divide is created between the biological and the cultural.

5. I use the labels "social constructivist" and "constructivist" here interchangeably. This is a conflation that I think will suffice for the analysis I'm doing here, but a richer discussion of this topic would require teasing out the differences between those who label themselves social constructivists and those like Knorr-Cetina who have always embraced the label "constructivist" and Latour and Woolgar who, in their second edition of *Laboratory Life: The Social Construction of Scientific Facts*, removed the term "social" from the subtitle. As an astute reader can tell from my selection of theorists, I am most influenced by the work of those who embrace the label "constructivist" and insist on removing the modifier "social," and I think their work is closer in spirit if not in fact to the position I am attempting to support in this chapter.

6. For examples of analyses of gender, see Haslinger 1993 and Tuana 1996a; for race and racism see Mills 1997 and Zack 1993; for cognitive authority see Addelson 1991.

7. My term "material-social," is borrowed from Haraway's hyphenated notion of "material-semiotic" first introduced in "Situated Knowledges" and developed in her later work, particularly *Modest_Witness*. Though I employ "social" as a broader term that includes the semiotic, it is the hyphenating of the term that is crucial as a visual reminder that these are not two separate processes or phenomena but are always part of a complex interaction.

8. The metaphysic I advocate is also embraced by John Dewey (see especially his *Logic*), Alfred North Whitehead, and many contemporary biologists including Richard Lewontin (see Levins and Lewontin 1985).

9. My account here is derived from Vaughn et al. 1992.

10. I am influenced here by the work of Polanyi in *The Tacit Dimension* (1996). See also my discussion of primary health care providers in "Revaluing Science."

11. For an examination of the material agency of laboratory instruments, see Andrew Pickering's *The Mangle of Practice*. Studies that examine the material agency of the more-than-human world beyond the scientific lab are more difficult to find. A good beginning can be found in the work of David Abram, *The Spell of the Sensuous*, and Andrew Light's work on place. My own work has been influenced by the unpublished dissertation of Christopher Preston, *The Epistemology of Place*.

12. Rose and Gamble, 1994.

13. There are efforts to expand the metaphor. Donna Haraway, for example, in *Modest_Witness* employs the term "coconstructivist" to attempt to remind us that the process is richly interactive. Nevertheless, these efforts often fall on deaf ears. See, for example, Demeritt.

14. I do not intend to suggest here that science labs are not places. They are. However, current research on the notion of "place," engendered in large part by the work of Ed Casey, has employed the notion of "place" to refer to "natural" places. I do not wish to replicate a problematic cultural/natural split concerning place, but I do want to acknowledge that far more work has been done on the impact of places that have been heavily impacted by human constructions, like labs and architecture, than places that have not been so impacted.

15. My account here is influenced by the work of Christopher Preston in his unpublished dissertation "Epistemology and Environment: The Greening of Belief." See also the work of Andrew Light, Vine Deloria, and Edward Casey.

16. Gollnick, Tipton, and Karpovich 1964; Mathews and Wooten 1963.

17. A parallel conception of ontology can be found in Lorraine Code's work in process, *Responsible Knowing, Ecological Imagining, and the Politics of Epistemic Location,* in which Code examines what she calls "the ecological subject." This ecological subject is, for Code, "marvelously corporeal" (in the words of Annette Baier) and fundamentally interdependent, active, resistant and reactive, accountable; created out of sociality and itself creative of the forms of sociality in which it participates. "For this subject, interdependence among human beings and with the rest of 'nature' is a given: its benefits to be fostered, its privations and abuses to be addressed. They are neither to be repudiated nor transcended in illusory gestures of self-sufficiency, nor elaborated into a nostalgic immersion of self in nature or in Others. Acknowledging the partiality of their knowings and self-knowings and their effects (however small, however local) ecological subjects are well placed to 'own' their cognitive and moral activities, responsibly" (Code unpublished ms. 5–6). It is Code's goal to provide an account of an epistemology adequate to this ecological subject. According to Code, "the transformative potential of ecosystem-oriented thinking can be realized only by active participants who take on the burdens and blessings of identity, place, materiality, and history, to work within the locational possibilities and limitations, found and made, of human cognitive-corporeal lives. Ecological thinking distances itself from any search for a priori or transcendent principles and truths, to relocate inquiry, 'down on the ground' where knowledge is made, deliberated, circulated" (Code 5).

18. The quotes in this passage are from Levins and Lewontin 1985, 99–100.

19. See the articles of Code and Heldke in this volume for a rich articulation of the notion of epistemic responsibility.

REFERENCES

Abram, David. 1996. *The spell of the sensuous: Perception and language in a more-than-human world.* New York: Pantheon.

Addelson, Kathryn Pyne. 1991. *Impure thoughts: Essays on philosophy, feminism, and ethics.* Philadelphia: Temple University Press.

Alston, William P. 1996. *A realist conception of truth.* Ithaca, N.Y.: Cornell University Press.

Berger, Peter L., and Thomas Luckmann. 1966. *The social construction of reality: A treatise in the sociology of knowledge.* New York: Doubleday.

Boyd, Richard. 1983. On the current status of scientific realism. *Erkenntnis* 19: 45–90.

Casey, Edward S. 1993. *Getting back into place: Toward a renewed understanding of the place-world.* Bloomington: Indiana University Press.

Demeritt, David. 1998. Science, social constructivism and nature. In *Remaking reality: Nature at the millenium,* ed. Bruce Braun and Noel Castree. London and New York: Routledge.

Deloria, Vine. 1994. *God is red.* Golden, Colo.: Fulcrum.

Dewey, John. 1991. *Logic: The theory of inquiry,* ed. Jo Ann Boydston. Carbondale and Edwardsville: Southern Illinois University Press.

Halperin, David M. 1990. *One hundred years of homosexuality and other essays on Greek love.* New York and London: Routledge.

Hankinson Nelson, Lynn. 1990. *Who knows: From Quine to a feminist empiricism.* Philadelphia: Temple University Press.

———. 1993. Epistemological communities. In *Feminist Epistemologies,* ed. Linda Alcoff and Elizabeth Potter. New York: Routledge.

Haraway, Donna. 1997. Modest_Witness@Second_Millennium.FemaleMan©_Meets _OncoMouse™. New York, London: Routledge.

———. 1998. Situated knowledges: The science question in feminism and the privilege of partial perspective. *Feminist Studies* 14: 575–99.

Haslinger, Sally. Unpublished ms. Gender and race: (What) are they? (What) do we want them to be?

Horwich, Paul. 1990. *Truth.* Cambridge: Basil Blackwell.

Ihde, Don. 1991. *Instrumental realism: The interface between philosophy of science and philosophy of technology.* Bloomington: Indiana University Press.

Knorr-Cetina, Karin D. 1977. Producing and reproducing knowledge: Descriptive or constructive? *Social Science Information* 16: 669–96.

———. 1981. *The manufacture of knowledge: An essay on the constructivist and contextual nature of science*. Oxford and New York : Pergamon.

——— 1992. The couch, the cathedral, and the laboratory: On the relationship between experiment and laboratory in science. In *Science as practice and culture*, ed. Andrew Pickering. Chicago: University of Chicago Press.

Kuhn, Thomas S. 1962. *The structure of scientific revolutions*. Chicago: University of Chicago Press.

Kulp, Christopher. 1997. *Realism/antirealism and epistemology*. New York: Rowman and Littlefield.

Latour, Bruno, and Steve Woolgar. 1979. *Laboratory life: The social construction of scientific facts*. Beverly Hills: Sage.

Levins, Richard, and Richard Lewontin. 1985. *The dialectical biologist*. Cambridge, Mass.: Harvard University Press.

Light, Andrew, and Jonathan M. Smith. 1997. *Space, place, and environmental ethics*. Lanham : Rowman and Littlefield.

Maloiy, G. M. O., N. C. Heglund, L. M. Prager, G. A. Cavagna, and C. R. Taylor. 1986. Energetic cost of carrying loads: Have African women discovered an economic way? *Nature* 319: 668–69.

Mills, Charles. 1997. *The racial contract*. Ithaca, N.Y.: Cornell University Press.

Pickering, Andrew. 1995. *The mangle of practice: Time, agency, and science*. Chicago: Chicago University Press.

Polanyi, Michael. 1966. *The tacit dimension*. Garden City, N.Y.: Doubleday.

Putnam, Hilary. 1978. *Meaning and the moral sciences*. London and Boston : Routledge.

Rose, Jessica, and James G. Gamble. 1994. *Human walking*. Baltimore: Williams and Wilkins.

Scheman, Naomi. 1993. *Engenderings: Constructions of knowledge, authority, and privilege*. New York and London: Routledge.

Searle, John R. 1995. *The construction of social reality*. New York: Free Press.

Tuana, Nancy. 1996b. Revaluing science: Starting from the practices of women. In *Feminism, science, and the philosophy of science*, ed. Lynn Hankinson Nelson and Jack Nelson. Dordrecht; Boston: Kluwer.

———. 1996a. Fleshing gender, sexing the body: Refiguring the sex/gender distinction. *Southern Journal of Philosophy* 35: 53–71.

van Fraassen, Bas C. 1980. *The scientific image*. Oxford: Clarendon.

Vaughn, C. L., B. L. Davis and J. C. O'Connor. 1992. *Gaitlab*. Champaign, Ill. : Human Kinetics.

Whitehead, Alfred North. 1929. *Process and reality: An essay in cosmology*. New York: Free Press.

Zack, Naomi. 1993. *Race and mixed race*. Philadelphia: Temple University Press.

CHAPTER ELEVEN

PARTICIPATORY KNOWLEDGE
AND THE WORLD IN VIRGINIA WOOLF

LOUISE WESTLING

In a sense the whole of philosophy, as Husserl says, consists in restoring a
power to signify, a birth of meaning, or a wild meaning, an expression of
experience by experience, which in particular clarifies the special domain
of language. And, in a sense, as Valéry said, language is everything, since it
is the voice of no one, since it is the very voice of the things, the waves,
and the forests.

—Merleau-Ponty (1968, 155)

Environmental philosophers, feminist theorists, and "Ecocritics" have turned
their attention increasingly in recent years to our culture's destructive objecti-
fication and denigration of the nonhuman world, a heritage that can be traced
back at least as far as Plato's dialogues, with their fictions of human transcendence.[1] Yet similar critiques were underway much earlier, driven by loss of faith
in nineteenth-century progressivism, by Darwinian narratives of human evolution within the dynamic matrix of the living earth community, and also by popular accounts of the New Physics in the 1920s and 1930s. As early as 1927
Virginia Woolf offered a profound critique of the Platonic heritage of Occi-
dental philosophy in *To the Lighthouse* when she satirically characterized the
sterility of such thinking "about subject and object and the nature of reality"
through the eyes of artist Lily Briscoe.

Woolf anticipated the present movement toward reembodiment of consciousness by suggesting a dynamic epistemology of enmeshment in the web of

life in her fiction. From her earliest diaries to her final novel, written as German bombs fell on England and threatened to destroy everything she valued, Virginia Woolf was writing her way toward an expression of her own sense of the indeterminacy and mystery of perception. In 1908 she wrote in her journal that she was working to "achieve a symmetry by means of infinite discords, showing all the traces of the minds [sic] passage through the world; & achieve in the end, some kind of whole made of shivering fragments; to me this seems the natural process; the flight of the mind" (Woolf 1990, 393). By 1925 she had developed that idea further, making the much-quoted claim that "Life is not a series of gig lamps symmetrically arranged; life is a luminous halo, a semitransparent envelope surrounding us from the beginning of consciousness to the end" (Woolf 1925, 189). Accordingly, the task of the novelist is to "record the atoms as they fall upon the mind in the order in which they fall . . . [and] trace the pattern, however disconnected and incoherent in appearance, which each sight or incident scores upon the consciousness" (1925, 190).

Woolf eagerly embraced the New Physics as soon as it became accessible to nonspecialists.[2] Far more than most other modernists, she integrated the radical ontological and epistemological perspectives suggested by quantum physics into her writing, because they accorded so much with her own sense of things. In the process she began to dramatize phenomenological concepts of participatory reality similar to those later defined by Maurice Merleau-Ponty. Like her contemporary John Dewey, Woolf believed that *art is experience,* part of the interaction of our living being with and within the matrix of the whole living world. Her aesthetic concept of "moments of being"—intense awareness set apart from the "cotton wool" blurriness of ordinary consciousness—is much like Dewey's sense that heightened experience is art in germ, signifying "complete interpenetration of self and the world of objects and events," a dynamic stability that is "rhythmic and developing" (Dewey 1934, 19).

Read together, Woolf, Dewey, and Merleau-Ponty help us begin to recover in modern form something like the ancient recognition of the dynamic interplay between human life and the myriad other lives and energies surrounding us. They suggest a reorientation of humanistic understanding that ought to be considered as radical as the reorientation of scientific thought brought about by quantum physics. It is a deeply ecological way of thinking, informed by the New Physics but also parallel to recent developments in biology such as the work of Lynn Margulis and other proponents of James Lovelock's Gaia Hypothesis (Margulis and Sagan 1986 and 1997; and Lovelock 1979 and 1988).

From the beginning of her career, Virginia Woolf was concerned about the multiplicity of consciousness and the dynamism of the world around her characters. Her diaries are full of landscape descriptions, commentaries on the weather, and self-conscious musings about how she might capture in her writing the human mind's experience of these vibrant realities. In 1903 she likened the English Downs "to the long curved waves of the sea. It is as though the land here, all molten once, & rolling in vast billows had solidified while the waves were still swollen & on the point of breaking. From a height it looks as though the whole land were flowing" (Woolf 1990, 192). Humans seem to her to have had no effect on the real shape of the place, and villages seem to have sunk into hollows between the waves. The fields around Salisbury strike her as rising, swelling, and falling, "like some vast living thing, & all its insects & animals, save man, are exquisitely in time with it. If you lie on the earth somewhere you hear a sound like a vast breath, as though it were the very inspiration of earth herself, & all the living things on her" (1990, 203). Writing is an activity so fused with her experience of earth and sea and sky that she thinks of it in terms of landscape or waves. When she looked out at the hills above Florence while on a 1908 trip to Italy, for example, she thought at once of the Renaissance literature that had been produced in that setting: "I positively saw the long smooth sentence [of classic prose] running like a ribbon along the road . . . & curving freely over the bare slopes of the hills" (1990, 397). She thought of style as being a simple matter of rhythm: "A sight, an emotion, creates this wave in the mind, long before it makes words to fit it" (Woolf 1977, 247).

As early as *The Voyage Out* (her first novel, published in 1915), she was experimenting with points of view outside ordinary human awareness. The novel's protagonist Rachel Vinrace has a sense of the vast life beyond human apprehension or control—of "mammoths pastured in the fields of Richmond High Street" many thousands of years before London existed, or of "something alive" under the streets, in the sewers, in the wires surging through the modern city (Woolf 1948, 67). At another point the narrator's gaze moves away from the ship on which her characters sail the Atlantic, until the people on board look like insects or lumps, cormorants, or cows (1948, 87). Later her narrative presence floats through a sleeping hotel, describing the life of the night flowing through when all its human inhabitants are sunk in sleep, while outside wild animals are abroad and the wind blows purer and fresher over the hills and woods than under human eyes in daylight (1948, 111). Rachel asks her fiancé Terence Hewett whether he ever thinks "that the world is composed entirely of vast blocks of matter, and that we're nothing but patches of light" (1948, 292).

Similar experiments and ideas occur in *Jacob's Room* (1922) and *Mrs. Dalloway* (1925), but it is in the "Time Passes" section of *To the Lighthouse* that Virginia Woolf most boldly ventures to give agency and even sentience to forces of weather and time, and to other living creatures and entities such as rats and weeds, mold and mildew. In such a context, the tragedies of the novel's human protagonists appear as only the most belated parenthetical asides. Encompassing ten years of life (and death) in the Ramsay family, this twenty-page section was planned from the earliest stages of the novel's conception in Virginia Woolf's mind, as a narrow corridor between two blocks focusing closely on a family (Lee 1992, xiv).

The short span of this corridor in pages has an immensely ironic relation to its huge subject and profound effect, for it contemplates the vast forces of the nonhuman world that flow over, and eventually erase, every life and all the intricate structures of the human community, particularly of course those seen in the richly detailed portrait of the Ramsay family. "Time Passes" is a careful extension of Woolf's earlier efforts to consider the world free of people and flowing with elemental energies and rhythms.[3] It is a project on which she worked until the end of her life.

Before looking closely at "Time Passes," we need to acknowledge the philosophical context Woolf establishes for the novel's unfolding action. Mr. Ramsay, the novel's father/philosopher, is a satiric portrait of Woolf's own father, Sir Leslie Stephen, whose work on *The Dictionary of National Biography* is parodied by Mr. Ramsay's doubts about whether he can move his logical system from Q (the point he has succeeded in reaching) to R and onward toward the faintly glimmering Z in the distance beyond his mental capacities (Woolf 1992c, 39).

Clearly Mr. Ramsay's philosophical exertions are part of the transcendental Platonic heritage of Western culture. Other commentators have found the influence of Hume and of G. E. Moore in Woolf's portrait of Mr. Ramsay (Beer 1996, 29–47), but Plato is the father of them all, as Stevie Davies has shown (Davies 1989, 66–99). Andrew Ramsay's explanation of his father's work to painter Lily Briscoe provides a comic visual mark of this heritage: first he says that it is about "subject and object and the nature of reality," but when Lily cannot understand, Andrew suggests, "Think of a kitchen table then, when you're not there" (Woolf 1992c, 28). From then on Lily carries in her mind the picture of a scrubbed kitchen table lodged in the fork of a pear tree. This image alludes to the well-known passage in Plato's *Republic X* (Plato n.d., 360–74) where Socrates asks his disciple about the formal essence of a table or a bed. Stevie Davies characterizes *To the Lighthouse* as Woolf's "most deeply and consistently Platonist work" filled with yearning for the transcendent reality of the Ideas or Forms behind the shadows held between a fire and the wall of the cave in *Republic VII* (Davies 1989, 70). On the contrary, it seems to me that the image of the table in the tree could only have been meant to be ridiculous, demonstrating the deadness and rigidity of human structures made from living things. Furthermore, we cannot ignore the gender implications Woolf has provided in Andrew's condescending suggestion that Lily try to imagine a domestic object in a tree when she fails to comprehend the spare "masculine" terminology of "subject and object and the nature of reality" (Woolf 1992c, 28). Mrs. Ramsay's fertile enmeshment in the world stands behind this reference, because Woolf clearly means to associate Lily's embodied imagination of the living tree with a passage coming a few pages later that defines Mrs. Ramsay in terms of a fountain of life and "a rosy-flowered fruit tree laid with leaves and bouncing boughs into which the beak of brass, the arid scimitar of . . . the egotistical man, plunged and smote, demanding sympathy" (1992c, 43–44). Her husband's philosophical work is presented as a lonely heroic quest which separates him from the rest of life and makes him an egotistical tyrant dependent on his wife's nurture. The transcendent Platonism he seeks is a sterile, linear abstraction that does violence to the wholeness of the living world. Woolf's aggressive, phallic images of masculinity accompany this kind of thinking and suggest its destructive consequences, in contrast to the organic fullness, flexibility, and dynamism of the fountain and fruit tree that figure forth Mrs. Ramsay's and Lily's intuitive, embodied intelligence.

As most readers have agreed, Lily Briscoe is the unifying artistic consciousness of the novel, and she is less conventionally "female" than Mrs. Ramsay. In placing Lily's understanding in so central a role, Woolf dissociates the novel's implied epistemology from any kind of feminist essentialism, in a similar way to that in which she moves away from focus on the feminine toward the end of *A Room of One's Own*, to insist on the need for an androgynous vision for the writer (Woolf 1929, 100–10). For Woolf, as for John Dewey, embodied experience is the primary reality, source of all thought and art. Lily's incapacity for abstraction signals Woolf's own effort in the novel to reembody human consciousness, or, in Laura Doyle's words, "to turn inside out the unnamed, body-transcending core of traditional Western philosophy and narrative" (Doyle 1994, 42). *To the Lighthouse* moves toward a new kind of understanding partially realized in Lily's consciousness but even more directly approached through Woolf's effort to capture the nonhuman forces that sweep into the house as sleep and darkness fall upon it in "Time Passes."

"Time Passes" is divided into ten short sections, each perhaps standing for one of the ten years between the first narrative block of the novel ("The Window") and the last ("The Lighthouse"). This narrow corridor of time opens out from the night that falls on the Ramsays and their guests in Part 1, into the many nights of autumn darkness and winter, flowing into a movement of seasons and years, during which the forces of wind, rain, and mildew desolate the increasingly dilapidated house.

"So with the lamps all put out, the moon sunk, and a thin rain drumming on the roof a downpouring of immense darkness" begins that first night. In section 2 it floods in profusion through the sleeping house, creeping in at keyholes and crevices, stealing into rooms, swallowing shapes and colors, confounding identities of bodies and minds (Woolf 1992c, 137). We see all this through an impersonal consciousness that personifies little airs and lights that creep through the rooms, toy with flaps of wallpaper, brush, muse, and question all human artifacts with ghostly movements among the sleeping bodies of the characters we have known with such intimacy in the long preceding section of the novel. This action of one night (section 2) moves into a new section of many nights succeeding one another as autumn advances toward winter. Trees are ravaged and tattered by winds that are followed by mellow harvest moons and the illusion of peace, broken finally by nights of storm and destruction. By this point, the possibility of questioning is transferred to human agents—sleepers who might awaken and walk upon the sand to question the natural chaos of the season, seek to bring the night to order and make the world "reflect the compass of the soul" (1992c, 140). But the narrator makes it clear that transcendental philosophical inquiries into "subject and object and the nature of reality" are completely out of place here (Doyle 1994, 62). Mr. Ramsay's heroic efforts to reach Z or place a firm stake in the flood of time are brought to sudden consternation when unexpectedly the section ends in two bracketed sentences casually announcing the death of Mrs. Ramsay (Woolf 1992c, 139–40).

Peace reigns in the deserted house through section 4, with only the clammy sea airs moving among the shrouded forms of furniture and light and shadow playing along the walls, and across the blankness of the mirror that once reflected human forms. Only the nonhuman remains, wrapped in an indifferent air of pure integrity. A green shawl that Mrs. Ramsay had used to veil the skull her son James had hung on the wall loosens and falls partly away, suggesting that the comfort of human illusions has also begun to fall away with her death and the passage of time. Two sections later it is spring, reviving the usual hopes and energies of the season. In brackets the wedding of the Ramsays' daughter Prue is announced, ushering in descriptions of spring's lengthening evenings when hopeful men indulge "imaginations of the strangest kind"

> —of flesh turned to atoms which drove before the wind, of stars flashing in their hearts, of cliff, sea, cloud, and sky brought purposely together to assemble outwardly the scattered parts of the vision within. In those mirrors, the minds of men, in those pools of uneasy water, in which clouds for ever turn and shadows form, dreams persisted, and it was impossible to resist the strange intimation which every gull, flower, tree, man and woman, and the white earth itself seemed to declare (but if questioned at once to withdraw) that good triumphs, happiness prevails, order rules. (Woolf 1992c, 144)

Here Virginia Woolf seems to be calling up Romantic traditions of nature's sympathy with human needs. In fact, however, she inverts such habits of pathetic fallacy, by suggesting that human thought mirrors the nonhuman world, rather than the other way around. Thus men imagine the transubstantiation of flesh into atoms, and their minds whirl with images of stars, cliff, sea, and sky. This bewildering confusion and interpenetration of forms and substances parodies our anthropomorphic projections but also points toward a different kind of human interrelation with nature—a truly reciprocal one that overwhelms ordinary understanding. We should notice Woolf's ironic parenthetical reference to earth's withdrawal from any assertion of goodness and order. Indeed, after a brief assertion of spring's rainy sympathy with the sorrows of mankind, we learn in another bracketed sentence that the bride, Prue Ramsay, has suddenly died of "some illness connected with childbirth" (Woolf 1992c, 144). The advancing summer is troubled by "ominous sounds like the measured blows of hammers dulled on felt" which further loosen Mrs. Ramsay's old green shawl and crack the tea cups. These must be the muffled resonances of artillery from across the English Channel. Another bracketed pair of sentences announces blandly that a shell has exploded in France, killing twenty or thirty young men including the promising young mathematician Andrew Ramsay (1992c, 145). Thus the Great War makes itself known in a sardonic aside that brings the narrator to muse again about the possibility of Nature's sympathy with human beings.

> Did Nature supplement what man advanced? Did she complete what he began? With equal complacence she saw his misery, condoned his meanness, and acquiesced in his torture. That dream, then, of sharing, completing, finding in solitude on the beach an answer, was but a reflection in a mirror, and the mirror itself was but the surface glassiness which forms in quiescence when the nobler powers sleep beneath? Impatient, despairing yet loth to go (for beauty offers her lures, has her consolations), to pace the beach was impossible; contemplation was unendurable; the mirror was broken. (1992c, 146)

This flat denial signals the end of Romantic optimism and ushers in section 7, another succession of seasons and return of spring, this time strange, eyeless, and terrible. The universe seems to be ruled by brute confusion and wanton lust, and the mind of man cannot reflect it with any comprehension. In spite of occasional visits of an old cleaning woman, by section 9 the house seems to be left "like a shell on a sandhill," bereft of human life and settling into an eternal night in which toads nose their way into the kitchen, thistles begin growing in the larder, swallows nest in the drawing room, and rats settle in behind the wainscots while plaster falls by the shovelful. "What power could now prevent the fertility, the insensibility of nature?" asks the narrator, before answering that nothing withstands either these forces of decay or the new wild lives that make the house into a place of Nature. The house is on the brink of falling into the depths of darkness and oblivion (1992c, 149–51). "But there was a force working; something not highly conscious; something that leered, something that lurched" (1992c, 151). That something merges into the forms of two cleaning women, Mrs. McNab and Mrs. Bast, who come back to restore the house for the Ramsays. Unexpected, unknowable energies return us to the familiar human realm where the house is shored up for its returning inhabitants. The Ramsays who come back after ten years are a sadly depleted lot. Their lives are shadowed by loss and dwarfed by the interlude that "Time Passes" describes—those ten years in which the enormous forces of the nonhuman world and the carnage of World War I tore away the illusions of knowledge, control, and transcendence.

Around the same time that Virginia Woolf was probing these questions about the relation of humans to the vast and humbling forces of the world, John Dewey and phenomenologists such as Edmund Husserl and Martin Heidegger were also moving away from the disembodied idealism that Mr. Ramsay represents and that has dominated Western intellectual life since Plato. As early as 1929, Dewey was insisting that aesthetic and moral traits extend into all of the natural world and "testify to something that belongs to nature as truly as does the mechanical structure attributed to it in physical science" (Dewey 1929, 2). For him, human concepts are not the names of real essences: "Permanence, essence, totality, order, unity, rationality, the *unum, verum et bonum* of the classic tradition, are eulogistic predicates" that represent "an artificial simplification of existence" (1929, 28). Consonant with Einstein's discoveries about the relation of mass and energy, Dewey saw mind and matter as different characteristics of natural events (1929, 74), and he argued that symbols are not empty signs but rather incarnations (1929, 82). His 1934 book *Art as Experience* builds on these assumptions about the enmeshment of all human activity in the rest of the living world, defining experience as "the result, the sign, and the reward of that interaction of organism and environment which, when it is carried to the full, is a transformation of interaction into participation and communication" (Dewey 1934, 22). Art is prefigured in the very processes of living—including those of all animals and even plants—and form in the arts "is the art of making clear what is involved in the organization of space and time prefigured in every course of a developing life-experience" (1934, 24). Form thus grows out of natural processes of rhythmic conflict and fulfillment in animal life, and our ideas and purposes are generated by organs inherited from our evolutionary heritage (1934, 24–25).

In a philosophical approach that parallels Dewey's insistence on the physical, bodily center of art and mind, Husserl developed a phenomenology that led in turn to the participatory epistemology of Maurice Merleau-Ponty in its insistence on the body as locus of knowledge (Abram 1996, 35–45).

Merleau-Ponty developed an ontology that erases traditional distinctions of mind and body, spirit and matter, human and natural. "We have relearned to feel our body," Merleau-Ponty writes in *Phenomenology of Perception* (1986); "we have found underneath the objective and detached knowledge of the body that other knowledge which we have of it in virtue of its always being with us and of the fact that we are our body. In the same way we shall need to reawaken our experience of the world as it appears to us in so far as we are in the world through our body, and in so far as we perceive the world with our body" (Merleau-Ponty 1986, 206). Not long before he died, he explicitly called for the destruction of the objectivist ontology of the Cartesians and set out to achieve it himself (Merleau-Ponty 1968, 183).

Merleau-Ponty's final work, *The Visible and the Invisible* (1968, published after his sudden death in 1961), focuses attention on a concept of "the Flesh" which includes the body of the whole world. David Abram calls this "the mysterious tissue or matrix that underlies and gives rise to both the perceiver and the perceived as interdependent aspects of its own spontaneous activity" (Abram 1996, 66). This is just the kind of embeddedness Woolf has conjured in "Time Passes" on so cosmic a scale that individual human lives appear as brief presences awash in the vast sea of dynamic being. In fact, from *The Voyage Out* (1948) to *Between the Acts* (1969) the sea is the master metaphor surging through everything she wrote. Mrs. McNab and Mrs. Bast can be understood in this context as natural expressions of unknowable forces that heave up wars like other destructive weathers, absorb an Andrew or Prue Ramsay as easily as a wind or a dissolving iceberg. Merleau-Ponty said in *Phenomenology of Perception* that "we are the upsurge of time" (Merleau-Ponty 1986, 428), suggesting the same kind of brief appearances of definite shape and sentience that mark each discrete living being in the world for its particular duration in "Time Passes."

The fact that Woolf moves in "Time Passes" to deny the possibility of Nature's reflections of human emotion does not mean a denial of the possibility of harmony or relation. It is a stage in her progress toward the vision of her last novel, *Between the Acts*, in which all beings and phenomena are actively engaged with each other. *Between the Acts* is a series of embedded dramas, or plays within plays, in which all of geologic history and human history and English history interpenetrate each other and the lives of one rural family within its village community, in turn embedded within the lives of all the animals and plants, weathers and colors and landscapes that constitute that world. In fact Woolf suggests that a cesspool or murky fishpond can function as the central metaphor for all living processes, including artistic creation. The novel is also engaged in richly dialogic interchange with a living though fragmented English literary history, particularly through the village pageant but also through Woolf's passionate engagement with Shakespeare. *King Lear*, in all its anguished questioning of Nature and human existence, reverberates constantly in the interstices of Woolf's narrative language, as do echoes of Prospero's farewell to his art in *The Tempest*. As Shakespeare suggests about his own "insubstantial pageant faded," the village play staged in the novel—and by extension all works of literature— are clouds floating across the sky, taking brief shape and then moving and being dispersed by the wind as they drift along. The indeterminacy of the novel's picture of art and its meaning, indeed of language itself, seems an uncanny anticipation of Merleau-Ponty's definition of the proper language of philosophy in *The Visible and the Invisible*. There he claims that "the words most charged with philosophy are not necessarily those that contain what they say, but rather those that most energetically open up on Being, because they more closely convey the life of the whole and make our habitual evidences vibrate until they disjoin" (Merleau-Ponty 1968, 102). Rather than attempting to make words control or fix meaning, precisely capturing "what they say," Merleau-Ponty feels that the most appropriate uses of language must open on Being to help us see and question our assumptions. This is a radically interrogative use of language that opens us up to the uncertainty of the world. Woolf's narrative persona and her characters question and question the meaning of their lives and the meanings of Miss La Trobe's pageant. A central refrain of the pageant is the phrase "scraps, orts, and fragments" which seems to indicate all we can know and all that culture can preserve. Yet meaning is shaped from these fragments by the characters in the novel, and by ourselves as readers negotiating the silences and confusions, as well as the various propositions and symbolic suggestions of the text.

Between the Acts is set on the eve of World War II, with the menace of world affairs intruding by sinister signals increasingly toward the end, punctuating the closing ceremonies like harbingers of violent weather to come. It posits nonhuman forces and beings as crucial players in the human drama, both in the village pageant written by Miss La Trobe and in the world of its audience. Swallows, trees, cows, clouds, and rain interweave their existences with the activities of the June day in 1939 that is the scene of the novel. Again and again during the pageant, the wind blows the words away as the chorus of villagers chant their lines. Yet from time to time, cows lend their voices to fill up the spaces when the wind renders the villagers' words inaudible. "From cow after cow came the same yearning bellow. The whole world was filled with dumb yearning. It was the primeval voice sounding loud in the ear of the present moment" (Woolf 1969, 140). Again, the rain that comes as sudden relief during the gap of "ten mins. of present time" (1969, 179) that La Trobe has allowed in her pageant is "the other voice speaking, the voice that was no one's voice" (1969, 181). This idea is very close to the final sentence of the epigraph from Merleau-Ponty with which I began: "And, in a sense, as Valéry said, language is everything, since it is the voice of no one, since it is the very voice of the things, the waves, and the forests" (Merleau-Ponty 1968, 155). By the end of Woolf's novel it is clear that humans are only animals like their prehistoric ancestors eking out a life among the mammoths and rhododendrons in what is now Picadilly. Lucy Swithin, whose gentle intelligence and reverence tie modern humans to their ancient ancestors, makes her last appearance reading in her Outline of History, "Prehistoric man, half-human, half-ape, roused himself from his semi-crouching position and raised great stones." And then we turn to Giles and Isa Oliver, alone with their married antagonisms:

> Alone, enmity was bared; also love. Before they slept, they must fight; after they had fought, they would embrace. From that embrace another life might be born. But first they must fight, as the dog fox fights with the vixen, in the heart of darkness, in the fields of night. . . . The house had lost its shelter. It was night before roads were made, or houses. It was the night that dwellers in caves had watched from some high place among rocks. Then the curtain rose. They spoke. (Woolf 1969, 218–19)

I am sure Virginia Woolf would have been delighted by the recent discovery of the nine-thousand-year-old skeleton called Cheddar Man and the DNA evidence of his common ancestry with forty-two-year-old Adrian Targett, a history teacher in the town of Cheddar at the present time (*The Register-Guard* 1997, 20A). This is exactly the kind of background she carefully—and ironically—draws for the Oliver family. The Olivers are "latecomers" with only two hundred years' habitation of Pointz Hall, and they are unaware that the fishmonger's boy who delivers their luncheon fish has a name recorded in the Domesday Book, or that some ancient skeleton like Cheddar Man could be buried in the murky depths of their lily pond or in the earth beneath their house or garden.

John Dewey's sense of an aesthetic intrinsic to all the living world, perhaps even including rocks, electrical forces, and winds as well as animals and plants, and Merleau-Ponty's concept of communal unity can stand as an illuminating backdrop for Woolf's elucidation of a participatory consciousness immersed in the Flesh or the Body of the World in the same primal way that our prehistoric human ancestors experienced it. This is a relationship we share with all other creatures, as Woolf implies in the "Time Passes" section of *To the Lighthouse* and in her interweaving of the lives of humans and birds, cows and fish, trees and weather in *Between the Acts*. Merleau-Ponty defines a similar human "coexistence or *communion*" (Merleau-Ponty 1986, 213; emphasis added;) with all the things and beings—an engagement of the sensing body in the world of primal being. "This environment of brute existence and essence is not something mysterious: we never quit it, we have no other environment" (Merleau-Ponty

1968, 116–17). Unlike the hierarchical, transcendent separateness of Platonic humanism, the new epistemology shared by Virginia Woolf, John Dewey, and Maurice Merleau-Ponty stresses enmeshment, reciprocity, dynamism, and continuity as the qualities of our knowing and being. Merleau-Ponty believed in the active power of the world to call us to attention, and he saw our relationships with things as sacred. "If the qualities [of a thing] radiate around them a certain mode of existence, if they have the power to cast a spell and what we called just now a sacramental value, this is because the sentient subject does not posit them as objects, but enters into a sympathetic relation with them, makes them [her] own and finds in them [her] momentary law" (Merleau-Ponty 1986, 214). As he explained this respectful, dynamic relationship near the end of his life, Merleau-Ponty claimed that we can only know things by attending to the ways in which they offer themselves to us. They only do so, he believed, "to someone who wishes not to have them but to see them—not to hold them as with forceps, or to immobilize them as under the objective of a microscope, but to let them be and to witness their continued being" (Merleau-Ponty 1968, 101). This kind of interrogative, participatory engagement lies at the heart of Virginia Woolf's work and is the kind of vision she seeks to shape in *Between the Acts*. The emphasis of all her fiction on the fragmentary quality of perception, the myriad possible perspectives on reality and thus the relativity of any one view, and her acceptance of indeterminacy dramatize an epistemology congruent with the lessons of modern physics and ecological science. She would have rejoiced to learn that her efforts to overthrow the reductionist Platonism of Western philosophical tradition were being seconded by the philosophies of John Dewey and Maurice Merleau-Ponty. Woolf was acutely aware of the gendered history of abstract philosophy, as we have seen in her treatment of Mr. Ramsay's work in *To the Lighthouse*, but she did not want to substitute one essentialism for another. Her interest in quantum physics and her stress on the need for an androgynous mind indicate that she understood the problem of knowing to be a general human one, and the embodied aesthetic of John Dewey, like Maurice Merleau-Ponty's description of our intertwining within the flesh of the world, help to develop the radical ecological epistemology toward which her novels gesture.

Notes

A revised version of this chapter was published in *New Literary History* as "Virginia Woolf and the Flesh of the World," 30.4 (Autumn 1999): 855–75.

   1. Shepard 1991; Merchant 1980; Ehrenfeld 1978; Solnit 1994; DuBois 1988; Oelschlaeger 1991; Abram 1996; Westling 1996; and King 1990.

   2. Beer 1996, 112–24; Lee 1996, 554; and Pridmore-Brown 1998, 408–21.

3. Stevie Davies sees "Time Passes" as "the mourning central part" of the Modernist pastoral elegy that is the whole effort of *To the Lighthouse*, but while the novel can be profitably read in that way, it is only one of many valid approaches (Davies 1989, 121–38). I think that "Time Passes" needs to be considered for itself as a meditation on the place of humans in the world.

Davies also reads "Time Passes" as an ironic passage which both mocks human narcissism with its references to the mirrors that no longer reflect the flawed forms of the humanly visualized Real, and simultaneously presents a realm of "pure integrity" in which the Platonic Forms "reveal themselves and unite before the mindless mirror" (Davies 1989, 76–77). As my discussion of Mr. Ramsay's work makes clear, and as I explain in examining "Time Passes," I see Woolf's effort in a completely contrary light.

References

Abram, David. 1996. *The spell of the sensuous: Perception and language in a more-than-human world.* New York: Pantheon.

Beer, Gillian. 1996. *Virginia Woolf: The common ground.* Ann Arbor: University of Michigan Press.

Davies, Stevie. 1989. *Virginia Woolf: To the lighthouse.* Penguin Critical Studies. Harmondsworth: Penguin.

Dewey, John. 1929. *Experience and nature.* New York: Norton.

———. 1934. *Art as experience.* New York: Perigee.

Doyle, Laura. 1994. These emotions of the body: Intercorporeal narrative in *To the lighthouse. Twentieth-Century Literature* 40: 42–71.

DuBois, Page. 1988. *Sowing the body: Psychoanalysis and ancient representations of women.* Chicago: University of Chicago Press.

Ehrenfeld, David. 1978. *The arrogance of humanism.* New York: Oxford University Press.

King, Ynestra. 1990. Healing the wounds: Feminism, ecology, and the nature/culture dualism. In *Reweaving the world: The emergence of ecofeminism,* ed. Irene Diamond and Gloria Feman Orenstein. San Francisco: Sierra Club.

Lee, Hermione. 1992. Introduction, Virginia Woolf. *To the lighthouse.* London: Penguin.

———. 1996. *Virginia Woolf.* London: Chatto and Windus.

Lovelock, James. 1979. *Gaia: A new look at life on earth.* New York: Oxford.

———. 1988. *The ages of Gaia.* New York: Norton.

Margulis, Lynn, and Dorion Sagan. 1986. *Microcosmos: Four billion years of evolution from our microbial ancestors.* New York: Summit.

———. 1997. *Slanted truths: Essays on Gaia, symbiosis, and evolution.* New York: Copernicus.

Merchant, Carolyn. 1980. *The death of nature: Women, ecology, and the scientific revolution.* New York: Harper.

Merleau-Ponty, Maurice. 1968. *The visible and the invisible,* trans. Alphonso Lingis. Evanston, Ill.: Northwestern University Press.

———. 1986. *Phenomenology of perception,* trans. Colin Smith. London: Routledge.

Oelschlaeger, Max. 1991. *The idea of wilderness.* New Haven, Conn.: Yale University Press.

Plato. n.d. *The republic,* trans. B. Jowett. New York: Modern Library.

Pridmore-Brown, Michele. 1998. 1939–40: Of Virginia Woolf, gramophones, and fascism. *PMLA* 113, 3: 408–21.

Shepard, Paul. 1991. *Man in the landscape.* Orig. pub. 1967. College Station: Texas A&M University Press.

Solnit, Rebecca. 1994. *Savage dreams: A journey into the landscape wars of the American west.* New York: Vintage.

The Register-Guard. Eugene, Oregon. March 9, 1997: 20A.

Westling, Louise. 1996. *The green breast of the new world: Landscape, gender, and American fiction.* Athens: University of Georgia Press.

Woolf, Virginia. 1925. *The common reader.* London: Hogarth.

———. 1929. *A room of one's own.* New York: Harcourt.

———. 1948. *The voyage out.* Orig. pub. 1915. New York: Harcourt.

———. 1969. *Between the acts.* New York: Harcourt.

———. 1977. *Letters, volume 3 1923–1928,* ed. Nigel Nicolson and Joanne Trautmann. New York: Harcourt.

———. 1990. *A passionate apprentice: The early journals 1897–1909,* ed. Mitchell A. Leaska. New York: Harcourt.

———. 1992a. *Jacob's room.* Orig. pub. 1922. London: Penguin.

———. 1992b. *Mrs. Dalloway.* Orig. pub. 1925. London: Penguin.

———. 1992c. *To the lighthouse.* London: Penguin.

PART IV

WHOSE STORIES? WHICH BIASES?

CHAPTER TWELVE

RATIONAL IMAGININGS, RESPONSIBLE KNOWINGS: HOW FAR CAN YOU SEE FROM HERE?

LORRAINE CODE

INTRODUCTION

The epistemic subject is a shadowy figure in orthodox Anglo-American theories of knowledge. Not only is it irrelevant to wonder who he is, it amounts merely to a diversion from the main tasks of epistemology to ask where and how he is located, or to claim epistemic significance for the feelings and motivations that prompt his knowledge-making projects.[1] He is, and for epistemological purposes, *should be* disconnected from situational idiosyncrasies and from the distractions of affect, human relationships, and personal, social, or cultural history. More specifically for my purposes here, a stark objectivity requirement that traditionally stands as a condition *sine qua non* for knowledge properly so called underwrites the expectations, first, that he can and will expunge imagination and interpretation from his cognitive projects in order to escape the ineluctably subjective threat they pose to a process that has to transcend subjectivity if it is to yield knowledge; and second, that his perceptual knowledge is universally replicable, without variation or interference, by any knower in comparable circumstances.

This knower utters the knowledge claims that derive from his (controlled) observations in formal, monological propositions that are publicly testable against evidence that is equally available to everyone. For classical empiricists, such observation-derived data comprise the building blocks of which knowledge is made: "simples" usually caused by such medium-sized material objects as coins, envelopes, or colored patches, that become foundational for more complex knowledge claims. When observations move to the laboratory, a presumption accompanies them according to which information-processing from controlled input to statistically variant output offers the best available, standard-setting objective knowledge. A knower cannot, on this model, know anything well enough to do anything with it or about it; nor does the exemplary status accorded such knowledge claims reveal how these empirical "knowns" figure in his life. Rarely do other people count as part of what he knows, except in recognitions—that this is a man but that is a robot—or in laboratory investigations of standardized, quantifiable behavioral responses, all of whose (subjective) specificities are deemed epistemologically insignificant. Rooted in his observation post, which is strictly separated from anything he claims to know, this epistemic subject is restricted in his knowings to what he can see from there.

This—admittedly somewhat caricatured—sketch of the orthodox epistemic subject offers the starkest, thinnest of outlines. My intention in presenting it is not to gloss over recent departures from this model, in naturalized and socialized epistemologies, in post-Wittgensteinian theories, and in revivals of pragmatism. Instead, I am suggesting that idealized versions of this hybrid of Baconian, Cartesian, and positivistic lineage exert a continuous pull on regulative epistemic principles even within theories committed to modifying or evading its reductive excesses.[2] Yet my purpose is not just to call epistemology to account for being "too abstract," scientistic, remote from ordinary epistemic lives: this project is well advanced in feminist and other postcolonial theories. I am interested in some ongoing effects of these epistemic restrictions in places where responsible knowing makes a difference—often a vital difference—to people's lives. For this epistemic subject does not travel well into places where knowing people in real, yet "extraordinary," situations is the issue. Such knowings pose problems for theories whose infinitely replicable subject constructs his knowledge around uncontested assumptions that everyone is just like *him*, and that anyone can "stand in" for anyone else, as knower or known. In short, I am proposing that *imaginative-interpretive* sensitivity to human specificities and commonalities is integral to knowing people well enough to act responsibly with them, toward them, or for them; and that imagining is at least as rational a component of these processes as observational knowing and its multiples.

My focus, then, is on the intricacies of subjectivity: both of subjects knowing and subjects known, taking my starting point from Barbara Johnson's introduction to *Freedom and Interpretation: The Oxford Amnesty Lectures 1992* (1993), whose contributors were invited to "consider the consequences of the deconstruction of the self for the liberal tradition," to ask whether the self "as construed by the liberal tradition still exist[s]," and if it does not, "whose human rights are we [=we Amnesty activists] defending?" (1993, 2). They were to address an apparent inconsistency, then, between the defense of human rights that is at the core of Amnesty International's mandate, and postmodern deconstructions of the humanistic subject that contest the very idea of a unified human self as bearer of rights.

My underlying thesis in what follows is that the self of the liberal tradition (the autonomous bearer of rights, the rational self-conscious agent, and thence the orthodox empiricist knower) has only ever existed in narrowly conceived theoretical places, abstracted from the exigencies of human lives. Of special significance for my purposes is his principled isolation from affective engagement with the exigencies that surface insistently in experiences of trauma, and in everyday moments marked by the vulnerability and trust that demand responsible knowing. The deconstruction of the self in postmodern thought, I will suggest, is matched if not exceeded by ordinary and extraordinary assaults on integrated subjectivity that occur routinely just below the polite surface of the liberal tradition, for which "autonomous man" is emblematic of all that is humanly admirable.[3]

The epistemologies of liberal-empiricist societies offer scant resources, either in professional or in secular situations, to epistemic subjects who need to know people responsibly not only because their rights are under threat, but because their very selves are under pressure. With their commitment to maintaining an objectivity that requires detachment from the "object of knowledge," these epistemologies work with a model of knowledge-and-subjectivity within which knowledge is achieved by a legislated purging of affect, and subjectivity is uniform, yet rarely individuated. In knowledge, affect could only compromise objective clarity; affect in the person(s) to be known would be chaotic, unstable, unknowable. Thus even the idea of affective knowledge becomes oxymoronic. Such epistemic assumptions block putative knowings that are prompted and informed by, or dependent on, very specific functionings or malfunctionings of affectivity: of pain, sorrow, fear, suffering. Thus orthodox epistemic subjects cannot know well enough to be able to respond appropriately/effectively, in situations that occur "at the limits" of ordinary experiential expectations. For it is neither the self as one-time rights bearer nor the self as theoretically dispersed that pushes most urgently at the boundaries of received, objectivist knowledge, but the self struggling to reconstruct itself from trauma. This is a self whose disintegration also puts the affective/imaginative self-certainties of its would-be (humanistic) knowers into question just when those putatively more "stable" selves most need to hold steady, in order to know well.[4]

Pertinent to addressing this impasse in empiricist-liberal knowing is a conceptual contrast Barbara Johnson introduces. She writes:

> While the Anglo-American ("liberal") tradition tends to speak about the "self," the French tradition tends to speak about the "subject." . . . The concept of "self" is closely tied to the notion of property. I speak of "my" self. In the English tradition, the notions of "self" and "property" are inseparable from the notion of "rights." . . . The French tradition, derived most importantly from Descartes's "I think, therefore I am," centers on the importance of reason or thought as the foundation of (human) being. Where the "self," as property, resembles a thing, the "subject," as reason, resembles a grammatical function. . . . [I]n the sentence "I think, *therefore* I am," what is posited is that it is *thinking* that gives the subject being. (1993, 3)

Here I examine some moral-political-epistemological implications of Amnesty's question to its contributors that bear on issues of "individuals" and individuality, framed within and against Barbara Johnson's self-or-subjectivity dyad.

Paul Ricoeur highlights some of these implications in his lecture, "Self as *Ipse*" (1993), where he appeals to "the notion of narrative identity . . . [as] the indispensable link between the identity of a speaking and acting subject and that of an ethico-juridical subject" (1993, 114). Narrative identity is, by definition, temporally situated in its own evolving specificity; and socially located in its utterances that connect "an 'I' and a 'you' " (1993, 111), and in its openness to the third-person narratives from which people learn about themselves. Thus in response to Amnesty's question, Ricoeur proposes a revisioned, addressive-dialogic selfhood *enacted* in an ability to take present, and future, responsibility for its thoughts and deeds: a subject for which "recognition is constitutive of both the self and his/her other" (1993, 119). In its emphasis on reciprocity and responsibility, Ricoeur's project suggests one way of opening out the orthodox model of knowledgeable selfhood interpretively, imaginatively, into narrative articulations that go beyond monologic affirmations of rights and self-ownership. In its recognition of how identity is shaped by what matters, and to whom, the project moves away from the suppression of affect and specificity to which I have referred. The dialogic, *interpretive* grounding of the project, with its appeal to the imaginative variations on identity "enhanced by literature" (1993, 115), suggests that imaginative knowings can yield more than rehearsals of the ready-made scripts available in the dominant liberal social imaginary only if self, subjectivity, and epistemic agency are radically rethought.

Even the Amnesty question holds the knowings that it problematizes to deconstructions and fragmentations of selves at a level more theoretical, less subjectively basic, than the oppression, torture, abuse, and rape that are Amnesty's own mandate to address, where victims, and others who attempt to know them and their circumstances, must deal with disintegrations far more radical than theoretical deconstruction: traumas that make owning one's capacities and actions far less matter-of-course than liberal presuppositions assume. Hence the need to engage with the intricacies of epistemic and moral subjectivity.

As a sort of bottom line for this inquiry, I favor preserving some version of rights talk as an ultimate court of appeal, together with the cognate language of rationality-as-objectivity, while extracting them from their intrication with the implausible individualism that attaches to self-ownership and epistemic autonomy.[5] I read "subjectivity" against these ideas to expose their limitations. But "self-or-subject" is neither a tidy distinction, nor does it function dichotomously in this chapter or elsewhere. Both rights talk (=talk of the self) and discourses of enacted, located subjectivity variously inform feminist and other antioppression, postcolonial analyses: there need be no forced choice between them. Thus, the Amnesty question about rights relates to how these locutions—"self-or-subject"—are enacted, against and within one another. As Amnesty activists also must, I consider how "limit experiences"— experiences that traverse and interrogate the viable extension of "norms" that are embedded in normalizing discourses—contest the standard liberal epistemology, ontology, and morality of "the self." These experiences demand radical rethinking of subjectivity not just in philosophy, but in lives where subjectivity is under pressure from story lines too difficult to bear, sustain, or imagine "from here." Amnesty activists need to practice a peculiarly imaginative, discursively responsive knowing that is wary of replicating the very silencings and other oppressions it aims to counteract. Questions about violence, political oppression, and torture open out into vexed questions about how practitioners and other putative knowers who are situated in comfort and stability, can know such radically "other" situations well enough to act/judge/advocate. Frequently, it appears that they can, even in the absence of experiential congruity. But how can that be, given the limits of locational specificity?

In the next section I begin to develop a critical response to this question, through a reading of Mark Johnson's *Moral Imagination* (1993). My aim is to show how certain entrenched assumptions about "the imagination" in the social imaginary of the affluent masculine liberal Western world both enable and thwart attempts to think through these issues. Specifically, I contend that responsible imagining is more and other than a mere stretching, an additive or

variational extension of empirical seeing: indeed, that imagination thus construed cannot enable epistemic subjects to imagine rationally or know responsibly beyond a narrowly delineated "here."

"ORDINARY LIVES"

Mark Johnson develops an innovative analysis of the workings of imagination
in "ordinary" people's everyday cognitions. He "naturalizes" the account with an
appeal to cognitive science's demonstrations that "We human beings are imaginative creatures, from our most mundane, automatic acts of perception all the
way up to our most abstract conceptualization and reasoning" (1993, ix): that
imagining is integral to the "discriminations" that enable people to act "sensibly
and responsibly toward others" (1993, x). Drawing on experimentally revealed
"prototypical" and "nonprototypical" conceptual structures that shape human
reasoning across a range of situations, Johnson contends that imagination is no
enemy of reason: concepts and reasoning are "grounded in . . . bodily experience
and . . . structured by various kinds of imaginative process" (1993, 1). Reason
devoid of imagination, he claims, lacks the conceptual-theoretical scope to go
beyond simple, exemplary cases to "those that are either nonprototypical or
completely novel" (1993, 3). Thus Johnson deplores erasures of imagination
from the governing conceptions of rationality in objectivist epistemologies and
moral philosophies.

　　As in his coauthored book *Metaphors We Live By* (Lakoff and Johnson
1980), Johnson contends that people interpret their lives through socially entrenched metaphors of "common moral understanding" (1993, 52). This understanding evolves within a metaphorics, an open-ended, malleable system
of metaphors and sedimented imaginings that embody a communal sense of
how things are, and frame moral perceptions and deliberations. Knowing
emerges as "imaginative exploration and transformation of experience" not,
then, as a "pigeonholing of cases under a set of fixed rules" (1993, 80) or descriptions, with the consequence that the sheer plethora of "possible fram-
ings" for any situation enjoins modesty in claims to knowledge (1993, 12) and
cautions against reductivism. Hence good moral decisions depend on the
quality of the imaginings that inform them. Nor is imagination merely subjective: it is as communal as it is "individual."[6]

　　For Johnson, objectivists work with an "impoverished conception of
reason . . . [and] an equally problematic correlative view of the self . . . [which]
cannot account for . . . the moral identity of a person [as] an ongoing, culturally
and historically situated, imaginative process of thought and action" (1993,
126); for how "we grope around for our identity, which is never a fixed or fin-

ished thing" (1993, 147). What it knows and how it acts matters for this epistemic (and moral) subject, for the self is "at stake in moments of choice and deliberation," which is an "activity of self-understanding, critical self-reflection, and self-formation" (1993, 148). Human beings, thus, are both "*constituted* by sedimented cultural practices, institutions and meanings . . . and *constituting* beings who can . . . transform . . . structures of meaning and action" (1993, 161). Such constitutive activities manifest themselves in "narrative unities" (1993, 154) that frame and reframe people's self-understandings: these epistemic subjects are storytellers about their lives.

Johnson thus goes a considerable distance toward contesting the caricatured activities (=passivities!) of orthodox epistemic subjects with which feminist epistemologists also take issue. His is a richly innovative analysis of the imaginings most readily available in the normal operative spaces of "ordinary lives" in Western societies: spaces that are at once hospitable to "most people's" everyday experiences, and sources of the conceptual frames, the "common sense," and the media imagery out of which they construct their sense of self, community, and world. His work offers a valuable corrective to the exclusions of imagination integral to postpositivist moral epistemologies, even as it suggests how theorists might fill some of the gaps in the experience-remote theories that call forth feminist and postcolonial critique. I have read Johnson's text as a resource for developing a successor epistemology cognizant of the place of imagination in knowing, and this reading has been productive. Yet these points of consonance also highlight some dissonances I now address.

Johnson is persuasive in showing that the knowings of a generic knower are as imaginative as they are conventionally rational. He locates these proposals within ordinary lives, and substantiates them with evidence from experimental psychology that "naturalizes" his conclusions. Yet my hesitations about going further with him are responses to tacit assumptions in the text that represent the scope of his conclusions as broader than the premises of the inquiry permit. An analogy with standard S-knows-that-p knowledge claims will clarify this point. Such knowledge claims—"Susan knows that the door is locked"—perform an exemplary function within circumscribed observational frames where perceptual evidence warrants straightforward conclusions, and in uncontestable multiples of such evidence-derived, empirically verifiable knowings. But their epistemic pertinence diminishes in situations whose complexity differs in kind, not just degree, from what could be derived from accumulations of such claims. Nor is it easy to discern their pertinence to the specificities of situations and events that disrupt the settled frame within which such knowings pass as paradigmatic. S-knows-that-p claims are representative, exemplary across a far narrower range than epistemologists tend to allow.[7]

Comparable restrictions on the representative status of "ordinary lives" circumscribe Johnson's inquiry. His implicit assumptions about such lives show by contrast and omission that epistemic subjects can, in fact, be liberated from their rootedness in an unspecifiable "here" only by means of thoroughly revisionary sociopolitical analyses that contest the traditional liberal assumptions about selfhood and self-ownership to which Barbara Johnson refers. In the next sections I move in and out of Mark Johnson's text, showing how it contributes to reconfiguring the place of imagination in knowing; indicating where it sustains beliefs inimical to, and indeed often obstructive of, the development of politically effective successor epistemologies.

CONTRA JOHNSON, AFTER ALL

Donna Haraway's observation that "Knowledge from the point of view of the unmarked is truly fantastic, distorted, and so irrational" (1991, 193) accounts for some of the problematic effects of Johnson's position. We "imaginative creatures" appear in this text within an epistemic-ethical frame that departs only minimally from orthodox liberal thought. True, the imagination he analyzes stretches ahead of and backward away from the imaginer: it is neither time-, place-, nor even body-bound; thus it seems to release the epistemic subject from his rootedness to one spot. Johnson heralds this potential release within a cognitive science frame—he naturalizes it, sometimes situates it ecologically, locates it within narrative structures. Having advocated many of these same moves, I have looked to this text for a way of reconfiguring knowledge and subjectivity imaginatively, relationally, and ecologically, that would be continuous with my epistemological project (see Code 1996). Yet even with so many of the ingredients in place, the mix does not quite work; and the reasons are instructive well beyond the scope of the discussion in *Moral Imagination*.

Especially telling among these reasons is one of the overarching metaphors "we" live by: "life is a journey," which Johnson explains thus:

> In our culture, living a life is conceived of as a massive purposeful activity made up of a huge number of intermediate actions directed toward various purposes. We are expected to have goals ... and to formulate life plans that make it possible for us to attain [them]. . . . A PURPOSEFUL LIFE IS A JOURNEY is perhaps the dominant metaphor by which we structure our experience, understanding, and language concerning our ongoing life projects. (1993, 39)

But whose culture is this? Whose experience? Who expects to formulate life plans, have ongoing life projects? claim recognition for their validity? live so smoothly that they will easily go through? Their number has always been restricted to a privileged group; in the social upheavals and collapse of the social support systems in the 1990s, even for the affluent, disruptions have more often been the norm. The metaphor is class, race, able-bodied, and gender specific: according to my students, it is generation specific as well.[8]

In short, Johnson's examples, which are drawn mainly from the lives of right-thinking affluent White Western men, perpetuate an illusion that rational imaginings and responsible knowings "in general" fit easily within the ready-made frame of "our" lives, presented in the text so as to sustain an assumption of straightforward self-ownership. The "vanilla" imaginings on which his argument depends bypass the necessity, urgent in feminist and postcolonial theory and practice, of imagining the unimaginable.[9] He takes "our shared" moral intuitions, thoughts, principles, even experiences, for granted, in a benignly "evolving environment" to which "we" adapt in the course of life's journey. Thus his examples reinforce assumptions of universal sameness that render human differences not so different after all; and although his appeals to imagination in knowledge and morality break through the seamlessness of malestream objectivism in many of the ways that feminists have advocated, just below the surface, there are problems. Johnson does well with imagining the familiar, less well with imagining the strange, where "strange" means alien to the experiences of an articulate White American man. Indeed this conceptual apparatus can neither make the familiar strange, nor approach the strange except by making it familiar. In consequence, Johnson's epistemic and moral subject remains fixed in place after all, unable to see very far from there, and—appearances to the contrary—"there" is no unmarked, innocent place. Nor, more significantly, does this epistemic subject see that he cannot see: his imaginings remain imperceptibly rooted in the here and now, despite Johnson's best intentions.

The "person" who inhabits this text, then, is implicitly male, and a liberal "self." Noting that "women have not been granted the same prototypical status as men with respect to moral personhood,"[10] that "'phallocentric' and racist biases . . . pervade Western culture" (1993, 99), Johnson proposes ways of imagining beyond the stratified, stereotyped assumptions that these recognitions record. Yet although it may sound like a tired old story, it is the practices of "we-saying" to which he tacitly appeals that keep the imaginative subject firmly in his place. References to an unidentified, universalizing "we," "us," and "our" are jarring in their unselfconscious frequency. Given what "we" can unquestioningly assume, think, expect, do, there is little doubt that "we" are able-bodied adult educated affluent White men, and there is considerable doubt about the scope—even the imaginative scope—of the "we." In one sense this might not matter, for it could be read to show that Johnson's is a *situated* position on knowledge and imagination. But only a casual reading of situatedness would suggest such a conclusion. It is integral to Haraway's conception of *situated knowledges* that knowers take responsibility for the implications and effects of situatedness; that they recognize the impossibility of an innocent positioning. Yet although Johnson contends that "our very prototypes are in dispute" (1993, 99), he assumes that they are "ours"—everyone's: a locution that might be a mere slip of the pen were the "we" and "our" not so silently aggregated.

Prototypes, Johnson asserts, "*can* supply what we need to make intelligent moral decisions," via "principles of extension . . . from the central to the noncentral members within a category" (1993, 190; italics in original). To this end, he grants a pivotal place to "imaginative empathetic projection into the experience of other people": to putting ourselves "in the place of another" (1993, 199). Here, then, is another potential point of intersection between feminist imaginings and Johnson's position. Feminists, too—and I among them—have debated the desirability and the dangers of empathy (see Ferguson 1984; Code 1995a). Empathy is desirable for promoting a social order that is more than merely instrumental, for enabling respectful, affective engagement across the myriad differences that responsible knowings have to acknowledge; yet at the same time it is dangerous in affirming the center's capacity to coopt, appropriate, own the experiences and situations of Others. Such dangers resurface in Johnson's assumption that "we" can "inhabit [other people's worlds] . . . in imagination, feelings, and expression" (1993, 200). Despite the part that he believes empathy plays in breaking the boundedness of self-certainty, Johnson remains caught within the liberal assumption that, as Nicola Lacey aptly puts it, "a single individual can 'get inside' the experiences of others, imagine what their lives might be, *without ever having actually to listen to anyone else*" (1998a, 65; italics in original). "Hard cases," harder than those Johnson adduces, show that there is no easy resolution.

The hooker's tale, which he apparently includes in order to unsettle the homogeneity of the "we," is one such case. In his analysis of a story in which a hooker tries to "reconstruct the narrative of her actual lived experience . . . [to] explain . . . herself and her actions from a *moral* standpoint" (1993, 154; italics in original), Johnson reads past textual evidence of the effects of a systemically embedded sex/gender system in shaping her story of how it is to be a woman in a sexist society, accustomed to giving "sexual favors" in order to "attract, hold a man." Glossing over their specificity within the politics of a gender order, he draws the hooker's experiences into "our" narratives, to illustrate how "*we ordinary humans* understand, deliberate, and evaluate within . . .

narrative contexts, even though we are seldom aware of this" (1993, 160; italics in original). Thus he evokes the idea that "we" are constituted by cultural practices more in the name of an implicit human sameness than in imaginative engagement with the radical experiential differences that separate "us." Despite his plea for a self-knowledge aware of its "limitations, and blind spots" (1993, 187), these reduce both in his reading of the hooker's tale—and in a briefer allusion to the "limited, situated freedom" of an Afro-American woman in the American South of the 1950s—to differences that merely mask "our" commonalities; to a freedom "we all possess" (1993, 162).

Representing human development as gradual change with "infrequent . . . moments of more radical and rapid transformations" (1993, 109) presupposes a stability of lives lived evenly, from beginning to middle to end. Adaptability, and imaginative techniques for achieving it, assume a process within a frame that holds fast. Yet Johnson does not make clear how the frame *could* hold in conceptual (=prototype) crisis; in "gaps, disjunctions, reversals, fractures" (1993, 170), which for feminists and other postcolonial theorists-activists count more as the norm than the exception. Lives fragmented in fractured processes cannot adapt so readily, cannot keep on "weaving together the threads" (1993, 152). Nor, as feminists know well, are "our" narratives always, or even so usually, "our own" as assumptions about narrative unity imply (e.g., 1993, 164). "The power of fictional narrative to develop our moral sensitivity, our ability to make subtle discriminations, and our empathy for others" (1993, 197) comes up against its own limitations when lives and/or events defy narrative elaboration beyond an imaginative rootedness that is unaware of its own fixity, and when tellers can never be sure that anyone is listening. "We," whoever we are, delude ourselves if we think that such events are merely extraordinary. Johnson's smooth narratives of ordinary self-ownership expose the poverty of an imagination that merely extends out from positions at the center: that fails in its monologic tellings to negotiate the reciprocity and recognition—the relationality—that for Ricoeur, are constitutive of the self and his/her other.

Thus because Johnson conceives of imagination as *belonging to* someone, it remains oddly individualized even through his affirmations of its communal, public character: its putative commonality fails to exceed the sum of its parts. Here especially, the English tradition of the liberal self has to make way for thinking within the language of *subjectivity*, of enactment, which Barbara Johnson traces to a continuation of the French (Cartesian) tradition (1993, 3). Thus she observes that "while Descartes saw a *coincidence* of human thinking with human being, Lacan sees a *disjunction* . . . an illusion of the stable self [that] motivates a lifelong attempt to "catch up" to the image." In a Foucauldian disciplinary society, she notes, this subject becomes "a function of what a given society defines as thinkable" (1993, 6).

Despite his innovative proposals, then, which might have worked toward redefining the thinkable, Mark Johnson remains conservatively, statically within what is readily thinkable in affluent White liberal societies. In consequence, the conceptual apparatus he develops offers no way of thinking beyond the limits of the social imaginary that is regulative within such societies. Although he effectively defies the restrictions that make "*rational* imaginings" merely oxymoronic, his imaginative knowers live and imagine within the self-certainties of late capitalism, individualism, and the transparent, bounded, and unified "self construed by the liberal tradition" (recalling the Amnesty phrase): within the American dream, where everyone has a life plan and the freedom to pursue it; where knowledge enables mastery over the "external" world and morality enables mastery over "the self." These certainties underwrite and frame the orthodox epistemologies of the mainstream with their impersonal, interchangeable objectivity, and the moral theories that appeal to autonomy, individual rights, equality of opportunity, and standardized conceptions of human decency and "the good life."

RATIONAL IMAGININGS, RESPONSIBLE KNOWINGS

The complex of interlocking assumptions that presume universal human sameness and discount singular experiences at the limits of what the society defines as thinkable is held in place by a hegemonic imaginary: an *instituted social imaginary*.[11] A social imaginary is somewhat analogous to a Kuhnian paradigm or a Foucauldian episteme; but it is neither about normal science, nor only about how knowledge is spread out before the knower. It is about systems of metaphorics and interlocking explanations-expectations within which people somewhere, in specific time periods and geographical-cultural situations, enact their knowledge and subjectivities. Imaginaries are self-reinforcing rather as self-fulfilling prophecies are. Ongoing "successes" within them, an undisturbed smoothness of "life's journey" that continually sustains the dream, consolidate their sense of rightness. In one structural feature, however, they resemble both paradigms and epistemes: pressures, destabilizations, ruptures, breaks—from above, within, or below—repeated explanatory stress, can become so insistent that the imaginary, ultimately, can no longer accommodate it in its seamlessly enveloping story. It becomes clear that the center cannot hold: and this despite the fact that a tenacious belief that the center *must* continue to hold still informs the replicability and universalizability requirements that sustain the regulative normativity integral to the epistemologies that the orthodox epistemic subject silently inhabits. How, then, to dislodge it?

Consider how the Amnesty Lectures, and three essays in which Susan Brison develops a first-person philosophical analysis of a rape (*her* rape), contest the stability of the dominant social imaginary and the limitations of what is thinkable within it. These examples show something of the difficulty, even with an intelligently imaginative conceptual apparatus, of knowing responsibly "from here." They serve as reminders that despite professional philosophy's professed unconcern with the specificities of subjectivity, some specificities in fact draw its attention sharply enough to prompt it to relegate certain events, certain testimonials, to the categories of the nonrational, the merely particular: to cast them as aberrant episodic disturbances; to disqualify their tellers as reliable knowers of the stories of "their own" lives.

Brison demonstrates that the personal, in its full affective particularity, is indeed philosophical—epistemological—in her analyses of self and subjectivity in disintegration, striving for a liveable reintegration, in posttraumatic stress following sexual violence (Brison 1993; 1995; 1997). She tells this story of rape and gradual recovery frankly and bravely, in the first person, recreating a very ordinary daytime walk in the French countryside that became the scene of a brutal rape, after which she was beaten and left for dead. In the narrative process, Brison rejects the comfortable option of distancing herself from the story in the interests of generality or objectivity. Thus she breaks the philosophical taboo that keeps the subject, whether as knower or as known, hovering silently in the wings, speaking only in the third person as though into a void. She addresses her readers, offers them "imaginative access to what is, for some, an unimaginable experience" (1993, 5), asks them to *listen*, to try to know how an experience beyond the limits of their imaginings can disrupt the self in the assuredness of its self-ownership. Her essays affirm that it is not only or even principally the deconstructions of postmodernity that fragment the presumed unity of the subject, but unimaginable everyday, ordinary events. Indeed, Brison reminds her readers of "the every-dayness of sexual violence" (1993, 7), in an account that should dislodge the standard knowing subject from the certainties built into the epistemic imaginary he inhabits; fracture the structures that hold it together; destabilize the belief that "life is a journey" at whose way-stations and at whose end people simply arrive in the fullness of time. Ironically, its very every-dayness "leads many to think that male violence against women is natural" (1993, 7); and yet—recalling the tenacity of the assumption that the center must hold after all—she observes that "while most people take sexual violence for granted, they simultaneously manage to deny that it really exists" (1993, 7).

Barbara Johnson notes that "Torture . . . becomes an interference with the tortured one's narrative self-determination" (1993, 12); a fragmentation of narrative unity that also must challenge the complacency of assuming that "life is a journey." Analogously, Brison's theme is "the disintegration of the self experienced by victims of violence" (Brison 1993, 7). She depicts "the undoing of the self" in the undermining "of its most fundamental assumptions about the world" (1995, 38); the severing, when trauma is of human origin, of "the sustaining connection between the self and the rest of humanity" (1997, 14). Her essays present a chronicle of the willed unknowings that too much particularity evokes within professional philosophy marked by a "disciplinary bias against thinking about the personal" (1995, 38) and assured of its power to achieve the exclusions of corporeality and affect that keep particularity off its agenda. Likewise, she shows how secular listeners filter out experiential details that they cannot accommodate within the metaphors *they* live by; how they try to "explain the assault in ways that leave [their] world view unscathed" (1993, 11). In short, her analyses expose some consequences of the fact that orthodox epistemic subjects are trained only to know *instances* not particulars; and to fit those instances into ready-made universals, generalities.

Yet some of Amnesty's critics take it to task on this very issue, arguing that its concentration on particular victims blunts its effectiveness, allows it to ignore the larger political-economic structures that produce victimization and suffering. Thus, in his lecture, Wayne Booth explores the vexed issue of uniqueness in an intellectual climate that withholds the label "knowledge" from what it deems excessive particularity. He frames his inquiry around a paradox about how to represent human violations as "fundamentally, *universally* wrong" in a world cognizant of "human variety and the elusive nature of the self" (1993, 70; emphasis added). Booth worries that "Amnesty's program must be suspect if the victim's worth is to be found *only* in his or her individual uniqueness" (1993, 87; emphasis added). And thus the epistemological paradox that runs both through Brison's essays and the Amnesty questions. Knowing only generalities, instances, fails to enable epistemic subjects to imagine well enough to respond adequately to the particularities of suffering, the specificities of a situation whose horror is exacerbated by its being so unlike anything hitherto known or imagined. Yet attributions of radical particularity, of utter uniqueness, risk placing the events thus described beyond the boundaries of what is sayable, communicable: risk affirming an incommensurability that would, in fact, be unspeakable.

On this issue, a structural disanalogy between Brison's essays and the Amnesty lectures requires comment: Brison speaks for herself, from the urgency of a unique specificity, whereas Amnesty advocates for its victims, represents and argues for their particularity. Epistemologically, both forms of speaking are fraught with difficulties: personal narratives for the identity of teller and tale that precludes the distance of dispassionate objectivity; advocacy for the elusiveness of accurate representation when vested interest produces analogous failures of distance. Yet these are the difficulties within which imaginative epistemic subjects have to negotiate. For neither of these speakings (which is in each example explicitly *addressive*, hence no formal propositional utterance into a void) is indifferent to the ears on which it falls; neither looks merely for detached assent to an indifferent truth; each seeks a second-person acknowledgment from and of (an)other(s) as a *you* so engaged as to make knowing possible. Nor must this acknowledgment only be personal. Brison professes relief—epistemic relief I will call it—at receiving acknowledgment from doctors and lawyers: a response with its counterpart in Amnesty's practices of seeking engagement with its victims from specific people, also addressively, as in its letter-writing campaigns. And each, albeit again differently, looks to knowings that can become sensitively communal even in their explicit particularity, for the affirmations that they, differently, seek.

What then to do? "We" may indeed be imaginative creatures, but prototypes and hegemonic imaginaries can block responsible imaginings at least as frequently as they enable them. Booth is resistant to the proffered alternative of framing the solution in the language of deconstruction. He fears that "the world's ubiquitous torturers will welcome the rumor that advanced thinkers in the most advanced nations find no solid reality in that victim who cringes and weeps before their dry eyes" (Booth 1993, 77). By contrast, in a 1998 essay Nicola Lacey notes that the liberal assumption of self-ownership in criminal law, with its focus on "an individualised notion of [sexual] consent" and its assumption of sexual autonomy "assumes the mind to be dominant and controlling, irrespective of material circumstances"; thus it leaves "no space for the articulation of the affective and corporeal dimensions of *certain* violations of autonomy"[12] (Lacey 1998c: 117). These are provocative thoughts in their suggestion that *both* subsumption under generalities *and* deconstruction into scattered specificities erase the self-as-knowable from epistemic consciousness, analogously, if from opposite directions. The paradox admits of no easy resolution.

It is clear, however, that resistance to particularity is more than just a policy for ensuring objectivity: it functions also to preserve the detached dislocation of epistemic subjects whose practices of dealing only with instances require from them neither response nor responsibility. The need for an epistemology capable of engaging with particularity has to unsettle the epistemic subject; to require *him* (and now her) to come out of the shadows. Events and subjectivities such as those I have discussed here generate questions that must undermine the self-certainty of the subject's vanishing act—into the shadows, into an allegedly ubiquitous "we." Fully visible/audible specificities require him *and now her* (for the generic self dissolves) to engage in ways that put his/her subjectivity also on the line; to assume responsibility for what and how he/she claims to know.

These processes are complicated by the fact that, ironically, orthodox epistemic subjects cannot bear too much truth. Nor, as habitual speakers of their knowledge claims as though into a void, are they trained in the *listening* that makes imaginative empathy possible. Brison notes that people in their ordinary lives "are not taught to empathize with victims" (1993, 11). Yet the traumatized self in its fragility and vulnerability is often, she shows, "resilient enough to be reconstructed with the help of empathic others" (1997, 12). Empathy as she appeals to it, however, is no (Johnsonian) matter-of-fact, self-assured putting oneself in the position of another. In the circumstances she recounts, empathic subjects are responsible for knowings that are precisely *not* prototypical: not of generalities, but of particularities, specificities, whose very singularity pushes at the boundaries of the ready-made descriptions that "prototypical conceptual structures" (recall Johnson) make available.

This imaginative empathy, I am proposing, is less about knowing than about *believing*, in a reconfigured sense of "belief" in which the standard definition of knowledge as justified true belief undergoes a reversal.[13] Consider the locution, odd to an orthodox epistemologist's ears: "I always knew that X, but I did not believe it," where X could stand for the details and/or subjective effects, of rape, torture, trauma. For Brison, a palpable willingness to *believe* her, to enter into the story and become her interpretive community, her reality check, allows her to know her story so that she can own it, put herself together around it, if perhaps never in that old unified way that promises easy self-ownership. Remaining caught within patterns of incredulity keeps her sense of reality and of self shattered and in suspense.

Amnesty, likewise, has to insist on the details of particularity because its addressees have also to *believe* enough (which again is different from knowing enough) to exert engaged political pressure: to put themselves on the line in defiance of abusive practices. Yet its project, too, is both individual in insisting on the full particularity of the known, and not purely individual in appealing to commonality and social responsibility: not, then, so unrelievedly unique as its critics charge. It has to advocate well enough to enable its addressees to imagine fully and rationally enough, to engage their participation—*and yet also*—as Brison too must, it has to call a society to account for holding open a place for acts of violence against women/against political dissenters, condoned by a social imaginary that sustains hierarchies of vulnerability and power. The issue is about knowing that particularity is always insistently particular, *this* one whose torments need to be imagined in their specificities, who asks an "us" to imagine how it is for a "you"; and at the same time, and equally, part of/symptomatic of larger structures of power and privilege, listening and silencing. A victim is neither reducible to a symptom of a sick society nor knowable only as "a case, a statistic"; but she or he has to be understood that way as well. Either way, knowers—epistemic subjects—have to emerge from the shadows, not only in their self-possession as interlocutors in a (possible) conversation, but more fully as subjects enacted in their knowings, whose subjectivity is in process around whatever stability it may achieve at its core; mobile in its positionings within and in relation to people it has to know.

These examples contest the limits of imagination, and with it of coherent monologic storytelling, stable epistemic assumptions, and the fixity of subject-object positions in knowings that matter more than knowing cups on tables. Just as significantly, they contest assumptions of liberal individualism and self-ownership that contribute, also, to holding the orthodox epistemic imaginary in place. Booth observes that neither tortured nor torturer "is bounded by the skin that is being pricked or that is holding the electric prod. Both of them are 'societies,' both have experienced plot lines entailing world views that are now being shattered" (Booth 1993, 93). From positions scripted into ordinary "plot lines," it is impossible for knowing subjects to know uniqueness, singularity, strangeness just by extrapolating or reaching out from here. Responsible epistemic practices have to move in an arc, not a linear path: along a trajectory of seeing and hearing that begins, somehow from *there*—as in María Lugones's "world"-traveling (Lugones 1989), where the respectfully engaged traveler is no mere tourist nor anthropologist, aspiring only to observe without taking part, or changing any of her/his entrenched beliefs. The guiding assumption will be that knowing can never be infallible or complete, yet that it can often be "good enough" to inform effective, transformative practice.

In some senses, the position I have sketched is pessimistic about understanding across differences: though its pessimism bespeaks a healthy skepticism, not a despair in the face of incommensurability. Things are less commensurable than the unmarked "we"—represented by Mark Johnson—have blithely assumed. But radical incommensurability is not a tenable claim, in view of the extent to which "we" demonstrably succeed in practice—albeit variably—in navigating knowledgeably within what seem to be common circumstances and situations.

Yet some philosophers will take issue with my framing these issues so that *cognition* (=*knowing*) functions both as the problem and the cure: with my addressing them within an epistemological frame. The experience-and-affect-remote character of standard epistemologies, to which I have referred, partially explains these hesitations. Thus, for example, Sandra Bartky objects to philosophers' attempts to conceive "the resolution of the problem of difference . . . in largely cognitive terms" (1997, 178), contending that cognition as it is commonly understood is simply incapable of engaging with the affective quality of lives that fall outside the norms of epistemic sameness. With reference to orthodox empiricist-positivist epistemology, her objections are well taken. Bartky resists conceiving of knowing as "the mere acquisition of [more] knowledge," advocating in its place "a knowing that transforms the self who knows, a knowing that brings into being new sympathies, new affects as well as new cognitions and new forms of intersubjectivity . . . in a word . . . a knowing that has a particular affective taste" (1997, 179). Without denying the differences between our positions, I suggest that the reconfigured picture of knowledge I have drawn, with its emphasis on responding *knowingly*, is consonant with her view:

that this transformative, revisionary epistemological project has aims in common with hers, despite our differences.

The very possibility of responding knowingly depends on listening well.
Yet even though good listening is integral to knowings that transform the self
who knows, who is sensitive in hearing narratives of identity and trauma, epistemologically, listening is surprisingly unthought, undertheorized. The attuned
conversations of close friends afford a more ordinary model than those I have
discussed, though it has to be read obliquely into asymmetrical relationships
(such as those between Amnesty advocate and victim) that contrast with the
more (ideally) symmetrical quality of friendships. But good listening is often as
tactile as it is auditory: thus neither purely objective, nor perfectly rational. It does
not lend itself easily to conceptual analysis, though phenomenologically it is well
known: it shelters and encloses, without requiring the *literal* touch that becomes
invasive in relations of power asymmetry. It creates a palpably safe space that invites and honors trust; preserves a (reconfigured) language of "knowing," even as
it departs from the accumulation-of-information sense. It retains what I call a
"normative realist" component that respects the integrity of tellers and listeners,
even though it may interrogate and reinterpret both tellings and hearings.

Narrative identities, then (recalling Ricoeur), are as much about imagin-
ers and listeners as about narrators: about conditions of imaginative uptake and
response, without which they could not escape the monologic mold of the cognition whose inadequacy Bartky deplores. In an evocative reading of Nawal El
Saadawi's story of undergoing a clitoridectomy as a small child, Bartky writes
that to have any idea of this experience "I must imagine . . . what it was for her
to have *felt* this terror, this absolute incomprehension in the face of the cruelty
of those she trusted." Most strikingly, in this imagining, she observes, "I do not
think of myself at all. Nor is my imagining really mine in any but the most trivial sense" (1997, 192). Such imagining breaks the boundaries of self-certainty
to leave prototypes and self-ownership far behind. Nor does it amount simply
to letting the Other speak, granting the Other subjective status, with the con-
descension of self-satisfied rightness that such magnanimous lettings imply.
The other is already speaking. It is a matter of listening, and not from here but
from as close to there as a sensitive imagining can go.

CONCLUSION

It need not be said that this chapter is inconclusive. It maps the promise and
pitfalls of imaginative extensions of knowledge and epistemology beyond immediately available observational evidence and assumed homogeneity. Rather
than engaging with feminist analyses—by Sabina Lovibond, Michèle Le

Doeuff, Drucilla Cornell, and Susan Babbitt—it looks to Mark Johnson's analysis of imagination, because its location closer to the hegemonic mainstream confirms the tenacity of a social imaginary that needs to be disrupted. It offers some cautionary tales, sets in motion a redirected line of reasoning, warns against premature conclusions. It pulls me back to thinking about epistemic responsibility (see Code 1987), needing not just to expose irresponsible epistemic practices but to develop guidelines for more responsible, deliberative, inductive, and engaged epistemic practices. This is where I will go from here.

But it is hard not to conclude on a note of pessimism that contrasts both with Mark Johnson's claims for the imagination and with an "ungrounded optimism" that Susan Mendus, for example, reads in Richard Rorty's equally self-assured praise for "the ability to think of people wildly different from ourselves as included in the range of 'us'" (Mendus 1996, 58; citing Rorty 1989, 192). The collapse of the welfare state in the affluent Western world goes with a breakdown of face-to-face local and global communication that is more about listening than it is about speaking: a crisis of listening in the age of soundbytes. "We" are bombarded with information, pronouncements, analyses of how things are—and also by a sense that even as there is more and more talk there is less and less listening. Perhaps for me the problem is exacerbated by living in arch-Conservative Ontario, where the social support systems are disintegrating, and nobody listens except to pick up "bits" and distort them to their own ends. To keep mindful of the problems that a would-be responsible, imaginatively rational epistemic subject has to struggle with, it is salutory to read Mark Johnson—and Richard Rorty—against the background of Trinh T. Minh-ha's reminder: "On one plane, we, I, and he, may speak the same language and even act alike; yet, on the other, we stand miles apart, irreducibly foreign to each other" (1989, 48). The epistemic imperatives these meditations invoke count as reminders of how wary we, all of us, must be of assuming that we can see very far from here.

NOTES

Thanks to Patricia Johnson for prompting me to think about the epistemic subject; to Murray Code and Peta Bowden for comments on an earlier version of this chapter; and, for engaged listening and helpful questions, to audiences at the University of Dayton, the University of Oregon, the Canadian Society for Women in Philosophy, and Trent University.

1. I use the masculine pronoun throughout this initial account because, in the tradition of which I am writing, knowers were (and often still are) presumptively male.

2. For recent feminist critiques of the pull of this model, under the label "realism," see Lloyd 1995 and Barad 1996.

3. See in this connection Code 2000.

4. Compare my discussion in Code 1995a.

5. Here I am in accord with Ricoeur, who claims that "human rights do not necessarily rely on the presupposition of a 'liberal' self . . . [on the] self that *atomistic* political philosophies take for granted . . . a rational self . . . equipped with rights prior to engaging in any form of societal life." (1993, 119).

6. This system of communal imaginings is what Michèle Le Doeuff (1989) and Cornelius Castoriadis (1994), in different contexts, call "an imaginary." Mark Johnson quotes Putnam, for whom Kant "is doing what he would have called 'philosophical anthropology,' or providing . . . *a moral image of the world*" (1993, 65).

7. See in this regard Code 1995c.

8. For an analysis of the class and race specificity of "life plans" see also Walker 1998.

9. My use of the adjective "vanilla" here is meant to capture the bland ordinariness of Johnson's imaginings, their failure to disturb or disrupt. It contrasts, though I think not conflictually, with Diana Meyers's use of the term in Meyers 1997.

10. It is interesting that women would be "granted" it, while (some) men just have it.

11. The terminology is due to Cornelius Castoriadis (1991, 62). He characterizes the instituted social imaginary as follows: "The socialization of individuals—itself an instituted process, and in each case a different one—opens up these individuals, giving them access to a *world* of social imaginary significations whose instauration as well as incredible *coherence* goes unimaginably beyond everything that 'one or many individuals' could ever produce. These significations owe their actual (social-historical) existence to the fact that they are *instituted*."

12. Lacey cites Brison (1997) in her excellent discussion of law's impotence to deal with the harms of rape.

13. See Code 1995b for a discussion in a different context of this reversal.

REFERENCES

Barad, Karen. 1996. Meeting the universe halfway: Realism and social constructivism without contradiction. In *Feminism, science, and the philosophy of science*, ed. Lynn Hankinson Nelson and Jack Nelson. Amsterdam: Kluwer.

Bartky, Sandra. 1997. Sympathy and solidarity: On a tightrope with Scheler. In *Feminists rethink the self*, ed. Diana Tietjens Meyers. Boulder, Colo.: Westview.

Booth, Wayne. 1993. Individualism and the mystery of the social self; Or, does amnesty have a leg to stand on? In *Freedom and Interpretation: The Oxford Amnesty Lectures 1992*, ed. Barbara Johnson. New York: Basic.

Brison, Susan J. 1993. Surviving sexual violence: A philosophical perspective. *Journal of Social Philosophy* 24, 1: 5–22.

———. 1995. On the personal as philosophical. *APA Newsletter on Feminism and Philosophy* 95, 1: 37–40.

———. 1997. Outliving oneself: Trauma, memory, and personal identity. In *Feminists rethink the self*, ed. Diana Tietjens Meyers. Boulder, Colo.: Westview.

Castoriadis, Cornelius. 1991. Individual, society, rationality, history. In *Philosophy, politics, autonomy: Essays in political philosophy*, ed. David Ames Curtis. New York: Oxford University Press.

———. 1994. Radical imagination and the social instituting imaginary. In *Rethinking imagination: Culture and creativity*, ed. Gillian Robinson and John Rundell. London: Routledge.

Code, Lorraine. 1987. *Epistemic responsibility*. Hanover, N.H.: University Press of New England.

———. 1995a. I know just how you feel: Empathy and the problem of epistemic authority. In Lorraine Code, *Rhetorical spaces: Essays on (gendered) locations*. New York: Routledge.

———. 1995b. Incredulity, experientialism and the politics of knowledge. In Lorraine Code, *Rhetorical spaces: Essays on (gendered) locations*. New York: Routledge.

———. 1995c. Taking subjectivity into account. In Lorraine Code, *Rhetorical spaces: Essays on (gendered) locations*. New York: Routledge.

———. 1996. What is natural about epistemology naturalized? *American Philosophical Quarterly* 33, 1: 1–22.

———. 2000. The perversion of autonomy and the subjection of women: Discourses of social advocacy at century's end. In *Relational autonomy*, ed. Catriona Mackenzie and Natalie Stoljar. New York: Oxford University Press.

Ferguson, Kathy. 1984. *The Feminist case against bureaucracy*. Philadelphia: Temple University Press.

Haraway, Donna. 1991. Situated knowledges: The science question in feminism and the privilege of partial perspective. In *Simians, cyborgs, and women: The reinvention of nature*, ed. Donna Haraway. New York: Routledge.

Johnson, Barbara, ed. 1993. *Freedom and interpretation: The Oxford Amnesty Lectures 1992*. New York: Basic.

Johnson, Mark. 1993. *Moral imagination: Implications of cognitive science for ethics*. Chicago: University of Chicago Press.

Lacey, Nicola. 1998a. Theories of justice and the welfare state. In *Unspeakable subjects: Feminist essays in legal and social theory*, ed. Nicola Lacey. Oxford: Hart.

———. 1998b. Unspeakable subjects, impossible rights: Sexuality, integrity and criminal law. In *Unspeakable subjects: Feminist essays in legal and social theory*, ed. Nicola Lacey. Oxford: Hart.

———. 1998c. Sexual integrity and the criminal law. In *Unspeakable subjects: Feminist essays in legal and social theory*, ed. Nicola Lacey. Oxford: Hart.

Lakoff, George, and Mark Johnson. 1980. *Metaphors we live by*. Chicago: University of Chicago Press.

Le Doeuff, Michèle. 1989. *The philosophical imaginary*, trans. Colin Gordon. Stanford: Stanford University Press.

Lloyd, Elizabeth A. 1995. Feminism as method: What scientists get that philosophers don't. *Philosophical Topics* 23, 2: 189–220.

Lugones, María. 1989. Playfulness, world travelling, and loving perception. In *Women, knowledge, and reality*, ed. Ann Garry and Marilyn Pearsall. Boston: Unwin Hyman.

Mendus, Susan. 1996. "What of soul was left, I wonder": The narrative self in political philosophy. In *Literature and the political imagination*, ed. John Horton and Andrea T. Baumeister. London: Routledge.

Meyers, Diana Tietjens. 1997. Emotion and heterodox moral perception: An essay in moral social psychology. In *Feminists rethink the self*, ed. Diana Tietjens Meyers. Boulder, CO: Westview.

Minh-ha, Trinh T. 1989. The language of nativism: Anthropology as a scientific conversation of man with man. In *Woman, native, other: Writing postcoloniality and feminism*, ed. Trinh T. Minh-ha. Bloomington: Indiana University Press.

Ricoeur, Paul. 1993. Self as *Ipse*. In *Freedom and interpretation: The Oxford Amnesty Lectures 1992*. New York: Basic.

Rorty, Richard. 1989. *Contingency, irony and solidarity*. Cambridge: Cambridge University Press.

Walker, Margaret. 1998. Career selves: Plans, projects, and plots in whole life ethics. In *Moral understandings: A feminist study in ethics*, ed. Margaret Walker. New York: Routledge.

CHAPTER THIRTEEN

THE EPISTEMOLOGY OF MORAL VOICE: DISPLACING HEGEMONY IN MORAL/LEGAL DISCOURSE

SUSAN HEKMAN

DIFFERENT MORAL VOICES

In recent years the problem of "differences," particularly the differences among women, has dominated feminist theory and politics. The unitary concept of "woman" that informed feminist thought in the 1980s has become suspect; charges of exclusion, implicit hierarchy, and racism abound. In the wake of Elizabeth Spelman's *Inessential Woman* (1988), few feminist theorists employ the concept of woman without qualification; many have abandoned it altogether. Some feminist theorists have criticized this development, arguing that we need to retain general concepts such as "woman" in order to engage in social critique. At this point, however, the trend seems irreversible— differences are everywhere.

It is significant, then, that one aspect of feminist theory has been almost unaffected by the move toward differences: feminist moral theory. When feminists first began discussing moral theory they emphasized the exclusion of women from moral and political discourse. Feminists argued that the tradition of moral philosophy, by defining morality in terms of rationality and women as irrational, barred women from morality altogether.

The feminist discussion of moral theory changed radically, however, with the publication of Carol Gilligan's *In a Different Voice* in 1982. Gilligan's work placed the moral difference between men and women at the center of feminist discussions. Her discussion of women's moral voice resonated strongly with many women; defining the "care" voice of women has subsequently become one of the central themes of the discussion of women and morality. Although discussions of the care voice are not the only preoccupation of feminist moral theory, the predominance of this issue is significant for the future of feminist theory. One way of characterizing this development is that feminist moral theory has moved from debunking the one true morality of masculinist moral theory to proclaiming a successor morality: the care voice.

In one respect this development is not surprising. The attempt to replace the justice voice of modernity with the care voice of women has its roots in the tradition of moral discourse that has evolved in Western thought. Although the twentieth century has seen numerous attempts to deconstruct modernist epistemology, to define multiple paths to truth, a parallel effort in moral discourse has been decidedly lacking.

Deconstructing the unitary epistemology of Western thought is, admittedly, a challenging task. But there is a sense in which such an endeavor is academic, the concern of philosophers removed from the "real world." Deconstructing the hegemonic unitary conception of moral truth, however, is a different order of things. Moral discourse has real-life applications; the threat of moral anarchy constrains discussions of multiple moral voices. Despite contemporary discussions of "moral relativism," most moral philosophers feel compelled to come up with some definitive answer to the question What is moral? The discussion of the care voice in feminist moral theory is no exception. Discussions of the different moral voice of women have revolved around the replacement of the justice voice with the feminine voice of care. Epistemologically, this alternative remains within the parameters of the hegemonic moral tradition: one true, universal definition of morality is replaced with another; the epistemology of one true moral voice is unaltered. Although some feminists (significantly, Gilligan herself) have argued that there are two equally valid moral voices, the epistemological significance of this argument is rarely explored. The possibility of more than two moral voices, furthermore, almost never arises. In other words, what is missing from the discussion of care and justice is the issue that has dominated contemporary feminism: differences, not difference.

It is not difficult to cite examples of this phenomenon. A symposium on care and justice was held at the 1994 American Political Science Association convention and published in a subsequent volume of *Hypatia*. In this symposium two of the best-known "care" theorists, Joan Tronto and Virginia Held, explored the question of the best or most comprehensive framework for moral, political, and legal questions. Held argued that care is the "most basic" moral value, the wider moral framework into which justice should be fitted (1995, 131). Tronto took a different approach but, like Held, concluded that the care approach is the "best" framework for moral and political judgments (1995, 141).

Discussions of the feminine moral voice of care have been a fruitful development in feminist thought. They begin the necessary task of deconstructing the hegemony of the justice voice. But attempting to displace this hegemony by proclaiming the superiority of the care voice is not an effective strategy for feminist moral theory. By arguing that the moral voice of care is superior to that of justice, that is, that it is the better and more comprehensive moral framework, these feminist discussions perpetuate the hegemonic moral and epistemological assumptions of the Western tradition. What is required, however, is an epistemological alternative that provides an understanding of multiple moral voices that can incorporate differences nonhierarchically.

Articulating this alternative must begin with an approach to the epistemology of the care voice that does not involve defining a hierarchy of care and justice. Gilligan's work itself provides the basis for such an approach. Gilligan's argument rests on the assertion that gender is constitutive in the formation of moral voice; her approach suggests that morality is particular and contextual, socially constructed. This understanding of morality offers a sharp contrast to the impartial, abstract paradigm that defines the justice voice. The hegemonic discourse of the justice voice defines the moral realm as disembodied, transcending all social and cultural influences, including gender. Indeed, it assumes that the removal of social and cultural influences is a necessary prerequisite to the definition of moral principles. Gilligan counters this not just by suggesting that the feminine voice of care is constructed, but by defining moral voice per se as constructed. In her formulation both the care and the justice voice are constructed in conjunction with the formation of the gendered self. Thus in an epistemological sense Gilligan is not integrating another moral voice into existing moral discourse but redefining the moral realm itself.

Gilligan does not develop the epistemological implications of her position. But the significance of her position is reinforced by the fact that, despite her emphasis on the care voice, she refuses to privilege the care voice over the justice voice. Although Gilligan's work has spawned a literature whose central presupposition is the superiority of the care voice, Gilligan herself does not take this position. She consistently asserts that the two moral voices are equally valid, not that the voice of care is superior. She frequently reiterates her claim that her goal is to replace a unitary moral discourse with a discourse of nonhierarchical duality. Although she does not explicitly acknowledge it, however, Gilligan's refusal to privilege one voice offers a clear contrast to the hegemonic moral discourse, a discourse predicated on the existence of a single, universal standard of moral judgment. This discourse cannot tolerate the existence of two, much less many, moral voices or standards. Once more, Gilligan is not integrating but redefining morality.

Gilligan's insistence on both the social constitution and the equality of the two moral voices suggests an alternative moral epistemology that places differences at its center. Gilligan focuses on the constitutive force of gender in the formation of moral voice, arguing for the validity of the different voice of women.[1] But once the different construction of moral voice is posited, two questions immediately arise. First, if one social influence, gender, is constitutive in the formation of moral voice, why not others as well? Once we argue for the constitutive role of gender, it seems obvious that other social factors—class, race, ethnicity—will also be constitutive of moral voice. Second, if gender is constitutive of moral voice, isn't it the case that gender is coded differently according to a variety of social factors? There is not one gender coding, but many; the gender coding that a White, middle-class woman will encounter will be quite different from that of a woman of a different race and class.[2] Once Gilligan deconstructs the disembodied rationality of the justice voice and jettisons a single, universal standard, the road to a moral epistemology of differences is open. Gilligan focuses on the difference that gender makes in the moral realm. But her approach suggests that more differences than those between men and women are epistemologically significant in the construction of moral voice.

Contemplating a moral epistemology of multiple moral voices, however, raises disturbing questions. If we embrace such an epistemology and, hence, reject a universal standard, how would we choose among moral voices? How could we declare anything to be "right"? How could a legal system function? I am not alone in asking and attempting to answer these questions. Several contemporary feminist moral theorists are exploring the reconstruction of moral theory without a single "true" morality. Thus, for example, Marilyn Frye (1991) argues that women do not need "'ethics" if ethics is "getting it right" in moral theory. She argues instead for a plethora of ethics, not just one. Annette Baier (1985) argues against Kant that we must look to anthropology, sociology, and psychology to find out what morality *is*. Margaret Walker argues for a morality defined in terms of human beings searching for shareable interpretations of responsibility (1989, 20).[3] Even feminist moral theorists concerned primarily with the care voice have moved away from the assertion of a single woman's moral voice (Ruddick 1989; Noddings 1989).

My purpose in the following is to build on these theories, articulating a moral epistemology of multiple voices. Two related problems are central to this task. The first is defining an alternative moral epistemology of multiple moral voices and exploring how the hegemony of the universal, abstract moral paradigm can be displaced by such an epistemology. In order to address this question I focus on legal discourse, the embodiment of the justice voice in the

Western tradition. The second is defining how to choose among moral voices, how to decide which moral voice is appropriate in a particular moral context. I address this question elsewhere (Hekman 1999).[4]

In *What Can She Know?* (1991) Lorraine Code argues that moral theory cannot be separated from the epistemological theory in which it is grounded. In the spirit of this insight I look to two twentieth-century epistemologists as guides for the reconstruction of feminist moral theory. I turn to the work of Hans-Georg Gadamer and Stephen Toulmin for several reasons. Like Code, I want to emphasize the link between epistemology and moral theory. This link is clarified by directly applying an epistemological theory to moral issues. Further, although the feminist moral theorists I cited above advocate multiple paths to moral truth, this thesis has not been sufficiently developed. In contrast, the advocacy of multiple paths to truth in Gadamer and Toulmin is well developed and explicit. Using their theories as a kind of template in moral theory clarifies the issues at stake, particularly from a feminist perspective. In other words, if we can see the multiple paths clearly in epistemology they might become clearer in moral theory as well.[5]

In *Truth and Method* (1975) Hans-Georg Gadamer attacks the notion that truth is defined in singular terms, arguing instead that there is more than one path to truth. Specifically he asserts that the exclusive association between truth and the scientific/logical method is misguided. Against this unitary epistemology he proposes a hermeneutic epistemology of location and context. Our experience of truth, he asserts, is not limited to the abstract, universalizing method defined by logic and the natural sciences; that truth, he asserts, is the exception rather than the rule.

What might be called Gadamer's deconstruction of modernist epistemology has two principal thrusts. First, he suggests an alternative, hermeneutic epistemology that posits many paths to truth. Second, he turns the modernist argument on its head by suggesting that the abstract, universalizing method, far from constituting the single paradigm of all truth, is, instead, an exception, even an aberration. Our paradigmatic experience of truth, on Gadamer's account, is contextual and particular. This point is encapsulated in his concept of "prejudice," the prejudgments that he defines as making all understanding possible. His hermeneutic approach presupposes that we always understand out of a context, a particular location that defines meaning for us. From Gadamer's perspective, then, the "truth" defined by the method of the natural sciences and logic is an unusual and infrequent occurrence, not a paradigm but an irregularity.[6]

There are striking parallels between Gilligan's approach to moral theory and Gadamer's definition of truth. Implicit in Gilligan's work are assumptions that transform moral epistemology in the same way that Gadamer's work transforms epistemology. At the core of Gilligan's argument is her contention that morality is always contextual, that the moral voices of situated subjects are constituted by their experiences. Like Gadamer, Gilligan argues that the abstract, universalizing model is an aberration rather than the typical case. The striving for abstraction that characterizes the justice voice, the attempt to formulate moral arguments that eschew connection and context, she claims, is an "adolescent ideal" (1982, 98). Her contrast between the justice voice and the care voice is rooted in her understanding of how the different gendered experiences of girls and boys in our society produce different moral voices. The modernist tradition against which Gilligan is arguing asserts that autonomous, abstract justice, "true morality," is an essential, universal human trait. Against this Gilligan argues that both moral voices are the product of social and discursive forces. She asserts that it is not the case, as women have been told, that women's situatedness prevents them from perceiving moral truth. Rather, her point is that both the autonomy characteristic of men's moral voice as well as the connectedness characteristic of women's are constituted by their different locations.

Another way of putting this point is that Gilligan's work reveals that modernist moral theory misunderstands the nature of moral truth in the same way that Gadamer reveals the misunderstanding of truth implicit in Enlightenment thought. Gilligan rejects the modernist presupposition that moral truth is singular and universal, abstract and autonomous. Rather she asserts, in a Gadamerian spirit, that it is hermeneutic: local and contextual. A Gadamerian reading of Gilligan suggests that her work is not an effort to "get it right" in moral theory, to replace the justice voice with the care voice, but, rather, to introduce an alternative moral epistemology that posits many (or at least two) paths to moral truth. This reading produces an understanding of moral truth that is situated, particular, and, most importantly, multiple.

My second epistemological guide is Stephen Toulmin. Like Gadamer, Toulmin attacks the paradigm that defines a single path to truth. In *The Uses of Argument* (1958) he examines the claim that grounds modernist epistemology: "logic is the laws of thought" (1958, 3). In a careful analysis of the structure of various kinds of arguments he develops the thesis that what he calls the "Court of Reason" can be approached by different paths. His principal point is that although the force of an argument is invariant, judging the *strength* of any particular case is "field dependent," that is, relative to the appropriate evidence (1958, 38). The target of Toulmin's argument is the deification of a particular kind of argument, what he calls the "analytic syllogism." The analytic syllogism, like the concept of truth that Gadamer attacks, is defined by its simplicity and abstraction. Conceding that simplicity has its merits, Toulmin nevertheless argues that by treating the simplest argument as the paradigm of all truth "we may end up thinking that, for some regrettable reason hidden deep in the nature of things, only our original peculiarly simple arguments are capable of at-taining to the ideal of validity" (1958, 144).

Toulmin echoes Gadamer's argument that this paradigm, far from defin-ing the typical case, is instead exceptional. The development of logical theory, Toulmin asserts, began with a special class of arguments: unequivocal, analytic, formally valid arguments with a universal statement as a formal premise. The characteristics of this class of arguments have been interpreted by logicians as signs of special merit. But, Toulmin argues, "analytic arguments are a special case, and we are laying up trouble for ourselves, both in logic and epistemology, if we treat them as anything else" (1958, 145). Toulmin's goal is to open the "Court of Reason" to arguments that do not conform to the analytic syllogism and its "timeless truths."

Both Gadamer and Toulmin are, in effect, deconstructing modernist epistemology by arguing against the hegemony of the abstract, universalizing paradigm that defines truth. They question rather than presuppose the hege-monic status of the modernist paradigm; they highlight this hegemony and ex-pose its unfounded assertions. Specifically, they reveal the Achilles heel of that paradigm: its exceptional character. Although the universal, abstract model of epistemology is hegemonic, it is also, in practice, an exception, an aberration. These epistemological arguments bring an important perspective to questions of moral epistemology. What Gilligan calls the "justice voice" in moral dis-course is, like the abstract model of truth, hegemonic in Western thought. The justice voice defines what moral truth is; any other definition is ruled out. The work of Gilligan and other feminist theorists of the care voice have revealed the limitations of this definition and begun the task of defining an alternative. They have argued for an understanding of moral truth as local and contextual, rooted in the concrete situations of moral subjects.

But these arguments are just the first step. Defining an alternative moral epistemology in the face of the deep-rootedness of the justice voice is a daunt-ing task. The principal obstacle to this task is the threat of moral anarchy, the fear that unless we define another, singular and true path to morality we are inviting chaos and disorder. Unless this threat can be successfully negotiated, no alternative moral epistemology can emerge.

DIFFERENT LEGAL VOICES

The most concrete embodiment of the hegemony of what Gilligan calls the justice voice is the structure of the legal system in Western democracies. The law concretizes the abstract impartiality of the justice voice in the institution of the rule of law: the impartial judge assessing the facts of a case and applying a universal law. The law also offers a graphic example of Gilligan's analysis of the gendering of the justice voice. One of the principal goals of Western rationalized legal practice is to eradicate the particular in favor of the impartial and universal as much as is humanly possible. Jurors are carefully questioned regarding their connection to the case at hand; they are excused if such a connection exists. They are questioned about their ability to render an "impartial" judgment. Likewise, judges are expected to recuse themselves if they have any connection to a case. Even more significantly, until quite recently women were assumed to be incapable of the abstraction from particulars necessary to achieve impartiality and thus excused from jury duty altogether. In short, the law actualizes the gendered division between abstract masculinity and particular femininity.

If feminists want to destabilize this hegemony and begin the process of defining an alternative moral epistemology, then the law presents the greatest challenge to that effort. It seems obvious that if our legal system does not rely on a single, universal standard to legitimize legal judgments, the very fabric of society will be threatened. The ideology of the rule of law provides just such a clear cut and stable legitimation of moral/legal judgments in our society. At the root of that ideology is a belief borrowed from the justice voice: if we abstract from the particulars of individual cases and our own particular circumstances and apply universal principles, then "truth" will win out. Although even the advocates of this ideology concede that this is only sometimes (its critics would say rarely) the case, it nevertheless exerts a powerful influence in our moral and legal systems. Because of the reality and immediacy of the law, furthermore, it appears to be one area in which contemplating a moral epistemology of multiple moral voices is both ill-conceived and dangerous. It thus provides the clearest test of such an epistemology.

Gadamer and Toulmin described the hegemony of the abstract, universalizing paradigm in epistemology. Max Weber does much the same for the hegemony of a similar paradigm in Western legal discourse: the impartiality model. Weber's examination of the evolution of legal practices in the West is a function of his comprehensive examination of the development of rationalism in the West. In this case Weber wants to find out why the West developed a highly rationalized legal system while other societies did not. In his analysis Weber ignores issues of gender; for Weber gender is not a significant category of social analysis. Reading Weber across feminist discussions of the masculinization of reason and rationality, however, is revealing. From a feminist perspective the story Weber is telling is a description of how feminine qualities have been subverted in Western thought and how the masculine definition of rationality has achieved almost undisputed dominance. But Weber's analysis is also useful from a feminist perspective because it suggests a concrete strategy for destabilizing the hegemonic moral/legal discourse of the West. Weber's analysis reveals the presence of, in a sense, other legal voices. I want to turn this to feminist purposes by arguing that we can and should legitimize these voices, paving the way for multiple paths to moral/legal truth.

Weber's analysis of the character and evolution of Western legal practices has two purposes. First, he wants to define the unique character of Western law: rationality. Weber defines two senses in which Western law can be described as rational: generalizability—the reduction of reasons relevant in the decision of concrete cases to one or more principles—and systematization—the integration of all legal propositions into a seamless web (1978, 655–56). In contrast to this he defines "irrational" lawmaking and lawfinding as occurring when a "decision is influenced by concrete factors of the particular case as evaluated on an ethical, emotional, or political basis rather than by general norms" (1978, 656). It would be difficult to find a clearer statement of the gendering of moral epistemology that has characterized Western thought since Plato. The abstract and universal (masculine) is defined as the ideal and only true form, the particular and concrete (feminine) as its opposite and inferior.

Weber's second task is to explain how this rational legal practice developed in the West. What emerges from his account is, significantly, not the story of an inexorable process of development toward the present rationalized system, but, rather, a complex picture of the play of conflicting forces. Weber discusses a range of rationalizing tendencies but focuses particularly on the development of academic law teaching. He argues that it was the academization of the law that resulted in the uniquely abstract character of our legal system. The law's removal from concrete cases, he argues, produced "a far-reaching emancipation of legal thinking from the everyday needs of the public" and the "blind desire for logical consistency" (1978, 789).

But Weber documents opposing forces as well. English common law, German customary law, and the practice of jury trials resisted the formalization of legal practices, preventing the complete rationalization of the law; calls for substantive rather than formal justice could not be completely silenced. For my purposes the most revealing aspect of Weber's analysis in this respect is his discussion of "Kadi" justice. Weber defines Kadi justice as the adjudication of individual cases by charismatic justice or informal judgments rendered in terms of concrete ethical principles (1978, 976). Two elements of this definition are significant. First, cases are settled not by reference to a systematic code of laws, but by the unique qualities of individual cases. Second, the criteria of justice are substantive and concrete ethical standards, not abstract, universal principles.

Weber's discussion of Kadi justice is far from historically accurate. The operation of Kadi justice in Islamic countries involved the application of divine law as revealed in the Koran; it operated under extreme procedural limitations that allowed no judicial discretion. Weber took elements of this actual institution and, in the spirit of his ideal typical methodology, developed an ideal type for his own specific purposes: contrasting substantive, particularistic, and flexible justice to procedural, rationalized justice. For Weber the ideal type of Kadi justice is not the Islamic judge but the Biblical Solomon: the all-wise judge who acts not on the basis of formal laws but according to his perception of the course of justice in each particular case.

Although elements of what Weber calls Kadi justice remain today— English common law, many jury decisions, and justices of the peace—the formalizing tendencies of Western law have been successful in both marginalizing and discrediting this form of justice. Significantly, Weber does not question the normative implications of this trend. He is unequivocal in his judgment that Kadi justice is a throw-back to an inferior, primitive stage in the development of legal practices characterized by kinship groups before the evolution of modern states. "The primitive formalistic irrationality of these older forms of justice," he states, was cast off by the emerging authority of princes and magistrates (1978, 809).

Both Gadamer and Toulmin argue that, despite the exceptional character of the abstract, universalizing paradigm in epistemology, it has established hegemony as the only path to truth. Weber finds a similar pattern in legal discourse and practice. Much of his analysis involves a description of how various approaches to legal issues vied for dominance and how formal rationality, despite its uniqueness and the infrequency with which it occurred, overcame other approaches and established hegemony. The hegemony of the "blind desire for logical consistency" that Weber documents is the legal manifestation of Gadamer's description of the identification of truth with scientific method and Toulmin's description of the hegemony of the analytic syllogism. Their analyses differ in that Weber applauds this development while Gadamer and Toulmin deplore it. The cases are similar, however, in that the paradigm they describe is at the same time hegemonic and aberrant.

Weber's analysis also parallels aspects of Gilligan's approach. Although they are far from identical, there are significant similarities between what Gilligan and other feminist moral theorists have labeled the care voice and Weber's discussion of Kadi justice. In Weber's ideal type of Kadi justice the judge pays attention to the unique qualities of individual cases and relies on concrete rather than abstract principles. Both of these qualities are central to Gilligan's description of the care voice. She defines the care voice in terms of its attention to the particular aspects of concrete moral problems and its rejection of abstract principles. Another similarity lies in Weber's definition of Kadi justice as primitive, irrational, and inferior, a throw-back to underdeveloped legal practices. Critics of the care voice have described it as an inferior moral practice lacking in definitive criteria. Weber argues that the rejection of Kadi justice was justified by its lack of definitive criteria; the critics of the care voice make much the same argument. Finally, Weber's documentation of the absence of substantive justice from formalistic legal practice parallels Gilligan's account. Weber states: "Formal justice and the 'freedom' which it guarantees are indeed rejected by all groups ideologically interested in substantive justice. Such groups are better served by Kadi-justice than by the formal type" (1978, 813). This statement helps explain why feminists and other protest groups have found the legal system inadequate to their goals. It also explains why feminists have theorized the care voice to oppose the formalism of the justice voice. Weber's analysis reveals why it is only by appeal to this voice that feminists and other advocates of social change can attain their goals.

CONCLUSION

In front of the Supreme Court Building in Washington, D.C. stands a statue of a blindfolded woman, whom the sculptor named "Contemplation of Justice." The woman is holding the scales of justice in her hand. Opposite her is a statue of a man, "Guardian of Authority of Law." The statue of the woman is the visual representation of Weber's argument that the paradigm of our legal thought is the impartial, rational observer (portrayed here, interestingly, as a woman, albeit supported by male authority) adjudicating by reference to universally applicable laws; the rule of law, not men. Weber's analysis documents the establishment of this hegemony of the impartial judge in Western legal practice. But although his work is limited to the evolution of legal discourse, it has implications that far exceed this domain. The impartial judge of the rationalistic Western legal tradition is a function of the paradigm that defines the hegemonic discourse of Western moral thought. Gilligan's work demonstrates this very clearly. The justice voice is defined by its abstraction and reliance on universal principles. The hegemony of this voice, furthermore, is almost unquestioned. Gilligan's analysis documents that, for both men and women, the highest stage of the justice voice is simply what morality *is*.

In her discussion of this issue Judith Sklar puts this point very succinctly: "The value placed on impartiality is, lastly, supreme. The impartial observer is the hero of moral theory, as the impartial judge is the embodiment of justice" (1964, 61–62).

The analyses of the evolution and structure of the ideal type of the impartial observer by Gadamer, Toulmin, and Weber reveal the extent of its hegemony. But they also reveal its vulnerability and, hence, suggest strategies for displacing that hegemony. It is my argument that reading Gilligan's argument across these analyses clarifies the strategies of displacement implicit in her account. In *Truth and Method* Gadamer argues that defining truth as the exclusive product of logic and the scientific method violates our experience of truth; we experience truth in a variety of ways not limited by this paradigm. Gilligan makes much the same kind of argument in her analysis of women's moral voice. She details the structure of women's moral deliberations, deliberations guided by care, connection, and particularity rather than abstract justice. She then asks us to accept these moral deliberations as a moral discourse equal to that of the justice voice. Another way of putting both of these arguments is that if we look at what we actually *do* in the realms of epistemology and morality, we find a variety of methods, not one alone. The argument that both Gadamer and Gilligan are advancing is that we should accept these alternative practices as equally valid.

Weber's analysis of the evolution of legal thought leads to a similar conclusion. The hegemony of the impartial observer and the rule of law is unquestioned; other legal practices are marginalized and devalued. But this is not the whole story. Although devalued in theory, these alternative legal practices are nevertheless utilized; they form the basis of a significant number of decisions in our legal system. In his analysis Weber documents the continued existence of substantive justice in the Western legal tradition. An analysis of contemporary legal practices could add to this list: family courts and adjudication through mediation are examples of legal practices that deviate from the impartiality model. In addition, some Western democracies have adopted a kind of hybrid legal system to deal with the particular situation of native peoples.[7] What these practices reveal is that courts arrive at decisions using methods that include but are not limited to the impartiality model. And, most significantly, these decisions have legitimacy in our legal and political system; the existence of multiple paths to legal judgments does not diminish the legitimacy of those judgments.

What I am arguing here is that if we look at what we actually do—in epistemology, morality, and the law—we can learn a valuable lesson from these practices. If we look beyond the ideology of impartiality we will see that, in practice, multiple paths to truth exist in each of these areas. We experience truth outside the realm of logic; we act morally on considerations other than abstract justice; and legal decisions are grounded in considerations other than impartial justice. We already engage in these activities; we recognize their legitimacy in practice if not in theory. My argument is that making that recognition explicit, and, specifically, granting these practices theoretical as well as practical legitimacy, can lead to a new understanding of epistemology, morality, and the law. This is an understanding, furthermore, that will displace the hegemony of the impartiality model. In a Wittgensteinian spirit I am arguing that we should look at what we do rather than what the philosophers say we should do.

These arguments are, quite obviously, only a beginning. We are a long way from an acceptance of multiple moral voices and a fundamental rethinking of our legal system. But looking at the complexity of the system that we already possess, as Weber, Gilligan, and, in epistemology, Gadamer and Toulmin do, is an important first step. We need to understand the full extent of the hegemony of the impartiality model before we can begin the task of displacing it. And that task will be facilitated by using tools that we already possess.

Notes

1. It should be noted, however, that in her more recent work Gilligan has become more sensitive to the influences of race, class, and ethnicity in the constitution of moral voice (Gilligan et al. 1990).

2. For an elaboration of these arguments see Hekman 1995.

3. See also Addelson 1991; Hoagland 1988.

4. In *The Moral Theory of Poststructuralism* (1995), Todd May develops a moral theory that rejects the transcendentalism of finding one right answer. Although his project has much in common with mine, he does not deal directly with the question that concerns me here: the interaction of multiple moral discourses within one society.

5. I do not find the contemporary approach of "moral relativism" useful in this regard. The problem with this approach from a feminist perspective is that it ignores the fact that must be the starting point of the feminist critique: the hegemony of the justice voice and the devaluation of alternative and, especially, "feminine" approaches to morality. Moral relativists ignore questions of power and subjectivity that must be central features of a feminist moral theory (Hekman 1995).

6. See Hekman 1986.

7. The Canadian practice of sentencing circles and the Mexican reliance on family and community courts are examples (Nadar and Metzger 1963).

References

Addelson, Kathryn. 1991. *Impure thoughts: Essays on philosophy, feminism and ethics.* Philadelphia: Temple University Press.

Baier, Annette. 1985. *Postures of the mind: Essays on mind and morals.* Minneapolis: University of Minnesota Press.

Code, Lorraine. 1991. *What can she know? Feminist theory and the construction of knowledge.* Ithaca, N.Y.: Cornell University Press.

Frye, Marilyn. 1991. A response to *Lesbian ethics:* Why ethics? *Hypatia* 5, 3: 132–37.

Gadamer, Hans-Georg. 1975. *Truth and method*. New York: Continuum.

Gilligan, Carol. 1982. *In a different voice*. Cambridge, Mass.: Harvard University Press.

Gilligan, Carol, Nona Lyons, and Trudy Hanmer. 1990. *Making connections*. Cambridge: Harvard University Press.

Hekman, Susan. 1986. *Hermeneutics and the sociology of knowledge*. Notre Dame, Ind.: Notre Dame University Press.

———. 1995. *Moral voices/moral selves: Carol Gilligan and feminist moral theory*. University Park: Penn State Press.

———. 1999. *The Future of differences: Truth and method in feminist theory*. Cambridge: Polity/Blackwell.

Held, Virginia. 1995. The meshing of care and justice. *Hypatia* 10, 2: 28–32.

Hoagland, Sarah. 1988. *Lesbian ethics: Toward a new value*. Palo Alto, Calif.: Institute of Lesbian Studies.

May, Todd. 1995. *The moral theory of poststructuralism*. University Park: Penn State Press.

Nadar, Laura, and Duane Metzger. 1963. Conflict resolution in two Mexican communities. *American Anthropologist* 65, 584–92.

Noddings, Nel. 1989. *Women and evil*. Berkeley: University of California Press.

Ruddick, Sarah. 1989. *Maternal thinking*. Boston: Beacon Press.

Sklar, Judith. 1964. *Legalism*. Cambridge: Harvard University Press.

Spelman, Elizabeth. 1988. *Inessential woman*. Boston: Beacon Press.

Toulmin, Stephen. 1958. *The uses of argument*. Cambridge: Cambridge University Press.

Tronto, Joan. 1995. Care as a basis for radical political judgments. *Hypatia* 10, 2: 141–49.

Walker, Margaret. 1989. Moral understandings: Alternative "epistemology" for a feminist ethics. *Hypatia* 4, 2: 15-28.

Weber, Max. 1978. *Economy and society*, ed. Guenther Roth and Claus Wittich. Berkeley: University of California Press.

CHAPTER FOURTEEN

Objectivity and the Role of Bias

Susan E. Babbitt

In Chinua Achebe's *Anthills of the Savannah*, Achebe tells the following
story: Once upon a time the leopard who had been trying for a long time
to catch the tortoise happened upon him on a solitary road. AHA, he said;
at long last, prepare to die. And the tortoise said: *Can I ask one favour before
you kill me?* The leopard saw no harm in that and granted it. But instead of
standing still as the leopard expected the tortoise went into strange action
on the road, scratching with hands and feet and throwing sand furiously in
all directions. *Why are you doing that?* asked the puzzled leopard. The
tortoise replied *Because even after I am dead I want anyone passing by this
spot to say, yes, a fellow and his match struggled here.*
                                                                —Achebe 1988, 128

In Achebe's story, the tortoise doesn't fight for his own existence. He knows
he's going to die. Instead, he fights for the interpretation that is given to his
death. The point of Achebe's anecdote about the tortoise is that there is power
in the control of the story: At one level, there is the struggle for existence, the
political struggle, which the tortoise has already lost. At another level, there is
the struggle for the importance of that political struggle, for the story that can
make that political struggle meaningful as a struggle of a certain sort.

The tortoise knows that he is not in fact a match for the leopard. Yet the
tortoise believes that others can come to believe that in fact a fellow and his
match struggled there. The tortoise wants to bring it about that a particular
story possesses credibility, eventually, even though he knows, at least in the political sense at hand, that the story is not now true.

297

Thus, the tortoise is biased toward an interpretation of his death that does not, so far, have much going for it. He wants his death to be represented as something other than what it is—as a struggle between a fellow and *his match*—in order, perhaps, to promote other goals and other sorts of understanding. Indeed, there is no reason to think that a tortoise is a match—in a physical fight—for a leopard. But the tortoise has defined and claimed for himself a view that might promote such reason. And he acts on it.

In this chapter I consider the role of *bias* in the pursuit of more adequate understanding. It is fairly commonplace now to acknowledge that we always rely upon some standpoint, or perspective, when we make observations and interpret information. Often, we must make an effort to take different perspectives. There are those, for instance, who write about how the world looks different depending on whether they take one or another aspect of their identity to be important—their White part or their Latin part, and so on. And they talk about "border crossing," of seeing things from one perspective one day and from another the next, depending on who is listening and what the context is. But sometimes, proper understanding requires, not consideration of difference, but rather concern about the perspective according to which we see some differences as more important than others in specific ways.[1] And occasionally it is necessary to assume a direction of development—single-mindedly, like the tortoise's sand throwing—in order to ascribe importance in a more adequate way.

This topic illustrates a difficulty in understanding certain experiences and struggles. When we try to be objective, we try not to be *un*biased, but rather to be biased in an appropriate way. I am not unbiased when I try to evaluate my students objectively, for I am predisposed toward specific criteria of evaluation, and I give more importance to some information about them (results of the test) than other information (e.g., appearance). I have to take a position about what matters in order to be objective, and I should do so according to the right sorts of standards. My aim in this chapter is to identify a complexity involved in the emphasis on storytelling, namely, the need sometimes to make explicit moral judgments about the relative importance of stories, and to urge that it be acknowledged philosophically.

In the following I draw upon an example of a story *about* some stories to suggest that we must sometimes, in order to properly appreciate stories, take a moral and theoretical position *about* those stories first. I draw upon the example to try to suggest that we *do* do this in any case, in practice, and to make some remarks about the theoretical implications. Precisely in situations in which dominant expectations rule out the meaningfulness of important struggles, understanding of such struggles is not best achieved through the collecting of stories, at least not through the collecting of stories as a primary goal. For in order to hear some stories *as* important, we often need *not* to hear other stories, or at least not to take them as seriously. We do therefore—in the very appreciation of difference and multiplicity—take specific moral positions in rather exclusionary ways.

DEVELOPMENT, STORIES, AND MARITZA

Some development theorists, critical of post World War II theories of development, have criticized the role of a single dominant worldview in development theories; namely, the view according to which we think of "the North" as developed largely on the basis of consideration of economic wealth. The idea is that an unstated, single dominant view of how the world divides up—into developed North and undeveloped South—suggests that development requires accumulating wealth, as in the North. And feminist scholars have been concerned that relying on such a world view makes it difficult for First World women to acquire adequate understanding of Third World women, and their real needs and aspirations (e.g., Mohanty 1991, 51–80). Thus, some have proposed a kind of particularism, such as emphasis on concrete, local practices (Escobar 1995), or the particular and varied standpoints of women (Mueller 1987). The suggestion is that resistance to the detrimental effects of a single worldview depends on promoting particular views about human needs and interests, emerging from a wide variety of situations and backgrounds.

A recent, influential study of women and development urges that the best way to arrive at an understanding of *human* development is to investigate the personal stories of women from many different backgrounds and cultures (Nussbaum and Glover 1995). Recognizing that the problems of women in developing countries call for new forms of analysis, theorists urge an approach to development that moves beyond utilitarian economics to identify a number of distinct components of a human being's quality of life, including life expectancy, maternal mortality, access to education, access to employment, and the meaningful exercise of political rights (e.g., Sen 1993, 30–53). They argue that the capabilities approach is superior to utilitarian-economic or cultural-relativist approaches to development in analyzing women's problems and in generating creative solutions.

Martha Nussbaum's proposal, for instance, is that we ask ourselves what are the characteristics of a human being? What does a human being do as such? Put another way, what are the forms of activity, of doing and being that constitute the human form of life? Nussbaum suggests that inquiry begins by examining a variety of self-interpretations of human beings. Especially valuable are myths and stories that situate the human being in the universe with beasts on one hand and gods on the other, stories that ask what it means to live as a human being set apart from the rest of the world of nature and with limitations that derive from membership in the world of nature. The idea is that people in many different societies share a general outline of such a conception and that we can identify it by collecting the stories we all tell each other: "This convergence gives us some reason for optimism, that if we proceed in this way, using our imaginations, we will have in the end a theory that is not the mere projection of local preferences, but is fully international and a basis for cross-cultural attunement" (Nussbaum 1995, 74).

I suggest that one complication to this suggestion about acquiring understanding is that some stories and myths are not able to be heard, and some are not able to be heard as morally relevant, unless we first apply a conception of human development to the context in which stories are being told.

Consider the following example: In her award-winning collection of stories *Alguien Tiene Que Llorar,* Cuban author Marilyn Bobes tells the story of Maritza, an architect who wants to construct alternative buildings because she believes that getting up every morning to see buildings that are all the same renders a person intolerant (Bobes 1995, 7–24).[2] We do not hear the story of Maritza from Maritza's point of view because Maritza is already dead, having committed suicide. Instead, we hear about Maritza from the point of view of her friends, or at least of those people who were closest to her. We start with the impressions of Daniel, who is looking at a picture of a fifteenth birthday, the fifteenth being the birthday at which girls "come out" to society to be presented to men. Maritza, he says, was already marked for death at the time of the party, decades ago. She stands out above the others physically and her face is the only one that "is not a birthday face," that is, the only one not expressing the significance of the coming-out party. The stories begin and end with the impression of Daniel, the only male. Daniel's impressions set the stage by being primarily about Maritza's looks and how people responded to them. For we learn as the story proceeds that appearances constitute an important criterion for evaluating and understanding Maritza. Daniel, we learn, is in love with Cary, who is the most respectful of and influenced by Maritza. Daniel's impressions end the story: Noting how devastated Cary is by Maritza's death and recognizing Maritza's talent and influence, Daniel is primarily concerned with how Cary looked at the funeral, the color and tone of her skin, for instance.

Cary, who is closest to Maritza, tells us that Maritza was never like the rest of them; she refused to prepare herself for the "future auction" (Bobes 1995, 9), meaning the pursuit of men. Maritza wore clothes that were flowing and disguised her body; she didn't carry makeup. Cary is influenced by her. They go together to the lonely stretches of beaches that Maritza likes to frequent on cold, grey days. Maritza tries to convince Cary that she (Cary) is making a mistake to let men be the determining factor in her life. Maritza tells

Cary that Cary has talent as a writer, and tells her specifically what her talent consists in. She wants to help Cary develop herself. But when they talk about Maritza's beliefs about love and self-realization, Cary finds it hard to follow Maritza's reasoning. For Maritza's ideas and interpretations are different from others'. Some of her ideas are new to Cary. Maritza believes that the more realized a person is, the less she needs to depend on another to be happy. Love is an invention, she believes, to placate the losers (women), and people who think they are in love are really wanting approval. Love is too uncertain a feeling to possess such a "major protagonistic role" as it does in women's lives, according to Maritza. Maritza herself has been in love, she admits to Cary, but Cary says that she could not ask Maritza about it because by the time they got to that part of the conversation, Cary was not even sure what they were talking about. It is to Cary that Maritza says, as in the title, "Someone has to cry" ("alguien tiene que llorar"). Maritza tries to persuade Cary that if someone has to cry, it could just as well be the other person.

Alina and Lazara, two other companions of "the fifteenth," both remark on Maritza's questionable sexuality. Alina tells us that she always suspected that something was wrong with Maritza but that Maritza always kept it inside. She says that she went to the funeral out of respect and good manners but that respect and good manners do not require that her name be put on the wreath. Alina, married with three kids at the time she tells her story *about* Maritza, states cruelly and self-righteously that Maritza was clearly deviant and, like a deformed child, was better off dead. A woman without children, she says, can never realize herself.

Lazara, in contrast to Alina, respects and loves Maritza, but like Alina, Lazara thinks Maritza's sexuality immoral. For Lazara says that even if Maritza were gay, she was still a good person, as if being gay and being good are somehow opposed. Lazara recognizes and appreciates Maritza's distinctness for she also says that she would like to have been like Maritza, that Maritza was not like the rest of them, letting herself be taken in by people who did not respect her.

The story of Maritza is powerful, not for what it represents, but for what it doesn't represent and, we might suspect, what cannot easily be represented, and that is Maritza herself. Maritza is already dead at the time of the remembrances of her friends, but even if she were not, it is not clear how Maritza could have told her own story. The point is not that individuals can only tell their own stories, that, for instance, because Maritza is dead, we can never know the real Maritza. Even if Maritza *were* available and even if Maritza *did* tell her own story, the story would be hard to understand.

The story told in "Alguien tiene que llorar"—the one story (told about the many stories)—tells us that it is hard to get a satisfying picture of Maritza because the norms and values that inform the stories *about* her are also those which Maritza herself, for the sake of self-realization, is committed to resisting. Marilyn Bobes's story *about* the stories about Maritza tells us something about *how* Maritza's story is hard. It does this by organizing the other stories. The one story *about* the various stories takes a *position* on those stories.

In the last two paragraphs of the story, Daniel remarks on how he felt as he stood with Cary and Lazara beside the grave, the only people remaining. We gather from the fact that Daniel remains at the grave that he feels and perhaps possesses closeness to Maritza. His main impressions, however, are of the appearances of Maritza and Cary, and of how Cary's skin has faded. He recognizes Cary's devastation, but his reflections are about her looks. In the final sentences, Daniel says that he knew that Cary "flew" with the thoughts and ideas of Maritza and he remarks that he would like to have been there. Until yesterday, he says, that would have been possible, but now it is not.

The arrogance of Daniel's final statement—that it was possible for him to have access to Maritza's ideas as long as she was alive—summarizes the devastating difficulty of Maritza's position: Maritza was what was not acceptable or expected in her society, and she realized that for her to go ahead in her society required changing the form of the society itself, changing, for example, the buildings: When people rise up every day seeing buildings that are all the same they become, themselves, intolerant of difference. We might understand Maritza as someone who had explicitly confronted the norms and values of her society in her own life. She had thought through and had tried to persuade at least Cary that it was mistaken to think that women *ought* to be in love with men, that romantic love was the most important value. And Maritza knew that struggling against norms and values was hard, that "someone had to cry." Now, Daniel, for instance, could see that Cary "flew with Maritza." And he could see that Maritza was someone special. But Daniel also thinks that if only he had been able to be there, to listen, he would have had access to her difference. The powerful tragedy of Maritza's life is not that she could not be understood by those closest to her, but that, except for Cary, those closest to her could not see that there was any particular difficulty in understanding her; they thought she was *merely* different.

There are two sorts of philosophical questions about moral understanding raised by examples of people whose expectations for themselves are in conflict with expectations generated by social norms and values. First, there are questions about how an individual understands and gives significance to her own life and experiences, for instance, how someone like Maritza takes responsibility for the meaningfulness of her commitments and identity (e.g., Card 1996). Second, however, there is a question about how other people understand those whose lives and expectations are out of synch. One possibility is that such people are misunderstood by others, and just dismissed. They might, say, be considered eccentric or weird. The deeper, and sadder, possibility is that people *think* they have understood someone when they have not in fact understood what most needs to be understood. Worse than being misunderstood or discounted as crazy is to be understood in a way that disallows recognition that there is something that *still needs* to be understood.

The only one who could see that, as Maritza said, someone has to cry, was Cary. And Cary is the one who, after Maritza is dead, does not dare to try to explain why Maritza died. Cary says to Lazara something about self-realization, but she does not try to explain what might have happened to Maritza. Only Cary, of all the friends and companions, understands that there is pain in understanding, that it is difficult, that it means that someone will be hurt. Only Cary understands that it is *hard* to understand Maritza and that she has not *yet* understood. The particular story that ends the general story about Maritza is that of Daniel who provides the cruel dismissal of Maritza's struggle by saying that if only he had been able to listen he would have had access to Maritza's thoughts.

DIFFERENCE AND JUDGMENTS OF IMPORTANCE

Maritza was understood to be different. But being different is easy compared to the pursuit of meaningfulness that engaged Maritza. When one is different, one is still part of the community, understandable on the basis of shared standards of sameness and difference. Probably everyone experiences themselves as different from their community in important ways at some point in their lives. Maritza tried to redefine standards of sameness and difference. And Cary, who recognized Maritza's struggle, at least tacitly, also recognizes the difficulty of explaining it, of creating awareness in others. In a later story, Cary says about her own struggle to understand, and in response to those who see her as living a life of sin, that "the real road of sin is to try to understand" (Bobes 1995, 36).

The story of Maritza tells us *about* a story that cannot easily be told, given the norms and values that define the society in which Maritza lives. The problem for development theory is not that stories like Maritza's are important and need to be considered if problems for women are to be more adequately understood, although this is an important insight. The deeper problem for development theory is that unless a story of a particular sort is told about the story of Maritza, for instance, we might not recognize that there exists a story of a certain sort that has not *yet* been told. The story of "Alguien tiene que llorar" is, in effect, not a story about Maritza herself, for we realize that we do not understand Maritza; rather, it is a story about the context in which Maritza struggled to realize certain goals, such as self-realization, greater social understanding of diversity, creative and intellectual achievement, independence. We learn from the stories, and how they are organized (around the photo of "the fifteenth"), that Maritza's context is one in which women are supposed to love men, auction themselves off to men, concern themselves with appearances, and in which it is expected that women without children will never manage to realize themselves. In Maritza's case, we understand that a story relevant to understanding the real needs of women has not been properly told, and should be. But we realize this, not by hearing stories about Maritza, but rather by hearing a story about the context in which some stories about someone like Maritza are easier to accept, because of the context, than others.

Cary, for instance, first knew Maritza as did the others, as different, as a woman not interested in men, not ready to make herself an object, independent, committed to ideas. But Cary's understanding of Maritza is deeper, more respectful, although Cary, as has been noted, does not offer an explanation for Maritza's death. Maritza tries to explain to Cary that women cannot realize themselves as persons within existing expectations about love and relationships, for women are always expected to need, and to act out their need for a man. Maritza believed love was a pact among the losers who were, after all, women. Cary writes that she did not understand all this, and moreover that she thought Maritza was wrong about love. But Cary understood through Maritza that there were things she didn't understand, and that these things that she didn't understand mattered. Cary engaged with Maritza's ideas to the point that she could not ask Maritza who she (Maritza) had been in love with because Cary no longer knew what it was that they were talking about. Cary had therefore understood that Maritza's ideas and aspirations involved different understandings of fundamental values, that she embraced values of different substance, and that she defended her values. More important than this, though, was that Cary developed respect for Maritza as a result of which she believed that it was important that Maritza maintained different values, and that she, Cary, understood her. Cary did not understand Maritza but she came to believe that understanding Maritza was worth pursuing.

What Cary acquired of significance from Maritza is not obviously beliefs, or information. What was significant about the relationship was not that Cary had *access* to Maritza's views. She might easily have had access to Maritza's ideas and have misunderstood or failed to appreciate their significance. Whichever of Maritza's beliefs could have been understood by Cary could also have been explained away by Cary, if she had wanted to explain them away. What Cary seems to have acquired from Maritza is recognition that there was something important that needed to be explained and that was not yet adequately explained. The short story does not provide enough details to explain Maritza's influence on Cary. But it raises a question about a particular sort of difficulty about understanding others, of different values and traditions. What distinguishes Cary's understanding of Maritza from the others is not that Cary understood more, but that she understood that there was more, specifically, of importance to be understood about Maritza that had not yet been understood.

Cary came to understand through Maritza that there are goals for which it is important to discover a relevant sort of meaningfulness—goals, for instance, of self-realization. Alina offers an explanation for Maritza's death, or at least for her deviance. According to Alina, "women who don't have children never manage to realize themselves." Now, this is not an unreasonable explanation. It may even be true that within the society of Alina and Maritza, a woman without children cannot realize herself. It may be true, for instance, that women who don't have children are just too odd, given the social structures, to be able to realize themselves as persons. Moreover, we know from the stories that are told about Maritza, particularly about the pressures on women to present themselves as objects for men, that Alina's story would be credible within her society. According to Alina, women without children never manage to realize themselves, but according to Cary, Maritza's struggle is just that, to realize herself—and it is without children and a man. For Alina, Maritza is different because she does not realize herself, because she does not have children and a man. For Cary, Maritza realizes herself *and* she has no children. So, from Cary's perspective, Alina is wrong. But Cary's understanding depends on the importance she attributes to Maritza, and to the fact that she really likes Maritza. Cary's understanding, to the extent that she has understood anything, is explained by her very strong bias, toward Maritza's importance and, in some unidentified sense, the correctness of Maritza's views.

If Cary had simply appreciated Maritza's difference, she would not have recognized the importance of Maritza's struggle. Like the tortoise, Cary recognized that there was a story that needed to be told about importance, even though Cary herself could not tell it. One problem this raises epistemologically is that Cary needs to be in a position to understand Maritza's struggle *as* one of self-realization, or something like it, before she can give Maritza's struggle the appropriate significance relative to, say, Alina's explanations. Alina says that a woman without children cannot realize herself. So, according to this story, Maritza is not realizing herself, whatever else she may be doing. Cary rejects Alina's story because she sees Maritza's life as important, even though she cannot provide the full explanation about *how* it is important.

Cary needs to be able to see Maritza's struggle as being of a certain sort *first* in order for her to recognize that it constitutes a challenge to the view expressed by Alina, the view of the society in general. Alina's story does, after all, accommodate Maritza's difference. Maritza *is* different in not having a male partner or wanting children. According to Alina, Maritza's differences mean that she cannot realize herself, whereas for Cary, Maritza's example means that there is something wrong with Alina's view of self-realization. Cary doesn't have an alternative explanation about Maritza's death that can rival Alina's. What Cary has is a belief about the importance of such an explanation, still to be discovered. Cary doesn't agree with or entirely understand what Maritza does and thinks. What explains her belief in the importance of an alternative explanation is that Cary has engaged with Maritza to the extent of perceiving her *as* a certain sort of person, even if she cannot identify what sort that is.

EXPECTATIONS AND THE CASE OF CUBA

Cary has understood Maritza better than the other members of the group. But what Cary has understood is that she has not understood Maritza adequately. Cary might well have thought she understood. It would have been easier for Cary to tell *some* story about Maritza's death. That Cary does not tell a story about why Maritza died expresses a commitment toward a certain possibility for meaningfulness, not currently available. Richard Miller points out that in order to get at the truth about someone who is being widely slandered and lied about, you'd have to really like the person (Miller 1991, 747). The problem is not just that a balanced, passive view would be a distorted one in such cases of widespread false beliefs, but also that the dominant view in such cases is likely to be powerful, having to do with how people see themselves, thus being harder to identify and resist.

In some cases of understanding, there must first be resistance to available, more comfortable explanations and, second, commitment to narrowly focused, *biased* pursuit of a specific sense of importance and meaningfulness. Che Guevara identified *narrow* focus as necessary, in cases of systemic injustice, for human freedom. Writing in the early years of the Cuban revolution, he tried to describe the role in human freedom of specific, focused striving for the conditions that make possible imagination of human development (Guevara 1970, 367–84). Given that the commitment of the Cuban revolution was to thoroughgoing revolution, Che Guevara tried to address the question of justification. He aimed to answer those who worried that a revolutionary commitment, requiring the bringing about of new values and the development and imposition of new perspectives, moral, social, and political, necessarily involved arbitrariness. His point was that the simple fact that a revolution involves, at least to some extent, an imposition of values, and a narrow, specific, *directed* focus, is not enough to establish that it undermines individual freedom. For human freedom, in situations of injustice, *always* involves narrowly focused struggle for direction. For such direction is required for understanding.

Che Guevara's point was expressed by Mirta Rodríguez, discussing the situation of women in Cuba during the "special period," the period of economic hardship in Cuba resulting from the disappearance of the Soviet Union and the Eastern European bloc. Rodríguez says that Western readers will have a hard time imagining the shortages of goods in Cuba and what it is like for everyone to be resorting to the underground market. The point is that while it is hard for American readers to imagine the difficulties of life for women in Cuba, it is also hard for American readers to appreciate the significance of the difficulties. And Rodríguez says in her concluding paragraph: "To understand would require having been immersed in superior ideals; perhaps having been an internationalist, prepared to fight and die for foreign peoples, having believed in the possibility of the 'new man' that Che Guevara thought we could create here. As life becomes more difficult, people think about these things. All this gives coherence and internal force to the decision to resist" (Rodríguez Calderón 1995, 18–19).

There is a point here about interpretation that might be missed. One point of the article is that the situation for women in Cuba *is* hard, very hard. Rodríguez presents the facts about hardship, describes the situation and provides anecdotes. The idea of the final paragraph, though, is the difficulty of imagination. Rodríguez says that while it is hard for North American readers to imagine the difficulties, it is still harder to imagine the *significance* of the hardships. One part of understanding has to do with the possession of information. In the case of Cuba, we don't always possess the necessary information. But there is also the problem of the importance of information. Rodríguez suggests that readers cannot imagine the meaningfulness in terms of which such events acquire importance relative to other events.

Moreover, Rodríguez suggests that if we could make relevant judgments about importance, we would ask different questions. She says that people do not adequately understand the situation of women in Cuba if they do not know what it is like to believe in Che Guevara's "new man," or to be immersed in internationalist values. Now, she does not say that people must, in order to understand, know what it means to realize these values. She says that, to understand, people must know what it is like to *believe* in them—to think that they are important. Like the relationship between Cary and Maritza, there is something epistemologically significant about the recognition of the importance of certain values, even if they are not yet understood. Rodríguez suggests that readers would understand the situation differently if they understood what

the commitment to such values meant, regardless of whether such a commitment can ever be realized. Indeed, Che Guevara's idea of the "new man" *is* the
idea that to understand, one has to be willing to be engaged, to be transformed
in a specific direction of development.

Che Guevara wrote that what people fail to imagine, if they have not
been involved in such a revolutionary process as that in Cuba, is "esa estrecha
unidad dialéctica existente entre el individuo y la masa, donde ambos se interrelacionan, y a su vez la masa, como conjuntos de individuos, se interrelacionan
con los dirigentes" (Guevara 1970, 370).[3] What needs to be lived to be appreciated is the *narrow* dialectical unity, a dialectical unity defined by a particular
direction of movement, not, for instance, by relationships between all existing
ideas and forces. One might think that, in order to have free deliberation, one
should seek a "dialectic" among all the available voices, a kind of exchange with
equal resources, as defended by some liberal political theorists. Liberals argue
that with free exchange and equal resources, the best view will win out. But
Che Guevara realized, as have feminist theorists more recently, that in an unjust system, equal resources does not mean equal expressive opportunity, even
in the absence of explicit coercion and with complete information. Freedom
from restrictions, and the ability to organize and express oneself as one pleases,
is not real freedom for everyone. For some views, under systemically unjust social conditions, are much more difficult to make plausible. And some possibilities for human development are not imaginable, under unjust conditions, just
as Maritza's self-realization was unimaginable. In such situations, really free
discussion and deliberation requires the bringing about of more adequate conditions, and this requires more narrow, exclusionary pursuit.

Anthropologist Claude Lévi-Strauss, writes in one of his accounts: "The
whole village left, leaving us alone in the abandoned houses with the women
and children" (Noël 1994, 27). He writes as if the women and children are not
part of the village. Lévi-Strauss's sentence provides an example of how some
people are invisible as a result of, among other things, the concepts we apply
when we interpret our experience. Thomas Kuhn pointed out, and it is now
well known, that when we do not possess a concept for something, we do not
see it as existing (Kuhn 1962). We may look at something without seeing it *as*
the thing that it is. Such a point has implications for moral and political theory,
as well as the philosophy of science. For if some people do not even figure into
discussions, say, about justice, we have to pay attention to development of perspective, of appropriate categories for unifying experience, for classifying events
and phenomena, and seeing them as certain sorts.

The point about the "narrow dialectic" is not so unfamiliar. Che Guevara
seems to be suggesting that unless one is participating in a certain direction of
investigation, drawing on relevant background beliefs, one is not in a position

to appreciate the significance of certain events and phenomena. The idea is not just that one has to be there, to be engaged, in order to know what is going on. Instead, the suggestion of the *dialectic* is that one has to participate in such a way that one is influenced by the specific results of one's participation, so as to provide grounds for evaluating that participation. What is not imagined by those who have not lived the connection, Guevara says, is "esa dialéctica estrecha," the *narrow* dialectical unity that exists (Guevara 1970, 370), and the fact that it is within a particular focusing of direction, of purpose, that relevant aspects of similarity become identifiable. That is, it becomes possible to unify events and phenomena in ways relevant to that dialectic, and then to identify and appreciate the results. The notion of dialectical unity has to do with the fact that the imaginability of human possibilities depends on changing conditions, on the imposition of meanings and values, and that the measure of success of such change and imposition has to do with what sorts of cognitive, social, even emotional capacities result.

Worries about manipulation and repression constitute a crux of liberal defenses of a certain view of democracy and respect for human rights. There is a powerfully attractive idea (at least on the face of it) that it is always best for people to live their lives "from the inside," with true beliefs (Kymlicka 1991, 12). It is assumed that if we acknowledge that it is sometimes better for people's lives to be transformed as a result of changing conditions, there is a risk of justifying arbitrary coercion and manipulation. But the idea that it is always best to live one's life "from the inside," with true beliefs, is naive if one considers the enormous damage done to some individuals' abilities to act, to dream, to hope, to imagine, in systemically unjust societies. Guevara's suggestion was that people's desires, interests, and capacities can be transformed as a result of changing conditions, and that they must be if the history of a society, and its defining norms and values, involve deep injustice. There is also the idea that people, to be free, must be able to understand such changes, that the ultimate object of such change is that people be able, at least eventually, to control their lives in relevant ways.

I have suggested that what is distinct about Cary's relationship with Maritza is that Cary knew that there was something specific that she did not understand about Maritza's views and which, moreover, was important. Cary, in other words, related in such a way with Maritza that she developed cognitive needs: she acquired interests and desires as a result of her experience with Maritza which demanded explanation. Cary's relationship with Maritza was one that *created* an explanatory burden for Cary because it transformed Cary's interests and expectations in ways that raised further questions—about self-realization, love—which in order to be pursued required further explanatory resources.

Cary goes on to try to realize herself through her writing, through her creativity, and not through her relationships with men. As she describes it, it is both hard and confusing. In particular, it is hard to express. In the story in which Cary describes her life after Maritza, she expresses her own thoughts without punctuation, in long run-on sentences, while Alina's thoughts *about* Cary, in the same story, are written conventionally. It might look as though Maritza's influence on Cary was detrimental. For Cary ends up confused. If there is increased understanding, it is not obviously understanding *of* something in particular. Rather, it would seem that what understanding Cary acquires as a result of her relationship with Maritza, and what might constitute understanding *of* Maritza, is an orientation toward what is important, and an expectation that it can be understood as important.

In the case of Cuba, for instance, it is not enough to consider empirical evidence; it is also necessary to consider the conceptual and practical background that explains the importance given to evidence. Moreover, one has to consider the fact that relevant philosophical assumptions are now very powerful, that they constitute the basis for a worldview, informing the way people see themselves and interpret stories and experiences. We always interpret the world on the basis of background beliefs and traditions, and in the particular case of Cuba we have to become aware of certain beliefs and traditions, if we are to be fair.

Speaking to the United Nations in 1960, Fidel Castro invited the audience to suppose "that a person from outer space were to come to this assembly, someone who had read neither the Communist Manifesto of Karl Marx nor UPI or AP dispatches or any other monopoly-controlled publication. If he were to ask how the world was divided up and he saw on a map that the wealth was divided among the monopolies of four or five countries, he would say, 'The world has been badly divided up, the world has been exploited'" (Castro 1992, 72). The suggestion is that without the aid of ideology or propaganda, or at least without the aid of certain ideologies and propaganda, someone from outer space might have good reason to think something is *wrong* with the way the world is divided up.

Now, it would seem that Fidel Castro's point here is interesting not primarily because it refers to a different perspective, or the suggestion of one, but rather because it refers to the difficulty of properly understanding something that is obviously true. The truth of the claim that the world is divided up badly is hard to dispute; its truth is somewhat obvious. But its *understanding* is difficult. It might be possible for someone from outer space to think it *matters* that the world is wrongly divided up because someone looking from outer space would not have expectations generated by how the world is currently divided up. Such a person would be reasoning without a certain set of expectations. The suggestion seems to be that someone from outer space might see differences in a different way and might indeed find certain differences irrelevant. The point in this case, however, is not that they *could* be irrelevant from another perspective but that they *are* in fact irrelevant and that the only way this might be properly understood would be from the perspective of outer space.

The question of properly understanding certain truths may be more important in some cases than questions about their possession. Fully understanding the true statement "The world is divided up badly" requires not only a desire to understand how the world *ought* to be divided up but also, more fundamentally, a commitment according to which it *matters* that the world is divided up wrongly. The problem is not just that one has to see that there is an issue before one can appreciate the usefulness of the information. The more important problem is what is *involved* in seeing that there is an issue. Thus, it would appear that what is significant for the acquiring of understanding is not so much the discovery or identification of truth, but rather the commitment to the kinds of directions of development—particularly human development—that can make the right sorts of truths relevant. The difficulty of understanding that the world is divided up wrongly, even if one believes correctly that it is, is that such understanding requires an interest in the kind of possibilities for human existence its pursuit would make possible.

When people talk sympathetically about Cuba, for instance, it is common to say that although Cuba is not democratic, although the Cuban government does not respect the autonomy of its people (e.g., Stiff 1997), the Cuban revolution has succeeded in bringing about a social system that provides better medical care and education than many developed countries. Indeed, the statistics that generally follow the "but" which follows the claim that Cuba is not democratic indicate that in fact Cuba takes better care of its smallest and weakest citizens than probably any country in the world. One could think that this is a story about democracy and respect for autonomy, and many do. One might think that if "democracy" has to do with the people ruling themselves, and if "autonomy" has to do with individuals controlling their own destinies, it is hard to see how it can be irrelevant to democracy or autonomy what happens to people when they are in the most helpless states. But we often listen to the facts about Cuba and think somehow that recognized successes in caring generally for the weak and the sick do not *matter* to democracy, that these issues are just not the same sort of thing.

The Cuban Revolution involves two struggles: one to go forward politically and socially, maintaining and furthering gains in social justice; the other is for the story to be told about the struggle so far, and its strengths and weaknesses. For according to one way of understanding the world, the political/social

struggle in Cuba *cannot* be a struggle for social justice, for it cannot be democratic. There is in the first place a struggle for survival of a certain sort, but there
is also a struggle for the story according to which the Cuban Revolution is a
struggle of that sort.

CONCLUSION

Development theory, as an area of enquiry concerned about fairly assessing cultural norms and traditions, must come to grips with the need for direction, and
not primarily the need for multiple perspectives and appreciation of difference.
In some situations, such as that of Maritza's personal struggle, we have to *pursue*
the possibility of a certain sort of meaningfulness, in order even to identify it.
General understanding of human possibilities requires recognizing that in some
cases, as in Maritza's struggle, what seems chaotic and hopeless is a claim to personal integrity, to a specific sort of unity of existence. In other cases, such as those
in the position of the tortoise, it may be moral and political integrity, a unifying
vision. The point has been that if we do not have an adequate story about these
stories, we may not be able to expect them to be anything other than what they
seem to be at first glance—stories about failure, stubborn confusion, and death.
Moreover, to pursue such a story—about stories—we often have to be already engaged with and to expect its correctness, that is, to be relevantly biased.

Development theory—to the extent that it is about human flourishing,
about individuals' needs for self-realization—needs to recognize that there is
sometimes struggle for control of the story, as Achebe's anecdote suggests.
Sometimes we need to try to control the story in order that other stories become
possible. But the tortoise does not act arbitrarily. The tortoise has been engaged
with the leopard for a long time, just as Cary engaged with Maritza. And the
tortoise has interests and orientation resulting from that engagement. He also
has beliefs about the general situation of tortoises and leopards. The problem—
epistemologically—is that the tortoise cannot take a "balanced" view, hearing all
the different sides. Neither can Cary, as regards Maritza. For the "balanced
view"—expressing existing expectations—already rules out significant interpretations. Instead, they take a single-minded, directed approach, partly out of desire to pursue a singular story, which might make possible other stories.

I have made reference to the case of Cuba particularly because, whatever
the result of a struggle for political existence, there is still also an ever important question about the story to be told about that struggle and about the lives
lived in commitment to it. Cuba raises the question of perspective urgently, for
those who care about Cuba, because Cuba's fight against neoliberal institutions
and imperialism has been insistent and explicit. When some Cubans say about

the prospects of socialism that "we have no choice, we must continue dreaming," they might be referring to problems of deliberation in a situation in which, not only must one pursue new human possibilities, but one must also try to develop or discover the kind of story that can make one's pursuit morally imaginable and plausible. Whatever one thinks of the Cuban revolution, Cuba raises questions about what is involved in effective moral evaluation of a social and political struggle which is ruled out of importance by dominant expectations.

In certain situations of understanding it is important to recognize the struggle for the story, for the theoretical and moral perspective, and the narrowly focused, *biased* commitment required to achieve it. In the case of Cuba, and for many women in situations like that of Maritiza, there is a struggle not just for existence, but for the story to be told about that struggle and its moral and political significance. In listening and giving importance to stories, we need to be aware of the more singular stories that explain why some stories are so much easier to hear and believe than others. And we need sometimes to be hierarchical, exclusionary, and relentless in resisting the explanatory comfort of our often implicit, more broadly unifying stories.

Notes

This chapter is an earlier, shorter version of chapter five of *Artless Integrity: Moral Imagination, Agency and Stories* (Lanham, MD: Rowman and Littlefield, 2001). For discussion of the issues of this chapter, I am grateful to Marilyn Bobes, Juscarid Morales Fernández, Ernesto Tornín, and audiences at Carleton University, Ottawa and the Casa de las Americas in Havana. I am indebted to the Social Sciences and Humanities Research Council of Canada for support for the broader project to which this chapter contributes.

1. I have discussed this in Babbitt 1999, 235–54.

2. I am indebted to Barbara Schubert for introducing me to the work of Marilyn Bobes and to Juscarid Morales Fernández for discussing the stories with me at length, helpfully explaining the *cubanismos*.

3. "This narrow dialectical unity existing between the individual and the masses, where each interrelates, and at the same time the masses, as groups of individuals, interrelate with the leaders."

References

Achebe, Chinua. 1988. *Anthills of the savannah*. London: Picador.

Babbitt, Susan. 1999. Moral risk and dark waters. In *Racism and philosophy*, ed. Susan Babbitt and Sue Campbell. Ithaca, N.Y.: Cornell University Press.

Bobes, Marilyn. 1995. Alguien tiene que llorar and Este vez tienes que hacerme caso. In *Alguien tiene que llorar.* Havana: Casa de las Americas.

Card, Claudia. 1996. *The unnatural lottery: Character and moral luck.* Philadelphia: Temple University Press.

Castro, Fidel. 1992. The case of Cuba is the case of every underdeveloped country. Address to the General Assembly, Sept. 26, 1960. In *To speak the truth.* Fidel Castro and Che Guevara. New York: Pathfinder.

Escobar, Arturo. 1995. *Encountering development: The making and unmaking of the Third World.* Princeton, N.J.: Princeton University Press.

Guevara, Ernesto. 1970. El socialismo y el hombre en Cuba. In *Ernesto Che Guevara: Obras 1957–1967, Tomo 11.* La Habana: Casa de las Americas.

Kuhn, Thomas. 1962. *The structure of scientific revolutions.* Chicago: University of Chicago Press.

Kymlicka, Will. 1991. *Liberalism, culture and community.* Oxford: Clarendon.

Miller, R. W. 1991. Fact and method in the social sciences. In *The Philosophy of Science,* ed. Richard Boyd, Philip Gaspar, and J. D. Trout. Cambridge: MIT Press.

Mohanty, Chandra. 1991. Under Western eyes: Feminist scholarship and colonial discourses. In *Third World women and the politics of feminism,* ed. Chandra Mohanty, Ann Russo, and Lourdes Torres. Bloomington: Indiana University Press.

Mueller, Adelle. 1987. Peasants and professionals: The social organization of women in development knowledge. PhD. Diss. Ontario Institute of Studies in Education.

Noël, Lise. 1994. *Intolerance: The parameters of oppressions.* Montreal and Toronto: McGill-Queen's University Press.

Nussbaum, Martha, and Jonathan Glover, eds. 1995. *Women, culture and development: A study of human capabilities.* New York: Oxford University Press.

Rodriguez Calderón, Mirta. 1995. Life in the special period. In *NACLA Report on the Americas* 29, 2 (September/October).

Sen, Amartya. 1993. Capabilities and well-being. In *The quality of life,* ed. Martha Nussbaum and Amartya Sen. New York: Oxford University Press.

Stiff, Jennifer. 1997. *The question of national autonomy: The case of Cuba.* Paper presented at North American Society for Social Philosophy conference at Queen's University, July 20, 1997.

CHAPTER FIFTEEN

The Struggle to Naturalize Literary Studies: Chicana Literary Theory and Analysis

Judith Richards

Racism is especially rampant in places and people that produce knowledge.
—Gloria Anzaldúa, *Making Face, Making Soul. Haciendo Caras*

The story I am telling is a story of this sort: a reading I put forward for discussion, rather than a final telling.
—Lorraine Code, *Rhetorical Spaces*

Recent feminist theoretical projects in philosophy and literary studies indicate a commitment to avoiding analytical frameworks that suppress the natural diversity of human voices, contexts, and experiences. With this goal in mind, many scholars in both disciplines are currently exploring how to evaluate physical, social, and discursive evidence for the purpose of positing theoretical statements that articulate commonalities without losing the authenticity of the individual example, or that through evaluation (re)establish positions of domination in the academy. In this regard, interdisciplinary debates have focused on the conventional paradigms used to depict relationships between the subject and object of analysis, through questions that explore the ideological components of representation and evaluation, and their connection to "real world" issues. Underpinning these revisionist projects are shared queries: who speaks? from where? and how does the critical evaluation of enunciations interface with the processes of their production? With these questions theorists in both fields have begun to articulate models for how to proceed normatively on the basis of the diversely specific, how to hypothesize for decision-making purposes in a manner that privileges the unique location and subject without recreating reductive hierarchies.

This chapter will explore cross currents in contemporary feminist episte-mology and Chicana literary theory, drawing on philosopher Lorraine Code's recommendations for a more productive approach to naturalism in epistemo-logical theories and Gloria Anzaldúa's analyses of multicultural projects in lit-erary studies. It will become clear that Code's deconstruction of the reigning scientific practices linked to knowledge theories and Anzaldúa's critique of Anglo-centric multicultural studies can be put in dialogue with each other in order to further our understanding of how nondiscriminatory knowledge the-ories might promote progressive human interaction on the local and global level. Developments and issues pertinent to contemporary discussions of nat-uralism will be outlined in the next section in preparation for examining their connection to similar concerns in literary studies.

WHOSE NATURALISMS, WHOSE STORIES?

Feminist philosophers interested in unveiling the exclusionary principles sup-porting traditional knowledge theories are examining the historical and intel-lectual development of epistemology as an ally of the physical sciences. As Code describes, "mainstream epistemologists commonly assume that knowl-edge properly so-called must be modeled on scientific criteria . . . [and] con-strued in stringent objectivist terms" (1991, 32). Particularly physics, the science most closely associated with classical epistemology, was thought to be the most applicable in theorizing the physical attributes of the world. Implicit in the legacy of this epistemology is an a priori universal reason that finds cor-respondence in the knowable world, and is empirically available to human sub-jects through systematic observation by a viewer whose cognitive structuring and subsequent evaluation are thought to be free of inflection by their social and cultural context. Serving historically as model of this abstract, impartial knower have been affluent or at least well-educated and economically privi-leged males of European descent, whose life experiences and intellectual premises are seen to be interchangeable with those of other knowers, regardless of cultural, ethnic, gender, racial, and other characteristics. Yet, as Code ob-serves, it is a matter of record that the Enlightenment and subsequent theories

of rational autonomy excluded those whose circumstances or personal characteristics did not correspond to those of the ideal subject.[1]

Code contends that the solidity and longevity of conventional naturalisms is largely due to their rhetorical successes, rather than metaphysical
truths. Consequently, as she observes throughout her work, "malestream" discourses have survived despite their logical twists and lapses. Principal examples
of this phenomenon in standard knowledge theories are the separation of the
viewer from the object of study "throughout investigative, information-gather-
ing and knowledge construction processes" (1991, 32), the conviction that "simple, basic observational data . . . provide the foundation of knowledge because
perception is invariant from observer to observer, in standard observation conditions," which results in the interchangeability of knowers and the self-evident
world in which they reside (1991, 6), and the gendering of the subject of
knowledge via the consistent alignment of reason with masculinity in the construction of the ideal knower, in contrast to "feminine" mental activities such as
emotion, intuition, and interpretation.[2]

Further, the use of binary oppositions in methodologies supporting conventional epistemologies has functioned to ignore epistemic claims and evidence originating in what Code calls "the excluded middle [ground]." The
archetypal dichotomy, the Platonic mind-body distinction, later reinforced by
Descartes's "pure" intellect connected to the human soul, has successfully pro-
tected reason "from aspects of experience deemed too trivial and particular for
epistemological notice" (1995, 215). In this practice, naturally predictable and
"demonstrable" evidence leads to the decontextualization and reification of
what is "known." And likewise, mainstream dichotomous thought—in constructs such as public-private, light-dark, right-wrong, masculine-feminine,
virgin-whore, culture-nature, academy-world—reinforces support for social
and ideological structures that preserve White, masculine hierarchies, social
norms, and privilege, and designate "the disadvantaged places reserved for
women and other less privileged people" (1991, 28). From this view, ambiguity
is intolerable; elements not fitting sanctioned classifications are overridden or
recast and appropriated into existing categories.

Code's work on the renaturalizing of epistemological procedures is essentially demythologizing: it exposes the contrived essence of neutrality claims
made in principal Anglo-American theories, which in turn reflect researchers'
refusal to acknowledge the inevitable ideological imprint on investigative projects. In her 1993 article "What Is Natural about Epistemology Naturalized?"
Code explores the long-standing connection between science and epistemology
with specific regard to conventional understandings of naturalisms. In this essay,
her principal concern is to demystify the paradoxical twist inherent in the
premises of principal Anglo-American epistemologies, which have proceeded

artificially by claiming to derive from and pertain to what constitutes human nature, while at the same time naturalizing "the very attributes and actions that they purport to discover and thence to recommend" (1993, 7). In other words, homogenous groups of researchers, already certain about what and who is natural in knowledge production, claim to investigate with scientific objectivity what is natural in human cognitive behavior. More natural and thus socially progressive, in Code's view, would be the admission of points of view in research as a principal element in theorizing activities. Instead, as is currently clear, the failure of conventional naturalism to recognize itself as a construct has weakened science's connections to actual human learning situations, producing and sustaining "an epistemological monoculture . . . whose consequences are to suppress and denigrate ways of knowing that depart from the stringent dictates of scientific knowledge-making" (1993, 15). For Code, then, recidivistic naturalisms have promoted projects constructed on premises that in practice have placed community survival in danger by promoting circular rather than exploratory reasoning as normative.

In light of the solid and lofty connection of knowledge to the physical sciences, Code reasons that an appropriate point of departure for renaturalizing epistemologies is to be found in the equally self-contradictory discourse on which standard analyses are built. Thus, she recommends an interdisciplinary approach for new projects, in the anticipation that social and psychological analysis and recent narratological insights might more accurately provide the diverse range and shifting parameters of actual human cognitive activities in their multiple settings.[3] The strength of these revised procedures, as Code explains, lies in their localized orientation: far from the conventional touchstones of idealized abstraction and a priori conditions for knowledge, they seek the plethora of information to be found in diverse and contextualized interpretations of physical, social, and human nature (1993, 3).

Code proposes methodological as well as conceptual shifts in knowledge theories. Since the concept of pure objectivity is demonstrably both impossible and unwise (1995, 162–65), she argues for multiply-informed interpretation as a rich, informational tool. While current arguments in philosophy see the "interpretive twist" as a direct link to epistemological chaos and anarchical relativism, she argues that interpretation is—and always has been—a component of conventional knowledge projects, since experiments are always tested and evaluated in response to contact with the particularities of the material world (1991, 68). Indeed, she argues, given the complexity and uniqueness of natural environments and human nature, evaluative projects must require, rather than rule out, interpretative thinking. As a result, the naming and description of the researcher's perspective, instead of being destructively relativistic, serves to initiate dialogues that allow communities to conceptualize on a broader and more accurate scale. For these reasons, in Code's view, interpretation "is as 'natural' and as evidence-reliant as the other activities that naturalists study; and it is just as essential to survival . . . [in that it] uncovers and reveals the contingency of motivations, power structures, and extra-scientific assumptions that are often so embedded in experimental design and in narrative structures as to seem merely a matter of course" (1993, 10).

In this vein, Code notes that the interpretive twist in epistemological practices challenges epistemologists to devise new ways of positioning themselves as theorists. In contrast to those who hold the universalistic "view from nowhere," the researcher who acknowledges the plurivocality of nature will take into account the complexity of the equally situated viewing activity itself, and consequently seek ways to position and reposition herself "within the structures she analyzes, to untangle the values at work with in them and to assess their implications" (1991, 70). On this basis, in contrast to the standard, abstract model, this researcher anticipates only a partial accuracy from her view of evidence, which offers at the least, an imperfect picture of the real world, and at best, a representative format that encourages the juxtaposition of evaluations in order to discover in a democratic fashion the best way to proceed. In such a discussion, claims of value-neutral objectivity are treated as one kind of interpretation of data, rather than the best available form of thought.

Another important dimension of Code's argument for the epistemic value of interpretive activity in research projects is her removal of the traditional distinction between philosophizing and storytelling. A principal reason for this historical separation is, she maintains, discomfort with the disparity in reporting results that "can vary with the interpreter(s) in ways that objective (formal) reasoning is believed to escape" (1995, 229). Moreover, theories have always been a kind of storytelling disputed by other stories, since "disputed versions about the nature of the world have always been considered worthy of rigorous philosophical discussion, themselves dependent upon the historically and culturally mutable narratives (= interpretations) in which they are embedded" (1995, 229–30). That is, objective conclusions discovered by pure reason have always passed through the interpretive filter of some kind of descriptive narrative (1991, 58).

"Storied" theories are built around details and anecdotes that tell of their origins, and show and explain their reasoning. In particular, autobiographical narratives, which Code calls "genealogical epistemologies," offer an abundance of evidence for the researcher, in that they provide "descriptive justifications of reasoning and knowledge claims and, through [their] own internal logic, establish some (organic) degree of normativity" (1995, 155). And once again, while the limits of epistemologies produced in this fashion include the partial nature of evidence provided, their authority is admittedly connected to *a* view, rather than *the* view, of reality, and thereby openly elicits discussions about counterevidence.

As a result, when Code talks about the "interpretive twist" that will re-orient the claims of natural epistemologies in the real word, she is referring to the need to recognize, and thus build on, the essential continuity between epis-temology and the circumstances of its production. Moreover, her realignment of rigorously interpretive evidence with reasoned narrative in epistemological projects makes clear "the relevance of narrative as an epistemological resource" (1995, 170). In the end, she concludes, while not a perfect process, the inter-dependent and negotiative modes required to process knowledge in this man-ner at least have reason to engage and compete with the repressive dynamics in elitist, monocultural, hierarchical models.

Underpinning Code's discussion of the merits and limits of feminist philosophers' recommendations for naturalizing epistemologies is an ongoing concern about the role of theory itself in projects that claim to be liberatory. On the one hand, since survival depends on the human processing of informa-tion available in local environments, the goal of epistemology, she claims, should be to help people to understand and cultivate their informational pro-cessing capacities (1993, 3). In this light, theory seeks to develop conceptual frameworks that are descriptively rich enough (evidence and justification) and sufficiently empirical (analysis of context) to enable people to think even what might appear at first to be contradictory thoughts (1993, 9)—in other words, that interpretive and naturalistic thinking will proceed in a mutually informa-tive fashion (1993, 10). As a result, theoretical processes, rather than products, will become standard practices, and the interaction between knowledge pro-duction and social well-being will create new community resources.

However, on the other hand, since historical evidence indicates that clo-sure is inherently an element in theory making, Code has formulated a provocative, alternative recommendation in the essay "Remapping the Epis-temic Terrain." Here she proposes that philosophers take a respite from theory making, in favor of proceeding "descriptively" with the productive tension be-tween the actual ambiguity and specificity available in real-world situations. Her goal in doing without epistemological theory is to create space for new critical practices that "can take into account the positions people occupy on [their own] epistemic terrain." Otherwise, she fears, the resourcefulness of these accounts will go unnoticed when filtered through prescribed views (1995, 306–307). In the discussion of Anzaldúa's theory-making recommen-dations that follows, I will return to Code's uneasiness with the tendency for closure in theory making.

In summary, Code's principal achievements in the project of reorienting epistemology in the world it purports to describe are the demystification of the exclusionary practices embedded in traditional knowledge theories, the posit-ing of the epistemic gold mine and social resource that is self-reflective narrative, and the dialogical processes she recommends for deciding how to proceed wisely in the evaluation and application of knowledge—all constitutive elements in the discussion of how persons and communities might best proceed for *mutual* survival.

Culture Wars as Epistemological Struggle

the india in you, betrayed for 500 years / is no longer speaking to you
—Gloria Anzaldúa, *Borderlands/La Frontera*

Code's position that the production of "genealogical" narratives is a rich epistemic activity serves Chicana feminist literary theory well in its contentions that knowledge theories are locally produced versions of what is known, who knows and how, and that likewise, authority and legitimacy—or evidence and justification—are locally conceded. This same concept is reflected in many Chicana writers' insistence on grounding literary theory in Chicana testimonial writing, in order to tease out the historical, geographical, cultural, and political complexity that shapes it. Like Code, Chicana theorists are concerned with unveiling the real and different locatedness of multiply-oppressed subjects who in their daily lives must battle the practices of dominant discourses in which they have a negligible presence, if they figure at all. In addition, through their writing, many Chicanas seek to make visible the art, literature, and theories that have always informed their work and communities and that therefore have already contributed to human spirituality and survival. In recent publications Chicana writers have explored issues concerning the emergence of their writing into mainstream texts and courses. Principal among concerns they have recognized in academic circles are the possibility of theorizing equitable conversations between the local and the dominant without re-creating hierarchies of truth and authority, and the creation of dialogue wherein culturally contextualized Chicanas are authoritative and others—particularly Anglos, White feminists, male Chicanos, and other women of color—listen and learn.[4]

In light of the historical development of mainstream, "American" literary theories, many Chicana critics question whether even current deconstructionist and feminist approaches to reading texts are capable of registering the complexity and originality of differently-located works, or of challenging the dynamics of racism and sexism underpinning the same academy that oppresses rather than encourages them as learners. Indeed, as I will claim here, requesting of dominant academic practices a nondiscriminatory approach to "new" literatures and critical discourses means invoking the same sort of paradoxical twist that Code faces in her renaturalizing project.

In 1981, addressing not only the Euro- and andro-centric but also the White feminist norms prevailing in the academy, Gloria Anzaldúa and Cherríe Moraga published *This Bridge Called My Back: Writings by Women of Color*. Constituting a watershed in feminist theory, the anthology's insistence on the recognition of pluralism in "women's" literary production initiated an egalitarian shift in the articulation of what constitutes U.S. literature, and of *how* to read it? and *who* reads it well? Since *Bridge*, U.S. feminist literary theories have undergone radical changes, including recognition of the multifaceted nature of identities, the complex construction of gender and representation of sexuality, and of the very different national sites from which critical analyses and literatures emerge. Challenges yet to be met in the creation of inclusive academic practices include the tendency of Anglo feminists to consider their experiences normative for all women, the concomitant under-representation of lesbians and women of color in mainstream discussions of theory, and separatist dynamics within emerging marginal groups themselves.[5]

U.S. Latina publications, themselves enriched by diverse roots in Mexican, Puerto Rican, Cuban, and Dominican cultures, have become principal contributors to increasingly heterogeneous conversations within universities and publishing houses, with works whose notable artistic merit parallels their compelling value as sociopolitical testimony. In particular, Chicanas, whose colonial experience in the United States collectively began in 1848 with the annexation of one-third of Mexican national territory, are contributing narratives of resistance to the neocolonial impact of Anglo academic discourses on the production and analysis of Chicana literatures. As a result, in spite of so-called culture wars, the current national boom in the publication of ethnic and racial minority women's writing means that Latinas are vying with White and minority male writers for prime commercial space in bookstores and television interviews, as well as for representation on academic reading lists.

In literary studies, the concept of revised naturalisms as used by feminist epistemologists is most clearly pertinent in response to ongoing debates about multiculturalism in academic disciplines, as well as in institutional and commercial populations. Diversity projects have been implemented to more accurately reflect the communities these elements serve, and the race-class-gender categories of analysis are no longer uncommon evaluative optics. On the other hand, some successes notwithstanding, Anzaldúa fears that the current practice of sprinkling diversity throughout institutions and their literatures may be a move that actually avoids rather than addresses the real challenges involved in dismantling ingrained discrimination. "We want so badly to move beyond Racism to a 'postracist' space . . . but we are only prolonging the pain and leaving unfinished a business that could liberate some of our energies" (1990, xxii).

Perhaps as a consequence of postponed change, strong nationalistic sentiments shape much of Chicana literary discourses, among them the assertion that Chicanas will be the "best" critics of Chicana creative writing. Many anticipate that evaluation of Chicana texts by Chicana scholars will articulate and promote characteristics and practices authentically representative of Chicana experiences, including barrio and migrant life, border dwelling, language and cultural conflicts, and the daily negotiation of multiracial identities. And yet, as Anzaldúa laments in several of her essays, despite its long struggle to count as part of the pluralistic presence in U.S. culture and literary canons, some literary production by Chicanas, while conceptually pluralistic and egalitarian, has in its articulation and application embraced, rather than rejected, exclusionary and reductive practices (1990, xxvi). For her, the (re)imposition of normative standards for who *can* read Chicana writing *correctly*, know *authentically* its *complete* cultural significance, and describe *authoritatively* its signifying strategies, are moves that threaten to contradict the reformative beliefs they claim to hold. In the following discussion I will describe Anzaldúa's principal strategies for engaging and disassembling racisms, and her recommendations for how Chicanas might move progressively into academic disciplines and theory.[6]

For Gloria Anzaldúa, discussions that seek resolution in singularity work against the real racial, cultural, linguistic, gender, and class mixtures comprising the identities of many Latinas. Like Code's refusal to treat knowledge as information gained in isolation and articulated in monologic statements, Anzaldúa's position constructs knowledge and subjectivity on the mutual relations and interaction of diverse groups located on the borders between allegedly discrete territories and attributes. Specifically, it is the overlapping, rubbing up against, or collision of one element or identity or set of beliefs and discourses with another, on the margins and slippery edges of places and beliefs, that constitute what Code describes as the interdependent relationships that shape persons' identities. For Anzaldúa this kind of interdependency functions as an erosion of boundaries, a natural resistance to being contained in artificial categories. Two concepts critical to her representation of the natural untidiness of physical and social realities are *mestizaje*, or mixture, a Spanish-language word that refers to the third culture and race created in the violent union of Spanish and Mexican peoples; and the Borderlands, the line of demarcation between Mexico and the United States, a sign of the actual geographic places she has inhabited, as well as the overlooked zones in-between specific, definitive categories of people, places, and things.

As a point of departure for self-description and analysis, *mestizaje* intervenes in conventional dichotomies by occupying the ambiguous spaces between their polarities. For example, as a racial and cultural mixture, the *mestiza* is what

she is not: "you / are neither *hispana india negra española* / ... *eres mestiza,
mulata,* half-breed / caught in the crossfire between camps / while carrying
all five races on your back / not knowing which side to turn to, run from"
(1987, 194). In this way, *mestizaje* serves as a productive category of analyses
in general, teasing out new insights and meanings from standard ontological
and epistemological paradigms. Not a conventional balancing of opposites, nor
a synthesis, it is "a third element which is greater than the sum of its severed
parts" (1987, 79–80), and thus, for Anzaldúa, an apt point of departure for the
reinvention of a concept that is pliant enough to embrace the actually uncontainable components of all that she is and is not.

Anzaldúa uses "the *new mestiza* consciousness" (1987, 79–80) to establish
a contrast with the one that has never been articulated (at least in Western
terms). Through this optic she encounters the natural elusiveness and endless
ambiguity of identity as a concept, and thus the difficulty in finding words adequate to the notion: "As a *mestiza* I have no country, my homeland cast me
out; yet all countries are mine because I am every woman's sister or potential
lover" (1987, 80); "I ... / continually walk out of one culture / and into another / because I am in all cultures at the same time" (1987, 77). Principal experiences of these sites are the sense of "juncture ... where phenomena tend
to collide [and] the possibility of uniting all that is separate occurs" (1987, 79).
This consciousness, inflected by tolerance for contradiction, flux, agitation, and
ambiguity, are both the *mestiza's* reality and coping strategies: "She learns to be
an Indian in Mexican culture, to be Mexican from an Anglo point of view ...
to juggle cultures, [to operate] in a pluralistic mode [that] turns ambivalence
into something else" (1987, 79). In this view, the practices by which standard
Anglo-American epistemologies have regulated and regularized the natural
heterogeneity of persons and cultures stand in marked contrast to the evidence
of mixtures in Anzaldúa's *Borderlands,* where normative description would be
of negligible use, and indeed unnatural.

In a similar manner, as Anzaldúa explains, the linguistic and narrative
ramifications of *mestizaje* deconstruct conventional beliefs in the unity of
mainstream discourses on both sides of the border. While Chicano Spanish is
said to be "incorrect," for her it is a living language and thus uncontainable. Her
list of the languages she herself speaks includes working-class and slang English, standard Spanish and English, North Mexican Spanish, Southwest Chicano Spanish, Tex-Mex, and Pachuco (1987, 55). Additionally, coming into
voice, taking up the pen, talking back to the machista elements in her first culture as well as to the monocultural academy, are moves that require choices:
"with which voice (the voice of the dyke, the Chicana, the professor, the master), in which voice (first person, third, vernacular, formal) or in which language
(Black, English, Tex-Mex, Spanish, academese)" (1990, xxiii).

Life on the Borderlands: The Aquisition of Agency

only I remain / a person of the middle / who battled in a brown-colored life, / battled in a life colored white, / and become strong . . . enough to say: / don't call me for the Chicanos, / nor for my parents, / nor for women. / summon me for myself, / one woman
—Marina Rivera ("Mestiza" 1993, 100)

Meant to clarify political and racial differences, the United States-Mexico border is meant to determine who belongs and who does not. And yet, while this political boundary signifies the production of other arbitrary dichotomies that psychologically oppress those on the wrong side (white-brown, legal-alien, American-other, English-Spanish, safe-unsafe) border dwellers like Marina Rivera's "person of the middle" occupy spaces that override not only geographical but also racial and gender boundaries. As a result, Anzaldúa's Borderlands, sites on "this thin edge of / barbwire" (1987, 3) that scars lands and peoples, are actually rich locations for knowledge production, complex situations where multifaceted, multiracial persons devise strategies for community building and survival on both sides of the wire. A model of border crossing in her own racial and linguistic mixtures, the *mestiza*—more than the *mestizo*, who still claims masculine privileges—embodies a natural resistance to Enlightenment (and Conquest) depictions of the world. Likewise, the construction of agency and the production of border knowledges by *mestiza* subjects is an activity that in itself contests Western epistemologies.

Like the recommendations that Code proposes, to shift knowledge theories to new epistemic localities where the knowledge people need to live and act well is actually produced (1994, 158), Anzaldúa claims the Borderlands as productive sites of knowledge that will serve not only border dwellers well, but also provide a model for productive coexistence in the increasingly boundaryless twenty-first century: "the future will belong to the mestiza . . . because [it] depends on the straddling of two or more cultures . . . creating a new mythos—that is, a change in the way we perceive reality, the way we see ourselves, and the ways we behave" (1987, 80).

As Anzaldúa describes it, border crossing is both a personal and a political activity. The *mestiza* self-consciously reconstructs herself and her surroundings; undertaking a conscious rupture with all oppressive traditions of all cultures and religions, "[s]he reinterprets history, . . . shapes new myths, . . . adopts new perspectives toward the darkskinned, women and queers . . . strengthens her tolerance (and intolerance) for ambiguity, . . . is willing to . . . make herself vulnerable to foreign ways of seeing and thinking, . . . surrenders all notions of safety, of the familiar" (1987, 82). Here, Anzaldúa specifies what is required of the epistemic subject in revolt, the danger inherent in shedding received knowledges, fear of being rejected by her family, or thrown out of the academy.

The methodologies of the mixed-race consciousness subvert definitive borders and flourish in ambiguity. Locating oneself is as much a function of perception as of geographies. The *mestiza* appropriates invisibility in order to reorient herself; she goes underground, inside, elsewhere, instead of confronting and thus colliding with Western, intellectual solidity. Likewise, the path of change is subjective, elusive, interpretive, and negotiative. Writing, particularly autobiographical narrative, is an instrument of exploration, self-knowledge, and survival; through the writing process, the *mestiza* acquires knowledge through the intersection of her multiple selves (Chicana, tejana, india, española, lesbiana, femenista). This plurality, the result of the "infinite divisions" (Bernice Zamora's phrase) informing self, place, and perception, allows the knower to cross multiple boundaries, reverse herself, and return again. Furthermore, as Anzaldúa explains, components of her identity can be used as bridges that traverse otherwise uncrossable borders. By example, through the optic of her lesbian self, "I am all races because there is the queer of me in all races" (1987, 81). In this way, the *mestiza* narrator discovers power and knowledges that elide Western perspectives, by straddling cultures and beliefs, breaking down the subject-object dualities, and playing with the always elusive third possibility. At times there occur, as Anzaldúa describes, rare moments when the continual juggling of blendings and contradictions achieves equilibrium, a sensation of "spanning abysses" when she experiences temporary acts of intellectual, emotional, and discursive equipoise (1983, 209).

Anzaldúa's epistemic style is representative of the constellated self she claims. It reflects a process built around the interaction of knowledges, embodied, spiritual, and acquired. Her narrative personas address a "you" whose referent is both oppressed women of color and her own, various selves in formation: "I write to record what others erase when I speak, to rewrite the stories others have miswritten about me, about you. . . . To discover myself, to preserve myself, to make myself" (1983, 169). Here, by addressing the otherness she, too, lives, using the text as a cultural, political, and personal mirror, Anzaldúa uses writing to enter and explore alternative, more inclusive environments. A principal strategy of her epistemological revolution, egalitarian writing strategies heal and nurture the violated self while also unleashing forces that in a larger sense can facilitate community change.

In her most recent anthology, *Making Face, Making Soul. Haciendo Caras* (1990), Anzaldúa uses her introductory essay to discuss theory making and its practices in the Anglo academy. One of her goals in creating the book was to discuss the role of theory in repressing voices and erasing faces in academic institutions and, in response, to encourage women of color to tap into their own border-crossing experiences as new sites for theory making.

Pertinent to this argument is Anzaldúa's analysis of the meaning of "theory." It refers to the effective inseparability of both the theory-making process and product, a variety of ways to construct a conclusive perspective: a *set* of knowledges, a *mental* viewing, "a formulation of *apparent* relationships or underlying principles . . . verified to *some* degree." Theory as an object, used by individuals, is inescapably subjective: one *has* theory, and *holds* "considerable evidence in support of a formulated general principal" (1990, xxv; emphasis added). Thus scrutinized, since "[w]hat is considered theory in the dominant academic community is not necessarily what counts as theory for women-of-color" (1990, xvi), the description of knowledges and their acquisition from new locations will authenticate what is understood as American literature(s) and reveal the natural plurivocality supporting them. Further, this overriding of conventional knowledge boundaries is a move that will also rewrite other disciplines through mixed and nuanced categories of analysis (race, class, gender, and ethnicity). Here Anzaldúa identifies the advantage of knowledge from the margins and the crossroads, where strength lies in informed visions, shifting perspectives, emerging evidence, optics that see through deceptions imposed on the past and unveil the power of self-description when we "give up the notion that there is a 'correct' way to write theory" (1990, xxvi). "Making face," or theorizing oneself into the world, corresponds to creating an agency, "cultivating our ability to affirm our knowing . . . step[ping] into new terrains where we make up the guidelines as we go . . . looking at our shadows and dealing with them" (1990, xxvii).

Important in the goal to occupy theory from one's own location is Anzaldúa's unveiling of the strong links between literature and the selective reality of academic politics. From the Borderlands, "academese" is difficult to engage since it "presents its conjectures as universal truths while concealing its patriarchal privilege . . . [and] hushes our voices so that we cannot articulate our victimization" (1990, xxiii). Equally problematic is the academy's tendency to use the term "melting pot" as a synonym for multiculturalism, a theoretical way to avoid the serious dismantling of racism (1990, xxii). Moreover, she explains, both White and non-White students are taught to read through the conventional White, male optic. In response, with *Making Face*, Anzaldúa sought to create a book that "would teach ourselves and whites to read in nonwhite narrative traditions (1990, xviii). In this picture, when Chicanas write themselves into theory, they emerge from the blank spaces in mainstream paradigms, where unmarked whiteness produces "sign[s] of Racism unaware of itself" (1990, xvi). The process of "making face," then, recognizes and names theory and theory making as principal instruments of oppression, and, therefore, important sites from which to intervene in oppressive academic practices.

Consistently evident in Anzaldúa's theoretical recommendations is inclusive language—"we," "our," "us," a nonhierarchical practice that establishes an interactive relationship with the reader. As a critic, she not only applies what she knows but invites dialogue by positioning herself face to face with her reader—a move that recalls the practice of "making face." This activity, she explains, speaks to vulnerable areas of the body that bear the imprints of acculturation, such as instructions for being "*mujer, macho*, working class, Chicana. As *mestizas*—biologically and/or culturally mixed—we have different surfaces for each aspect of identity . . . carved and tatooed with the sharp needles of experience" (1990, xv). Frequently a mask covers several layers of "faces," deformed by internalized oppressions and self-hatred and separated by interfacings, buffers between them "where our multiple-surfaced, colored, racially gendered bodies intersect and interconnect" (1990, xvi). Imposed, received faces, and thus identities, begin to be shed and new communities formed when writing begins; both artistic narrative and critical writing provide linkage to disparate aspects of identity, and make the subject accessible to others who are also struggling.

In this view, theory is a living and therefore complex activity that need not follow any set pattern. Intensely self-reflective, "there is no difference between writing creative writing and writing critical theory. It's all creative. I bring in my sense of history, the history of all the different cultures that I'm involved in, the family history and . . . the autobiographical" (1990, xxv). Likewise, the visceral link between mind and body overrides conventional, divisive categorizations that weaken a writer's connection to her memories; the intellect needs the gut and adrenaline, she writes, in order to keep it in touch with the anger that is a crucial element in breaking out of oppression (1990, xviii).

Like Code's community-based epistemic paradigm, Anzaldúa's living theory reflects a present-tense, progressive ontology whose epistemological resources are both embodied and discovered through interactive exchanges. A healing process, the overlap between theory and storytelling clarifies power structures and discourses, solves problems, and looks for alternatives. Writers then envision new stories to explain the world, from their own perspectives, projecting different value systems "with images and symbols that connect us to each other and to the planet" (1987, 81). In addition, for both Code and Anzaldúa, self-reflective narrative is an important epistemic resource. It works simultaneously back into histories (personal and cultural), forward to the time when the feminist *mestiza* consciousness will be a leader in the structuring of global survival, and inward to the creative self that is always reconstructing (retheorizing) itself. In this way *la conciencia mestiza* is an epistemic process that seeks equilibrium though self-scrutiny and nonhegemonic practices. Importantly, it is also a non-utopian mode: it candidly observes that the infinitely fragmented self, which is creatively flexible, also experiences the daily (re)negotiation of self as an enervating activity.

FROM PHILOSOPHY AND LITERARY STUDIES:
AN ENLIGHTENED TOLERANCE FOR AMBIGUITY

> We have grown up and survived along the edges, along the borders of so
> many languages, worlds, cultures and social systems. . . . Those of us who
> try to categorize these complexities inevitably fail.
> —Tey Diana Rebolledo, "The Politics of Poetics"

In a manner similar to Code's goal that epistemologies address individual and local specificities without constructing new hierarchies, Anzaldúa argues that Borderland knowledges, in themselves naturally uncontainable, will take turns being important. In this section, by way of summary and conclusion, I will look at how Code's and Anzaldúa's epistemological subjects use texts to remap themselves, and what kinds of sites they identify as optimum for further development of nonexploitative environments.

For both Code and Anzaldúa the operative meaning of naturalism is the negotiated process of what counts as knowledge and how it comes to count. In its broadest sense, such a naturalism is always located specifically at the crossroads of what is unique to each subject—of the shifting pattern of sociocultural intersections she experiences, and how she recognizes and represents them. In these naturally unique sites, the normative conditions of interactivity cultivated by Code's new epistemic subject are of relevance to Anzaldúa's *mestiza* border dweller as well. Both use narrative activity as integral to the project of the subject's knowing herself in relation to her environments; both describe as a central goal the destabilization of the self-certainty inscribed in monovocal, unstoried projects; and both concord in the premise that what counts as natural is qualitative decision-making dependent on descriptive evidence and recommend that judgments about the nature of human agency be assessed in keeping with local circumstances. Interlocutors in these storied locations, then, will naturally contest hegemonic claims and negotiate with other, self-identifying subjects, since the assumption that anything or anyone might be *wholly* self-announcing will prove to be information inadequate for local needs.[7] Anzaldúa's *mestiza* project reinforces Code's proposition that theory making and self-reflective writing are similar activities, and that recognition of this naturalizing phenomenon is crucial if

unstoried versions, dominant in such places as the academy, are to be effectively challenged and altered.[8]

Here, reminding us that narrative descriptions are never value-free, Code
emphasizes that it is their dialogic quality that allows storied epistemologies to
arrive at normative statements, since contesting them requires interlocutors
whose claims would also have to explain the provenance for their own moral
and rhetorical positions (1991, 16).[9]

One question pertinent to Code's and Anzaldúa's depictions of located
knowledges points to their perhaps utopian goal of serving communities and
environments *well*. In response Anzaldúa's *mestiza* consciousness offers not solutions but rather the continual re/negotiation of that which produces living
well, through the characteristic plurality of all knowledges and mixtures of locations pertinent to knowers, even when these knowledges are contestatory. For
this reason, the imposition of useless abstractions is unlikely to prevail *on the
local level*. In a similar fashion, Anzaldúa's concerns about separatism and coun-
terstances are well served by Code's continual return to local descriptions of experience and place. In this view, even when it appears that racial and gender
characteristics can regularize narrative agency, Chicana critics who maintain that
only other Chicanas can read Chicana texts well are ignoring the unique mixes
that inform their specific, ethnic localities.[10] Likewise, in a manner that recalls
the classical practices of malestream epistemologists, Chicanas who hold that
they are the best readers of their own literary production are effectively resorting to a priori descriptions and the ranking of knowledges. And further, these
reductive measures suggest that there is a set of monocultural phenomena la-
belled *Chicanisma*, waiting "out there" for the ideal (Chicana) knower. Likewise,
this monocultural position will have difficulty in arguing with the academy that
Chicanas are also good readers of Anglo or other women's writing.

An important site of discussion between these two theorists is Code's
proposal for a hiatus in the production of epistemological theory, in order that
marginal knowledges might have unfettered intellectual space in which to develop and become audible. From Anzaldúa's point of view, a possible response
to this idea recalls that of feminists to poststructuralist critics in the 1970s, who
declared that the (concept of the) author was dead. Feminists, on the other
hand, argued vehemently that killing off the author was not an appealing move
to those just assuming narrative authority. And, indeed, the coincidence between the increasing presence of marginal voices in mainstream reading lists
and the malestream critics' patricide did not go unnoticed. In like manner, Anzaldúa might argue with Code that the relinquishing of theory, and therefore
of visions from diverse locations heretofore unrepresented in histories and
philosophies, is a move that might be seen as prejudicial.

Overall, Code's and Anzaldúa's theoretical models, when put in conversation with each other, offer a rich source of ideas from which epistemologists and critics in other disciplines might gather insights for furthering the production of theories of respectful coexistence. Code's hope that equitable epistemological models will put philosophy progressively in service to communities and their well-being can take heart from Anzaldúa's vision of the ways that "border" knowledges naturally take turns being important and that inherently shifting—or *mestiza*—identities never solidify—two important dynamics in the flexibility and creativity required for global survival and progressive international diplomacies.

Notes

1. In "Critiques of Pure Reason," from *Rhetorical Spaces* (1995), Code explains the historical contradiction between Enlightenment beliefs in democratic goals and the sociopolitical circumstances that consistently prohibited their realization: "Ideas of reason that govern the history of philosophy so as to underwrite received conceptions of knowledge, objectivity, formal validity, and moral authority are modelled upon, and generate models for, the best socially sanctioned realization of white male achievement in the professional and propertied class of affluent societies. . . . Although in principle Enlightenment reason promised emancipation to all, the nature of that emancipation, and the methods of achieving it, were tacitly modelled on the lives and circumstances of propertied white men, and dependent for their realization or access to intellectual and material resources just like theirs. . . . [Thus] its purity was always only an illusion, deriving as it did from an idealized reading of the circumstances of its advocates, and exerting an exclusionary force over 'others' who failed to qualify as participants because their circumstances were different" (1995, 213).

2. "Reason is discursively constructed as an object of descriptive and normative analysis . . . in discourses whose symbols and metaphors shape and are shaped by dominant ideals of masculinity" (Code 1995, 215).

3. See Mieke Bal (1993, 293–320) for a productive application of Code's interdependent theory of acculturation and knowledge production, which Code calls "second personhood" (1991, 82–87). My application in other essays of Bal's insights to Anzaldúa's use of the text as an instrument of self-discovery treats the text itself as an interlocutor, a concept that parallels Code's egalatarian paradigm.

4. See Richards (1998).

5. For discussion of these issues in Chicana critical theory, see Richards (1998).

6. The majority of Anzaldúa's work is directed toward White women and women of color. However, since her self-descriptions clearly locate her also in *chicanismo* and Chicana issues, in this chapter I am specifically naming Chicanas as the theoretical subjects well served by her work.

7. The philosophical insights guiding this discussion are assisted by Code 1994, 160.

8. She writes, "social issues such as race, class and sexual difference are intertwined with the narrative and poetic elements of a text, elements in which theory is embedded . . . [and through which] we create new categories for those of us left out or pushed out of the existing ones" (1990, xxvi).

9. In *Making Face*, Anzaldúa provides a specific example of normativity being tested: "One of the changes that I've seen since *This Bridge Called My Back* was published is that we no longer allow white women to efface us or suppress us. Now we do it to each other" (1990, 142).

10. Several years ago at an MMLA meeting in Chicago, I participated in a discussion resulting from an English professor's paper on Cherríe Moraga's *Loving in the War Years*. Hispanists also on the panel (including a specialist in peninsular literatures) somewhat smugly admonished the speaker to "know" cultures better before tackling a Chicana text. Their suggestion referred to the English professor's explanation to the audience that *chorizo*, mentioned in Moraga's book, was a Mexican sausage. Since the Hispanists knew that chorizo originated in Spain, and was therefore Spanish, the speaker's error was cast as egregious. Having read *Loving in the War Years*, I pointed out that Moraga herself footnotes *chorizo* as a Mexican sausage. In this situation, an analysis of who knows, and how, was essential for community—and professional— well-being.

REFERENCES

Anzaldúa, Gloria. 1987. *Borderlands/La frontera: The new mestiza*. San Francisco: Aunt Lute.

———, ed. 1990. *Making face, making soul. haciendo caras: Creative and critical perspectives by feminists of color*. San Francisco: Aunt Lute.

Anzaldúa, Gloria, and Cherríe Moraga, eds. 1981. *This bridge called my back: Writings by radical women of color*. New York: Women of Color.

Bal, Mieke. 1993. First person, second person, same person: Narrative as epistemology. *New Literary History* 24, 2 (Spring): 293–320.

Code, Lorraine. 1991. *What can she know? Feminist theory and the construction of knowledge*. Ithaca, N.Y.: Cornell University Press.

———. 1993. What is natural about epistemology naturalized? *American Philosophical Quarterly* 33, 1: 1–22.

———. 1995. *Rhetorical spaces: Essays on gendered locations*. New York and London: Routledge.

Rebolledo, Tey Diana. 1996. The politics of poetics: Or, what am I, a critic, doing in this text anyhow? In *Chicana creativity and criticism: New frontiers in American literature,* ed. María Herrera-Sobek and Helena María Viramontes. Albuquerque: University of New Mexico Press.

Richards, Judith. 1998. Toward Chicana critical theories: Seeking equilibrium in the analysis of infinite complexities. *College Literature* 25, 2: 182–90.

———. 1999. Gloria Anzaldúa. *Significant contemporary American feminists: A biographical sourcebook*, ed. Jennifer Scanlon. Westport, Conn.: Greenwood.

Rivera, Marina. 1993. Mestiza. In *Infinite divisions: An anthology of Chicana literature*, ed. Tey Diana Rebolledo and Eliana S. Rivero. Tuscon: University of Arizona Press.

CHAPTER SIXTEEN

Epistemological Deliberations: Constructing and Contesting Knowledge in Women's Cross-Cultural Hair Testimonies

Lanita Jacobs-Huey

Introduction

Life within "societies structured in dominance" has implications for the way knowledge is generated, shared, and validated among all women (Davis 1981; Jouve 1991; Frankenberg 1993), including women of color (hooks 1981; Anzaldúa 1990; Chow 1993; Visweswaran 1994; hooks 1996; Hurtado 1996). In her discussion of Black feminist thought, Patricia Hill Collins stresses the interdependence of experience and consciousness for Black women in the United States: "Black women's concrete experiences as members of specific race, class, and gender groups as well as our concrete historical situations necessarily play significant roles in our perspectives of the world" (1990, 33). Black women's marginalization on the basis of race, gender, and class has also influenced the ways they have approached and used various *ways of knowing* in cross-cultural contexts to empower themselves.

This chapter examines several instances wherein Black and White women negotiate ideologies and practices around Black hair and hair care. I am centrally concerned with African American women's lay and expert narratives about hair as an index of their personal, professional, and in some cases, political identities

(Bonner 1991; Mercer 1994; Rooks 1996). I will argue that their narratives of hair are, in many ways, filtered through their *experiences of marginalization* as a collective of women who are under-represented in Eurocentric standards and representations of beauty. These shared experiences socialize them into similar ways of knowing and experiencing their bodies, particularly hair. African American women's ways of knowing their bodies and strategies for using this knowledge also emerge from lay and professional *epistemological communities* (Nelson 1993). These communities are overlapping in that African American women draw upon their own experiences of race and gender-based marginalization, both in society and in the hair-care profession, to construct counterevidence to privileged ideologies and practices around hair and hair care. As their hair narratives are constructed in critical response to White women's commentaries, I describe the *critical role of audience* in shaping the way African American women collaboratively construct ways of knowing Black hair in their cross-cultural dialogues. To the extent that Black women legitimize their shared knowledges about Black hair, their collaborative narratives can be considered *counternarratives* to "master," or Eurocentric, notions of beauty or, alternatively, what Nancy Goldberger (1996) calls *privileged epistemologies* or socially valued ways of knowing for establishing and evaluating truth claims.

It is important to mention, at the outset, that African American women are diverse in both their hair-care experiences and means of articulating those experiences. To resist essentializing women in this multisited study as a monolithically marginalized group, I use narrative analysis to illuminate the different epistemic stances they employ to construct their counternarratives. My findings offer an ethnographically based framework for understanding race and gender oppression as a matrix through which subjective counterknowledges are "coconstructed" (Duranti and Goodwin 1992) and legitimized by African American women of diverse class backgrounds. Further, by drawing from actual dialogues between African American and European American women, this research provides a more authentic understanding of how epistemic stances conveyed in *naturally occurring interaction* can serve to engender discord or unity among women of diverse backgrounds.

THEORETICAL BACKGROUND

Narrative analysis is a useful analytical strategy toward this end for several reasons. Personal narratives are mediums through which speakers constitute their cultural selves, histories, and ways of knowing (Briggs 1996; Bruner 1991). As speakers, we tell narratives for their potency to explain, rationalize, and delineate past, present, and possible experience (Bauman 1986; Duranti and Brennais 1986; Ochs 1994; Baquedano-López 1997). In so doing, we do not merely depict events temporally, but we often display epistemic stances and disposi-tions toward those events through verbal and nonverbal forms of talk (Goff-man 1981). Narratives are also a means through which marginalized speakers can act as agents who not only generate knowledge, but also contest privileged epistemologies. In these ways, narratives emerge from experience, yet, at the same time, shape experience (Ochs and Capps 1996).

Partha Chatterjee (1993) likewise reminds us that narratives may consti-tute forms of resistance to "master" or hegemonic storylines. Such stories or counternarratives derive political force as oppositional responses to grand histor-ical narratives. Counternarratives also debunk "official" narratives of everyday life, or what Michael Peters and Colin Lankshear describe as "legitimating stories . . . which herald a national set of common cultural ideals" (1996, 2). Patricia Baquedano-López's (1998) ethnographic study of a Los Angeles parish accord-ingly demonstrates how Latina instructors teach cultural narratives in Spanish, despite administrative pressures to adopt a mainstream Eurocentric curriculum and standard language in classroom instruction. These counternarratives cele-brate Latino students' culture and language in the face of encroaching English-only legislation at both the local and statewide level. Marcyliena Morgan (1995) uses a similar concept, "camouflaged" narratives, to describe the means through which older, southern African Americans opposed implicit rules governing lan-guage, which dictated that they veil public and private descriptions of racial op-pression. Through the use of indirectness and other forms of linguistic camouflage, these narratives serve to deconstruct and interrogate life under hege-mony. And like counternarratives, these camouflaged narratives act as veiled con-testations of past and present experiences. Finally, Susan Gal (1995) suggests that aspects of women's everyday talk and women's voice or consciousness can be un-derstood as strategic responses, often resistance, to dominant cultural forms. In this sense, women's talk can reflect the political essence of counternarratives. This analysis is concerned with African American women's use of counternarratives to debunk privileged ideologies around hair and beauty practices, which are directly and indirectly invoked by European American women.

Data

Data for this analysis was collected over the past four years as part of a larger study of African American women's linguistic and cultural practices around hair. I focus on three interactions that feature African American and European American women in the process of producing and sharing subjective knowledge in real-life settings. In their dialogues, African American women collaborate in a series of counternarratives that critique mainstream narratives about hair and simultaneously marginalize the status of the European American conversants. African American women's counternarratives can be thematically represented by the following epistemic stances: Hair is (just) hair and Hair is *not* just hair. While these claims may appear contradictory, they both serve to oppose mainstream, liberal feminist stances that often naively celebrate "choice" without understanding how privilege and exclusion are intricately intertwined in dominant ideologies about women's hair care and hairstyle choices.

Analysis

Episode One: Hair Is Hair

In the first interaction, African American women diversely affiliated with Black hair care adopt the stance *Hair is hair* to problematize a White cosmetology student's professed ignorance of Black hair. This exchange, depicted sequentially in transcripts 1 through 3 (below), was recorded during an early-morning hair-weaving demonstration at a Los Angeles hair show and involved four African American women and one European American woman. Each of the four African American women (fictitiously named Linda, May, Kesha, and Joyce) and the European American woman (fictitiously named Carla) are affiliated with the beauty industry. May is a licensed stylist who specializes in braiding and weaving. In the interaction (see figure 16.1), she is using a loom to demonstrate how to create a weft for hair weaving. Kesha, who is standing next to Carla, markets Black hair-care seminars and publications. Linda and Joyce are both young licensed stylists and Carla is a cosmetology student at a local community college.

I have a lot of black friends, OKAY. The interaction begins when May acquaints herself with the women and attempts to recruit them as participants in a

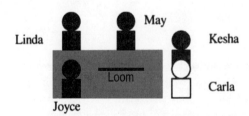

Figure 16.1. Spatial Arrangement of Participants

statewide network of licensed braiders. She first asks Joyce how long she has
been braiding. May then directs her attention to Carla and asks her what is her
particular niche. Carla responds by expressing a desire to learn how to "work
with Black hair," which May reframes as a desire to become a Black-hair specialist. Carla also laments the fact that many White stylists lack the desire to
learn how to "mess with Black folks' hair." When May asks her to speculate on
why this is so and offers a hypothesis (i.e., doing Black hair may be a challenge
for White students), Carla responds, "I don't know if it's much of a challenge. I
have a lot of Black friends OKAY." Carla's latter response offends many of the
African American women, who I observed exchange puzzled looks and orient
physically away from Carla. I later learned that many of them perceived that her
comment reflected the naiveté of one who claims to understand the complex
plight of Black people by referencing the fact that "some of my best friends are
Black." Though Carla does not engage in such grand presumptions here, her response is deemed defensive without merit, and thus worthy of the same scorn.

　　Carla's controversial proclamation, however, does not deter May's line of
inquiry, or her conversational fervor. While the other African American women
temporarily orient their attention to passersby, magazines, or each other, Carla
and May critique the phenomenon of White students who shy away from instruction and practice on Black patrons. Perhaps conscious of the other women's
momentary disregard for their conversation, May revoices Carla's preceding responses to the entire group to encourage ongoing dialogue. She states: "So what
she's [Carla] saying yeah that she'd like to learn more and so I guess it's a challenge you know [she] wants to learn more about it." In doing so, May favorably
characterizes Carla's desire to learn more about Black hair care. She also re-
inserts her implicit explanation that learning to do Black hair may, in fact, be
considered a challenge by Carla and other White cosmetology students.

　　When we examine African American women's ensuing narratives, particularly how they invoke participant frameworks (Goodwin 1980) that privilege their
own cultural narratives about hair over more mainstream ones, I believe we see evidence of counternarratives at work. African American women share a series of
narratives which generally broaden the critique of White stylists who shy away
from black hair care and also celebrate the versatility of Black hair. Taken together,
these outcomes serve to indict mainstream ideologies and practices within the
wider cosmetology profession, which privilege European hair textures and styles.
These ideologies and practices allow Carla and other non-Black stylists to become
licensed without developing skills in styling African American hair textures.

It's a myth that . . .[Black hair is difficult to work with]. As explained above, Carla
has already corroborated with May in the critique against White stylists who
are allegedly scared of working with Black hair. However, Carla's positionality

as a collaborator in this stance is marginalized, and at times even ignored, since the African American women's counternarratives are coconstructed around experiences and physical attributes (i.e., Black hair) to which Carla has little or no access. This, along with their use of cultural speaking styles, serves to limit the extent to which Carla can speak on these topics, thus relegating her to the margins of the discussion. We see this happening in transcript 1 when, after several uncomfortable moments, Joyce decides to speak.[1]

Transcript 1

```
1   Joyce:   It's a it's a myth that um
2   May:     Go ahead
3   Joyce:   that there be hhh that people just get caught in sometimes you know
4            We know as now that I hear you say the word
5            I can say that I'm a Black hair specialist
6            because I don't do naturally straight hair
7            but what I find
8            is that by going to other haircolor companies
9            because I learn how to do all that
10           so I can color that hair right for weaving
11           and I end up being the only Black stylist there
12           so I *do* understand that
13           but what I try to do is um is just let them know
14           that I have the *same* uh inhibitions sometimes
15           so we can get together
16           we can trade information
17           they can call me
18           I can talk to them
19           you know and go back and forth
20           and that'll help eliminate some of that fear
21           because the fear just come from not knowing
22           without the truth
23  Joyce:   I know the truth
24           <we know that our hair is very easy to work with
25           and uh [very nice to work with
26  May:              [It's so it's so versatile
27  Joyce:   yes
28  May:     Black hair is so versatile
29  Joyce:   yes
30  May:     that's what it is
31           We can do so much with it
```

Joyce conveys both a sympathetic and critical stance toward White stylists who are ambivalent about styling Black hair

Joyce's narrative becomes a collaborative celebration of the versatility of Black hair, a narrative to which Carla has limited access

32	Joyce:	yeah
33	May:	We can make it look like cotton in one week
34	Joyce:	that's right
35	May:	and the next week, turn around, *it's silky!*
36	Joyce:	bone straight
37		that's right
38	Kesha:	mm hmm (.) mm hmm
39	May:	ha ha so our hair is interesting

Joyce's narrative is multilayered, invoking shifting participant frameworks (Goodwin 1990) throughout its course. Joyce initially debunks what she calls a "myth," itself a politically laden framing of the belief that Black hair is a difficult medium. May both anticipates and ratifies Joyce's description, offering the response cry (Goffman 1974) "Go ahead" in line 2. Then, using the first-person narrative, Joyce affirms herself as a "Black hair specialist," a term first introduced by May in response to Carla's professed interest in Black hair care. Here, Joyce and May are in explicit dialogue. Joyce then sets up an affiliative frame with White stylists who are allegedly ambivalent toward Black hair. She invokes her own experience as the only Black stylist in hair-coloring seminars and expresses her understanding of the inhibitions facing White stylists. While Joyce understands these inhibitions, however, she does not excuse them. Rather, in lines 7 through 22, she proposes a strategy of information sharing to debunk the "myth," alleviate the "fear," and eventually uncover the "truth" about Black hair. This is a vivid prelude to an alternative ideology about Black hair; it is one which is explicitly constructed against widespread "myths" that stigmatize Black hair. How this construction takes place is of particular interest.

Disclosing the "truth" about Black hair is actually a collaborative undertaking by May and Joyce. Beginning in line 24, Joyce constructs a framework for participation which, by the referential nature of her commentary, restricts participation in the sequence to the African American women present. This restriction of participant frameworks is indexically realized through her use of the pronouns "we" and "our" to describe those present who have Black hair (i.e., African American women) and those who have skills in Black hair care. Significantly, May not only corroborates Joyce's positive description of Black hair, she also assumes the role of primary narrator in line 26. In their reversal of roles, Joyce now collaborates in May's description of Black hair through back-channeling cues ("that's right," "bone straight, that's right"). Kesha also participates in the coconstruction of Black hair as versatile and interesting. At line 38, she endorses the narrative in progress with "mm hmm (.) mm hmm." Despite Carla's previous alignment with African American women's stance toward Black hair care, she has fewer rights to speak in this sequence given that she is not a part of the "we" group who knows that "our hair" (i.e., Black hair) is an easy medium with which to work.

Some White people are afraid of working with curly hair textures. In setting up a contrastive frame between "truth" and "myth," Joyce disrupts official narratives that marginalize Black hair, problematizes White stylists who are fearful of Black hair care, and ignites a narrative celebration of the versatility of Black hair. Joyce and May's call-and-response sequence affirming the versatility of Black hair may, in fact, be an extended attempt to articulate the fact that while Black hair may be different, it is in no way inferior. In these ways, Joyce's narrative conveys the illocutionary and pragmatic force of a counternarrative. While Carla is thus far a marginal participant, she resurfaces in the dialogue's progression. In the next sequence of talk, depicted in transcript 2, Carla reenters the conversation and attempts to insert the ideology that race is not so much a factor in White stylists' inhibitions, as much as is their lack of familiarity with curly hair textures.

Transcript 2

40	Carla:	There are some White people with overly kinky you know curly hair
41	Kesha:	oh Yeah
42	Carla:	and the White students don't want to work on them either
43		because they're scared
44		I don't know what they're scared of
45	Kesha:	But see our culture is changing *so much*
46		you have all these interracial couples and all things like that
47		<u>You Don't Know</u> *what* is coming up you know
48		and so you have to be able to be versatile as a hair stylist
49		to work with all kind of hair textures you know
50		[*((looks pointedly at Carla))*
51		[>black white< (.) that's not even an issue
52		[*((points toward Carla))*
53		[It's *hair*

Carla's second verbal contribution to the discussion occurs at line 40. Here, she broadens her description of the inhibitions of White cosmetology students. White students are not only hesitant to service Black patrons, but also White clients who have "overly kinky" or "curly" hair textures. While Carla is representative of the generic group of White cosmetology students she critiques, she distances herself from those who are "scared" to style naturally curly hair by stating, "*I* don't know what *they're* scared of" (my emphasis). Through this stance, Carla ideologically aligns with Kesha, May, and Joyce who have thus far critiqued cosmetology students who are reportedly fearful of doing Black hair, as well as the "myths" that ground their perspectives.

Implicit in Carla's comments, though, are several potentially offensive characterizations which, I believe, compel Kesha to use counternarrative to reprove Carla. Carla initially describes curly hair as "overly kinky," which carries with it the controversial insinuation that hair can actually be too kinky. Within African American communities, the term kinky is also an in-group characterization of a very curly texture of Black hair (see Smitherman 1994). Since this term often carries a negative connotation, its use by Carla could be deemed offensive. Carla's commentary thus far presumes that some Whites, but all Blacks, have overly kinky hair. Kesha takes issue with this implicit assumption in lines 45 through 53. Because there are biracial couples who presumably bear children with an even broader range of hair textures, Kesha suggests that all hair stylists must be versatile enough to service whomever enters their salon. It is striking to observe the way Kesha ends her commentary. She looks pointedly at Carla and states: "Black, White that's not even an issue." Then, while pointing toward Carla, she adds, "It's *hair!*" This epistemic stance problematizes semantic distinctions between hair textures, particularly those which are value-laden (e.g., "overly kinky") and race specific. As a modestly veiled reproof of Carla's narrative, Kesha's rebuttal acts in the pragmatic sense of counternarrative. Her counternarrative also continues the work of co-constructing an ideology which is celebratory of Black hair and critical of Eurocentric practices in the wider hair-care field.

I always had to work with Barbie. Another narrative shift occurs when Linda, who has thus far been largely silent, begins a personal narrative about dolls. Her narrative is nostalgic, recalling a time during her childhood when the Barbie (read as "White") doll was all she had. Her narrative, depicted in transcript 3, also celebrates the advent of the Black Chrissy doll.

Transcript 3

54	Linda:	*((speaks softly))* It's not that they don't know how to do that
55		It's just that [they're not familiar]
56	Kesha	[They don't know how]
57	May:	Okay
58	Linda:	I would say that
59		ever since I um grew up
60		I've always had to work with Barbie
61		*((looks toward Carla and Kesha))*
62		So I kind of like had a wider range [because working with *her*
63	Kesha:	[Go ahead
64	Linda:	that was basically the texture of a Caucasian person's *hair*
65	May:	Yes [Yes Yes]
66	Linda:	[However]

Linda constructs a personal narrative of overcoming a problematic event; as a child for whom there were few Black dolls, she learned how to style her Barbie (read as "White") doll's hair

67		I *learned* how to work with that hair
68		and style it with water and grease
69		and make it pretty hhh
70		which I wanted my doll TO BE
71		because that's all I had
72		However, once my mom got me a Chrissy doll
73		I was able to get [BAsically
74	Kesha:	[All right Chrissy!
75		[*((claps hands, looks at Linda))*
76		[Remember the Chrissy?! heh heh
77	Carla:	[heh heh heh [heh heh
78	Kesha:	[GIRL WE'RE [GOING BACK! heh heh heh
79	Joyce:	[Right down to Chrissy Okay heh
80	Linda:	[*((smiling hesitantly, clasps hands, awaits lull in laughter))*
81		[the same the same thing
82		but then a little more on the [line of our hair
83		[*((looks toward Carla and Kesha))*
84		but [*Not*
85		[*((horizontal nod, signals "no" with hands))*
86		it at all
87		but then I had to learn . . . on my own
88		so I did get a range to deal in kind of like different styles
89		[*((looks at Carla))*
90		[but I don't think that for one reason our hair is any different
91	Kesha:	[Right
92	Linda:	[other than the fact that it is of [just a different texture
93		[*((accompanying vertical nod))*
94		and that is all

Marginal notes:

Linda's Chrissy narrative is an occasion for co-remembering among the African American women; this narrative event underscores their shared childhood experiences of marginalization and overcoming

Counternarrative subtext; appears to be directed at Carla

Linda initially frames her narrative to refute Kesha's prior claim that White stylists simply do not know how to do Black hair. She suggests that many White stylists' alleged ignorance is instead a result of their limited exposure to Black hair, both as children and, as we will later see, as professionals. To contextualize this argument, Linda discloses her early impressionable experiences with Chrissy, the first Black doll on which she practiced hair grooming. While her narrative is launched as a personal narrative (i.e., "I would say that ever since I grew up . . ."), it eventually becomes a narrative event, indeed an occasion for co-remembering between Linda and her African American peers. May, Joyce, and Kesha employ the cultural discourse style of call and response (Smitherman 1977; Collins 1990; Morgan 1998), in-group terminology (e.g.,

"Girl, we're going back!"), various continuers (e.g., "mm hmm," "Go ahead"), as well as more lengthy emphatic turns, to coconstruct Linda's narrative-in-progress. Reciprocally, Linda uses eye gaze to organize their orientation and participation in her narrative. The Chrissy narrative thus emerges as a collective and nostalgic account of their initial hair-grooming practices. It is also a means through which Black women discursively co-affiliate with one another by virtue of their shared childhood grooming experiences and discourse practices.

As a thinly veiled description of African American women's marginalization, the Chrissy narrative is imbued with the subversive force of "camouflaged narratives" (Morgan 1995). These African Americans' testimonies critique and explain their past as children for whom there were very few black dolls on which to practice hair care. Note, for example, the pragmatic force of several narrative tropes of marginalization and triumph that appear throughout Linda's narrative:

- (Lines 58–60) "I would say that ever since I um grew up, I've always had to work with Barbie"—*denotes Linda's marginalization as a child for whom there were few Black dolls*
- (Lines 66-70) "However I *learned* how to work with that hair and style it with water and grease and make it pretty hhh which I wanted my doll TO BE"—*inscribes a tale of overcoming despite limitations posed by the lack of Black dolls*
- (Line 71) "because that's all I had"—*reinforces Linda's marginalized status while, at the same time, rationalizes her need to "make do" with Barbie*
- (Line 88) "so I did get a range to deal in kind of like different styles"—*recounts a triumphant tale of surmounting various constraints (i.e., lack of dolls with Black hair textures) that could have rendered her solely proficient in styling European American hair textures*

The Chrissy narrative also functions as a counternarrative by exposing the privilege of other White stylists who, like Carla, have had the option to choose whether or not they wish to develop proficiency in Black hair care. For the African American women, the decision to become proficient in styling European American hair textures was never much of an option, as much as a prerequisite. (Thus, while Joyce does not "do naturally straight hair," she is nevertheless trained to do it. Similarly, while Linda's formal education in cosmetology did not offer much instruction in Black hair care, she nevertheless sought out opportunities to learn.) Moreover, this counternarrative appears to be explicitly directed at Carla, in particular, when in lines 90 through 94, Linda tells Carla, "but I don't think that for one reason that our hair is any different other than the fact that it is of just a different texture and that is all." While

Carla lacks direct culpability for the stance for which she is reproved, she nevertheless appears to be the central target of this counternarrative.

See you were blessed. In the final sequence, depicted in transcript 4, Joyce suggests additional factors which might color the current state of affairs within the beauty profession. Her personal narrative exposes her position of relative privilege among her African American peers. Linda responds to Joyce with a counternarrative that is a literal and symbolic extension of the Chrissy narrative. Carla's verbal contribution remains notably absent during the latter part of the exchange.

Transcript 4

95	Joyce:	I went to a community college cosmetology school	
96		and so my instructors were versed in all of it	Joyce's narrative describes her relative privilege as an African American cosmetology student who had the opportunity to choose the area in which she wanted to excel
97		and so I was the one who got to pick	
98		... what I wanted to excel in while I was there	
99		... and and a lot of the White students	
100		that got a chance to choose	
101		if they wanted to excel in Black hair	
102		... so we got a chance	
103		to choose what we want(ed)	
104	Linda:	See you were blessed	Linda's second narrative about continued difficulties with finding a doll with kinky hair accentuates differences between herself and Joyce and segues into an explicit counternarrative that proposes a strategy for promoting White students' exposure to both Black and White patrons
105		because most instructors	
106		and usually when you go	
107		I know for a long time	
108		it was hard to find a doll with even kinky hair	
109		so if it wasn't out there for you to work	
110		and learn	
111		and be educated on	
112		then how were you supposed to learn in these schools?	
113		So now if they would put	
114	May:	Yes!	
115	Linda:	different textures	
116		ALL different textures	
117		and make every student learn from all different textures	
118	Joyce:	that's (right)	
119	Linda:	then they those students as well can learn on all different textures	
120		they won't be intimidated by it	
121		because if you just only get one side—type of model	
122		then that's all they're gonna want to work on	

Narratives not only serve to engender unity among participants, but as Baquedano-López (1998) notes, they also organize diversity within a collective. This point is underscored in the last excerpt, where Joyce's personal narrative serves to differentiate her experiences from those of her African American peers. Following Linda's account of her belated exposure to Black dolls as a child, Joyce describes her own experiences as a cosmetology student. Her narrative implicates the curriculum and instructors in cosmetology schools in fostering either an apprehensive or a welcoming disposition toward Black hair care. Joyce's narrative also exposes her relative privilege as an African American student who was able to decide which hair textures she was exposed to in cosmetology school.

Joyce's narrative-telling captures the attention of Linda, who characterizes Joyce's experience as a blessing (line 104). Joyce's story is a catalyst for a second tale that, strikingly enough, resembles the Barbie/Chrissy narrative. As with Black girls who struggled to find dolls with features similar to their own, Linda asserts that many African American students face the challenge of "finding a doll with kinky hair" in cosmetology school (lines 107 through 112). To address this problem, Linda suggests that both curly and straight hair models be introduced in cosmetology schools to promote more equitable exposure to Black hair textures within the wider beauty profession. May's ensuing narrative, though not represented in the above transcript, enlists the women's support in a national campaign to make cosmetology board requirements for African American braiders more relevant to their craft. May's commentary extends the political subtext of Linda's narrative; she indicts the larger beauty industry, which marginalizes Afrocentric hair-care practices and hair styles.

Linda's and May's respective narratives are both charged with the oppositional undercurrent of the counternarratives previously discussed in transcripts 1 through 3. It is telling to examine how the other women, particularly Carla and Joyce, participate in this exchange. Carla remains a silent peripheral participant. However, whereas her gaze was directed at the women speaking in prior sequences, Carla's gaze is directed toward the floor throughout most of this exchange. Joyce, whose relative privilege might seem to align her more closely with Carla (and the other White stylists previously discussed), nevertheless maintains an affinity with May and Linda by conveying a supportive stance for the strategies they propose. Joyce's affiliative stance is conveyed through such means as back-channeling cues—i.e., "that's (right)" in line 118 and an attentive gaze. Kesha, though silent, also signals her participation in ongoing discourse through an attentive gaze. The differences between the African American women, thus, appear to be minimized as they coalesce around strategies to debunk "myths" and allay stylists' fear toward Black hair care within the wider hair care profession.

Episode Two:
Exposing White and Black Women's Respective Advantages

Y'all don't know how to do [Black hair]? In the second interaction, African American cosmetology students embrace concerns similar to the ones previously discussed. In particular, they challenge a White stylist's professed ambivalence about her ignorance of Black hair and implicate larger Eurocentric ideologies and practices around hair in the field of cosmetology. Students also affirm their own identities as extremely versatile and well-sought-after stylists. I recorded the interaction depicted in transcript 5 while conducting a year-long ethnographic study of a cosmetology school in Charleston, South Carolina. Two of the students, Katcha and Theresa, and their instructor interview two White stylists during a fieldtrip to a local salon.

Transcript 5

1	Katcha:	Do you train your staff?
2	Stylist 1:	They just have to be (trained)/(learned) in school
3		I mean heh heh I'm not trying to be smart
4		but I mean uh you *are* qualified heh heh
5		**We really do need an African American stylist in here** *badly*
6	Stylist 2:	We do!
7	Katcha:	Why?
8	Stylist 1:	Because we don't have one . . . I'm serious!
9		Heh heh
10	Teacher:	Do you have a lot of um African Americans coming in?
11	Stylist 1:	We have a lot of people
12		that walk in here wanting relaxers
13		and want lots of things
14	Katcha:	**Y'all don't know how to do that?**
15	Stylist 1:	I know how but I don't know feel comfortable like I know enough
16	Katcha:	*You didn't learn that in school?*
17	Stylist 1:	They didn't do a whole lot of that stuff when I went to school
18	Students:	mmmmm
19	Stylist 1:	They didn't.
20		Now they've started with more African American styling
21		and relaxers and more classes
22		because our class fussed so much
23		because we're like, 'How can you expect us to do it?'
24	Teacher:	So what school did you go to?

(marginal note alongside lines 8–14): Katcha critically probes White stylists' ignorance of Black hair care; she indirectly problematizes their relative privilege to choose their area of expertise

25	Stylist 1:	I went to X Beauty College
26	Teacher:	*((repeats the name of the school))*
27	Stylist 1:	Now they are pretty good about having the classes
28		because my friend . . . worked there
29		. . . She said she learned all of it.
30		She does African ethnic hair . . .

We have already seen how African American women adopt epistemic stances that "hair is hair" to co-construct counternarratives which oppose Eurocentric epistemologies and practices in cosmetology schools. It is also important to consider the strategies of their audience, particularly how White women's attempts to align with Black women act as catalysts for Black women's oppositional responses. Recall in the prior episode, Carla's attempts to reach common ground and align with the other women's problem are thwarted by her comment, "I have a lot of Black friends OKAY" and other potentially offensive references to Black hair as "overly curly." As these comments were perceived as racial slights by several of the African American women present, Carla is unable to establish her alignment with them in later conversation. In fact, despite her professed desire to learn to do Black hair, she becomes the indirect and, at times, more explicit target of a series of counternarratives that critique White stylists who are ignorant of styling Black hair.

A similar instance takes place in episode two. When Katcha asks one of the European American stylists whether or not they train their staff, the stylist responds by expressing her expectation that students be appropriately trained in cosmetology school prior to seeking employment. While conceding that her presupposition may sound "smart," she also assures the students that they are being appropriately prepared. This stylist's subsequent disclosure for the need of a Black stylist, though, is troublesome and prompts Katcha to inquire about her interlocutor's prior training. Katcha asks, "Y'all don't know how to do that?" referring to a relaxer, a chemical hair-straightening procedure used by many Black women. The stylist confesses her ambivalence, but Katcha is apparently unsatisfied with her answer. Katcha adds more poignantly, "*You didn't learn that in school?*" Katcha's question may be an indirect strategy for exposing the stylist's relative privilege. While the stylist assumes that the students are being appropriately prepared to handle the clients who enter their salon, Katcha and the other students have now learned that she is ill-prepared to service Black patrons.

The stylist's attribution of her ignorance to improper training does very little to deter Katcha and the other students' criticism. After the interview, several of the students indicated that it was unfair for them to be expected to master different types of hair, while their White colleagues gained experience in only one hair type. Their complaints were similar to Carla's and Kesha's critique of White stylists who, because of their ignorance, must turn African American clientele away. Further similarities between the epistemic stances conveyed by the African American women in episode one and two become all the more vivid when another student, Theresa, probes into the practical implications of the stylist's reported ignorance of Black hair care.

Transcript 6

31	Theresa:	Question! Being that . . . how many average a week
32		<how many people with ethnic—Black people
33		did you turn away a week because you don't have a Black stylist?
34	Stylist 1:	A lot a lot
35	Stylist 2:	A lot
36	Stylist 1:	Way too many
37	Theresa:	Give me a number—something. Twenty? Thirty?
38	Receptionist:	Around yeah . . . I would say fifteen to twenty, up in there
39	Stylist 2:	Our problem is that we had one very good Black stylist
40		who worked with us.
41		She's booth renting now.
42		She built up her clientele that big *((makes a wide gesture))*.
43		We just haven't been able to find one that will stay put you know
44	Stylist 1:	They get them [clientele] and then they leave
45	Theresa:	**Most Black hair stylists have a lot of clientele**
46		**because there's just so much versatility with the hair**
47	Stylist 1:	Yeah exactly. And there is I mean, there is . . .
48	Theresa:	**And we would probably make more money than you all**
49		**because we do . . .**
50	Stylist 1:	Yeah heh heh it is the truth
51	Stylist 2:	It's true it's very true!
52	Theresa:	It is! We do the tracks . . .
53	Katcha:	**It's it's more complicated**
54	Theresa:	We do this and (we're)/(they're) going to whip that out
55	Stylist1:	So you can charge more for it
56		and I'm telling you being an um African American stylist,
57		it won't take you anything to build up to a master stylist
58	Stylist 2:	Because the clientele is here

Upon learning that many Black clients are refused service, Theresa describes the relative advantage of Black stylists, since they serve patrons with extremely versatile hair. It is interesting to see Katcha co-construct this view by describing Black hair as "more complicated." Katcha and Theresa's co-narration bears a close resemblance to Joyce's and May's call and response sequence about the versatility of their hair in episode one. In my discussion with the students after the interview, I learned that this commentary was, in part, an attempt to educate White stylists to the fact that Black hair was a versatile medium and, hence, not to be feared. Though the stylists agree with Theresa's and Katcha's assessments and make other attempts to align with the students (as they simultaneously attempt to recruit them), it is ultimately their own ignorance of Black hair-styling procedures which constrains their ability to develop a rapport with the students.

Episode 3: Hair Is Not Just Hair

In the third interaction, African American women invoke the notion that *Hair is not just hair* to censure a White woman's claim that "hair is (just) hair" and independent of cultural symbolism or sociopolitical implications. In doing so, the African American women collaborate in the production of a counternarrative that invokes their shared marginalization as Black women who are, for the most part, rendered invisible (or exotic) in mainstream representations of beauty.

I have straight hair . . . so I get a perm. The interactions depicted in transcripts 7 and 8 occurred during a highly charged discussion of the politics of hair and identity on an African American listserv.[2] Prior to the interaction, listserv members debated such topics as whether Black women's hair styles were true reflections of their racial consciousness. Other discussions centered around the social, economic, and political factors at play in Black women's hair-style decisions. The interactions I discuss here include two sequences and commence when Lisa, a self-identified non-Black woman, responds critically to subscribers who advocate "natural" hair styles for Black women. Lisa espouses a mainstream feminist ideology that celebrates all women's right to style their hair without social repercussions. Subsequently, she is confronted by Njeri and Marla, both African American women, who find Lisa's position to be culturally insensitive.[3]

Transcript 7

1	Njeri:	Dear Lisa,
2		Thank-you for continuing this discussion from the perspective of a
3		non-Black woman. I will comment.

4		At 06:31 PM 5/8/95 -0700, Lisa wrote:
5	Lisa:	>I guess I qualify as one of the non-Black people on the list, I don't
6		>know if what I do to my hair merits any discussion, but here it is . . .
7		>I have straight hair that does nothing, I mean absolutely nothing.
8		>So, I get a perm, I mean, I always have a perm. I do this because
9		>when I look in the mirror, I like what I see. It doesn't matter what
10		>anyone else thinks, it matters what I think and I think the perm looks
11		>better. I really believe that most women do their hair for themselves,
12		>not for other people. I'm the one who looks in the mirror in the morning
13		>and I'm the one who has to live with my hair through the day, so it should
14		>be up to me to do what I want to it.
15	Njeri:	Okay, but you are not Black and therefore you don't appear to be able to
16		relate to the issues presented heretofore. I am assuming that you are a
17		European American, Lisa. I submit to you, that IF it is true that White
18		people have the power in America, then it really doesn't matter what you
19		do to your hair because you are a member of the power clan. Your people
20		made the rules. They made the rules for beauty, throughout the world, which
21		a majority of non-White people were forced to live under.

Lisa's feminist stance is articulated clearly in lines 5 through 14 where she celebrates her hair alternatives and affirms other women's right to wear their hair in any way that pleases them. Njeri's response in lines 15 through 21 directly challenges Lisa's cultural authority in the hair discussion. Lisa's identity as non-Black (and perhaps her self-described "straight hair" in line 7) leads Njeri to assume that Lisa is European American and hence, unable to relate to the role of hair as an ethnic signifier for African American women. Thus, although Lisa's self-effacing remark about having "straight hair" that "does absolutely nothing" depoliticizes women's hair-care practices in general, Njeri instead scolds Lisa for failing to acknowledge her power privilege as a White woman in dictating the standards of beauty in America. In this way, Njeri's post constitutes a counternarrative which, while exposing the privilege implicit in Lisa's epistemic stance that hair is (just) hair, also impedes Lisa's bid for ongoing dialogue around the idea that women should be able to choose their hair styles without regard to sociopolitical implications.

Hair for non-Blacks does not have the same . . . consequences as it does for [Blacks]. Soon after Njeri's posting, Lisa is confronted again, this time through an apparent call-and-response sequence between Njeri and an African American woman named Marla. Interestingly, while Marla's comments appear to predominate the message below, it is actually Njeri who is the editor, as it were, of this post. Njeri's comments are appended to quoted excerpts from Marla's prior post to Lisa. Her comments act as affirming response cries (Goffman 1974), which sporadically ratifies Marla's remarks. In this sense, Njeri's response cries serve to co-construct Marla's critique of Lisa's post.

Transcript 8

1	Njeri:	Thanks for helping me out here Marla!
2		At 04:34 AM 5/9/95 -0700, Marla wrote:
3	Marla:	>To: Lisa (a non-Black woman)
4		>Please understand that our discussion on "hair" may seem like
5		>an infringement of certain inalienable rights from your perspective
6		>as hair for non-blacks does not hold the same political, social, and
7		>emotional consequences as it does for us, from childhood thru present.
8		>Some of my (and perhaps others) childhood recollections include:
9		>* Sitting in a hard chair for long hours as an elementary school-aged
10		>child suffering the grueling process of "straightening" (hot comb on stove),
11		>hair grease sizzling, ears and neck burning—worrying endlessly about the
12		>enemy of water in all forms—"sweating it back," rain, swimming,
13		>showering/bathing;
14		>*Using a little White girl's brush to brush my beloved "bangs" at an
15		>elementary school age and having the teacher send the girl to the nurse's
16		>office with her brush to have it soaked in rubbing alcohol and hot water;
17	Njeri:	>Yes, break it down, Sister.
18	Marla:	>*The imagery that any truly sexy woman will "let her hair down"
19		>before becoming intimate; I could go on but won't cuz this is too long
20		>already. Suffice it to say that our natural texture of hair was and sadly
21		>still is still taught to many of us at our earliest recollections to be inferior
22		>and in constant need of being corrected to be socially acceptable.
23	Njeri:	Amen!
24	Marla:	>We mistakenly apply the mythology of White feminism in the form
25		>of its many "rights" to ourselves . . . this is not to say that the "right" to
26		>wear our hear [sic] however we want to does not exist for Black women
27		>and that any one's personal choices makes them inferior to those who
28		>make other choices, but that our discussion cannot be limited to political
29		>correctness and catch phrases and must delve deeper into our longstanding
30		>practices of self-hatred and self-abuse to be an honest discussion.
31		>You as a non-Black woman MUST respect and try to understand that
32		>the sentiments being expressed by some of us are based on our own

354 LANITA JACOBS-HUEY

```
33          >experiences in a racist and ignorant society that even today frowns
34          >heavily upon our natural attributes.
35          >Marla.
36  Njeri:  Well said.
37          Asante sana.
```

Marla, a proponent of "natural" hair styles for Black women, begins her post with an appeal; she encourages Lisa to try to understand the cultural significance of hair among Black women, who, unlike White women, face a separate set of economic, political, and social consequences for their hairstyle choices. However, the form of Marla's appeal in lines 4 through 7 again exposes Lisa's privilege as a non-Black individual. Marla states: "Please understand that our discussion on 'hair' may seem like an infringement of certain inalienable rights from your perspective. . . ." Marla then provides an expansive bulleted list of hers and other African Americans' painful childhood and adulthood experiences of being marginalized due to the texture and length of their hair.

When read (in the literal sense) in succession, Marla's bulleted narratives have the expressive force of call and response in a religious sermon. Njeri employs several religious and cultural "response cries" to affirm Marla's post. Njeri writes: "Yes, break it down, Sister" in line 17, "Amen!" in line 23, "Well said" in line 36, "Asante Sana" in line 37, and in line 1, Njeri thanks Marla for helping her redirect Lisa's interpretation of the hair discussion. At a larger level, Marla and Njeri's critique of Lisa's failure to understand the significance of hair for Black women parallels criticisms made by women of color of mainstream, liberal feminism (see Giddings 1984; Crenshaw 1992; Carby 1996). In fact, lines 24 through 34 of Marla's post to Lisa explicitly critiques "White feminism" for wrongfully assuming that all women share the same rights and positionalities in American society. Marla culminates her post with an appeal that Lisa expand her framework for understanding the politics of hair and identity for Black women.

SUMMARY AND CONCLUSION

Nelson (1993) has argued that we can learn much about knowledge and its production by understanding the communal and historical contexts in which it emerges (see Foucault 1980 Knorr-Cetina 1981; Mills 1994). Accordingly, the preceding analysis draws from ethnographic data of several hair-related conversations between African American and European American women. Many of these women situate their narratives sociohistorically by describing their experiences as children and cosmetology students for whom there were (both literally and metaphorically) few Black dolls on which to practice hair care.

Discourse analyses of women's everyday conversations offer an even richer portrait of *how* diverse women negotiate between various knowledges and their own experience to construct individual and collective stances about hair. African American women, in particular, employ such cultural discourse styles as call and response and indirectness in their (counter)narratives to align with one another and to critique mainstream ideologies about Black hair. European American women's unwitting expression of privileged epistemologies or their own racialized privilege are also the catalysts for African American women's expression of such epistemic stances as *Hair is (just) hair* and *Hair is not just hair.*

A close investigation of these seemingly polarized views, of when they are employed, and toward which ends, reveals congruence in the political efficacy of these claims. Namely, Black women coconstruct these stances to refute Eurocentric ways of knowing racialized and gendered bodies that are directly or indirectly invoked by White women. Black women's claims that *Hair is hair* and alternatively, *Hair is not just hair,* can also be understood in light of larger universal/particular debates about race. Universal arguments posit that African Americans are Americans and hence, subjects of the same rights and responsibilities as other citizens. In contrast, particularistic claims employ race-specific rhetorical strategies to explain how African Americans are different. People of color may deploy these different subject positions and ideologies for strategic purposes (see also Moore 1994). They may also negotiate the various meanings and social-political implications of these viewpoints—not simply in grand political debates about civil rights, but also in everyday interactions that pose the opportunity or need to move between universal and particularistic arguments about race (see Sandoval 1991 for a relevant and poignant exposition).

The ethnographic and discourse analyses that ground this study reveal additional insights about feminist epistemology which are unlikely to be "seen" or explored by more traditional philosophical approaches to epistemology. For example, intensive microlevel analyses of women's hair narratives uncover critical moments wherein women succeed in aligning and, in other cases, fail to align with others in the construction of subjective knowledges. The above analyses also illustrate how women make sense of their race/ethnicity, gender, and lived experience in order to substantiate or undermine particular knowledge claims. Moreover, the very nature of African American and European American women's hair narratives invokes, at a larger level, pertinent themes in feminist theory, including a) the enunciation of *difference* between women engaged in knowledge production/sharing and b) the dialectics of race, gender,

experience, and epistemology. Collectively, these findings suggest the promise
of social science research in documenting the microprocesses of knowledge
production that are valuable as part of an interdisciplinary and empowering dialogue about feminist epistemology.

NOTES

I would like to thank Elinor Ochs, Patricia Baquedano-López, and Stan Huey for their insightful comments on an earlier draft of this chapter. I also want to thank the editors of the
volume, Nancy Tuana and especially Sandi Morgen, for making several valuable suggestions
that strengthened the conceptual focus. Lastly, I would like to acknowledge support from
the Wenner-Gren Foundation, the National Science Foundation, and the Ford Foundation.

1. Transcript notations largely follow those noted by Ochs and Taylor (1995):

[	a left-hand bracket indicates the onset of overlapping, simultaneous utterances.
(( ))	double parentheses enclose nonverbal and other descriptive information.
( )	single parentheses enclose words that are not clearly audible (i.e., best guesses).
Underline	underlining indicates stress on a syllable or word(s).
Italics	italicized words or phrases indicates talk that is in some way animated or performed (i.e., sarcasm).
SMALL CAPS	small caps indicates louder or shouted talk.
:	a colon indicates a lengthening of a sound, the more colons, the longer the sound
>	the "greater than" symbol indicates text taken from listserv (internet).
<	the "less than" symbol indicates that the immediately following talk is "jump-started," i.e., starts off with a rush.
Heh heh/Ha ha	marks laughter.
Hh (hh)	the letter *h* marks hearable aspiration, the more h's, the more aspiration. Aspiration may represent breathing, laughter, etc.
(try 1)/(try 2)	this arrangement of words/phrases enclosed by parentheses *and* separated by a single oblique or slash represent two alternate hearings.

2. A more detailed and systematic analysis of this listserv discussion appears in
Jacobs-Huey (1998). In this manuscript, I describe listserv participants' use of African
American discourse styles and cultural hair terminology to constitute their racial iden-
tities, cultural knowledge, and their right to speak on the subject of hair.

3. In transcript 7, Njeri copies parts of Lisa's prior post, as evidenced by the >
symbol which precedes Lisa's comments.

REFERENCES

Anzaldúa, Gloria. 1990. *Making face, making soul/haciendo caras: Creative and critical perspectives by women of color.* San Francisco: Aunt Lute.

Baquedano-López, Patricia. 1997. Creating social identity through doctrina narratives. *Issues in Applied Linguistics* 8, 1: 27–45.

———. 1998. Language socialization of Mexican immigrant children in a Los Angeles Catholic parish. Ph.D. diss. Los Angeles: University of California.

Bonner, Lonnice Brittenum. 1991. *Good hair: For colored girls who've considered weaves when the chemicals became too rough.* New York: Crown.

Briggs, Charles. 1996. *Disorderly discourse: Narrative, conflict, and inequality.* Oxford: Oxford University Press.

Bruner, Jerome. 1991. The narrative construction of reality. *Critical Inquiry* 18: 1–21.

Carby, Hazel. 1996. White women listen! Black women and the boundaries of sisterhood. In *Black British cultural studies: A reader,* ed. Houston Baker Jr., Manthia Diawara, and Ruth Lindeborg. Chicago: University of Chicago Press.

Chatterjee, Partha. 1993. *The nation and its fragments: Colonial and postcolonial histories.* Princeton, N.J.: Princeton University Press.

Chow, Rey. 1993. *Writing diaspora: Tactics of intervention in contemporary cultural studies.* Bloomington: Indiana University Press.

Collins, Patricia Hill. 1990. *Black feminist thought: Knowledge, consciousness, and the politics of empowerment.* New York: Routledge.

Crenshaw, Kimberle. 1992. Whose story is it, anyway? Feminist and anti-racist appropriations of Anita Hill. In *Race-ing justice, en-gendering power: Essays on Anita Hill, Clarence Thomas and the construction of social reality,* ed. Toni Morrison. New York: Pantheon.

Davis, Angela. 1981. *Women, race, and class.* New York: Vintage.

Duranti, Alessandro, and Charles Goodwin. 1992. *Rethinking context: Language as interactive phenomenon.* New York: Cambridge University Press.

Duranti, Alessandro, and Donald Brennais. 1986. The Audience as co-author. *Text* 6, 3: 239–347.

Frankenberg, Ruth. 1993. *The social construction of whiteness: White women, race matters.* Minneapolis: University of Minnesota Press.

Foucault, Michel. 1980. *Power/Knowledge: Selected interviews and other writings 1972–1977,* ed. and trans. Colin Gordon. New York: Pantheon.

Gal, Susan. 1995. Language, gender, and power: An anthropological review. In *Gender articulated: Language and the socially constructed self,* ed. Kira Hall and Mary Bucholtz. New York: Routledge.

Giddings, Paula. 1984. *When and where I enter: The impact of Black women on race and sex in America.* New York: William Morrow.

Goffman, Erving. 1974. *Frame analysis: An essay on the organization of experience.* New York: Harper and Row.

———. 1981. *Forms of talk.* Philadelphia: University of Pennsylvania Press.

Goldberger, Nancy R. 1996. Women's constructions of truth, self, authority, and power. In *Constructing realities: Meaning-making perspectives for psychotherapists,* ed. H. Rosen and K. Kuehlwein. San Francisco: Jossey-Bass.

Goodwin, Marjorie Harness. 1990. *He-said-she-said: Talk as social organization among Black children.* Bloomington: Indiana University Press.

hooks, bell. 1981. *Ain't I a woman: Black woman and feminism.* Boston: South End.

———. 1996. *Bone Black: Memories of girlhood.* New York: Henry, Holt.

Hurtado, Aída. 1996. Strategic suspensions: Feminists of color theorize the production of knowledge. In *Knowledge, difference and power: Essays inspired by Women's ways of knowing,* ed. N. Goldberger, J. Tarule, B. Clinchy, and M. Belenky. New York: Basic.

Jackson, Michael. 1993. Knowledge of the body. *Man* (n.s.) 18: 327–45.

Jacobs-Huey, Lanita. 1998. BTW, how do YOU wear your hair? Identity, knowledge, and authority in an electronic speech community. Unpublished Manuscript.

Jacoby, Sally, and Elinor Ochs. 1995. Coconstruction: An introduction. *Research on Language and Social Interaction* 28, 3: 171–84.

Jacoby, Sally, and Patrick Gonzales. 1991. The constitution of expert-novice in scientific discourse. *Issues in Applied Linguistics* 2, 2: 149–81.

Jouve, Nicole Ward. 1991. *White woman speaks with forked tongue: Criticism as autobiography.* London: Routledge.

Knorr-Cetina, Karin. 1981. *The manufacture of knowledge: An essay on the constructivist and contextual nature of science.* New York: Pergamon.

Labov, William, and John Waletsky. 1968. Narrative analysis. In *A study of the nonstandard English of Negro and Puerto Rican speakers in New York City,* ed. William Labov, Paul Cohen, Clarence Robins, and John Lewis. New York: Columbia University.

Lock, Margaret. 1993. Cultivating the body: Anthropology and epistemologies of bodily practice and knowledge. *Annual Review of Anthropology* 22: 133–55.

Mercer, Kobena. 1994. Black hair/style politics. In *Welcome to the jungle: New positions in Black cultural studies.* Cambridge: MIT.

Mills, Sarah. 1994. Knowledge, gender, and empire. In *Writing women and space: Colonial and postcolonial geographies,* ed. A. Blunt and G. Rose London: Guilford.

Moore, Henrietta L. 1994. *A passion for difference.* Bloomington: Indiana University Press.

Morgan, Marcyliena. 1995. Just to say something: Camouflaged narratives of African American life. Unpublished Manuscript. UCLA.

———. 1998. More than a mood or an attitude: Discourse and verbal genres in African American culture. In *African American English: Structure, history and use,* ed. Salikoko Mufwene, John Rickford, Guy Bailey, and John Baugh. London: Routledge.

Nelson, Lynn Hankinson. 1993. A question of evidence. *Hypatia* 8, 2: 172 (18).

Ochs, Elinor. 1994. Stories that step into the future. In *Perspectives of register: Situating register variation within sociolinguistics,* ed. Douglas Biber and Edward Finegan. Oxford: Oxford University Press.

Ochs, Elinor, and Lisa Capps. 1996. Narrating the self. *Annual Review of Anthropology* 25: 19–43.

Peters, Michael, and Colin Lankshear. 1996. Postmodern counternarratives. In *Counternarratives: Cultural studies and critical pedagogies in postmodern spaces,* ed. Henry Giroux, Colin Lankshear, Peter McLaren, and Michael Peters. New York: Routledge.

Rooks, Noliwe. 1996. *Hair raising: Beauty, culture, and African American women.* New Jersey: Rutgers University Press.

Sandoval, Chela. 1991. U.S. Third World feminism: The theory and method of oppositional consciousness in the postmodern world. *Genders* 10(Spring): 1–24.

Smitherman, Geneva. 1994. *Black talk: Words and phrases from the hood to the amen corner.* New York: Houghton Mifflin.

———. 1977. *Talkin' and testifyin': The language of Black America.* Boston: Houghton Mifflin.

Visweswaran, Kamala. 1994. *Fictions of feminist ethnography.* London: University of Minnesota Press.

CHAPTER SEVENTEEN

STANDPOINT EPISTEMOLOGY
IN THE PHYSICAL SCIENCES:
THE CASE OF MICHAEL FARADAY

BARBARA L. WHITTEN

Most scientists accept, at least in principle, the argument that the scientific community is too White, too male, and too middle class, and that it would be more equitable if underrepresented groups had more opportunities in science. Feminist, racial, and postcolonial critics make a complementary argument—that *science* itself is adversely affected by the homogeneity of the scientific community. The scientific knowledge we construct would be more complete if the scientific community that constructed it were more diverse.

This argument is a version of feminist standpoint epistemology. There is a wealth of evidence to show that standpoint epistemology is being successfully applied to the biological and social sciences. Bonnie Spanier (1995) and Evelyn Fox Keller (1985) have shown how anthrocentric attitudes have limited our understanding of biological phenomena. Donna Haraway, in *Primate Visions* (1989), describes the great changes in primatology that resulted when the female students of Sherwood Washburn began to do field studies. Sandra Morgen (1997) argues that anthropology is becoming "decolonized" as the community of anthropologists grows to include women, people of color, and Third World scientists.

The application of feminist standpoint epistemology to the physical sciences, where the objects of inquiry are not gendered, is more difficult. Elizabeth Potter (1993) has shown how his social and political context influenced the work of the chemist Robert Boyle, but examples are few and far between.

In this chapter, I use feminist standpoint epistemology to analyze the life and work of Michael Faraday, in an effort to show that physics is affected by the social and cultural background of the physicist.

FEMINIST STANDPOINT EPISTEMOLOGY AND STRONG COMMUNITIES

Feminist standpoint epistemology was first proposed by Nancy Hartsock (1983). The idea is borrowed from Marxist analysis of class relationships. Consider the division of society into two classes of people, one of which has more access to power than the other. I'll call these "masters" and "slaves," though we'll see that this is a general framework. These two classes of people have different and, in many ways, complementary pictures of the world and of social relationships. Though both points of view are partial and distorted, the slaves' is less partial than the masters'. This is because it is necessary to slaves' survival that they understand masters, while masters have no such need to understand slaves. On the contrary, it is probably better for masters' peace of mind that they never look at the world from slaves' point of view, or consider slaves to have a point of view.

Though the masters' point of view is partial and distorted, it nevertheless structures social relationships and determines values in the society. This means that it cannot be simply dismissed as false. Because of the preceding argument, the slaves' standpoint is not acquired simply by being born a slave. It must be *achieved* through intellectual analysis and political struggle. It is not necessary to be born a member of the slave class to achieve this standpoint, though it is probably simpler for those who have experienced oppression to understand it. If the slaves' standpoint can be achieved, it will be a more complete view of the world and of human relationships than the masters' standpoint. And it has the potential of being liberatory and revolutionary (both intellectually and politically).

This is clearly a highly simplified model; no one would argue that all masters or all slaves are alike. But as a model it does allow some interesting and useful analyses. Marxists apply standpoint theory to relationships between the ruling class and the proletariat, and derive limitations on the meaning of labor and its exchange with capital. Nancy Hartsock applies it to gender relationships, arguing that since our society is stratified along gender lines, a feminist perspective gives us a truer picture of the patriarchal structure of our society than an androcentric viewpoint. Note this is a feminist perspective, not a woman's perspective. One need not be a woman to achieve a feminist standpoint, nor are all women automatically possessed of a feminist standpoint. Note also that this argument is not universal—it proceeds from the political, historical statement that our society is stratified along gender lines rather than from biological or moral arguments about the nature of all men or all women.

In *Whose Science? Whose Knowledge?* Sandra Harding (1991) takes this analysis one step further. If a feminist standpoint can provide us with new insights, can we not achieve still other insights by starting from the standpoint of particular women? In a racially stratified society will not the standpoint of feminists of color teach us important new things? In a homophobic society, will not the standpoint of lesbian feminists be valuable? What about Third World women? Disabled women?

It's easy to see the power of this starting point. Harding says that the scientist who starts from women's lived experience is in the position of Galileo, who couldn't point his telescope anywhere in the sky without seeing something new. But it's also easy to see the problem. If all these different kinds of women have distinctive and important feminist standpoints, then who exactly is fit to be a feminist scientist? Must one be all of these women at once?

Harding addresses this question in a chapter titled "Creating Oneself as Other." She explains how, by intellectual and political *activity*, I can learn to look at my own life through the lenses developed, for example, by African American thinkers. I find Harding's argument very appealing, but she underestimates the difficulty of this project. Trying to reinvent myself without appropriating or romanticizing others' experience is fraught with difficulty. As Lorraine Code concludes her chapter in this book, "how wary we, all of us, must be of assuming that we can see very far from here" (this volume, 279). And there is a time constraint. If I am to create myself as all possible "others," it is hard to see how I will have any time left over to do physics.

A way out of this difficulty is suggested by Helen Longino. In *Science as Social Knowledge* (1990), she argues that scientific knowledge is not simply an aggregation of the work of individuals. Rather, it is *social* knowledge, constructed by the scientific community as a whole. In order to become part of accepted scientific knowledge, a scientist's work requires acceptance, critical emendation, and modification by the community of scientists. The objectivity of science is a characteristic of the practice of the scientific community as a whole. The objectivity of individual scientists consists not only in our relationship to our observations, but in our willingness to submit our work to the critical attention of the scientific community.

Longino's insight that science is necessarily practiced by groups rather than individuals gives scientific knowledge a real but strictly limited objectivity. The transformative criticism of the community will remove the prejudices and assumptions of individual scientists. But communities can also make mistakes, and assumptions cannot be subjected to criticism if they are shared by all members of the community. This is particularly a problem in a community as homogeneous as the scientific community presently is.

Now we can put together standpoint epistemology with Longino's idea that science is necessarily practiced by a group. Suppose that the scientific community were a diverse group of people with a variety of different stand-points—what I call a "strong community," in analogy to Harding's strong objectivity. Then I could "get by with a little help from my friends." I have no intention of relieving myself of the responsibility of creating myself as other—I do think that taking on, as far as possible, the standpoint of others is a necessary part of doing feminist science. But my attempts to do this have been made much easier by the assistance of very patient friends who tell me, sometimes over and over again, where my analysis is going wrong.

Efforts to reduce the barriers faced by women and other excluded groups who wish to become scientists are therefore not only just; they are *necessary* to produce reliable scientific knowledge. I do believe that under-represented groups would be better off if we were offered more opportunities in science. But *science* would also be better off; the knowledge we construct would be more reliable, more authentic, more objective, if the scientific community included more diverse standpoints.

The argument so far is general and applies to all branches of science. The point that scientific knowledge can be limited by the homogeneity of the scientific community is well documented in the social and biological sciences. (See, for example, Haraway 1989; Keller 1985; Morgen 1997; and Spanier 1995.) It is less obvious that the study of atoms and stars and quarks can be influenced by the social and cultural location of the scientist. One might conclude (and many of my colleagues in physics do conclude) that the physical sciences are less affected by the social location of the scientist, and less susceptible to feminist criticism. Yet the single fact that physical science communities are the most White and most male of all academic communities renders this conclusion suspect.

However, the homogeneity of the physical science community does make standpoint epistemology harder to test. How can I find an example of a physicist whose physics is obviously affected by gender or color if virtually all physicists are White and male? I spent some time looking at the work of the few female physicists and of the even fewer physicists of color, without finding a good example. But when I turned to the variable of class, I found a perfect example, right in the mainstream of physics.

The Education of Michael Faraday

Michael Faraday was one of the most important of nineteenth-century physical scientists and one of the greatest experimentalists in all of physics. He has laws and units named after him in both physics and chemistry. He invented the electric motor and the electromagnetic generator—machines which, more than any other except the steam engine, formed the technological basis of the Industrial Revolution and made modern life possible. And his unusual class background is almost as well known as his work.

Michael Faraday was the son of a blacksmith, born in England in 1791. At the age of sixteen, when most budding scientists were in school, Faraday was apprenticed to a bookbinder—his formal education ended in grammar school. He spent his days learning the craft that would one day be his. But he spent his evenings educating and "improving" himself. He read eagerly the books that came into the shop to be bound. "There were plenty of books there, and I read them" (Williams 1971, 11). He learned of electricity from an article in *Encyclopedia Britannica,* and saved his few pennies to buy old bottles, which he used to construct a static-electric generator and perform experiments.

His master, George Riebau, liked apprentices with broad interests—three of his apprentices went on to do something other than bookbinding. He encouraged Faraday and gave him an important boost. He showed Faraday's notes on chemistry to a customer. The customer was impressed and gave Faraday tickets to a series of lectures by Sir Humphry Davy, an important and well-known chemist. Faraday attended his lectures, took detailed and careful notes, and bound them.

In the fall of 1812, when he was twenty-one, Faraday realized that his apprenticeship was almost at an end and he would no longer have the leisure for the pursuit of science. He wrote to a friend "I must resign philosophy entirely to those who are more fortunate in the possession of time and means. . . . I am at present in very low spirits" (Williams 1971, 40). He wrote to the Royal Society asking for a position—any position in science, no matter how menial. He didn't even receive an answer. He wrote to Davy at the Royal Institution, sending him a bound volume of his meticulous notes on Davy's lectures. Davy hired him as a temporary assistant when his eyes were damaged in a chemical explosion. Then in March, 1813, the regular laboratory assistant at the Royal Institution was dismissed for brawling, and Faraday was offered the position. He began with routine tasks, but as his ability was recognized he began to help out with the lectures and do more independent work. He would remain at the Royal Institution his entire career, and eventually become its director.

It is clear that Faraday did not receive a conventional scientific education, but we would be wrong to conclude that he was uneducated. As an apprentice he developed a system of learning that was influenced by Dr. Isaac Watts's *Improvement of the Mind* (Williams 1971, 12). Watts claimed that formal education places a student within a critical tradition, but the self-educated man must develop his own critical judgment. He emphasized careful observation of "fact." Faraday took these ideas very seriously and constructed lifelong habits. He said, "I was never able to make a fact my own without seeing it" (Williams 1971, 975).

Faraday's self-education left him with very clear ideas about how one should learn. In 1818 he described these ideas in an essay "On Imagination and Judgment." The function of the imagination is to produce possibilities and analogies for the mind. The senses provide the means for the examination of the external world. The key faculty is judgment. It accepts the gifts of the imagination and subjects them to critical scrutiny. Evidence provided by the senses allows judgment to control the imagination, find what is reliable, and reject what does not accord with experience. Education is the process of training the imagination. The result is a constant interplay between mind and the external world in which facts are not external givens but are called forth by judgment to test the claims of imagination (Williams 1971, 334–35).

Working-Class Standpoint

At the beginning of the nineteenth century, English society was in transition from an open aristocracy based on property and patronage to the more familiar class-based society of the Industrial Revolution. Social relationships were based in villages centered around a "great house," and tended to be personal (Perkin 1969). It was possible for a promising young man of the "lower orders" to better himself by acquiring a patron and receiving an appointment to a responsible and well-paid position, as Faraday did.

The scientific community did not become professionalized until later in the nineteenth century, so there was no standard way to become a scientist (Knight 1989). Faraday's path was unusual but by no means unique for his time, though if he had been born forty years later, he might have had more difficulties. Sir Humphry Davy, Faraday's own patron and mentor, came from "humble" origins and received his first scientific appointment through the influence of a patron. He became successful because of his brilliance in chemistry (and his good looks, which turned the public lectures of the Royal Institution, originally designed to bring the fruits of the Industrial Revolution to the working class, into society events). Davy was knighted and married a wealthy woman, and became a social success (Knight 1989).

We can see that Faraday faced barriers that did not exist for his middle- and upper-class contemporaries. Extraordinary scientist that he was—smart, hardworking, and meticulous and possessed of an astounding physical intuition—Faraday also had to be *lucky* to become a scientist. If he hadn't had a master like Riebau, who encouraged his interest in science, he wouldn't have been able to attend lectures, do experiments, and write notes. And if he hadn't caught the eye of Sir Humphry Davy, he would have ended his days as a bookbinder, perhaps doing experiments in the back room in his spare time.

Faraday's "humble origins" do not guarantee a working-class standpoint. What evidence do we have that his standpoint was different from other scientists? To answer this question, we first need to ask what are some elements of a working-class standpoint.

First, it is not a coincidence that we call this the "working" class. Consider the nature of the work itself—menial, ill-paid, often dirty, often dangerous (Tokarczyk and Fay 1993; Lang 1995). Faraday, the apprentice bookbinder and blacksmith's son, was certainly aware of the menial, dirty, dangerous aspects. His early work as a bookbinder left him with a manual cleverness that was a great part of his skill as an experimentalist. In 1846 Charles Wheatstone, himself a well-known scientist, wrote to Faraday about a series of experiments he would like to do. But he says, "I have also been somewhat deterred by the consideration that for such experiments to succeed a delicacy and dexterity of manipulation equal to your own would be required" (Williams 1971, 484).

John Sumser (1995) describes the concrete nature of working-class jobs. A working-class person creates from raw materials a finished product—a horse shod, a book bound—that either works or it doesn't. The work of supervisors and managers is more nebulous and is measured by less clear standards. Faraday recognized and respected the knowledge and skills of working people. Early in his scientific career he worked on several practical problems in chemistry; for example, the chemical composition of high-quality steel. As he began to study the problem, he would visit factories and speak to artisans about the process. He believed that the people doing the work had useful knowledge to offer (Williams 1971, 111).

A second important piece of a working-class standpoint is a sense of place, of community, of family, in contrast to the mobility and individualism of the middle class (Lang 1995). In nineteenth-century England, this emerging working-class consciousness was leading to a socialist vision of a society of productive independent workers joined together in a cooperative community, in sharp contrast to the middle-class ideal of the "self-made man" in competition with all those around him (Perkin 1969, 231).

Faraday did not share this political consciousness; he took very little notice of politics at all, but was generally conservative. He was not, for example, sympathetic to the revolutions of 1848, believing that they originated from "unworthy motives" rather than the desire for freedom from tyranny (Williams 1971, 357). But his ideal scientific community does sound very much like a socialist utopia. In 1829 he wrote that trade made people "vicious and selfish," whereas a life of science made one "liberal and amiable" (Williams 1971, 178). In 1850 he described to John Tyndall a republic of science where "different persons [are] working at the same matter. Each one gives views and ideas new to the rest. When science is a republic, then it gains; and though I am no republican in other matters, I am in that" (Williams, 1971, 597).

Though he was indifferent to politics, Faraday did have a strong sense of duty to his family and community. He was born into and remained a lifelong active member of a small, strict, nonconformist sect called the Sandemanian Church. He served as an elder in the church, and often preached. His letters to family and friends mention the doings of the church. He married a member of the church, the daughter of a silversmith, and remained close to his family.

Faraday did not, as Davy had, aspire to social position. Davy offered him entrée to society as well as to science. He eagerly accepted the latter but declined the former. He refused most social invitations, preferring to spend time with his family. He accepted many scientific honors, but refused a knighthood, and wished to "remain plain Michael Faraday to the last" (Williams 1971, 495).

Sharon O'Dair (1993) mentions the importance of books to a working-class youngster, offering a window to the life of the mind not otherwise easily acquired. We can picture the young Faraday in the evenings, reading the books that come into the shop, attending lectures on electrochemistry, arguing natural philosophy with his friend and fellow apprentice, Benjamin Abbott.

Most poignantly, working-class academics speak of a double vision, a sense of being a stranger in both worlds, of moving away from family and familiar things as they advance in an academic career (O'Dair 1993; LaPaglia 1995). Early in his work as Davy's assistant, Faraday accompanied Davy to Europe, serving as his personal and scientific assistant. His letters home clearly show the excitement of a young man who had never before been more than twelve miles from London. He comments on the places and people he sees, and discusses the chemistry he is learning from the distinguished European scientists. But those same letters show great homesickness—he writes to his family and friends with affection and longing, and complains when letters from home are delayed (Bence Jones 1870, chapter 3).

It is important to remember that, in a society where the aristocracy and the middle class controlled institutions and determined values, a working-class standpoint required intellectual work to achieve. Faraday, unlike Davy, embraced his background and his connection with his family. He respected the knowledge of other working-class people. And he respected his own painfully acquired learning and understood its power. He made this argument publicly; in 1854 he lectured on "Observations on Mental Education," to an audience that included Albert, the Prince Consort (Williams 1971, 335).

His self-education made him much more conscious than his conventionally educated contemporaries of what one knows and how one knows. His critical stance on conventional education and on his own process of self-education shows that he did the work necessary to achieve a working-class standpoint. We shall see in the next section that Faraday's double vision gave him a critical perspective on the science of his time and became one of his greatest strengths as a scientist.

THE DISCOVERY OF ELECTROMAGNETIC INDUCTION

We can see how Faraday's working-class standpoint affected his work if we read one of his most important papers, the First Series of *Experimental Researches in Electricity*. In this paper, completed in 1831, he describes the discovery of electromagnetic induction, thought by physicists to be his most important experimental work. Faraday was by this time forty; he had been working at the Royal Institution for eighteen years. He had done good work in chemistry and electromagnetism, and had been elected to the Royal Society.

Faraday had begun work on electromagnetism earlier when his friend Richard Phillips, editor of *Annals of Philosophy*, asked him to write a historical survey of experiments and theories of electromagnetism. In 1824 François Arago in France announced a new electromagnetic effect. Arago suspended a magnetic needle over a copper disc. When the disc was rotated, the needle rotated as well. This was explained as the induction of a magnet in the copper plate by the permanent magnet. The attraction between the two magnets caused the one to follow the other. But the attraction existed only when the disc was in motion, causing great difficulties with contemporary theories.

In August of 1831, Faraday began to study this problem seriously. He built a ring of soft iron with a coil of copper wire wound around each side of the ring. One of the coils, called the primary, is connected to a battery through a switch; the other coil, called the secondary, is connected to a galvanometer, which deflects when a current passes through it. Faraday detected a brief pulse of current in the secondary coil when the circuit in the primary is *completed*, and an opposite pulse when the circuit is *broken*, but no current when the circuit of the primary is *stable*. Faraday called this effect "volta-electric induction"; we call it electromagnetic induction.

In the same set of investigations, Faraday found that if a copper coil connected to a galvanometer is moved in the vicinity of a strong permanent magnet, a current is again detected. He built a device that turned constant rotation of a conductor in a magnetic field into a constant current. He called this a "dynamo"; we call it an electromagnetic generator. In every power plant a generator turns rotation (usually from a steam turbine) into electricity. By turning mechanical energy into electricity, we are able to separate the generation of power from its use—we can easily move energy around and use it to run sewing machines, refrigerators, computers, and other machines necessary to modern life.

At this point Faraday had established the basic idea of electromagnetic induction—any change in a magnet induces a current in a conducting wire. He went on to check his ideas by varying the conditions of his experiment. He used a Leyden jar, which produces static electricity, to replace the battery as a source of primary current. He constructed *fifteen* different devices (labeled A–O in his diary) to replace the wire coil. He used several different methods to detect the current in the secondary. He worried that there might be an undetectably small current in the secondary when the circuit is stable, so he borrowed the powerful compound magnet of the Royal Society to repeat his experiments. The effect of closing the circuit was now so powerful that the galvanometer needle whirled around many times. But still there was no detectable deflection when the primary current was constant.

In this example we see Faraday's approach to a scientific research problem, which grew directly from his understanding of the educational process. First, he read everything written about the problem (sometimes going back as far as thirty years). He repeated all the experiments described, looking for possible errors in the experimental technique and weaknesses in the theory. This extensive background work gave his own imagination time to operate, so by the time he was finished studying and testing the ideas of others, he had a more-or-less well-defined hypothesis. He devised critical experiments to refine and extend his ideas. Finally, he subjected his theory to extremely rigorous tests. His diaries are full of exhaustive checks on every possible parameter of an experiment.

All good experimentalists need to be careful and meticulous, as much as they need good intuition and a creative approach to measurement. But it was particularly important for Faraday. The electrochemistry of the early nineteenth century depended in complex and subtle ways on the materials that instruments were made of. Faraday and his contemporaries were investigating phenomena that depended on the atomic structure of materials. But they were doing this with *macroscopic* tools and with no clear understanding of what atoms are. This is clearly illustrated in one of Faraday's papers, where he supposes, for the sake of argument, that in a cubic inch of matter there are 2800 atoms (Faraday, 1844). According to current understanding of the atomic structure of matter, there are on the order of 10^{23} atoms per cubic inch; clearly, his idea of an atom is very different from ours.

In this situation it was easy to make mistakes, to confuse one effect for another, to find effects which depended on impurities, or to be carried away by enthusiasm for a theory. It was easy to erect an elaborate mathematical theory on an inadequate empirical base. Faraday's suspicion of unsupported speculation, his preference for experimental "facts," and his compulsive testing of his own and others' work gave him an advantage. As we shall see in the next section, he found things others missed, and he didn't find things others thought they had found. He made a series of extraordinary discoveries of electric, magnetic, and chemical phenomena—electromagnetic rotations, electromagnetic induction, the laws of electrolysis, diamagnetism.

Faraday's working-class standpoint was an important element in his success. His self-education made him self-conscious about the process of acquiring knowledge. His respect for experimental evidence grew directly from this consciousness. His suspicion of others' and his own assumptions made him compulsively test his conclusions. This made him a different kind of physicist, and physics is richer for his contributions.

The Invention of the Field

The discovery of electromagnetic induction shows that Faraday's working-class standpoint was a clear advantage. It could also be a handicap, as we'll see here.

Faraday's extraordinary series of discoveries had made his reputation as a scientist. But it was an odd sort of reputation. He was—and still is, to a large extent—thought of as a great empiricist, a person who disliked theory, refused to speculate, and particularly hated mathematics. This is partly due to Faraday's own self-assessment; he says over and over, in letters to friends and even in scientific papers, that he is not a mathematician. His diaries and papers contain elaborate descriptions of his apparatus and his techniques and his exhaustive search for errors. But there are only occasional quantitative measurements, and no equations at all.

Nevertheless, it is a mistake to think of Faraday solely as an experimentalist; he invented one of the most important theoretical ideas of the nineteenth century. In his 1831 paper on electromagnetic induction, Faraday mentions for the first time "lines of magnetic force." In a footnote he defines lines of force as those "which would be depicted by iron filings; or those to which a very small magnetic needle would form a tangent" (Faraday 1831, paragraph 114). This idea would develop into the concept of the field, and eventually become the basis for electromagnetic theory.

In order to see how revolutionary Faraday's lines of force were, we need to look briefly at the development of ideas about physical force. At the beginning of the nineteenth century, the prevailing theory of force was "action at a distance," proposed more than one hundred years previously by Isaac Newton to explain the gravitational attraction between the earth and the moon. The Universal Law of Gravitation says that the gravitational force between any two bodies is directly proportional to the product of their masses and inversely proportional to the square of the distance between their centers. The two objects can be separated by empty space, as are the earth and the moon. (We'll leave aside the complex question of the existence of aether and other subtle fluids.) The gravitational force somehow leaps across that space to attract the two bodies to each other. Newton himself had not been particularly happy with action at a distance as a theory of gravity, but Newton's reputation, plus a century of repetition, made the idea pretty unassailable by the end of the eighteenth century.

In 1789 Charles Coulomb showed how Newtonian ideas applied to electrical phenomena. Using a highly accurate torsion balance that he had invented, Coulomb carefully measured the electrostatic attraction and repulsion between two charged objects, and discovered that this force also obeys an inverse square law where the product of the charges replaces the product of the masses. It is also possible to express magnetic attraction and repulsion by an inverse square law, where the masses are replaced by the pole strengths of the two magnets. Three very different forces are shown to obey the same force law. They are similar in one other important respect; they are all *central* forces that push the objects directly toward or directly away from each other. (See figure 17.1.)

In 1820 Hans Christian Ørsted discovered that a current-carrying wire exerts a magnetic force on a compass needle. This demonstration that electricity and magnetism are connected to each other both excited and distressed the scientific community. The force is not central; it pushes the needle in a direction perpendicular to the wire, and appears to form a circle around the wire. (See Figure 17.2.) In 1821 Faraday discovered that a current-carrying wire placed near a permanent magnet will rotate. (This is the principal behind the electric motor, which turns electricity into rotation, the inverse of electromagnetic induction.) The connection between the magnet and rotation emphasized the circular nature of magnetic phenomena.

André-Marie Ampère, a well-known French physicist, set out to place this phenomenon on Newtonian grounds. Ampère's earlier work on the interaction between electrical currents had earned him the title "Newton of electricity." In his analysis of Ørsted's experiments, Ampère began by assuming

Figure 17.1. Electrostatic repulsion between two positively charged spherical poles. The force pushes the poles directly away from each other. Newtonian force theory describes central forces acting between distant poles.

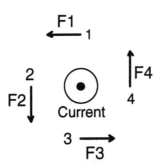

Figure 17.2. Magnetic force on a compass needle in the vicinity of an electric current. The current is in the center, coming directly out of the page. The arrows labeled F1, F2, F3, and F4 show the force on a compass needle located at points 1, 2, 3, and 4. This circular force is very difficult to reconcile with Newtonian force theory.

that electrical effects are primary, and a magnet is a collection of electric currents, on an undetectable molecular scale, flowing in a circle concentric to the axis of the magnet (Williams 1966, 65–66). Ørsted's electromagnetic effect is then reducible to the interaction between different currents. Upon this basis, Ampère erected a mathematical theory based on the primacy of central forces acting at a distance between charged objects.

This theory was favorably received by the scientific community. The emphasis on central forces between charges placed it firmly within the Newtonian tradition. Furthermore, central forces were much more amenable than circular forces to mathematical analysis, using the techniques of the day.

Faraday, unlike most of his contemporaries, was unimpressed with the mathematical rigor of Ampère's theory. He wrote to Ampère in 1825, "With regard to your theory, it so soon becomes mathematical that it quickly gets beyond my reach" (Williams 1971, 154). He cared more about what he could test in the laboratory than about remaining faithful to the Newtonian tradition. He bent a current-carrying wire into a circle and sprinkled iron filings on it. The filings formed curved lines of force that looked exactly like those around a bar magnet. This meant, to him, that Ampère's central forces could be derived from circular forces. Observable lines of iron filings were more real to him than Ampère's undetectable molecular currents.

Faraday's idea about lines of force was the germ of an alternative to Ampère's theory, and to the Newtonian idea of action at a distance. According to Faraday, a charged object creates a "strain" in the surrounding space; in modern terms we say that a charge creates an electric field. When a second charge is placed nearby, it is pushed away by the lines of force *at its own position*, not by the first object. The lines of force thus mediate between the two charges, eliminating action at a distance.

From the first mention of lines of force in the First Series of *Experimental Researches in Electricity* (it is characteristic that his definition is *operational*; he defined lines of force by saying how they are observed), Faraday used this picture of lines of force in space to guide his thoughts and his experiments. His ideas about lines of force became more sophisticated and clear as he studied electromagnetic induction and electrolysis. His explanation of the complex and subtle phenomenon of diamagnetism makes sense where other contemporary theories produced only gibberish.

Faraday's experimental success did not convince his contemporaries to adopt the field model of electromagnetic interactions. Sir George Airy, the Astronomer Royal, found Ampère's theory much more convincing:

> I can hardly imagine anyone who practically and numerically knows this agreement, to hesitate an instant in the choice between this simple and precise action, on the one hand, and anything so vague and varying as lines of force, on the other hand. (Williams 1971, 508)

An anonymous reviewer in *Athenaeum* was even more insulting:

> No mind ever reasoned well on the connexion of cause and effect in matters of quantity except a mathematical mind—a mind fitted, when properly exercised, to pursue a mathematical mode of investigation. But he [Faraday] is not fit, unaided as he is by mathematics, to handle matters which demand of the highest mathematicians the use of their most elaborate tools. *(Athenaeum* 1857)

Faraday's inability to convince his contemporaries of the usefulness of the field concept was in large part due to the language he used to describe it. Though he carefully described his experimental designs and results, he did not express his results in appropriate mathematical language. His well-known aversion for mathematics had become a serious handicap.

It was James Clerk Maxwell who made Faraday's ideas part of physics. Forty years younger than Faraday, Maxwell had been born in 1831, the year Faraday discovered electromagnetic induction. Unlike Faraday, he was the son of a landowner and a mathematical prodigy who published his first paper at age 14 and entered the University of Edinburgh at age 16. His first major paper, titled "On Faraday's Lines of Force," published in 1857, translated Faraday's "vague and varying" ideas into conventional mathematical terms which other scientists could understand. Maxwell gave full credit to Faraday:

> The conjecture of a philosopher so familiar with nature may sometimes be more pregnant with truth than the best established experimental law discovered by empirical inquirers, and though not bound to admit it as a physical truth, we may accept it as a new idea by which our mathematical conceptions may be rendered clearer. (Maxwell 1857, 187)

Maxwell continued to refine and clarify his field theory of electricity and magnetism through several more papers. These, unlike Faraday's, are highly mathematical and contain few experimental results, though he did use mechanical analogies that look very bizarre to a modern physicist. In 1873, after Faraday's death, he published *Treatise on Electricity and Magnetism*, a complete mathematical foundation of classical electricity and magnetism. This beautiful theory describes all electric and magnetic phenomena in terms of electric and magnetic fields. Faraday's idea of lines of force—a strain in space created by a charged object, which then acts on other objects—is the fundamental starting point of Maxwell's theory.

At the beginning of the twentieth century Einstein's theory of relativity made action at a distance completely untenable, but Maxwell's field theory survived. The field concept is central to modern physics; all of our current physical theories are field theories.

We see that in this case Faraday's working-class standpoint was both an advantage and a handicap. The education that emphasized observations made him less accepting of Ampère's theory, and made it easier for him to propose the alternative field theory. But his lack of mathematical background made his ideas unconvincing to his contemporaries. In order for field theory to become acceptable to the scientific community and thus, according to Longino, to become part of science, Faraday needed the help of a colleague who could express his ideas in conventional language.

Conclusion:
Strong Communities
and Standpoint Epistemology

Michael Faraday was a very great physical scientist whose contributions shaped our understanding of electricity and magnetism. He is often described as "uneducated," as if his background were a handicap. On the contrary, his "humble origins" gave him the opportunity to acquire a working-class standpoint that made his work unique and enriched physics.

I realize that this is a slippery argument; individual cases are hard to make. I cannot prove that Faraday's work would have been less valuable to physics if he had been born to an aristocratic family and educated at Cambridge. I cannot prove that physics would be different if Faraday had remained a bookbinder. Would someone else have discovered induction, electrolysis, and diamagnetism? Would Maxwell have invented the field without Faraday to suggest the idea? Would the idea have come from someone else? Or would we be thinking about physics in an entirely different way?

But I hope I have shown that Faraday's unparalleled skill in the laboratory grew directly from his working-class standpoint. Scientists need to be simultaneously inside and outside their scientific tradition. Scientists are of course people of their time, who take many of their ideas and questions and procedures from the tradition of their community. But important scientists are also expected to change that tradition—to add new questions and new kinds of answers. Faraday's working-class standpoint gave him a critical perspective on contemporary scientific practice and made it easier for him to look for creative alternatives.

We can also see that his working-class standpoint was in some ways a handicap. He could not communicate his ideas about lines of force in language that his contemporaries could understand, and they could not appreciate the power of his insight. He required the services of a translator—a conventionally educated man who *did* appreciate what Faraday had done, and could describe it in terms that less perceptive physicists could recognize.

Faraday, like all scientists, functioned within a community—science is practiced by groups rather than individuals. His ideas about fields did not become part of physics until a way was found to make them clear to the community of physicists. Faraday *needed* Maxwell to make his ideas available to his peers, just as he needed Riebau to encourage him and Davy to give him entrée into the world of science. Physicists love to tell stories of heroic loners—our media stars are Einstein, Feynmann, and Steven Hawking, often portrayed as iconoclastic rebels. But no scientist, not even the greatest, stands alone. Our work is based on that of our forebears, we require the encouragement and support of our contemporaries, and we need to find a way to communicate our results to our community.

No physicist doubts the value of Michael Faraday's contributions to physics. Perhaps we can see that these contributions were greater, not less, because of his unique standpoint. Perhaps we can extend this argument to women, people of color, and other excluded people. Perhaps we can appreciate that our beautiful science would be richer and stronger and more accurate if the community of physicists were a strong community that included many different standpoints of many different people.

Note

This project would not have been possible without challenges, help, and encouragement from my colleagues at Colorado College. Kathy Merrill has discussed my developing ideas with me, and read several drafts of this work. Bob McJimsey, Margi Duncombe, Andy Dunham, and Glenn Brooks have also been helpful.

I am grateful to Sandra Morgen and Nancy Tuana, the editors of this book, who offered useful suggestions. And I am indebted to the work of L. Pearce Williams. His wonderful scientific biography of Michael Faraday made it possible for this nonhistorian to begin to study Faraday's life and work.

References

Anonymous review. 1857. *The Athenaeum*, London, March 28.

Code, Lorraine. 1997. Rational imaginings, responsible knowings: How far can we see from here? Engendering Rationalities.

Faraday, Michael. 1812. Letter to T. Huxtable, 18 October. *The selected correspondence of Michael Faraday*, ed. L. Pearce Williams. Cambridge, England: Cambridge University Press, 1971.

———. 1825. Letter to A.-M. Ampère, 17 November. *The selected correspondence of Michael Faraday*, ed. L. Pearce Williams. Cambridge, England: Cambridge University Press, 1971.

———. 1829. Letter to J. A. Paris, 23 December. *The selected correspondence of Michael Faraday*, ed. L. Pearce Williams. Cambridge, England: Cambridge University Press, 1971.

———. 1831. First Series, *Experimental researches in electricity*. Three volumes. London. 1839–1855. The First Series was published in 1831 in *Philosophical transactions of the Royal Society*. The first volume of *Experimental researches in electricity* was published in 1839.

———. 1844. A speculation touching electrical conduction and the nature of matter. *London and Edinburgh Philosophical Magazine* 24: 136.

———. 1850. Letter to J. Tyndall, 19 November. *The selected correspondence of Michael Faraday*, ed. L. Pearce Williams. Cambridge, England: Cambridge University Press, 1971.

———. 1860. Letter to E. Becker, 25 October. *The selected correspondence of Michael Faraday*, ed. L. Pearce Williams. Cambridge, England: Cambridge University Press, 1971.

———. 1934. *Faraday's diary, 1820–1862: Being the various philosophical notes of experimental investigation*. London: G. Bell and Sons.

Haraway, Donna. 1989. *Primate visions: Gender, race, and nature in the world of modern science.* New York: Routledge.

Harding, Sandra. 1991. *Whose science, whose knowledge: Thinking from women's lives.* Ithaca, N.Y.: Cornell University Press.

Hasrtock, Nancy C.M. 1983. The feminist standpoint: Developing the ground for a specifically feminist historical materialism. In *Discovering reality: Feminist perspectives on epistemology, metaphysics, methodology, and philosophy of science,* ed. Sandra Harding and Merrill Hintikka. Dordrecht, Holland: Reidel.

Jones, Henry Bence. 1870. *The life and letters of Faraday* 2nd ed. London. Longmans, Green.

Keller, Evelyn Fox. 1985. *Reflections on gender and science.* New Haven, Conn.: Yale University Press.

Knight, David M. 1989. Davy and Faraday: Fathers and sons. In *Faraday rediscovered: Essays on the life and work of Michael Faraday, 1791–1867,* ed. David Gooding and Frank A. J. L. James. New York. American Institute of Physics.

Lang, Dwight. 1995. The social construction of a working-class academic. In *This fine place so far from home: Voices of academics from the working class,* ed. C. L. Barney Dews and Carolyn L. Law. Philadelphia: Temple University Press.

LaPaglia, Nancy. 1995. Working-class women as academics: Seeing in two directions, awkwardly. In *This fine place so far from home: Voices of academics from the working class,* ed. C. L. Barney Dews and Carolyn L. Law. Philadelphia: Temple University Press.

Longino, Helen. 1990. *Science as social knowledge: Values and objectivity in scientific inquiry.* Princeton, N.J.: Princeton University Press.

Maxwell, James Clerk. 1857. On Faraday's lines of force. *The Scientific papers of James Clerk Maxwell,* ed. W. D. Niven. New York: Dover, 1965.

———. 1873. *Treatise on electricity and magnetism.* New York: Dover, 1954.

Morgen, Sandra. 1997. Shaping the constitution of knowledge-producing communities. *Anthropology newsletter* (May), 1, 4–5.

O'Dair, Sharon. 1993. Vestments and vested interests: Academia, the working class, and affirmative action. In *Working-class women in the academy: Laborers in the knowledge factory,* ed. Michelle M. Tokarczyk and Elizabeth A. Fay. Amherst: University of Massachusetts Press.

Perkin, Harold. 1969. *The origins of modern english society, 1780–1880.* London. Routledge.

Potter, Elizabeth. 1993. Gender and epistemic negotiation. In *Feminist epistemologies,* ed. Linda Alcoff and Elizabeth Potter. New York: Routledge.

Spanier, Bonnie B. 1995. *Im/partial science: Gender ideology in molecular biology.* Bloomington: Indiana University Press.

Sumser, John. 1995. Working it out: Values, perspectives, and autobiography. In *This fine place so far from home: Voices of academics from the working class,* ed. C. L. Barney Dews and Carolyn L. Law. Philadelphia: Temple University Press.

Tokarczyk, Michelle M. and Elizabeth A. Fay. 1993. Introduction. *Working-class women in the academy: Laborers in the knowledge factory*. Amherst: University of Massachusetts Press.

Watts, Isaac. 1813. *The improvement of the mind: or, A supplement to the art of logic: Containing a variety of remarks and rules useful for the attainment and communication of useful knowledge in religion, in the sciences, and in common life, to which is added miscellaneous pieces*. New Brunswick: Lewis Deare.

Williams, L. Pearce. 1966. *The origins of field theory*. New York: Random House.

———. 1971. *Michael Faraday: A biography*. New York: Plenum.

———. (ed.) 1971. *The selected correspondence of Michael Faraday*. Cambridge, England: Cambridge University Press.

FEMINIST EPISTEMOLOGIES:
BIBLIOGRAPHY

Adams, Alison. 1995. Artificial intelligence and women's knowledge: What can feminist epistemologies tell us? *Women's Studies International Forum* 18, 4: 407–15.

Addelson, Kathryn Pyne. 1983. The man of professional wisdom. In *Discovering reality: Feminist perspectives on epistemology, metaphysics, methodology, and the philosophy of science*, ed. Sandra Harding and Merrill Hintikka. Dordrecht; Boston: D. Reidel. 165–86.

———. 1993. Knowers/doers and their moral problems. In *Feminist epistemologies*, ed. Linda Martín Alcoff and Elizabeth Potter. New York: Routledge. 265–94.

Addelson, Kathryn Pyne, and Elizabeth Potter. 1991. Making knowledge. In *Engendering knowledge: Feminists in academe*, ed. Ellen Messer-Davidow and Joan E. Hartman. Knoxville: University of Tennessee Press. 259–77.

Alcoff, Linda Martín. 1987. Justifying feminist social science. *Hypatia: A Journal of Feminist Philosophy* 2, 3: 107–27.

———. 1995. Is the feminist critique of reason rational? *Philosophical Exchange* 26: 59–79.

———. 1996. *Real knowing: New versions of the coherence theory*. Ithaca, N.Y.: Cornell University Press.

Alcoff, Linda, and Elizabeth Potter, eds. 1993. *Feminist epistemologies*. New York: Routledge.

Amorós, Celia. 1994. Cartesianism and feminism: What reason has forgotten; Reasons for forgetting. *Hypatia: A Journal of Feminist Philosophy* 9, 1: 147–63.

Anderson, Elizabeth. 1995. Feminist epistemology: An interpretation and a defense. *Hypatia: A Journal of Feminist Philosophy* 10, 3: 50–84.

Antony, Louise. 1993. Quine as feminist: The radical import of naturalized epistemology. In *A mind of one's own: Feminist essays on reason and objectivity*, ed. Louise M. Antony and Charlotte Witt. Boulder, Colo.: Westview. 185–226.

This bibliography is based on an earlier bibliography created for the NEH Summer Seminar on Feminist Epistemologies. I am grateful to William Cowling and Alex Stotts, who assisted me with the earlier version.

————. 1995. Is psychological individualism a piece of ideology? *Hypatia: A Journal of Feminist Philosophy* 10, 3: 157–74.

————. 1995. Comment on Naomi Scheman. *Metaphilosophy* 26, 3: 191–98.

Antony, Louise M., and Charlotte Witt, eds. 1993. *A mind of one's own: Feminist essays on reason and objectivity*. Boulder, Colo.: Westview.

Atherton, Margaret. 1993. Cartesian reason and gendered reason. In *A mind of one's own: Feminist essays on reason and objectivity*, ed. Louise M. Antony and Charlotte Witt. Boulder, Colo.: Westview. 19–34.

Babbitt, Susan E. 1993. Feminism and objective interests: The role of transformation experiences in rational deliberation. In *Feminist epistemologies*, ed. Linda Martín Alcoff and Elizabeth Potter. New York: Routledge. 245–64.

————. 1994. Identity, knowledge, and Toni Morrison's *Beloved:* Questions about understanding racism. *Hypatia: A Journal of Feminist Philosophy* 9, 3: 3–18.

————. 1996. *Impossible dreams: Rationality, integrity, and moral imagination.* Boulder, Colo.: Westview.

Baier, Annette. 1985. *Postures of the mind: Essays on mind and morals.* Minneapolis: University of Minnesota.

————. 1993. Hume: The reflective women's epistemologist? In *A mind of one's own: Feminist essays on reason and objectivity*, ed. Louise M. Antony and Charlotte Witt. Boulder, Colo.: Westview. 35–48.

Barad, Karen. 1996. Meeting the universe half-way: Realism and social constructivism without contradiction. In *Feminism, science, and the philosophy of science*, ed. Lynn Hankinson Nelson and Jack Nelson. Dordrecht; Boston Kluwer. 161–94.

Barber, Harriet. 1994. The market for feminist epistemology. *Monist* 77, 4: 403–23.

Bar On, Bat-Ami. 1993. Marginality and epistemic privilege. In *Feminist epistemologies*, ed. Linda Martín Alcoff and Elizabeth Potter. New York: Routledge. 83–100.

Barrett, Michele. 1992. *The politics of truth: From Marx to Foucault.* London: Polity.

Belenky, Mary Field, Blythe M. Clinchy, Nancy R. Goldberger, and Jill M. Tarule. 1986. *Women's ways of knowing: The development of self, voice and mind.* New York: Basic.

Bergmann, Sheryle. 1987. Feminist epistemologies. *Eidos* 6: 201–14.

Bickford, Susan. 1993. Why we listen to lunatics: Antifoundational theories and feminist politics. *Hypatia: A Journal of Feminist Philosophy* 8, 2: 104–23.

Bleier, Ruth. 1984. *Science and gender: A critique of biology and its theories on women.* New York: Pergamon.

Bordo, Susan. 1986. The Cartesian masculinization of thought. *Signs: Journal of Women in Culture and Society* 11: 619–29.

————. 1987. *The flight to objectivity: Essays on Cartesianism and culture.* Albany: State University of New York Press.

————. 1993. *Unbearable weight: Feminism, Western culture, and the body.* Berkeley: University of California Press.

Braaten, June. 1990. Towards a feminist reassessment of intellectual virtue. *Hypatia: A Journal of Feminist Philosophy* 5, 3: 1–14.

Braidotti, Rosi. 1991. *Patterns of dissonance*. New York: Routledge.

———. 1994. *Nomatic subjects: Embodiment and sexual difference in contemporary feminist theory*. New York: Columbia University Press.

Buker, Eloise A. 1987. Storytelling power: Personal narratives and political analysis. *Women and Politics* 7, 3: 29–46.

Campbell, Richmond. 1994. The virtues of feminist empiricism. *Hypatia: A Journal of Feminist Philosophy* 9: 90–115.

———. 1998. *Illusions of paradox : A feminist epistemology*. Rowman and Littlefield.

Cixous, Hélène. 1993. *Three steps on the ladder of writing*, trans. Sarah Cornell and Susan Sellers. New York: Columbia University Press.

Cixous, Hélène, and Catherine Clement. 1986. *The newly born woman*, trans. Betsy Wing. Minneapolis: University of Minnesota Press.

Clark, Ann. 1993. The quest for certainty in feminist thought. *Hypatia: A Journal of Feminist Philosophy* 8, 3: 84–93.

Clough, Sharyn. 1998. A hasty retreat from evidence: The recalcitrance of relativism in feminist epistemology. *Hypatia: A Journal of Feminist Philosophy* 13, 4: 88–111.

Code, Lorraine. 1981. Is the sex of the knower epistemologically significant? *Metaphilosophy* 12: 267–76.

———. 1987. *Epistemic responsibility*. Hanover: University of New England Press.

———. 1988. Credibility: A double standard. In *Feminist perspectives: Philosophical essays on method and morals*, ed. Lorraine Code, Sheila Mullett, and Christine Overall. Toronto: University of Toronto Press. 64–88.

———. 1988. Epistemology. In *A companion to feminist philosophy*, ed. Alison Jaggar. Cambridge: Blackwell. 173–84.

———. 1988. Experience, knowledge, and responsibility. In *Feminist perspectives in philosophy*, ed. Morwenna Griffiths and Margaret Whitford. Bloomington: Indiana University Press. 187–204.

———. 1991. *What can she know? Feminist theory and the construction of knowledge*. Ithaca, N.Y.: Cornell University Press.

———. 1993. Taking subjectivity into account. In *Feminist epistemologies*, ed. Linda Martín Alcoff and Elizabeth Potter. New York: Routledge. 15–48.

———. 1994. Responsibility and rhetoric. *Hypatia: A Journal of Feminist Philosophy* 9, 1: 1–20.

———. 1995. *Rhetorical spaces: Essays on gendered locations*. New York: Routledge.

———. 1996. What is natural about naturalized epistemology? *American Philosophical Quarterly*. 33, 1: 1–22.

———. 1998. How to think globally: Stretching the limits of imagination. *Hypatia: A Journal of Feminist Philosophy* 13, 2: 73–85.

Collins, Patricia Hill. 1990. *Black feminist thought: Knowledge, consciousness, and the politics of empowerment*. New York: Routledge.

———. 1991. Learning from the outsider within: The sociological significance of Black feminist thought. In *Beyond methodology: Feminist scholarship as lived research*, ed.

Mary Margaret Fonow and Judith A. Cook. Bloomington: Indiana University Press. 40–65.

Conway, Daniel W. 1998. The slave revolt in epistemology. In *Feminist interpretations of Friedrich Nietzsche*. University Park: Penn State University Press. 252–81.

Cook, Judith A., and Mary Margaret Fonow. 1986. Knowledge and women's interests: Issues of epistemology and methodology in feminist research. *Sociological Inquiry* 56: 2–29.

Dalmiya, Vrinda, and Linda Martin Alcoff. 1993. Are "old wives' tales" justified? In *Feminist epistemologies*, ed. Linda Martín Alcoff and Elizabeth Potter. New York: Routledge. 217–44.

Duran, Jane. 1991. *Toward a feminist epistemology*. Savage, Md.: Rowman and Littlefield.

———. 1993. The intersection of pragmatism and feminism. *Hypatia: A Journal of Feminist Philosophy* 8, 2: 159–71.

———. 1995. The possibility of a feminist epistemology. *Philosophy and Social Criticism* 21, 4: 127–40.

Fee, Elizabeth. 1983. Women's nature and scientific objectivity. In *Woman's nature: rationalizations of inequality*, ed. Marian Lowe and Ruth Hubbard. New York: Pergamon.

———. 1984. Critiques of modern science: The relationship of feminism to other radical epistemologies. In *Feminist approaches to science*, ed. Ruth Bleier. New York: Pergamon. 42–56.

Field, Terri. 1997. Feminist epistemology and philosophy for children. *Thinking* 13, 1: 17–22.

Fowlkes, Diane L. 1987. Feminist epistemology is political action. *Women and Politics* 7, 3: 1–4.

Fricker, Miranda. 1991. Reason and emotion. *Radical Philosophy* 57: 14–19.

———. 1995. Intuition and reason. *Philosophical Quarterly* 45, 179: 181–89.

———. 1998. Rational authority and social power: Towards a truly social epistemology. *Proceedings of the Aristotelian Society* 98: 159–78.

———. 1999. Epistemic oppression and epistemic privilege. *Canadian Journal of Philosophy. Supplementary* 25: 191–210.

Gatens, Moira. 1998. Modern rationalism. In *A companion to feminist philosophy*, ed. Alison Jaggar. Cambridge: Blackwell. 21–29.

Gergen, Kenneth J. 1988. Feminist critiques of science and the challenge of social epistemology. In *Feminist thought and the structure of knowledge*, ed. Mary McCanney Gergen. New York: New York University Press.

Gorham, Geoffrey. 1995. The concept of truth in feminist science. *Hypatia: A Journal of Feminist Philosophy* 10, 3: 99–116.

Gorz, Andre. 1976. On the class character of science and scientists. In *Ideology of/in science*, ed. Hilary Rose and Steven Rose. Cambridge: Schenkman. 34–46.

Grant, Judith. 1987. I feel, therefore I am: A critique of female experience as a basis for a feminist epistemology. *Women and Politics* 7, 3: 99–114.

Green, Karen. 1993. Reason and feeling: Resisting the dichotomy. *Australian Journal of Philosophy* 74, 4: 385–99.

Grosz, Elizabeth. 1988. The in(ter)vention of feminist knowledges. In *Crossing boundaries: Feminisms and the critique of knowledge*, ed. Barbara Caine, E. A. Grosz, and Marie de Lepervanche. Boston: Allen and Unwin. 92–104.

———. 1993. Bodies and knowledges: Feminism and the crisis of reason. In *Feminist epistemologies*, ed. Linda Martín Alcoff and Elizabeth Potter. New York: Routledge. 187–215.

———. 1994. *Volatile bodies*. Bloomington: Indiana University Press.

Haack, Susan. 1993. Reflections of an old feminist. *Reason Papers* 18: 31–43.

Hallberg, Margareta. 1989. Feminist epistemology—An impossible project? *Radical Philosophy* 53: 3–7.

Hammett, Jennifer. 1997. The ideological impediment: Epistemology, feminism and film theory. In *Film theory and philosophy*, ed. Richard Allen and Murray Smith. New York: Clarendon/Oxford University Press. 244–59.

Hampton, Jean. 1993. Feminist contractarianism. In *A mind of one's own: Feminist essays on reason and objectivity*, ed. Louise M. Antony and Charlotte Witt. Boulder, Colo.: Westview. 227–56.

Haraway, Donna. 1988. Situated knowledges: The science question in feminism and the privilege of partial perspective. *Feminist Studies* 14: 575–99.

———. 1989. *Primate visions: Gender, race, and nature in the world of modern science*. New York: Routledge.

———. 1990. A manifesto for cyborgs: Science, technology, and socialist feminism in the 1980s. In *Feminism/postmodernism*, ed. Linda J. Nicholson. New York: Routledge. 190–233.

———. 1991. *Simians, cyborgs, and women: The reinvention of nature*. New York: Routledge.

———. 1997. *Modest_witness@second_millennium.FemaleMan©_Meets_OncoMouse*[TM]: *Feminism*. New York : Routledge.

Harding, Sandra. 1980. The norms of inquiry and masculine experience. In *PSA 1980*, ed. Peter Asquith and Ronald Giere. East Lansing, Mich.: Philosophy of Science Association. 305–24.

———. 1983. Why has the sex/gender system become visible only now? In *Discovering reality: Feminist perspectives on epistemology, metaphysics, methodology, and philosophy of science*, ed. Sandra Harding and Merrill Hintikka. Dordrecht; Boston: D. Reidel. 311–24.

———. 1984. Is gender a variable in conceptions of rationality? A survey of issues. In *Beyond domination: New perspectives on women and philosophy*, ed. Carol Gould. Totowa, N.J.: Rowman and Allanheld. 43–63.

———. 1986. *The science question in feminism*. Ithaca, N.Y.: Cornell University Press.

———. 1986. The instability of the analytical categories of feminist theory. *Signs: Journal of Women in Culture and Society* 11: 645–64.

———. 1989. Feminist justificatory strategies. In *Women, knowledge and reality*, ed. Ann Garry and Marilyn Pearsall. Boston: Unwin Hyman. 189–201.

———. 1991. Who knows? Identities and feminist epistemology. In *(En)gendering knowledge*, ed. Joan E. Hartman and Ellen Messer-Davidow. Knoxville: University of Tennessee Press. 100–15.

———. 1991. *Whose science? Whose knowledge?* Ithaca, N.Y.: Cornell University Press.

———. 1993. Rethinking standpoint epistemology: "What is strong objectivity?" In *Feminist epistemologies*, ed. Linda Alcoff and Elizabeth Potter. New York: Routledge. 49–82.

———. 1998. *Is science multicultural? Postcolonialisms, feminisms, and epistemologies.* Bloomington: Indiana University Press.

Harding, Sandra, and Merrill Hintikka, eds. 1983. *Discovering reality: Feminist perspectives on epistemology, metaphysics, methodology, and philosophy of science.* Dordrecht; Boston: D. Reidel.

Hart, Carroll Guen. 1993. "Power in the service of love": John Dewey's *Logic* and the dream of a common language. *Hypatia: A Journal of Feminist Philosophy* 8, 2: 190–214.

Hartsock, Nancy. 1983. The feminist standpoint: Developing the ground for a specifically feminist historical materialism. In *Discovering reality*, ed. Sandra Harding and Merrill Hintikka. Dordrecht: D. Reidel. 283–310.

———. 1983. *Money, sex and power: Toward a feminist historical materialism.* New York: Longman.

———. 1987. Epistemology and politics: Minority vs. majority theories. *Cultural Critique* 7: 187–206.

———. 1998. *The feminist standpoint revisited and other essays.* Boulder, Colo.: Westview.

Harvey, Elizabeth D., and Kathleen Okruhlick, eds. 1991. *Women and reason.* Ann Arbor: University of Michigan Press.

Haslanger, Sally. 1993. On being objective and being objectified. In *A mind of one's own: Feminist essays on reason and objectivity*, ed. Louise M. Antony and Charlotte Witt. Boulder, Colo.: Westview. 85–126.

Hawkesworth, Mary E. 1987. Beyond methodological monism. *Women and Politics* 7, 3: 5–10.

———. 1987. Feminist epistemology: A survey of the field. *Women and Politics* 7, 3: 115–27.

———. 1989. Knowers, knowing, known: Feminist theory and claims to truth. *Signs: Journal of Women in Culture and Society* 14: 533–57.

Hekman, Susan. 1987. The feminization of epistemology: Gender and the social sciences. *Women and Politics* 7, 3: 65–84.

———. 1990. *Gender and knowledge: Elements of a postmodern feminism.* Boston: Northeastern University Press.

———. 1991. Reconstituting the subject: Feminism, modernism, and postmodernism. *Hypatia: A Journal of Feminist Philosophy* 6, 2: 44–63.

Held, Virginia. 1985. Feminism and epistemology: Recent work on the connection between gender and knowledge. *Philosophy and Public Affairs* 14, 3: 296–307.

Heldke, Lisa. 1987. John Dewey and Evelyn Fox Keller: A shared epistemological tradition. *Hypatia: A Journal of Feminist Philosophy* 2, 3: 129–40.

———. 1988. Recipes for theory making. *Hypatia: A Journal of Feminist Philosophy* 3, 2: 15–30.

———. 1992. Foodmaking as a thoughtful practice. In *Cooking, eating, thinking: Transformative philosophies of food*, ed. Deane W. Curtin and Lisa M. Heldke. Bloomington: Indiana University Press.

Heldke, Lisa and Stephen Kellert. 1995. Objectivity as responsibility. *Metaphilosophy* 26, 4: 360–78.

Hennessy, Rosemary. 1993. Women's lives/feminist knowledge: Feminist standpoint as ideology critique. *Hypatia: A Journal of Feminist Philosophy* 8, 1: 14–34.

Herman, Barbara. 1993. Could it be worth thinking about Kant on sex? In *A mind of one's own: Feminist essays on reason and objectivity*, ed. Louise M. Antony and Charlotte Witt. Boulder, Colo.: Westview. 49–68.

Holland, Nancy. 1995. Convergence on whose truth? Feminist philosophy and the "masculine intellect" of pragmatism. *Journal of Social Philosophy* 26, 2: 170–83.

Holler, Linda. 1990. Thinking with the weight of the earth: Feminist contributions to an Epistemology of concreteness. *Hypatia: A Journal of Feminist Philosophy* 5: 1–23.

Homaik, Marcia L. 1993. Feminism and Aristotle's rational ideal. In *A mind of one's own: Feminist Essays on Reason and objectivity*, ed. Louise M. Antony and Charlotte Witt. Boulder, Colo.: Westview. 1–18.

Irigaray, Luce. 1989. Is the subject of science sexed? Trans. Carol Mastrangelo Bove. In *Feminism and science*, ed. Nancy Tuana. Bloomington: Indiana University Press. 58–68.

Jaggar, Alison. 1983. *Feminist politics and human nature*. Totowa: Rowman and Allanheld.

———. 1989. Love and knowledge: Emotion in feminist epistemology. *Inquiry* 32: 151–76.

Janack, Marianne. 1997. Standpoint epistemology without the "standpoint"? An examination of epistemic privilege and epistemic authority. *Hypatia: A Journal of Feminist Philosophy* 12, 2: 125–39.

Keller, Evelyn Fox. 1983. *A feeling for the organism*. New York: W. H. Freeman.

———. 1984. *Reflections on gender and science*. New Haven, Conn.: Yale University Press.

Keller, Evelyn Fox and Christine R. Grontkowski. 1983. The mind's eye. In *Discovering reality: Feminist perspectives on epistemology, metaphysics, methodology, and philosophy of science*, ed. Sandra Harding and Merrill Hintikka. Dordrecht; Boston: D. Reidel. 207–24.

Kelly, Rita Mae, Bernard Ronan, and Margaret E. Cawley. 1987. Liberal positivistic epistemology and research on women and politics. *Women & Politics* 7, 3: 11–28.

Kruks, Sonia. 1995. Identity politics and dialectical reason: Beyond an epistemology of provenance. *Hypatia: A Journal of Feminist Philosophy* 10, 2: 1–22.

Lando, Iddo. 1994. Should there be separatist epistemology? *Monist* 77, 4: 462–71.

Langton, Rae. 1993. Beyond a pragmatic critique of reason. *Australian Journal of Philosophy* 74, 4: 364–84.

Lennon, Kathleen, and Margaret Whitford, eds. 1994. *Knowing the difference: Feminist perspectives in epistemology.* New York: Routledge.

Little, Margaret Olivia. 1995. Seeing and caring: The role of affect in feminist moral epistemology. *Hypatia: A Journal of Feminist Philosophy* 10, 3: 117–37.

Lloyd, Elisabeth A. 1993. Pretheoretical assumptions in evolutionary explanations of female sexuality. *Philosophical Studies* 69: 139–53.

Lloyd, Genevieve. 1984. *The man of reason: "Male" and "female" in Western philosophy.* Minneapolis: University of Minnesota Press.

———. 1993. Maleness, metaphor, and the crisis of reason. In *A mind of one's own: Feminist essays on reason and objectivity*, ed. Louise M. Antony and Charlotte Witt. Boulder:, Colo. Westview. 69–84.

———. 1998. Rationality. In *A companion to feminist philosophy*, ed. Alison Jaggar. Cambridge: Blackwell. 165–72.

Longino, Helen. 1989. Science, objectivity, and feminist values. *Feminist Studies* 14: 561–74.

———. 1990. *Science as social knowledge.* Princeton, N.J.: Princeton University Press.

———. 1993. Essential tensions—Phase two: feminist, philosopical, and social studies of science. In *A mind of one's own: Feminist essays on reason and objectivity*, ed. Louise M. Antony and Charlotte Witt. Boulder, Colo.: Westview. 257–73.

———. 1993. Subjects, power, and knowledge: Description and prescription in feminist philosophies of science. In *Feminist epistemologies*, ed. Linda Martín Alcoff and Elizabeth Potter. New York: Routledge. 101–20.

———. 1994. In search of feminist epistemology. *Monist* 77, 4: 472–85.

Longino, Helen, and Ruth Doell. 1983. Body, bias and behavior: A comparative analysis of reasoning in two areas of biological science. *Signs: Journal of Women in Culture and Society* 9: 206–27.

Longino, Helen, and Kathleen Lennon. 1997. Epistemology as a local experience. *Aristotle Society, Supplement* 71: 19–54.

Lugones, María. 1987. Playfulness, "world"-travelling, and loving perception. *Hypatia: A Journal of Feminist Philosophy* 2, 2: 3–20.

McCaughey, Martha. 1994. Redirecting feminist critiques of science. *Hypatia: A Journal of Feminist Philosophy* 8, 4: 72–84.

McDermott, Patrice. 1987. Post-Lacanian French feminist theory: Luce Irigaray. *Women and Politics* 7, 3: 47–64.

Messer-Davidow, Ellen. 1985. Knowers, knowing, knowledge: Feminist theory and education. *Journal of Thought* 20: 8–24.

———. 1991. Know-how. In *(En)Gendering knowledge: Feminist in academe*, ed. Joan E. Hartman and Ellen Messer-Davidow. Knoxville: University of Tennessee Press. 281–309.

Michelson, Elana. 1996. "Auctoritee" and "experience": Feminist epistemology and the assessment of experiential learning. *Feminist Studies* 22, 3: 627–55.

Miller-McLemore, Bonnie J. 1992. Epistemology or bust: A material feminist knowledge of knowing. *Journal of Religion* 72, 2: 229–47.

Mills, Charles. 1988. Alternative epistemologies. *Social Theory and Practice* 14: 237–63.

Minnich, Elizabeth Kamarck. 1990. *Transforming knowledge*. Philadelphia: Temple University Press.

Modrak, Deborah K. W. 1998. Aristotle's theory of knowledge and feminist epistemology. In *Feminist interpretations of Aristotle*, ed. Cynthia A. Freeland. University Park: Penn State University Press. 93–117.

Nagl-Docekal, Herta. 1999. The feminist critique of reason revisited. *Hypatia: A Journal of Feminist Philosophy* 14, 1: 49–76.

Narayan, Uma. 1989. The project of feminist epistemology: Perspectives from a non-Western feminist. In *Gender/body/knowledge*, ed. Susan Bordo and Alison Jaggar. New Brunswick, N.J.: Rutgers University Press. 256–69.

Nelson, Lynn Hankinson. 1990. *Who knows: From Quine to a feminist empiricism*. Philadelphia: Temple University Press.

———. 1993. Epistemological communities. In *Feminist epistemologies*, ed. Linda Martín Alcoff and Elizabeth Potter. New York: Routledge. 121–60.

———. 1993. A question of evidence. *Hypatia: A Journal of Feminist Philosophy* 8, 2: 172–89.

———. 1993. Who knows? What can they know? And when? *Reason Papers* 18: 45–56.

———. 1995. The very idea of feminist epistemology. *Hypatia: A Journal of Feminist Philosophy* 10, 3: 31–49.

———. 1998. Empiricism. In *A companion to feminist philosophy*, ed. Alison Jaggar. Cambridge: Blackwell. 30–38.

Nelson, Lynn Hankinson, and Jack Nelson. 1995. Feminist values and cognitive virtues: The case of neuroendocrinology. *PSA*, Vol. II. East Lansing, MI: Philosophy of Science Association.

Norwood, Vera L. 1987. The nature of knowing: Rachel Carson and the American environment. *Signs: Journal of Women in Culture and Society* 12, 4: 740–60.

Pakszys, Elzbieta. 1988. Feminism, sciences, epistemology: Three issues. *Communication and Cognition* 21: 141–43.

Pinnick, Cassandra L. 1994. Feminist epistemology: Implications for philosophy of science. *Philosophy of Science* 61, 4: 646–57.

Plumwood, Val. 1993. The politics of reason: Towards a feminist logic. *Australian Journal of Philosophy* 74, 4: 436–62.

Potter, Elizabeth. 1989. Modeling the gender politics in science. In *Feminism and science*, ed. Nancy Tuana. Bloomington: Indiana University Press. 132–46.

———. 1993. Gender and epistemic negotiation. In *Feminist epistemologies*, ed. Linda Martín Alcoff and Elizabeth Potter. New York: Routledge. 161–86.

Prokhovnik, Raia. 1999. *Rational woman: A feminist critique of dichotomy*. London; New York: Routledge.

Richards, Janet Radcliff. 1995. Why feminist epistemology isn't (and the implications for feminist jurisprudence). *Legal Theory* 1, 4: 365–400.

Rooney, Phyllis. 1991. Gendered reason: Sex, metaphor, and conceptions of reason. *Hypatia: A Journal of Feminist Philosophy* 6, 2: 77–103.

———. 1993. Feminist-pragmatist revisionings of reason, knowledge, and philosophy. *Hypatia: A Journal of Feminist Philosophy* 8, 2: 15–37.

———. 1994. Recent work in feminist discussions of reason. *American Philosophical Quarterly* 31, 1: 1–21.

———. 1995. Rationality and the politics of gender difference. *Metaphilosophy* 26, 1–2: 22–54.

Rose, Hilary. 1983. Hand, brain and heart: A feminist epistemology for the natural sciences. *Signs: Journal of Women in Culture and Society* 9, 1:7 3–90.

———. 1998. Beyond masculinist realities: A feminist epistemology for the sciences. In *Feminist approaches to science*, ed. Ruth Bleier. New York: Pergamon. 57–76.

———. 1988. Reflections on the debate within feminist epistemology. *Communication and Cognition* 21: 133–38.

———. 1994. *Love, power, and knowledge*. Bloomington: Indiana University Press.

Ruddick, Sara. 1989. *Maternal thinking: Toward a politics of peace*. Boston: Beacon.

———. 1993. New feminist work on knowledge, reason and objectivity. *Hypatia: A Journal of Feminist Philosophy* 8, 4: 140–49.

Russell, Denise. 1989. Feminist critique of epistemology. *Methods of Science* 22, 2: 87–103.

Sallah, Ariel K. 1988. Epistemology and the metaphors of production: An eco-feminist reading of critical theory. *Studies in the Humanities* 15, 2: 130–39.

Sanders, Kenny. 1993. Michele LeDoeuff: Reconsidering rationality. *Australian Journal of Philosophy* 71, 4: 425–35.

Scheman, Naomi. 1987. Othello's doubt/Desdemona's death: The engendering of scepticism. In *Power, gender, values*, ed. Judith Genova. Edmonton, Alberta: Academic. 113–34.

———. 1991. Who wants to know? The epistemological value of values. In *(En)Gendering knowledge: Feminists in academe*, ed. Joan E. Hartman and Ellen Messer-Davidow. Knoxville: University of Tennessee Press. 179–200.

———. 1992. Though this be method, yet there is madness in it: Paranoia and liberal epistemology. In *A mind of one's own: Feminist essays on reason and objectivity*, ed. Louise Antony and Charlotte Witt. Boulder, Colo.: Westview. 145–70.

———. 1993. *Engenderings: Constructions of knowledge, authority, and privilege*. New York: Routledge.

———. 1995. Feminist epistemology. *Metaphilosophy* 26, 3: 177–90.

Schott, Robin May. 1993. Resurrecting embodiment: Toward a feminist materialism. In *A mind of one's own: Feminist essays on reason and objectivity*, ed. Louise M. Antony and Charlotte Witt. Boulder, Colo.: Westview. 171–84.

Sells, Laura. 1993. Feminist epistemology: Rethinking the dualism of atomic knowledge. *Hypatia: A Journal of Feminist Philosophy* 8, 3: 202–10.

Shrader-Frechette, Kristin. 1995. Feminist epistemology and its consequences for polity. *Public Affairs Quarterly.* 9, 2: 155–73.

Smith, Dorothy. 1974. Women's perspective as a radical critique of sociology. *Sociological Inquiry* 44: 7–13.

———. 1979. A sociology for women. In *The prism of sex: Essays in the sociology of knowledge,* ed. Julia A. Sherman and Evelyn Torton Beck. Madison: University of Wisconsin Press. 135–87.

———. 1987. *The everyday world as problematic: A feminist sociology.* Boston: Northeastern University Press.

Soble, Alan. 1994. Gender, objectivity, and realism. *Monist* 77, 4: 509–30.

Solberg, Mary. 1997. *Compelling knowledge: A feminist proposal for an epistemology of the cross.* Albany: State University of New York Press.

Solomon, Miriam. 1994. Social empiricism. *Nous* 28, 3: 325–43.

Spivak, Gayatri Chakravorty. 1999. *A critique of postcolonial reason: Toward a history of the vanishing present.* Cambridge: Harvard University Press.

Stanley, Liz, and Sue Wise, eds. 1993. *Breaking out again: Feminist ontology and epistemology.* New York: Routledge.

Steinberg, Lynn Deborah. 1994. Power, positionality and epistemology: An antioppressive feminist standpoint approach. *Women: A Cultural Review* 5, 2: 295–307.

Stenstad, Gail. 1988. Anarchic thinking. *Hypatia: A Journal of Feminist Philosophy* 3, 2: 87–100.

Szabo Gendler, Tamar. 1996. On the possibility of feminist epistemology. *Metaphilosophy* 27, 1–2: 104–17.

Tanesini, Alessandra. 1999. *An introduction to feminist epistemologies.* Malden, Mass.: Blackwell.

Thalos, Miriam. 1994. The common need for classical epistemological foundations: Against a feminist alternative. *Monist* 77, 4: 531–53.

Thayer-Bacon, Barbara J. 1995. Navigating epistemological territories. In *Philosophy of education,* ed. Alven Neiman. Urbana, Ill.: Philosophy of Education Society.

———. 1997. Caring's role in epistemology: Fears of relativism. *Inquiry* 17, 2: 20–31.

Thompson, Audrey, and Andrew Gitlin. 1995. Creating spaces for reconstructing knowledge in feminist pedagogy. *Educational Theory* 45, 2: 125–50.

Tronto, Joan C. 1987. Political science and caring: Or, the perils of Balkanized social science. *Women and Politics* 7, 3: 85–98.

Tuana, Nancy, ed. 1989. *Feminism and science.* Bloomington: Indiana University Press.

———. 1992. The radical future of feminist empiricism. *Hypatia: A Journal of Feminist Philosophy* 7, 1: 99–113.

———. 1995. The values of science: Empiricism from a feminist perspective, *Synthese* 104, 3: 1–21.

———. 1996. Re-valuing science,.In *Feminism, science, and the philosophy of science,* ed. Lynn Hankinson Nelson and Jack Nelson. Dordrecht; Boston: Kluwer. 17–38.

Vintges, Karen. 1988. Do we need feminist epistemologies? *Communication and Cognition* 21: 157–62.

Walker, Margaret Urban. 1989. Moral understandings: Alternative "epistemology" for a feminist ethics. *Hypatia: A Journal of Feminist Philosophy* 4, 2: 15–28.

Wallace, Kathleen. 1993. Reconstructing judgment: Emotion and moral judgment. *Hypatia: A Journal of Feminist Philosophy* 8, 3: 61–83.

Walsh, Sylvia. 1997. Subjectivity vs. objectivity: Kierkegaard's *Postscript* and feminist epistemology. In *Feminist interpretations of Søren Kierkegaard*, ed. Céline Léon and Sylvia Walsh. University Park: Penn State University Press. 203–16.

Webb, Mark Owen. 1995. Feminist epistemology and the extent of the social. *Hypatia: A Journal of Feminist Philosophy* 10, 3: 85–98.

Whitbeck, Caroline. 1984. A different reality: Feminist ontology. In *Beyond domination: New perspectives on women and philosophy*, ed. Carol C. Gould. Totowa, N.J.: Rowman and Allenheld. 64–88.

———. 1984. Love, knowledge, and transformation. *Hypatia Women's Studies International Forum* 2: 393–405.

Worley, Sara. 1995. Feminism, objectivity, and analytic philosophy. *Hypatia: A Journal of Feminist Philosophy* 10, 3: 138–56.

Wylie, Alison. 1996. The construction of archaeological evidence: Gender politics and science. In *The disunity of science: Boundaries, contexts, and power*, ed. Peter Galison and David J. Stump. Stanford: Stanford University Press. 311–43.

Wylie, Alison, Kathleen Okruhlik, Leslie Thielen-Wilson, and Sandra Morton. 1990. Philosophical feminism: A bibliographic guide to critiques of science. *Resources for Feminist Research* 19: 2–36.

Young, Iris. 1990. *Throwing like a girl and other essays on feminist philosophy and social theory*. Bloomington: Indiana University Press.

Zerilli, Linda. 1998. Doing without knowing: Feminism's politics of the ordinary. *Political Theory* 26, 4: 435–58.

CONTRIBUTORS

Linda Martín Alcoff is Professor of Philosophy, Political Science, and Women's Studies at Syracuse University. Her most recent book is *Thinking from the Underside of History* coedited with Eduardo Mendieta (Rowman and Littlefield, 2000). She is at work now on *Visible Identities*, forthcoming with Oxford.

Susan E. Babbitt teaches Philosophy and Development Studies at Queen's University in Kingston, Ontario. She is the author of *Impossible Dreams: Rationality, Integrity and Moral Imagination* (Westview, 1996) and *Artless Integrity: Moral Imagination in the Drive for Unity* (Rowman and Littlefield, forthcoming) as well as various articles in moral psychology and epistemology. She is currently involved in two research projects in Cuba, where she spends a lot of time and to which she now takes groups of students.

Richmond Campbell is Professor and Chair of the Philosophy Department at Dalhousie University, Halifax, Nova Scotia, and an editor of *Canadian Journal of Philosophy*. He is the author of *Illusions of Paradox: A Feminist Epistemology Naturalized* and coeditor of *Paradoxes of Rationality and Cooperation: Prisoner's Dilemma and Newcomb's Problem*. His publications include articles in logic, philosophy of science, philosophy of mind, moral epistemology, and feminist theory.

Sue Campbell teaches Philosophy and Women's Studies at Dalhousie University. She has authored *Interpreting the Personal: Expression and the Formation of Feelings* (1997) and coedited *Racism and Philosophy* (1999). She is pursuing research on social memory.

Lorraine Code is Distinguished Research Professor in the Department of Philosophy at York University in Toronto, where she also teaches in the Graduate Programs in Social and Political Thought, and Women's Studies. In addition to numerous articles and four coedited volumes, she is the author of *Epistemic*

Responsibility (1987), *What Can She Know? Feminist Theory and the Construction of Knowledge* (1991), and *Rhetorical Spaces: Essays on (Gendered) Locations* (1995). She is General Editor of an *Encyclopedia of Feminist Theories* (Routledge, 2000). As a recipient of a Canada Council Killam Research Fellowship (1999–2001), she is writing a book with the working title *Responsible Knowing, Ecological Imagining, and the Politics of Epistemic Location.*

Susan Hekman is Professor of Political Science at the University of Texas at Arlington. She has published books and articles in the methodology of the social sciences and feminist theory, including, most recently, *The Future of Differences: Truth and Method in Feminist Theory.*

Lisa Heldke writes and teaches as a pragmatist feminist philosopher, at Gustavus Adolphus College in St. Peter, Minnesota. She is completing a book on the phenomenon of cultural food colonialism, with the working title *Let's Eat Chinese.*

Sarah Lucia Hoagland is Professor of Philosophy and Women's Studies at Northeastern Illinois University in Chicago. She is a member of two collectives, the Institute of Lesbian Studies and the Escuela Popular Norteña. She is author of *Lesbian Ethics*, and coeditor of *For Lesbians Only* with Julia Penelope and *Feminist Interpretations of Mary Daly* with Marilyn Frye.

Lanita Jacobs-Huey received her graduate degree in Linguistic Anthropology from the University of California, Los Angeles. Currently, she is Assistant Professor of Anthropology at the University of Southern California.

Sandra Morgen is Director of the Center for the Study of Women in Society and Professor at the Sociology Department at the University of Oregon. Her research expertise is in Women and Social Policy and Feminist Theory. Her book, *Into Our Own Hands: The Women's Health Movement in the U.S.* is forthcoming from Rutgers University Press in spring 2002.

Lynn Hankinson Nelson is Professor of Philosophy at the University of Missouri–St. Louis. She is coauthor (with Jack Nelson) of *On Quine* (Wadsworth, 2000), author of *Who Knows: From Quine to a Feminist Empiricism* (Temple University Press, 1990) and has published articles devoted to feminist naturalized philosophy of science. She is guest editor of a special issue of *Synthese* devoted to Feminism and Science, and coeditor (with Jack Nelson) of *Feminism, Science, and the Philosophy of Science* (Kluwer Academic Press, 1996 and 1997) and *Re-Reading the Canon: Feminist Interpretations of Quine* (Penn

State University Press, forthcoming). She is working on *Scientism Well Lost, Evidence Regained: Social, Naturalized, and Normative Philosophy of Science*.

Judith Richards teaches Latin American literatures at the University of Kansas. She is author of *Contemporary Feminists: A Bio-bibliography* (ed. Jennifer Scanlon, Greenwood Press) and has published in various journals including *Hispania, College Literature, Revista de Literatura Mexicana Contemporanea, Monographic Review/Revista Monografica*. Her research is in the areas of Mexican and Hispanic Caribbean women's writing; U.S. Latina writing; literary criticism and critical analysis. She is currently working on *Revolting Developments: Women's Novels of the Mexican Revolution*, an anthology of Spanish American women's short fiction, with Lynne Margolies, for Prentice-Hall.

Naomi Scheman is Professor of Philosophy and Women's Studies and Associate Dean of the Graduate School at the University of Minnesota. A collection of her essays in feminist epistemology, entitled *Engenderings: Constructions of Knowledge, Authority, and Privilege*, was published in 1993; and she is the editor of the forthcoming Wittgenstein volume in the *Re-Reading the Canon* series. Her current research, teaching, and administrative interests focus on the epistemological implications of the moral and political (un)trustworthiness of universities as sites of authoritative knowledge production.

Charlene Haddock Seigfried is Professor of Philosophy and American Studies and affiliated with Women's Studies at Purdue University. She is the author of *Pragmatism and Feminism: Reweaving the Social Fabric, William James's Radical Reconstruction of Philosophy*, and was a guest editor for a special issue of *Hypatia* on pragmatism and feminism. She is past president of the Society for the Advancement of American Philosophy and on the executive board of the Society for the Study of Women Philosophers. This past summer she was snorkeling with sea lions as part of leading a class in evolutionary theory in the Galapagos Islands and in Ecuador.

Nancy Tuana is Director of the Douglas Rock Ethics Institute and Professor of Philosophy at Penn State University. She works in the areas of philosophy of science, epistemology, and feminist science studies. She has published *The Less Noble Sex: Scientific, Religious, and Philosophical Conceptions of Woman's Nature* and *Woman and the History of Philosophy*. Her anthologies include *Feminism and Science, Revealing Male Bodies*, and *Feminist Interpretations of Plato*. She is currently coeditor of *Hypatia: A Journal of Feminist Philosophy* and series editor of the Penn State Press series *Re-Reading the Canon*.

Louise Westling teaches English and Environmental Studies at the University of Oregon. Her books include *Sacred Groves and Ravaged Gardens: The Fiction of Eudora Welty, Carson McCullers, and Flannery O'Connor* and *The Green Breast of the New World: Landscape, Gender and American Fiction.* At present she is exploring the possibility of theorizing an ecological humanism that intersects with developments in contemporary physics and phenomenology.

Barbara L. Whitten is Professor of Physics and Women's Studies at Colorado College. She received the Bachelor of Arts degree in physics from Carleton College, and the Doctor of Philosophy degree in physics from the University of Rochester. She is both a practitioner and critic of science. Her physics research is in computational atomic physics; she has worked on problems in laser physics, plasma physics, and Rydberg atom collisions. A lifelong feminist, she discovered the feminist critique of science about a decade ago, and has begun to teach and publish in that area. She is the mother of two children. Penelope is in tenth grade, a writer, artist, and swimmer. Jacob is in eighth grade, a computer expert and swimmer. She wishes for her children and her students to live in a feminist, multicultural world.

INDEX

Abram, David, 252, 253
Absolutism: metaphysical, 103
Abuse, sexual: childhood, 39, 151–169,
    156; memories of, 39, 151–169; recall-
    ing, 157; skepticism about, 152
Achebe, Chinua, 297
Adamson, Tim, 240*n3*
Addams, Jane, 100, 104, 119*n5*
Addelson, Kathryn, 176, 177, 181
Adler, Mortimer, 103
African American: audience role for, 336;
    experience, 74, 75; experience of race,
    336; interdependence of experience
    for, 335–357; marginalization, 7, 335,
    351; negotiation of ideologies around
    hair care, 335–357; use of counternar-
    rative, 337; ways of knowing, 336
Agency: aquisition of, 325–329; con-
    struction of, 325; in social identity,
    60
Alcoff, Linda Martín, 6, 9, 14, 18, 53–76,
    144*n2*, 201
Alguien Tiene Que Llorar (Bobes), 300
Alston, William, 222
Ambiguity: tolerance for, 329–331
Amnesty International, 263, 272, 274,
    276
Ampère, André-Marie, 372, 373
Anthills of the Savannah (Achebe), 297
Antony, Louise, 5, 13, 19*n5*, 195, 196,
    202, 204, 216*n1*
Anzaldúa, Gloria, 7, 315, 316, 321, 322,
    323, 329, 331*n6*, 332*n98*, 335
Arago, François, 369
Aristotle, 61, 100, 107

Art as Experience (Dewey), 252
Atkinson, Ti-Grace, 175
Authenticity, 77*n3*
Authority: acknowledging, 58; attitudes
    toward, 48*n32;* cognitive, 15, 16, 112,
    114, 176–177, 180, 224; dependence of
    knowing on, 30; entrenched, 27; epis-
    temic, 5, 27, 56, 58, 59, 181; knowl-
    edge and, 57; moral, 331*n1;* narrative,
    330; obedience and, 57; objectivity
    and, 25; power and, 15–16; rational,
    47*n25,* 57; of science, 128; socially rec-
    ognized, 26
Autonomy, 311; epistemic, 31, 33; indi-
    vidualism and, 265; rational, 317; of
    science, 182; sexual, 275; suggestibility
    and, 165; violations of, 275

Babbitt, Susan, 8, 15, 169, 279, 297–313
Bacon, Roger, 99
Baier, Annette, 42, 43, 46*n21,* 241*n17,*
    286
Bakhtin, M.M., 136–137
Baquedano-López, Patricia, 337, 347
Barad, Karen, 81, 82, 93–96, 133
Barash, David, 210
Bartky, Sandra, 277, 278
Being: bodily, 229; culturally constructed,
    236; language and, 254; moments of,
    246; patterns of, 229; qualities of, 256;
    in the world, 70
Belief: constraints on, 227; explanation
    of, 178; formation, 4, 56; gender and,
    4; inherited, 114; justified, 32, 37,
    45*n4,* 201; knowledge and, 54, 119*n3;*

397

objective grounds for, 206; political pressure and, 276; rational merits of, 178; in science, 37; sense of, 276; shared, 63; testimonial, 77*n1;* woman-affirming, 115

Bem, Sandra, 126

Bence Jones, Henry, 368

Between the Acts (Woolf), 253, 254, 255, 256

Bias: appropriate, 298; circularity and, 196–197; distinction between good/bad, 196, 197, 200, 206, 215; dominant, 195; elimination of, 60, 129, 196; epistemic role of, 8; evidence and, 197, 206–208, 210; in feminist projects, 154; of feminist therapists, 155–157; gender, 13, 195, 197, 201, 205, 206; as guides to truth, 13; in heart disease studies, 198–199; institutionalization of, 12; masking, 197; as norm, 197; normalization of, 12; objectivity and, 15; oppressive, 12; paradox, 13, 19*n5,* 195–216; perspective and, 198; phallocentric, 269; Problem of Circularity in, 196–197; Problem of Relevance in, 197; racist, 269; research, 155–157; systemic, 204–205, 206; truth and, 196, 203; understanding, 195, 298

Bledsoe, Caroline, 40, 135, 136, 137, 140–141

Bleier, Ruth, 11, 182, 186, 187, 188

Bobes, Marilyn, 300, 302

Bohr, Niels, 93, 133

Bonner, Lonnice Brittenum, 336

Booth, Wayne, 274, 275, 277

Bowman, Cynthia, 156

Boyd, Richard, 222, 223

Boyle, Robert, 361

Brennais, Donald, 336

Briggs, Charles, 336

Brison, Susan, 272, 273, 275, 276, 280*n12*

Brown, Laura, 167

Bruner, Jerome, 336

Bunkle, Phillida, 128, 137, 145*n15*

Calkins, Mary Whiton, 111

Campbell, Richmond, 13, 195–216

Campbell, Sue, 8, 16, 17, 39, 151–169

Carby, Hazel, 354

Casey, Ed, 241*n14*

Castells, Manuel, 61

Castoriadis, Cornelius, 280*n6,* 280*n11*

Castro, Fidel, 310

Certeau, Michel de, 146*n19,* 146*n20*

Chatterjee, Partha, 337

Chicana literary theory, 7, 315–331

China, 136

Chow, Rey, 136, 335

Circularity: bias and, 196–197; truth and, 200–202

Class: character and, 47*n29;* power differentials and, 202; privilege and, 8, 36; relationships of, 106, 362; social, 106; as social location, 7; working, 366–369

Code, Lorraine, 4, 6, 7, 8, 17, 24, 30, 47*n25,* 49*n36,* 56, 58, 76, 111, 112, 114, 119*n8,* 141, 146*n21,* 241*n17,* 261–279, 287, 315, 316, 317, 320, 329, 330, 331*n3,* 363

Cognition: abilities and sex difference, 181; affective dimensions of, 7, 277; agents of, 113; dysfunction in, 75; as enactment, 134, 136; everyday, 266; imagination in, 266; philosophical modes of, 105; practices of, 9; as representation, 134; social factors and, 181

Collaboration, 1

Collins, Patricia Hill, 40, 335, 344

Communities: committed individuals in, 6; construction of knowledge by, 227; diversity in, 14, 364; embodied, 234; epistemological, 336; faith in, 43; homogenous scientific, 361–377; human, 234; individuals in, 5; knowing, 5; living earth, 245; research, 205; research development and, 1; scientific, 363; social, 5; strong, 362–364, 375–376; variety of memberships in, 238

Competence: rethinking, 42

Conceptual coercion, 126, 127, 129

Consciousness, 104; embodied synthesis of, 70; foundation in perception, 71; intense awareness of, 246; mestiza, 330; multiplicity of, 246; multiracial, 326; new mestiza, 324; ordinary, 246; participatory, 255; racial, 351; raising, 127; reembodiment of, 245; working-class, 367; in the world, 70

Constructivism: artifactual, 235; strong, 229

Constructivism, social, 9, 221–239; constructions of, 224–229; embodiment hypothesis in, 229; emotion and, 224–225; interactionism and, 229–235; knowledge of the world and, 225–227, 229–235; ontological dimensions, 227–229; opposed to "natural," 223; social phenomena and, 224

Contextualism, 82

Cornell, Drucilla, 279

Coulomb, Charles, 372

Counternarratives, 336, 337, 339, 345, 351

Court of Reason, 288, 289

Credibility: epistemic, 53–76; social identity and, 55; trust and, 32

Crenshaw, Kimberle, 354

Cuba, 15, 306–312

Cultural: backgrounds, 14; difference, 133; discourse, 355; interpretation, 62; locations, 7, 364; meanings, 59; narrative, 337; norms, 15, 312; practices, 267, 271; relativism, 106, 133, 134; symbolism, 351; traditions, 15, 312; universalism, 13; values, 87

Cuomo, Chris, 145n13

Daly, Mary, 128

Darwin, Charles, 100, 102, 245

Davidson, Donald, 144n2

Davies, Stevie, 246, 257n3

Davy, Sir Humphrey, 365, 366, 368

Decision-making: rationality and, 100

Deep Ecology Movement, 145n13

Demeritt, David, 235

Democracy and Education (Dewey), 106

Dependency: complexity of, 42; difference and, 31; epistemic, 30, 35, 41; on expertise, 43; extent of, 29; extreme, 41–42; irrational, 41; marginality of, 30; of objectivity on social justice, 43; on oppressors, 41; on others, 29; in science, 41; trust and, 29–33

Descartes, René, 8, 31, 32, 33, 39, 42, 43, 46n21, 46n22, 90, 99, 130, 154, 158, 159, 162, 163, 264, 271, 317

Dewey, John, 10, 96n3, 96n5, 96n6, 101, 102, 103, 104, 105, 106, 107, 108, 111, 116, 117, 118, 119n5, 240n4, 240n8, 246, 249, 252, 255, 256

Difference: among women, 283; cultural, 133; dependency and, 31; experiential, 271, 303–306; gender, 202, 284; in perceptual access, 69; political, 325; racial, 9, 325; relational, 31; resolution of problem of, 277; science of, 128; sexual, 9, 177, 181, 187, 332n8; understanding across, 277; varied importance of, 15

Dingwaney, Anuradha, 62

Discourse: academic, 322; control of terms of, 48n35; cultural, 355; of disbelief, 153; dominant, 40, 48n35, 129, 143; hegemonic, 143, 293; of human science, 128; legal, 286, 289–293; literary, 323; of located subjectivity, 265; mainstream, 324; moral, 283, 284, 285, 289; of nonhierarchical duality, 285; political, 283; professional, 128; resistance and, 128; skeptical, 153; of suggestibility, 154

Discourse on Method (Descartes), 31

Discrimination: knowledge of, 67; social identity and, 60, 63, 68

Diversity, 14–15; attention to, 14–15; within a collective, 347; jury, 55, 56; of knowers, 14; knowledge and, 14; research and, 28; in scientific communities, 364

Duranti, Alessandro, 336

Einstein, Albert, 132, 133, 252
Ellison, Ralph, 74
Embodiment: cognitive impact of, 221; of consciousness, 245–246; emergent, 232; human, 230–232; idealism and, 252; interactionalist alternatives and, 229–235; role of, 9–10
Emotion: cognitive role of, 7; knowledge and, 212; material basis for, 224; reflections of, 253; social constructivism and, 224–225
Empathy, 7–9; dangers of, 270; defining, 276; desirability of, 270; imaginative, 276; lack of teaching about, 275
Empiricism: classical, 262; constructive, 223; dogmas of, 130; feminist, 183; orthodox, 101
Epistemic: ability, 75; autonomy, 31; credibility, 53–76; dependency, 30; judgment, 14, 70, 75; practices, 279; principles, 262; reliability, 56, 60; responsibility, 16–18, 279; restrictions, 262; self-sufficiency, 41; subject, 4, 262; values, 87
Epistemology: abandonment of, 5, 103; abstraction of, 262; alternative, 3, 14; choosing perspectives, 15; critiques of, 195; deconstruction of, 284; dependency and, 30; diasporic, 44; emphasis on, 111; essential nature, 103; genealogical, 319; goal of, 320; hegemonic, 114, 290, 292; of ignorance, 75; liberatory, 18, 26; of location, 287; modernist, 284, 287, 289; moral, 14, 75, 286; moral theory and, 287; of moral voice, 283–295; naturalized, 116, 119n9, 196, 320; object of knowledge, 263; privileged, 336; realism and, 223; renaturalization of, 318; reorienting, 320; of science, 41, 317; social, 30; social organization and, 6; as specialty, 103; standpoint, 68, 361–377; theories of, 330; traditional, 195; unitary, 287; "unmarked," 30
Epistemology, feminist, 2–4; common themes in, 3; development, 2; embodi-

ment hypothesis and, 9; family resemblance concept, 3; objectivity and, 12; removal of injustice and, 11; resuscitation of, 23–44; virtues in, 3
Escobar, Arturo, 299
Essentialism: critiques of, 82; feminist, 249
Ethics: teaching, 34
Existence: struggle for, 297; unity of, 312
Existentialism, 112
Experience: African American, 74, 75; art as, 246, 252; bodily, 70, 266, 336; border-crossing, 327; of childhood, 42; cognitive content, 73; cognitive significance of, 73; coherent, 130; concrete, 7; as constraint on beliefs and knowledge, 227; embodied, 249; empathetic projection into others', 270; exclusionary, 15; by experience, 245; experimental method and, 117; gendered, 108, 288; historical, 76; homogenization of, 61; identity and, 73, 77n3; imagination and, 266; individual contemporary, 61; inquiry into, 106; intentionality of, 73; interaction and, 226, 252; interpretation of, 104; invisible, 15; knowing and, 2, 7; knowledge and, 65, 75; lived, 62, 363; as making sense of information, 73; of marginalization, 336; masculine, 108; meaning of, 70, 73; mediated nature of, 76; narrative and, 337; nonvoluntary character of, 62; normative, 322; as ongoing process, 104; organizations of, 110; outcomes, 104; perceptual, 70, 91; possibility of, 109–110; reason and, 317; reconstruction of, 105; reinterpreting, 127; rendering intelligible, 61; shared, 336; significance of, 302; simultaneous doing/suffering in, 104; social identity and, 71; transformation of, 266; of trauma, 263; of truth, 287, 294; unifying, 308; universal, 42
Experts: dependence on, 43; moral character of, 33; in science, 29; training of, 43–44

False Memory Syndrome Foundation, 8, 16, 17, 39, 151–169, 169*n1,* 170*n2,* 171*n14,* 171*n17;* antifeminist rhetoric of, 153; argument from misdesign and, 157–163; institutional response to, 152; Scientific and Professional Advisory Board, 151; skepticism and, 154–157; strategies, 157–163; on suggestibility, 163–168

Faraday, Michael, 14, 364–377

Fausto-Sterling, Anne, 11, 177, 182, 184, 187, 188, 206, 207, 211

Fay, Elizabeth, 367

Femininity: claims about, 126; male-constructed concept of, 126; nature of, 126; social perceptions of, 142

Feminism: as liberatory politics, 27; political agendas in, 53; private healing and, 153; relation to objectivity, 27; unitary concept of woman in, 283; as zealotry, 152

Feminist: activism, 155; cognitive authority, 112; defining, 182; empiricism, 183; epistemology, 2–4; essentialism, 249; focus on value-neutrality, 131, 183; knowers, 136, 185; moral theories, 284; objectivity, 132; philosophy, 3, 53, 129–135, 214–216; political values, 185; power, 114; realism, 89–96; reconstructions of knowledge, 113; response to False Memory Syndrome Foundation, 152, 153; revolution, 114; science, 363; social factor, 178; standpoint epistemology, 361–377; theories, 112, 283; therapy, 39, 151–169; uses of knowledge, 110–111; values, 11, 182–189; work in recovered memory, 146*n25*

"Feminist Epistemology" (Scheman), 3

Foucault, Michel, 70, 72, 76, 77*n2,* 128, 144*n3,* 354

Foundationalism, 226

Frankenberg, Ruth, 335

Fricker, Miranda, 47*n25*

Frye, Marilyn, 286

Gadamer, Hans Georg, 57, 73, 127, 287, 288, 289, 290, 292, 294

Gaia Hypothesis, 246

Gal, Susan, 337

Gambia, 135, 136, 137, 145*n12*

Geertz, Clifford, 182

Gender: belief and, 4; bias, 13, 195, 197, 201, 205, 206; as central analytic category, 2, 4; construction of, 129, 224; difference, 202; essentialist views of, 119*n5;* experience and, 108; formation of moral voice and, 285, 286; inquiry and, 2; knowing and, 2; knowledge and, 317; marginalization and, 336; norms, 2; oppression, 336; power differentials and, 202; relationships of, 106, 362; as relevant axis of investigation, 185; research and, 15; roles, 126; as social location, 7; social roles and, 11; in social structure of institutions, 185; stereotypes, 205, 210; violence, 273

Giddings, Paula, 354

Giere, Ronald, 213

Gilligan, Carol, 14, 283, 284, 285, 286, 287, 288, 289, 290, 293, 294, 295*n1*

Gilman, Sander, 128, 146*n17*

Ginet, Carl, 45*n4*

Glover, Jonathan, 299

Goffman, Erving, 337, 341

Gold, Alan, 162

Goodwin, Charles, 336

Goodwin, Marjorie, 339, 341

Gorham, Geoffrey, 213

Gould, Stephen Jay, 131

Griffin, Susan, 125

Gross, Paul, 25, 26, 178, 182

Guevara, Che, 306, 307, 308, 309

Haack, Susan, 111, 175, 177, 178, 182, 191*n9*

Hacking, Ian, 235

Hall, Stuart, 62

Halperin, David, 224

Haraway, Donna, 26, 91, 96*n6,* 132, 135, 136, 235, 236, 237, 238, 240*n7,* 241*n13,* 268, 270, 361, 364

Harding, Sandra, 2, 12, 14, 26, 43, 68, 87, 108, 126, 146*n18*, 195, 198, 210, 211, 233, 234, 363, 364

Hardwig, John, 33, 34

Hartman, Betsy, 145*n13*

Hartsock, Nancy, 362

Hayles, Katherine, 231

Heidegger, Martin, 252

Hekman, Susan, 3, 14, 15, 283–295

Held, Virginia, 284, 285

Heldke, Lisa, 3, 10, 12–13, 81–96

Hermeneutics: pluritopic, 134

Heterogeneity: criterion of, 187; ontological, 185, 187

Hintikka, Merrill, 2

Hoagland, Sarah, 17, 18, 39, 40, 41, 44, 48*n35*, 125–143

Hobbes, Thomas, 41

hooks, bell, 335

Horwich, Paul, 222

Hubbard, Ruth, 11, 186, 187

Humanities: negligible social consequences of, 117

Hume, David, 46*n19*, 246

Hurston, Zora Neale, 140

Hurtado, Aida, 335

Husserl, Edmund, 245, 252

Hutchins, Robert, 103

Hypatia, 284

Idealism: transcendental, 54

Identity: of acting subject, 264; as background for outlooks, 63; constructions, 61; epistemic relevance of, 73; of ethico-juridical subject, 264; experience and, 73, 77*n3*; gendered, 71; as generative source of meaning, 61; interpretation of facts and, 69; interpretive nature of, 63; knowledge and, 62; Latina, 323; markers of, 59; meaning of, 61, 302; moral, 266; multifaceted nature of, 322; multiracial, 323; narrative, 264, 278; objective histories and, 63; perception and, 73; personal, 74; perspective and, 69; racial, 71, 74, 77*n3*; uniform outlook and, 63

Identity, social, 6, 14; credibility and, 55; differences in what is known and, 64; discrimination and, 60, 63, 68; disparate experience and, 61; epistemic ability and, 75; epistemic judgment and, 70; epistemic relevance, 59, 63; experience and, 71; grouping interpretive processes and, 74; as indicator of differences in perceptual access, 69; jury diversity and, 55; as legitimate feature in assessment, 60; perception and, 76; reference to agency in, 60; relevance of, 55, 60; subjectivity and, 60

Ihde, Don, 222

Imaginaries: hegemonic, 275; prototypical, 275

Imagination, 7–9; assumptions about, 265; as belonging to someone, 271; cognition and, 266; communal nature of, 266; erasures of, 266; expunging, 261; influence in memory, 39; judgment and, 366; knowledge and, 8; limits of, 276; memory and, 160; narrative and, 159; place in knowing, 268–272; privilege and, 8; reason and, 266; relations of epistemic dependence and, 154; suggestibility and, 164; training, 366; truth and, 159; workings of, 266

Imaginings: communal, 280*n6*; credibility of, 8; integral to discriminations, 266; moral decisions and, 266; rational, 261–279; responsible, 265; of the unimaginable, 269; "vanilla," 269, 280*n9*

Impartiality: criticism of, 195; discredited ideal of, 208; displacement of, 14; flawed ideal of, 195–216; ideal of, 6, 8, 12, 14, 197, 202; questions on, 11; realism and, 208–209; reinforcement of gender bias and, 195; research and, 12

In a Different Voice (Gilligan), 283–284

"In Search of Feminist Epistemology" (Longino), 3

India, 13, 136

Individualism, 30–31; autonomy and, 265; of early modernity, 41; liberal, 277; weak, 77*n1*

Information: experience and, 73; making sense of, 73; predispositions in interpretation, 69

Inquiry: as constitutive relation in reality, 93; context of, 92; defining, 85, 182; democratic processes of, 202; into experience, 106; as form of interaction in the world, 91; impartiality for, 195; intellectual, 195; as interaction between agents, 233; knowing as act of, 105; knowledge and, 109, 119*n5;* legitimate, 179; logic of, 111; methods of, 115; nature of context of, 89; objective, 85, 87, 92, 202; politicization of, 182; responsibility and, 85; "right and wrong" methods, 102; skepticism in, 153; theories of, 118*n2*

Interaction: biological, 10; community/culture, 234; complex, 10, 185; with environments, 234; everyday, 144*n1;* existence and, 222; experience and, 252; human, 235, 237, 239; inquiry as form of, 91; between knowledge production and social well-being, 320; material, 9, 229–235, 236; naturally occuring, 336; with nature, 234, 251; observer/object, 94; people/places, 233; phenomenon and, 94; pragmatism and, 240*n4;* in research, 232; with sciences, 25; social, 34; social constructivism and, 223, 224

Interactionism, 223, 224; complex phenomena in, 239; metaphysics of, 235–238; social constructivism and, 229–235

Intra-action, 94, 133

Jackson, Wes, 85–86

Jacobs-Huey, Lanita, 7, 335–357

Jacob's Room (Woolf), 246

James, William, 99, 100, 110, 119*n5*

Johnson, Barbara, 263, 264, 268, 271, 273

Johnson, Mark, 265–272, 277, 279, 280*n6*

Johnson, Samuel, 235

Jones, Ann, 142

Jones, James, 139

Judgment: of appearance, 58–59; decontextualized, 65; epistemic, 14, 70, 75; imagination and, 366; interpersonal, 56; legal, 290; moral, 285, 298

Justice: Kadi, 291, 292, 293; social, 43, 311, 312; values, 131; voice of, 284, 285, 286, 288, 289–293

Justification: assessing, 57; of belief, 32, 37; direct, 57; epistemic, 56, 57; interested/disinterested, 45*n4;* objective, 197, 202–206, 208, 211; relevance and, 202–206; of testimony, 77*n1;* working of, 38

Kadi justice, 291, 292, 293

Kant, Immanuel, 18, 53, 54, 55, 68, 280*n6,* 286

Keller, Evelyn Fox, 26, 182, 186, 206, 361, 364

Kellert, Stephen, 27, 47*n27,* 82, 85

Kipling, Rudyard, 136

Knight, David, 366

Knorr-Cetina, Karin, 225, 227, 228, 229, 232, 240*n1,* 240*n5,* 354

Knowers: distinct, 4, 6; engaged, 6–7; feminist, 136, 185; ideal, 317; imaginative, 272; knowing of, 267; male, 279*n1,* 317; orthodox empiricist, 263; reality of inquiry by, 90; sanctioned, 137; situated, 129–136, 139; social location of, 47*n27;* surrogate, 41, 43

Knowing: as acquisition of knowledge, 277; as act of inquiry, 105; collective, 77*n1;* communities, 5; consequences of, 105; constructed, 4; democratization of, 90; dependence on authority, 30; experience and, 2, 7; fixity of subject-object positions in, 276–277; forms of, 99; gender-specific ways of, 2, 119*n5;* generic, 4, 6, 30; imaginative, 8, 262, 267; as interdependency, 91; of knower, 267; language of, 132, 278;

listening and, 278; by men, 32; observational, 262; place of imagination in, 268–272; privilege and, 4; qualities of, 256; responsible, 261–279; situated, 129–135, 139; ways of, 336; world to be known and, 102

Knowledge: acceptability of claims, 35; acquisition, 5, 10, 77n1, 212, 277; affective, 263; application of, 321; authority and, 57; belief and, 54, 119n3; "bodily," 9; border, 325; cognition and, 7; constituencies for, 24; constraints on, 227; construction of, 7; conventional, 318; democratization of, 27; dependence on subjectivity, 65; distortion of, 5; diversity and, 14; embodied, 132, 133; emotional, 212; empirical, 144n1; evaluating, 321; excessive particularity and, 274; experience and, 65, 75; feminist accounts of, 16; gendering, 317; identity and, 62; imagination and, 8; imposition without consent, 27; influence of human perceptions, 222; inquiry and, 109, 119n5; interpretation and, 7; irrational, 268; justification for, 45n4; local, 6–7; located, 330; moral, 212; nonindividualist conception of, 5–6; nonpropositional, 7; object of, 263; objective, 41, 54, 106, 141, 169, 262; partial, 9, 70, 139; participatory, 245–257; perceptual, 75, 261; possibility of, 75; pragmatic theory of, 5, 104; privilege and, 16; processing, 320; production, 2, 14, 26, 117, 318, 325, 331n3; pursuit of, 31, 44; realist concept of, 212; reconfiguring, 268; reconstructions of, 113; replicable, 261; representational view of, 226; role of others in, 46n22; scientific, 126, 136, 363, 364; self, 271; situated, 96n6, 129–135, 270; "S Knows That p" model, 4–5; social, 363; social practices of, 6; social structures and, 4, 16; sociology of, 178; spectator theory, 100–101; subjective, 7, 355; testimonial, 6, 56, 58, 77n1; theories of, 99,

100, 106, 111, 115, 119n9, 261, 316; unavailable, 8; universal, 27; use of, 110; values and, 5, 13, 103
Kuhn, Thomas, 77n2, 126, 127, 130, 135, 188, 308
Kymlicka, Will, 309

Lacan, Jacques, 271
Lacey, Nicola, 270, 275, 280n12
Lang, Dwight, 367
Language: apolitical approach to, 54; appropriate uses of, 254; being and, 254; of deconstruction, 275; of enactment, 271; as everything, 245; expressive view of, 46n15; games, 127, 128, 130, 132; inclusive, 328; interrogative use of, 254; of knowing, 278; narrative, 254; of philosophy, 254; of rationality-as-objectivity, 265; of skepticism, 154; of subjectivity, 271
Lankshear, Colin, 337
LaPaglia, Nancy, 368
Latour, Bruno, 178–179, 226, 227, 228, 235, 240n5
Laudan, Larry, 178
Leder, Philip, 236
Le Doeuff, Michèle, 278–279, 280n6
Lehrer, Keith, 56, 57
Leibniz, Gottfried Wilhelm, 33
Lévi-Strauss, Claude, 308
Levitt, Norman, 25, 26, 177, 178, 182
Literary studies, 315–331
Lloyd, Elizabeth, 23, 37, 175, 178, 179, 188, 190n5
Location: cultural, 364; of cultures in nature, 233; epistemology of, 287; material, 9, 221–239; nonvoluntary character of, 62; of scientists, 364; social, 7, 47n27, 65, 69, 71, 364; of subjectivity, 265
Locke, John, 18, 53
Loftus, Elizabeth, 151, 156, 159
Logic: of discovery, 106; dominant, 143, 144n3; emergence from practice of, 140; empirical, 105; of inquiry, 111; naturalistic, 240n4; normative, 105;

phallic, 143; of rationality, 141; resistant, 139–143; scientific, 118*n1;* of validation, 106; Vienna Circle and, 54

Longino, Helen, 3, 5, 10, 11, 26, 111, 169, 184, 187, 188, 191*n11,* 202, 363

Lovelock, James, 246

Lovibond, Sabina, 46*n15,* 278

Lugones, María, 142, 277

MacIntyre, Alasdair, 144*n2*

Making Face, Making Soul. Haciendo Caras (Anzaldúa), 326, 332*n9*

Manning, Harvey, 82, 83

Marginalization: African American, 7, 335, 351; experiences of, 336; gender-based, 336; insights into reality and, 108; race, 336; shared, 351; social position and, 69; of Western rationality, 146*n20*

Margulis, Lynn, 246

Marshal, Gloria, 131

Marx, Karl, 46*n16*

Materialism, 19*n8*

Materiality, 9; complexities of, 221; emergent, 233; in feminist scholarship, 223; human, 221, 228–229, 230–232, 233, 234; of the more-than-human world, 221, 223, 230, 232, 234; as subject of investigation, 234

Maxwell, James Clerk, 373, 374

May, Todd, 295*n4*

Mead, George Herbert, 119*n5*

Meaning: attribution, 73; birth of, 245; construction of, 167; creating, 92, 134; cultural, 58–59; embedded, 127; of experience, 70; of identity, 61, 302; imposition of, 309; making, 40, 61, 137, 139; metaphorical, 88; narratives of, 76; representational theories of, 226, 235; structures, 267; transforming, 267; transparency of, 65; values and, 70; wild, 245

Meditations (Descartes), 31, 154

Memory; collective, 63; distortion, 157; doubt about, 161; false, 16, 153, 155,

159; group historical, 61; imagination and, 39, 160; malleability of, 8, 156, 157; politics of, 16; pseudo, 153; recovered, 16, 39, 146*n25,* 151–169; reliability of, 163; repression, 156; suggestibility and, 8; testimony, 162–163; visualization and, 8

Mendus, Susan, 279

Mercer, Kobena, 336

Merleau-Ponty, Maurice, 10, 70, 71, 72, 75, 77*n2,* 245, 246, 252, 253, 254, 255, 256

Merskey, Harold, 152

Mertz, Elizabeth, 156

Messer-Davidow, Ellen, 117

Mestizaje, 323–324

Metaphor: bridge-building, 226; construction, 226, 227, 232, 235; for living processes, 253; visual, 230; in Woolf, 253

Metaphors We Live By (Johnson), 266

Metaphysics, 110; assumptions of realist positions in, 221; of common moral understanding, 266; emphasis on, 111; feminist perspectives in, 2; of interactionism, 235–238; skepticism in, 163; social, 74

Meyers, Diana, 280*n9*

Mignolo, Walter, 133, 134, 141

Miller, Richard, 306

Mills, Charles, 74, 75

Mills, Sarah, 354

Minh-ha, Trinh T., 279

Modernity: justice voice of, 284

Mohanty, Satya, 61, 62, 69, 73, 136, 299

Moore, G.E., 132, 145*n9,* 246

Moore, Henrietta, 355

Moraga, Cherríe, 322

Moral: anarchy, 284, 289; authority, 331*n1;* character, 33; defining, 284; deliberations, 294; discourse, 284, 285; epistemology, 14, 75, 286; judgment, 285, 298; knowledge, 212; principles, 285; relativism, 284, 295*n5;* subjectivity, 265; theories, 283, 286, 295*n4;*

thought, 293; truth, 15, 284, 288, 289; understanding, 302; values, 284, 285

Moral Imagination (Johnson), 265

Moral voice(s), 295*n1;* of care, 284, 285, 288, 293; choosing among, 287; different, 283–289; epistemology of, 283–295; formation of, 286; gender and, 285, 286; of justice, 284, 285, 286, 288, 289–293; legal, 289–293; multiple, 285, 286, 290; of situated subjects, 288; of women, 284, 286

Morality: care voice of women in, 284; contextual, 285, 288; defining, 286; hegemonic tradition of, 284; issues of, 87; rationality and, 283; redefining, 286; responsibility and, 286; social construction of, 285; true, 288; women barred from, 283

Morgan, Marcyliena, 337, 344, 345

Morgen, Sandra, vii–viii, 361

Mrs. Dalloway (Woolf), 246

Mueller, Adele, 299

Multiculturalism, 19*n8,* 134, 322, 327

Narayan, Uma, 13

Narrative: abuse, 153; activity, 329; African American, 7; analysis, 336; authority, 330; autobiographical, 319, 326; collaborative, 336; cultural, 337; descriptive, 319, 330; experience and, 337; fictional, 271; genealogical, 321; of hair, 336; historical, 337; identity, 264, 278; imagination and, 159; langauge, 254; of meaning, 76; meaningful, 61; personal, 336; power of, 271; reasoned, 320; relevance as epistemological resource, 320; of resistance, 322; role of, 7–8; self-reflective, 320–321, 328, 329; social, 62; unity, 267, 271, 273, 347

Naturalism, 316–321, 322; empirical, 103; meaning of, 329; recidivistic, 318; understanding, 317

Needham, Lawrence, 62

Nelson, Lynn Hankinson, 5, 11, 16, 19*n5,* 56, 103, 111, 112, 113, 114, 115,

119*n5,* 119*n9,* 130, 131, 175–190, 226, 227, 354

New Physics, 245, 246

Newton, Isaac, 371, 372

Nietzsche, Friedrich, 68, 77*n2*

Nozick, Robert, 45*n1*

Nussbaum, Martha, 299, 300

Objectivism: alternatives to, 227

Objectivity: achieving, 40; alternative conceptions of, 24; attacks on, 27; authority and, 25; bias and, 15, 297–313; character of, 82; classical, 133; conception of neutrality as, 216*n1;* contextual values and, 45*n1;* as correspondence to reality, 96*n2;* critiques of, 11–13; data collection and, 40; defining, 81, 82–85, 96*n2;* dependence on social justice, 43; ensuring, 275; evidence and, 210; exclusion and, 40; expanded, 12–13; externalist account of, 34, 44, 47*n26;* feminist, 132; feminist science and, 175; history of, 27–28; inquiry and, 85, 87; instrumental value of, 26, 47*n26;* internalist account of, 29, 34, 35; maintenance of, 263; maximizing, 88; as moral concept, 87; need for, 25, 26; normative concept of, 24; persons and, 81; preservation, 23; processes, 81; promotion of, 81; pure, 318; rationality as, 265; reevaluations of, 129; reflexivity and, 209–212; as responsibility, 81; scientific, 27–29, 40, 129, 176, 318, 363; statements in, 81; strong, 12, 13, 14, 17, 198, 210, 364; threats to, 16, 23, 25; trust and, 23–44; truth-conducive, 13, 198–200; uses of, 25; values and, 13, 24, 87, 178, 198–200

Observation: agencies of, 133; contextless, 145*n14;* detached, 137; disembodied, 130; laboratory, 262; perspective in, 298; theory-dependence of, 130; value-laden, 130, 133, 134

Ochs, Elinor, 337

O'Dair, Sharon, 368

Oddsson, David, 48*n32*

Ofshe, Richard, 155, 157, 159, 160, 165
"On Imagination and Judgment" (Faraday), 366
OncoMouse, 236–238
Ontology: of heterogeneity, 185, 187; realist, 222, 235; of social constructivism, 227–229
Oppression: awareness of, 11; counteracting, 8; dependency and, 41; gender, 126, 336; imperialistic, 137; instruments of, 328; legitimization of, 133; multiple, 111; practices of, 114–115; pragmatism and, 103; race, 336; in science, 131; in systems of rationality, 17
Orsted, Hans Christian, 372, 373
Other, the: access to observe, 136; creating self as, 364; entitlement of access to, 136; experiences of, 270; knowledge of, 136; representation of, 134; situations of, 270; speaking, 278; subjugation of, 136; value of, 106

Park, Shelley, 153
Particularism, 299
Patriarchy: reinforcement of, 128; in science, 127; in society, 362
Perception: as access to truth, 71; boomerang, 138, 141; as culturally variable learned practice, 70; embodied, 71; foundation of consciousness in, 71; fragmentary quality of, 256; identity and, 71, 73; immediacy of, 73; indeterminacy of, 246; as interpretive exercise, 68; knowledge and, 75; learned, 71; moral, 266; organization of, 231; as orientation to world, 72; realist theory of, 225; scientific study of, 116; sense, 163; social identity and, 76; as social practice, 76; specificity of practice and, 71; variation in, 76
Perkin, Harold, 367
Perspective: bias and, 198; border crossing and, 298, 325; identity and, 69, 74; in interpretation of information, 298; multiple, 198; in observation, 298; of quantum physics, 246; on reality, 256

Perutz, M.F., 178
Peters, Michael, 337
Phenomena, 93–94, 96n7, 133; appreciating, 309; artificial, 227; constructed through lab interactions, 235; interaction and, 94, 239; limited understanding of, 361–377
Phenomenology, 70
Phenomenology of Perception (Merleau-Ponty), 253
Philosophy: abandonment of, 111; abstract, 256; alternative perspectives in, 112; analytic, 54; Anglo-American, 103; apolitical approach to, 54; continental, 54; epistemological turn in, 5; evolutionary model in, 100; feminist, 3, 53, 214–216; foundational, 117; gendered history of, 256; history of, 53; of inquiry, 106; language of, 254; pragmatist, 116; professionalization in, 54; reconstruction of, 102; of science, 2, 3
"Philosophy and Democracy" (Dewey), 106
Plato, 100, 245, 246, 252
Popper, Karl, 178
Porter, Bernard, 47n29
Positivism, 13; enlightenment, 130; extreme, 171n14; historical development, 47n27; logical, 47n27, 54, 102, 115, 118n1
Postmodernism, 112, 113
Poststructuralism, 330
Potter, Elizabeth, 361
Poussaint, Dr. Alvin, 37
Power: asymmetry, 278; authority and, 15–16; differentials, 202; diffusion of, 185; explanatory, 187; feminist, 114; hierarchies of, 276; of narrative, 271; relations, 108, 131, 278; role of, 15–16; social, 69; subordination, 212
Pragmatism, 3, 262; classic, 100; evolutionary model and, 102; interaction and, 240n4; nature and, 119n3; oppression and, 103; reconstruction of

philosophy by, 104; theories of science and, 100; as theory of inquiry, 118*n2*

Primate Visions (Haraway), 361

Privilege, 106, 269; contested, 337; exclusion from, 35; imagination and, 8; immunity from, 34; knowing and, 4; knowledge development and, 16; science and, 12, 29

Proctor, Robert, 128

Purism, 129

Putnam, Hilary, 222

Quine, Willard, 115, 119*n9*, 130, 144*n1*, 226

Race: construction of, 129, 224; marginalization, 336; oppression, 336; power differentials and, 202; privilege and, 36; self-deception in, 75; as social location, 7

Racism, 36, 61; classroom, 65, 66; constructed, 224; disassembling, 323; dismantling, 327; institutional, 67; in justice system, 36; ramifications of, 74; in research, 37; in science, 129; victim blame for, 66

Ramona, Gary, 161

Rationalism: development of, 290

Rationality, 31; aesthetic, 100; conceptual formulation in, 100; construed in individualistic terms, 178; decision-making and, 100; detached, 99; dimensions of, 99; dominant model, 18, 99; of dominant paradigm, 133; erasures of imagination from, 266; essence of, 82; essentialist definitions of, 82; feminist models, 99, 175; interactive, 100; morality and, 283; normative concept of, 24; as objectivity, 265; oppressive systems of, 17; perceptual input in, 100; practical, 100; pragmatist interpretation, 99–118; resistance to, 17, 18, 125–143; scientific, 128, 176; sense and, 128–129; theories of, 106; threats to, 16; transformation of self and, 106; Western law and, 291

Rawls, John, 48*n31*

Realism, 9; agential, 82, 133; classical, 134; convergent, 222; descriptive, 91; epistemology and, 223; evidence against/for, 91; external, 222; feminist versions of, 89–96; forms of, 81; impartiality and, 208–209; instrumental, 222; interactionist alternative to, 221–239; internal, 222; intra-acting and, 133; modified, 222; ontology and, 222; pluralistic, 214; prescriptive, 91; responsibility and, 89–96; semantic, 222; separation of representation and reality in, 212; suspicions of, 208; theories of, 222; truth and, 222; without truth, 212–214

Reality: absolute conception of, 46*n15*; agential, 134; apparent, 235; artificial, 227; as choice, 108; complexity of, 10; composition of, 94; embodied experience as, 249; emergent, 10; evidence for structure of, 91; experienced, 108; external, 108; fact and, 225; fixed, 91; human perspective in, 46*n15*; independent, 91, 92–93, 145*n9*; independent of inquiry, 93; inquiry as constitutive relation, 93; interactive, 93; laboratory, 227, 228; marginalization and, 108; nature of, 245, 250; ojectivity as correspondence to, 96*n2*; participatory, 246; perceptions of, 130; perspectives on, 256; primary, 249; subject and object of, 250; truth and, 198

Reason, 31; alleged universality of, 42; circular, 318; construction of, 331*n2*; embedded, 133; experience and, 317; exploratory, 318; as foundation of being, 264; generic images of, 231; ideas of, 331*n1*; imagination and, 266; importance of, 264; masculinity and, 317; sociological contexts of, 210; tradition and, 127–128; Western, 134

Rebolledo, Tey Diana, 329

Reductivism, 266

Reflexivity: epistemic ideal of, 197–198; objectivity and, 209–212

Relationships: class, 362; complex, 15, 185, 186; denial of different, 31; dialectical, 234; gender, 106, 362; hierarchical, 186; interdependent, 323; "lawlike," 186; linear, 186; natural, 186; between participants in inquiry, 12; power, 108, 131, 278; power/ knowledge, 15, 18; primacy of, 87–88; primary, 89; sexual, 74; social, 362

Relativism, 16, 45*n1*, 132; alternatives to, 227; anarchical, 318; defense of, 24; feminist science and, 175–190; as irrational position, 24; methodological, 179, 190*n4*, 190*n6*; moral, 284, 295*n5*

Reliability: epistemic, 56, 60, 74

"Remapping the Epistemic Terrain" (Code), 320

Representation: of beauty, 336, 351; propositional form, 212; realist theory of, 212, 225; theory of truth in, 226; view of knowledge in, 226

Repression: existence of, 156; of memory, 156

Research: AIDS, 37; androcentric assumptions in, 180, 188; bias in, 129, 155–157; on biological basis for sex differences, 181; collaboration and, 1; communities, 1, 205; contradictory evidence in, 131; development, 1; dismissal of feminist, 178; distorted results of, 12; diversity and, 28; dominance hierarchies in, 186; egg-sperm passive/aggressive debate, 205–206; empirical adequacy of, 10–11; ethics and, 34; evaluation of, 28; gendered, 15, 205; generation of hypotheses in, 205; impartiality and, 12; interaction in, 232; lack of trust in, 37; native informant in, 40; nonepistemic values in, 183; nonhierarchically structured, 202; obscuring truth in, 205; political considerations in, 28; racism in, 37; replicability in, 32; specialized, 144*n1*; Tuskegee syphilis experiment, 37, 139–140

Responsibility, 81–96; acknowledging, 86; epistemic, 16–18; expanding, 12, 86, 87, 92; fulfilling, 86; incompletable, 93; inquiry and, 85; lines of, 88; morality and, 286; narcissistic, 140; realism and, 89–96; variability in, 88

Richards, Judith, 7, 315–331

Ricoeur, Paul, 264, 271, 280*n5*

Rivera, Marina, 325

Rodríguez, Mirta, 307

Rooks, Noliwe, 336

Room of One's Own, A, (Woolf), 249

Rooney, Phyllis, 82, 87, 111

Root, Michael, 46*n19*, 46*n20*, 46*n24*, 49*n39*

Rorty, Richard, 103, 279

Russell, Bertrand, 18, 53, 54

el Saadawi, Nawal, 278

Sandoval, Chela, 355

Sartre, Jean Paul, 144*n4*

Scheman, Naomi, 3, 4, 6, 12, 23–44, 81, 82, 90–93, 96*n7*, 169, 225

Schmitt, Frederick, 77*n1*

Schneider, Herbert, 118*n1*

Science: androcentric, 12, 188; authority of, 128; autonomy of, 182; belief in, 37; change in, 126; cognitive authority and, 176–177, 180, 181; construction in, 223; contextual values in, 45*n1;* contradictory evidence in, 131; credibility in, 34, 36, 46*n24;* dependency in, 41; of difference, 128; empirical, 115; epistemology and, 178, 317; evaluation in, 25, 44, 116, 179; exemptions from local jurisdictions, 137; expertise in, 29; explanatory principles in, 178; fraud in, 32; good, 131; heart disease studies, 198–199; homogeneity of community in, 361–377; impartiality ideal in, 12; impersonality in, 35; integrity of results in, 34; interaction with, 25; misogyny in, 126, 127; natural, 287; nature of, 130; need for diverse communities in, 14; norms of, 28; objectivity and, 176, 363;

oppression in, 131; patriarchal paradigm in, 127; philosophy of, 2, 3; policing norms in, 46*n24;* political considerations in, 28; practiced by groups, 363; pragmatism and, 100; privilege and, 12, 29; production, 128; pseudo-explanations in, 178; racism/sexism in, 12, 129, 131, 144*n2,* 146*n17;* rationality and, 176; resistance in, 131; role of evidence in, 178; scientific method in, 129; sex differences in, 177; social factors in, 178, 179; as social practice, 27, 28, 44; sociology of, 178; specialized, 177, 181; standpoint epistemology in, 361–377; sustaining authority in, 176–177; theories of, 100; trust in, 29, 34, 35, 36; truth and, 29, 38–41; uncritical acceptance of, 25; understanding, 178, 179; unity of, 118*n1;* values in, 130, 131, 183, 195; wars, 175

Science, feminist: cognitive authority and, 176–177; discrediting, 182; empirical adequacy and, 185, 186; feminist values and, 182–189; non-disappearance of gender in, 187; objectivity and, 175; propaganda and, 175; rationality and, 175; relativism and, 175–190; role of evidence in, 183

Science as Social Knowledge (Longino), 363

Scott, Sara, 152, 153

Searle, John, 175, 177, 182, 222, 228

Seigfried, Charlene Haddock, 3, 5, 10, 99–118

Self: as-knowable, 275; concept of, 264; deception, 75; deconstruction of, 263, 265; disintegration, 273; essentialist views of, 119*n5;* fragmentation of, 265; gendered, 285; knowledge, 271; of liberal tradition, 263, 272, 280*n5;* ownership, 269, 275, 277, 278; property and, 264; rational, 280*n5;* realization, 303, 304, 305, 312; reflection, 267; sameness of, 8; substantive, 73; sufficiency,

41; transformation of, 106; understanding, 179, 267

"Self as *Ipse*" (Ricoeur), 264

Separatism, 132; conceptual, 17, 18, 126, 129, 133, 134, 142; epistemological, 40, 44; Lesbian, 127; as political strategy, 127; withdrawal as validation in, 129

Sexism, 36, 61; classroom, 65; constructed, 224; institutional, 67; natural selection and, 210; in science, 129, 131, 144*n2,* 146*n17*

Sexuality: biological, 184; as psychophysical entity, 224–225; relationships of, 106

Shapin, Steven, 31, 32, 34, 44, 61

"Significance of the Problem of Knowledge, The," (Dewey), 109

Silver, John, 53

Sisay, Kaddy, 135, 136, 137

Skepticism: False Memory Syndrome Foundation and, 154–157; in inquiry, 153; metaphysical, 163; on objectivity of values, 178

Sklar, Judith, 293

"S Knows That p" model, 4–5, 30, 267

Smith, Dorothy, 68

Smitherman, Geneva, 343, 344

Social: change, 107; class, 106; communities, 5; connection, 30; construction, 9, 130, 221–239; custom, 107; environments, 101, 232; ethics, 109, 110, 111; factors in science, 178; hierarchies, 107; identity, 6, 14, 55; imaginary, 272, 273, 279, 280*n11;* inequities, 28, 43; influence, 160; institutions, 27, 185; interaction, 34; justice, 43, 311, 312; knowledge, 363; landscapes, 176; location, 7, 47*n27,* 65, 69, 71, 364; metaphysics, 74; narrative, 62; norms, 302, 317; order, 18, 48*n31;* organization, 6; power, 69; prejudice, 60; relationships, 362; responsibility, 276; roles, 11; skepticism, 151–169; stratification, 15, 362; structures, 16; systems, 75; values, 12, 87, 302

Solomon, Miriam, 178
Sosa, Ernest, 57, 77n1
Spanier, Bonnie, 184, 205, 206, 361, 364
Spanos, Nicholas, 164
Spelman, Vicky, 138
Standpoint theory: conceptualized as like perspectives, 68; insights into reality in, 108; marginalization in, 108; questions in, 68; strong communities and, 375–376; working class and, 366–369
Stauder, Jack, 137
Stefansson, Kari, 48n32
Stepan, Nancy, 128, 146n17
Stewart, Timothy, 236
Storytelling, 7–9; appearances and, 300–313; importance of, 298; moral judgments and, 298; norms and values in, 301; philosophizing and, 319
Subjectivity: accounting for, 6; changes in, 142; in construction of knowledge, 7; in disintegration, 273; epistemic value of, 6; hidden, 64; integrated, 263; intricacies of, 263; language of, 271; location of, 265; moral, 265; reconfiguring, 268; social constitution of, 4; social identity and, 60; specificities of, 273; transcending, 261
Suggestibility, 163–169
Sumser, John, 367

Ten Essentials, 82, 83, 84
Testimony: credibility of, 36; dominant view of, 77n1; epistemological importance of, 46n19; importance of, 77n1; justification of, 77n1; knowledge acquisition from, 56, 58; lack of discussion on, 77n1; memory, 162–163; reliance on, 46n19
Theories: of acculturation, 331n3; of biological interaction, 10; Chicana literary, 7, 315–331; coherence, 228; of constructive empiricism, 223; critical, 113; development, 15, 299, 303, 312; emancipatory, 99; epistemological, 330; feminist, 283; feminist moral, 283, 284, 295n5; inferences from, 131;

of inferiority, 185; of justified belief, 201; of knowledge, 99, 100, 106, 111, 115, 119n9, 261, 316; liberatory, 11; logical, 289; of meaning, 226; moral, 283, 286, 295n4; of praxis, 111; queer, 19n8, 113; race, 19n8; of rationality, 106; of realism, 222; relativity, 132, 133, 134; of science, 100; spectator, 100–101; "storied," 319; of truth, 117, 226, 228
Therapy: cognitive behavioral, 156; competence of women therapists and, 152; distortion of, 39; feminist, 39, 151–169; feminist critics of, 153; hypnosis in, 164, 171n22; negligence suits in, 156; replacement by science, 157; suggestive, 154, 159
Third Meditation (Descartes), 43
This Bridge Called My Back: Writings by Women of Color (Moraga), 322
Thought: ecological, 241n17; epistemological, 114; as foundation of being, 264; interpretive, 320; laws of, 288; moral, 293; naturalistic, 320; as reconstruction of experience, 105; reflective, 102; scientific, 128; self-directive, 107; sociopolitical, 351
Tiles, Jim, 53, 54
Tiles, Mary, 53, 54
"Time Passes" (Woolf), 246, 249, 253, 255, 257n3
To The Lighthouse (Woolf), 245, 246, 255, 256, 257n3
Tokarczyk, Michelle, 367
Toulmin, Stephen, 287, 288, 289, 290, 292
Trigilio, Jo, 137
Tronto, Joan, 284, 285
Trust: appropriate, 42; barriers to, 30; as central epistemic issue, 30; coherence theory of, 228; consequences of, 31; considerations of, 31; credibility and, 32, 46n20; demonstrating, 35; dependency and, 6, 29–33; epistemic ability to decide, 54; epistemic centrality of, 6; epistemic importance of, 40–41;

ineliminability of, 33–38; in institutions, 36, 43; intersubjective, 59; justifiable, 42, 43; limits of, 39–40; in medical research, 37; misplaced, 34; multiple paths to, 284; objectivity and, 26, 39; rational grounding of, 25, 35; realist understanding of, 197; representational theories of, 226; in science, 29, 34, 35, 36; subordinated groups and, 47*n25;* suggestibility and, 164

Truth: access to, 71, 197; bias and, 13, 196; circularity and, 200–202; contextual, 15; decisions about, 103; defining, 287, 289; epistemic interpretation, 201; experience of, 287, 294; fixed, 103; imagination and, 159; inquiry and, 13; local, 15; moral, 15, 284, 288, 289; normative concept of, 24; objective, 29, 154; obscuring, 205; paths to, 287, 288; perception and, 71; proof of, 156; as property of propositions, 212; realism and, 13, 198, 222; recognizability of, 208; representational accounts of, 109, 226; scientific, 29, 38–41, 235, 287, 294; seeking, 182; theories of, 117; trackers of, 35; understanding, 311

Truth and Method (Gadamer), 287, 294

Tuana, Nancy, 1–18, 126–127, 130, 131, 221–239

Tyndall, John, 367

Underwager, Ralph, 156

Unity: communal, 255; dialectical, 308, 309, 313*n3;* of existence, 312; narrative, 267, 271, 273, 347

Universalism: cultural, 13; situated defense of, 47*n27*

Untermensch, 74

Uses of Argument, The, (Toulmin), 288

Values: androcentric, 11, 188; change as, 10; complexity as, 10; contextual, 45*n1,* 188; cultural, 87; defense of, 304; democratic, 130; determinants of, 362; embedded, 12; epistemic, 11, 87, 186,

188, 191*n11;* explicit, 188; facts and, 106; feminist, 11, 182–189; feminist science and, 182–189; fundamental, 304; imposition of, 131, 309; inherited, 7; instrumental, 47*n26;* justice, 131; knowledge and, 5, 13, 103; meaning and, 70; moral, 284, 285; nonepistemic, 178, 183, 184, 188; nonstandard, 195; objectivity and, 13, 87, 178; personal, 87; political, 11, 12, 185; rejected, 16; religious, 13; role in production of knowledge, 14; in science, 183; sexist, 11; social, 12, 87, 302; submerged, 188

Van Frassen, Bas, 162, 223

Vienna Circle, 53, 54, 115

Vincent, David, 47*n29*

Violence: gendered, 273; sexual, 280*n12;* social accountability for, 276; torture, 273

Visible and the Invisible, The, (Merleau-Ponty), 253

Visweswaran, Kamala, 335

Voyage Out, The, (Woolf), 246, 253

Wakefield, Hollinda, 156

Waldron, Jeremy, 48*n31*

Walker, Margaret, 286

Washburn, Sherwood, 361

Watters, Ethan, 160

Watts, Dr. Isaac, 365

Weber, Max, 290, 291, 293, 294

West, Cornel, 54

Westling, Louise, 3, 9, 10, 245–257

"What Is Natural about Epistemology Naturalized?" (Code), 317

Wheatstone, Charles, 367

White, Alan, 159

Whitten, Barbara, 14, 361–377

Whort, Benjamin Lee, 146*n21*

Whose Science? Whose Knowledge? (Harding), 363

Williams, L. Pearce, 366, 367, 373, 374

Williams, Patricia, 63, 64, 65, 66

Williams, Sherley Anne, 138

Wittgenstein, Ludwig, 3, 46*n15,* 126, 127, 132, 134, 144*n1,* 146*n25*

Wolpert, Lewis, 178
Woolf, Virginia, 9, 10, 245–257
Woolgar, Steve, 226, 227, 228, 240*n5*
Wylie, Alison, 45*n1,* 188, 189

Yabko, Michael, 164
Young, Iris, 71

Zamora, Bernice, 326